CONSTRUCTING A EUROPEAN MARKET

Constructing a European Market

Standards, Regulation, and Governance

MICHELLE P. EGAN

OXFORD

UNIVERSITY PRESS

OXFORD
UNIVERSITY PRESS

Great Clarendon Street, Oxford OX2 6DP

Oxford University Press is a department of the University of Oxford.
It furthers the University's objective of excellence in research, scholarship,
and education by publishing worldwide in

Oxford New York

Athens Auckland Bangkok Bogotá Buenos Aires Cape Town
Chennai Dar es Salaam Delhi Florence Hong Kong Istanbul Karachi
Kolkata Kuala Lumpur Madrid Melbourne Mexico City Mumbai
Nairobi Paris São Paulo Shanghai Singapore Taipei Tokyo Toronto Warsaw
and associated companies in Berlin Ibadan

Oxford is a registered trade mark of Oxford University Press
in the UK and certain other countries

Published in the United States
by Oxford University Press Inc., New York

British Library Cataloguing in Publication Data

Data available

Library of Congress Cataloging in Publication Data
Egan, Michelle P.
Constructing a European market : standards, regulations, and governance / Michelle P. Egan.
p. cm.
Includes bibliographical references.
1. European Union. 2. European Union countries—Economic policy. 3. Political
planning—European Union countries. I. Title.
JN30.E3 2001   341.242′2—dc21   00–068830
ISBN 0-19-924405-7

1 3 5 7 9 10 8 6 4 2

Typeset by Graphicraft Limited, Hong Kong
Printed in Great Britain by
T.J. International Ltd.,
Padstow, Cornwall

PREFACE

This book was completed with the help of many people. My greatest personal and professional debt is to Alberta M. Sbragia, Professor and Director of the Center for West European Studies and the European Union Center at the University of Pittsburgh, who provided generous guidance as I began to think about how markets are constructed. I am fortunate to have such an enthusiastic and creative mentor, and also to have benefited from the supportive environment within the University Center for International Studies and Department of Political Science. I am indebted to a number of past and present faculty at the University of Pittsburgh, including B. Guy Peters, Susan Hansen, Stephen Farber, and Bert Rockman, each of whom contributed important ideas at the early stages of the project. Their suggestions and comments have been invaluable in shaping the direction of my research, even though they may not entirely agree with the final analysis.

My colleagues at the School of International Service (SIS), American University, have also contributed to this project. In particular, SIS Dean Louis Goodman, Associate Dean Nanette Levinson, Linda Lubrano, and Quansheng Zhao have generously accommodated my fellowship leave requests and maintained a supportive atmosphere for faculty research.

I benefited from the support of a number of other institutions during the research process. Research grants and fellowships from the German Marshall Fund of the United States, the British Politics Group of the American Political Science Association, the European University Institute in Florence (Jean Monnet Fellowship), and the American Institute for Contemporary German Studies (Robert Bosch Fellowship in Contemporary Public Policy and Institutions) are gratefully acknowledged.

A large number of researchers in Europe and the United States have provided helpful suggestions for an interdisciplinary project. They include Giandomenico Majone, Stephen Woolcock, Kalypso Nicolaïdis, David Vogel, Martin Staniland, Albrecht Funk, Vivien Schmidt, Youri Devuyst, Suzanne Schmidt, Marc Smyrl, Kenneth Armstrong, Carl Lankowski, Philippe Schmitter, Mark Pollack, Francis Jacobs, Michael Shackleton, Claudio Radaelli, Andrea Lenshow, and Tony Zito. Phil Wilkin, Bibliographer at the University of Pittsburgh, and librarians at the European Commission Library in Brussels and Washington DC have been helpful with European documentation. Dominic Byatt of

Oxford University Press has been exceptionally supportive at crucial stages in the project, along with Amanda Watkins and Edwin Pritchard.

A special thanks to Jacques Pelkmans, Senior Research Fellow at the Center for European Policy Studies, who encouraged me to focus on the political economy aspects of standardization. CEPS also provided institutional support and a vibrant research environment during my stay in Brussels. Adrienne Héritier, Professor at the European University Institute and Director of the Max Planck Institute, Bonn, provided suggestions on my draft manuscript and a welcoming environment during my stay in Florence. Kurt Riechenberg of the European Court of Justice, and later Court of First Instance, provided extensive commentary on the case law regarding free movement of goods during his tenure as a Visiting EC Fellow at the University of Pittsburgh.

My research was also aided by the insight of numerous officials within European institutions, standards bodies, companies, and trade associations. Officials at CEN, CENELEC, ETSI, and EOTC were always willing to provide information and respond to questions regarding the complexities of standardization. The British Standards Institute was a generous summer host, enabling me to continue my research on standards and conformity assessment.

My family has patiently waited for me to finish this book, and now must watch me begin work on a new book on comparative market integration. Finally, my husband Bill Burros has learned more about the arcane world of standards than he ever imagined, providing advice and encouragement along the way. This book is dedicated to him.

CONTENTS

LIST OF FIGURES

LIST OF TABLES

LIST OF ABBREVIATIONS

AFNOR	Association Française de Normalisation
ANEC	European Association for Cooperation of Consumer Representation in Standardization
ANSI	American National Standards Institute
BSI	British Standards Institute
CCC	Consumer Consultative Council
CCITT	Consultative Committee on International Telephone and Telegraphy
CEN	European Committee for Standards (abb. from French) Comité Européen en Normalisation
CENELEC	European Committee for Electrical Standards (abb. from French) Comité Européen en Normalisation Électrotechnique
CEPT	European Conference of Post and Telecommunications
COCIR	European Coordination Committee of the Radiological and Electromedical Industry
DG	Directorate General (of European Commission)
DIN	Deutsches Institut für Normung
ECJ	European Court of Justice
ECSC	European Coal and Steel Community
ECU	European Currency Unit (replaced by Euro)
EEA	European Economic Area
EEC	European Economic Community
EFTA	European Free Trade Area
EOTC	European Organization for Testing and Certification
ESC	Economic and Social Committee
ETSI	European Telecommunications Standards Institute
ETUC/TUTB	European Trade Union Confederation Technical Board on Standardization
EU	European Union
FIEC	European Construction Industry Federation
HIMA	Health Industry Manufacturers' Association
IEC	International Electrotechnical Commission
ISO	International Standards Organization
ITU	International Telecommunications Union
NIST	National Institute of Standards and Technology (U.S.)

NTB	non-tariff barrier
OJ	Official Journal
SEA	Single European Act
SME	small and medium enterprise
UNICE	Union of Industrial and Employers' Confederations of Europe

1

Introduction

Contrary to expectations, the introduction of free markets, far from doing away with the need for control, regulation and intervention, enormously increased their range.

For Karl Polanyi, in his classic book, *The Great Transformation,* the history of the market is the history of unavoidable and uninterrupted market intervention.[1] Writing in 1944, Polanyi's analysis of markets led him to the conclusion that state intervention was necessary to provide a framework establishing not only the rules of the game, but also to address problems arising from the consequences of the market economy.

The operation of the market continues to be a cornerstone of contemporary debate as the internationalization of production and exchange, technology, and finance has resulted in the reconfiguration of political, social, and economic activities at the local, national, and international level. Whether it is processes of economic transition in Central and Eastern Europe, neoliberal reforms in Latin America, or the linkage between authoritarian regimes and economic growth among the Asian tigers, how markets are constituted and organized is the subject of intense scrutiny and analysis.[2]

The struggle over the shape and form of the market is equally salient at the regional level. Markets are politically instituted and socially regulated entities, and the effort at market-making in Europe over the past forty years has been less tumultuous but no less momentous in unifying disparate interests and market ideologies.[3] As early as 1953, Paul Reuter made the prescient observation that the common market was 'the least simple thing in the world' since it could not merely be 'opened', but needed to be 'established'.[4] Although this initially meant the elimination of trade barriers and the creation of a customs union, efforts in the 1950s and 1960s occurred against the backdrop of the mixed economy and welfare state that were central components of the post-war settlement.[5] As a consequence, governments were able to compensate and adjust for the increased competition and openness of national economies stemming from market integration.

Like other elements of the post-war order, European integration came under mounting pressure following the first oil shock and economic recession of 1973. Poor economic performance undermined both the budgetary foundations of welfare states and the emphasis on Keynesian demand management. The second oil shock in the late 1970s and the spread of a stagflationary combination of high inflation and unemployment prompted a vigorous challenge to politics as usual, and sparked varied responses to the economic crisis. The trade integration model, in particular, came under strain with increased recourse to protectionism. The result was a more inward-looking and defensive European polity; and also a less important entity in economic terms.

In the midst of this deep economic malaise, the limits of market integration seemed to have been reached. Yet European economies recovered as growth rates, productivity, and investment picked up rapidly. Interest in European integration grew as a consensus developed over the need to combat the loss of competitiveness and respond to the pressures of globalization.[6] It was in this environment that increased attention was once again given to the nature and effects of non-tariff barriers to trade, and particularly disparities between national standards and regulations.

This book examines this issue by looking at the political choices and economic strategies of constructing a market. The study demonstrates that the relationship between governments and markets cannot be understood without recognizing that a market is not organized by itself, but always operates within a political and legal framework that provides the rules of the game.[7] Although it is clear that the scope and nature of government regulation over markets in Europe has changed over time, as financial, technological, and ideological pressures have reduced the ability of governments to exercise jurisdictional control within their borders, this has not meant the complete absence of rules or what some have described as a 'stateless market.'[8]

My argument is that regulatory policies continue to condition market relations.[9] Although the European Union does not perform all of the functions of a modern state, it does engage in widespread economic and social regulation.[10] As the single most important function of the European Union, its regulatory role illustrates that market-making is more than simply pushing back the frontiers of the state. European market liberalization and market regulation are in fact intertwined, leading to the interesting paradox of 'freer markets, more rules'.[11] My analysis is thus largely congruent with the emerging body of literature that views the European Union as analogous to a 'regulatory state',[12] where the political economy of regulation is examined at both the domestic and international level.[13] Empirically, the focus of the book is to illustrate the efforts of the European Union to harmonize the diverse array of national regulations and standards and the resulting testing, certification, and licensing practices that affect the trade and distribution of goods and services in Europe. Because different national markets have developed distinctive and differing competitive norms and practices to sustain them, the integration process in Europe has sought to overcome these disparities through sustained market intervention.

As subsequent chapters illustrate, these regulatory efforts have not received the same level of political attention as privatization, deregulation, and globalization. This is in part because they often involve negotiations on small and seemingly insignificant technical issues, such as the labelling of food additives, colourings, and sweeteners, the safety level of electrical emissions and safety of toys, the noise level of airlines, and the designation of appropriate hallmarking for precious metals. While these are relatively arcane issues to most observers, they have moved to the forefront of economic policy and trade negotiations.[14] There has been a marked rise in the number of these disputes at both the regional and multilateral level. Disputes over domestic regulations and standards affecting imports or production and process methods are becoming increasingly contentious.

Setting standards is also difficult for public authorities, as it often requires balancing international competitiveness with legitimate domestic objectives such as safety, security, and soundness. Moreover, many of these regulatory barriers reflect legitimate differences between countries in terms of administrative culture, risk assessment, and patterns of state–society-economy relations.[15] Without some effort to coordinate different national standards and regulations, European markets would continue to be fragmented. Thus, European states have sought international policy coordination and harmonization of their regulatory frameworks for both products and services at the regional level.[16]

By studying regulatory policy, we learn more about the broad range of institutional arrangements that shape and influence economic behaviour, and this allows us to evaluate the way that the European Union[17] has coordinated markets, integrated economies, and fostered regulatory interdependence. As we shall see in subsequent chapters, the story that emerges is one in which governments have redefined their regulation of industry and transformed government–business–society relations in the process. Business is interacting with government in new ways, resulting in new forms of regulation. What is significant is that regulators and regulated are in this case the same, and the rules that govern their behaviour are increasingly the result of collective negotiation and bargaining among private interests. Although this conceptualization of market governance has been described in terms of private international regimes or private interest governments[18] the regulatory process is still mediated and steered by governments.[19] Understanding the institutional design and policy choices of European efforts to reconcile regulation and free trade is the core goal of this book.

Understanding regulation

While government control over certain sectors of the European economy was often taken for granted, alarm at the rapid growth, incoherence, and cost of these efforts has generated pressures for regulatory reform that imply a loss of power and authority for governments. Although the pattern and speed of regulatory reform has been uneven, many observers argue that the commitment to deregulation and the reduction of the state's regulatory role in industrial and financial affairs marks a shift in the pattern of state intervention from a 'welfare' state model to a 'competition' state model.[20] The picture painted by these observers is one in which a process best described as 'economic disengagement' has swept across the globe.[21] Governments—fearful of falling behind in a more competitive global economy—are implementing a variety of regulatory reforms as part of their efforts to cope with and foster structural adjustment. Governments are adopting reforms to eliminate or simplify burdensome rules, increase the use of market incentives as alternatives to traditional regulation, and devolve regulatory authority to local administrations, banks, regulatory agencies, or courts.[22]

When governments opt for market solutions to enable their industries to compete in the global market place, the political management of this process spills over into the domain of interstate or intergovernmental relations.[23] Governments then look for ways to increase regulatory cooperation and manage the political consequences of the operation of markets. Yet the debate on deregulation has overshadowed the continuing need for governments to establish boundaries around markets by providing, creating, and sustaining the rules for market governance. Liberalization of trade in the European Union has led to greater regulatory cooperation, as member states have been collectively involved in an exercise of regulatory rapprochement—or reregulation—at the Community level to counterbalance the impending loss of regulatory authority or sovereignty at the national level. The transfer of regulation to the European level is a cooperative solution to a broad range of problems, without which there could be market failure.[24] As Majone notes, because each member state has an incentive to regulate its national industries leniently, leading to weak and non-credible regulation as well as the proliferation of market distortions, the delegation of regulatory authority to the supranational level can overcome problems of credibility and collective agreement by shifting the responsibility away from national governments.[25] What has changed in the European case, as the following chapters demonstrate, is why, how, and at what level governments regulate industry.[26]

I argue that three factors are especially important in understanding why regulation provides the analytical building blocks to explain the construction of a European market.

First, as the most important and ambitious effort of the post-war period to reduce national trade barriers, the experience of the European Union illustrates the close relationship between regulatory and trade policies. In order to create a single market, the European Union has sought to limit the ability of its member states to exercise regulatory sovereignty. Domestic policies, which were previously neglected, are often considered impediments to trade, as disparities in national regulatory policies can hinder market access and restrict competition. These new forms of protectionism fall within what is known as the 'reserved powers' of states, and form part of the domestic regulatory agenda pursued by national governments. While many of these regulations have a sound basis in public policy, promoting such goals as the protection of health, safety, and the environment, they are under tremendous scrutiny as higher standards may be challenged as disguised protectionism and lower standards characterized as social or environmental dumping. Because disparities in regulation can hinder market access, restrict competition, and create arbitrage pressures, the possibility for beggar-thy-neighbour policies has led to intense concerns that competition among regulations may lead to a race to the bottom.[27]

Second, the integration process is driven by case law rulings. Legal scholars have highlighted the impact of legal 'rules' in fostering and achieving an integrated economy.[28] Legal rulings have sought to 'curb the parochial tendencies of the individual states' and played an indispensable role in maintaining free trade.[29] European case law has fostered an interstate market place by striking down mercantilist economic regulations imposed by national governments, freeing consequent market activity of many non-tariff barriers.

By ruling on the notion of trade restrictions and thereby delineating the degree to which states could circumvent European policy, the legal framework has shaped the environment in which both business and governments operate. European law is greatly influencing the nature and level of regulation, and in doing so, is determining the balance between integration and diversity. This involves balancing states rights and duties against regional integration and free trade. Since law plays a critical role in shaping the degree to which governments can regulate economic activity, the politics among governments is often played out in the legal sphere. Thus the evolution of the market and legal framework are closely intertwined, and European case law is an important factor in both promoting and hindering market integration.

Third, many studies of regulation, regardless of their disciplinary or analytic approach, emphasize either an economic argument of the power of markets over politics or a political argument of the power of economic interests over government.[30] These studies are primarily interested in exploring how private actors influence or 'capture' the policy process. Emphasis is placed on private goals, with private interests able to use or constrain public authority. However, the tendency to focus on the pressure group activities of firms does not account for patterns of decision-making that deliberately include private actors in the policy process. This regulatory arena must instead be understood in terms of intermediation and bargaining, since the institutionalized representation of interests can enhance the range of policy alternatives available to governments.[31] Because the patterns of negotiated rule-making are in fact diverse, governments can reduce their regulatory burden as the boundaries between public and private roles are increasingly blurred.[32]

Governments as political actors can use resources from both the public and private sector to bolster their regulatory goals and pursue their objectives.[33] The willingness to delegate important policy-making powers is in large part a recognition that regulation is not achieved by simply passing a law, but requires active involvement of regulated firms.[34] Because regulators lack information that only regulated firms have, firms themselves are acting like governments, by establishing regulations and codes of conduct in economic, environmental, and social areas. The growth of such business self-regulation is difficult to equate with the usual definitions of regulation perceived in terms of government activity, since it crosses the boundaries between providing a mix of public, private, or collective goods.

By studying regulatory developments through the interaction of law, markets, and governments on the one hand, and bargaining, calculation, and cooperation among firms on the other, it is possible to understand, evaluate, and assess the impact of market-building over time. This is particularly important as the movement from local to regional, national, or international markets has been a crucial factor historically in the process of economic development and growth.[35]

Markets and firms

While firms have increasingly played a role in shaping regulatory policy, they have also been forced to respond to changes in market rules. However, there have been surprisingly few assessments of the implications of free trade for corporate governance.[36] Chapter 10 in particular offers evidence of the impact and effects of the single market on corporate policies and strategies.[37] By tracing European efforts to remove non-tariff barriers to trade over the past forty years, this approach focuses not only on the *process* but also the *impact* of market-building in Europe. In marked contrast to many studies of European integration that tend to focus on the lobbying activities of business, the emphasis here is on the impact of market integration on economic strategies and behaviour. In focusing on the extent to which firms cooperate and realize the gains from trade, the analysis raises important questions concerning the strategic responses and ability of firms to take advantage of the single market.

Much of the economic research on integration (based on neoclassical assumptions) assumes that firms will exploit the economic opportunities created by removing barriers to trade. These analyses assume that firms will take advantage of changes in market structure, and that the resulting improvement in productivity and competitiveness will considerably enhance economic welfare and the general macroeconomic situation.[38] This analysis is undermined by the empirical evidence, as European efforts to remove regulatory barriers have not led to a frictionless, perfectly operating market. The task of market creation is extremely difficult given variations in the historical timing of regulatory development, in national institutional structures, and national legal traditions.[39] The success of the single market depends on whether negotiations on regulatory cooperation produce the necessary results and overcome problems of collective action to reach agreement on common European standards. The analysis presented here raises important questions about the 'success' of the EU in establishing a single market, and the degree to which firms have actually capitalized on changes in the European regulatory environment.

The use of comparison

Although this book is concerned with market-building in Europe, the argument is not confined to the European Union. The notion that market integration involves more than simply removing barriers to trade is rooted in a comparative and historical perspective. From a comparative perspective, the interrelationship between trade and regulation can be seen as one element of the debate about the distribution of regulatory competencies between different levels of government in the design and operation of federal or confederal systems. Economic theories of federalism have sought to determine the 'optimal' distribution of regulatory competencies among different levels of government.[40] This is based on the presumption that competition among different regulatory communities will determine the most efficient level and scope of government regulation. Each level of government should be assigned those functions that in principle it can best perform. In much the same way, the European Union is seeking to define the distribution of policy competencies among different levels of government. Scholars of European integration have also raised concerns about efficiency, collective action, and the problems of 'joint decision-making' to highlight the constraints under which integration takes place in a multi-level or federal type system.[41]

From a historical perspective, the way in which the European market 'has been painstakingly stitched together is reminiscent of the creation of a single market in the United States'.[42] Assessments of the construction of the American market have focused on issues of political economy and legal decisions surrounding the removal of restrictions to interstate commerce.[43] However, when the American market was constructed in the nineteenth century, the emphasis in political economy was on the removal of barriers to trade between nation-states. The historic attack on tariff policies and the advocacy of free trade has traditionally focused on international barriers to trade and not intra-national barriers. But this does not mean that internal barriers were or are insignificant. On the contrary, experience in the early American republic indicated that decentralization of decision-making fostered constant trade disputes. To overcome these restrictions, the federal government sought to prohibit states from erecting barriers to interstate trade, encouraging the growth of a 'common market'.

While the American jurisprudence regarding interstate commerce strikes a familiar chord with the European Union, as both have clauses concerning the free movement of goods, the American common market has been established with much less interference upon the sovereign powers of individual states. As Scheiber concludes, 'American federalism provided a benign framework favoring business institutions and fostering "benevolent" promotional or supportive policies by rival state governments'.[44] As we look at the difficulties faced by the EU, it is useful to remember that the American market is also 'imperfect' with some barriers or restrictions to cross-border state trade still in evidence, and that the strength of the American common market varies across sectors.[45] Although not a fully-fledged comparative study, a comparative 'lens' provides a useful way of understanding the importance of politics in shaping markets, and identifying those aspects of the market-building process that are sufficiently similar to warrant further study.

Plan of the book

Studies of European integration are often bifurcated between political science and economics. Political scientists are generally concerned with political institutions and policy-making, and economic institutions, particularly markets, tend to be woefully understudied, whereas economists tend to downplay the importance of institutions and rules in constraining economic behaviour.[46] Borrowing elements from both fields, as well as law and business, this book provides a historically based account of how the 'single product market' in Europe has come into being.

Chapter 2 outlines the analytic and conceptual underpinnings of the book, addressing the intersection of market liberalization and re-regulation. It includes an extensive review of the regulatory literature, most of which is based on the American political process. These theories are either state driven, focusing on the role of government in shaping market behaviour, or interest group driven, focusing on the influence of private interests which 'capture' the policy process. By contrast, the market-building process in Europe has been more complicated, and requires an examination of the ways in which governments and firms have used each other.

Chapter 3 focuses on the costs of market fragmentation in Europe. It reviews the economic impact of removing barriers to trade in industrial product markets. This chapter highlights the impact of regulatory barriers to trade on firms, and provides some empirical evidence of the benefits expected to accrue from market integration. This is followed in Chapter 4 with a discussion of early efforts in the 1960s and 1970s to tackle barriers to trade through harmonization. The push for convergence or harmonization of national policies in Europe was driven by the understanding that, without such regulatory intervention by governments, there would be no single market and trade conflicts would escalate. Chapter 4 illustrates the tremendous difficulties that the policy of harmonization encountered, and how regulatory reform enabled the EU to achieve a more appropriate match between its policy objectives and outcomes.

Chapter 5 builds on this argument, by highlighting the important role of law in fostering an integrated market. By tackling protectionism, addressing trade discrimination, and developing legal principles to balance state sovereign powers with the need for regional markets, the case law of the Community has played a key role in bringing about a single market. Chapters 6, 7, and 8 detail the impact of legal rulings in fostering regulatory reform. Chapter 6 highlights the relaunch of European integration in the 1980s and the critical new ways in which the EU tackled regulatory barriers to trade. That process involved states and firms in a complex 'new approach' to deal with the discriminatory effects of regulatory policies. Chapter 7 explores the operation of this new policy, focusing on how the setting of standards for market access has taken account of societal actors. As a result, the once clear-cut borderlines between the public and private spheres have become increasingly blurred. The reaction to this policy is explored in Chapter 8 through a series of case studies, with particular attention paid to difficulties in reaching collective agreement on common standards. The emphasis on the tension between competition and collaboration among those involved in setting regulatory standards is important, since it raises questions about the extent to which a single market has been achieved.

Chapter 9 focuses on the shortcomings of the new approach, and discusses reform efforts to deal with the slow progress towards achieving a single market. Highlighting both European proposals for regulatory reform and industry reactions to them, the chapter provides key insights into the complex and contested nature of negotiated rule-making in the European context. Chapter 10 provides a preliminary assessment of the impact of market integration upon corporate policies and strategies, an important issue that has not been adequately addressed in the single market literature. The survey findings are mixed, indicating that while many barriers to trade remain, there are also positive assessments of the single market programme. What the findings also reveal is that problems of mutual credibility and trust are still problematic for companies doing business in Europe, and that regulatory changes have impacted on corporate policies and strategies quite dramatically beyond the boundaries of the European market.

The Conclusion discusses the difficulties of achieving some form of accommodation between the interests of government, business, and society. The politics of market-building is an often contentious dialogue about the best ways to reconcile regulation and free trade. Market-building involves not only the allocation of authority between different levels of government, in a way that promotes the free exchange of goods without intruding on the legitimate regulatory powers of individual member states, but also an acknowledgement that the corporate strategies and activities of firms are a major determinant in the nature and direction of European integration. New factors such as delegation, oversight, and accountability have become highly consequential.[47] While the willingness to delegate important policy-making powers is in some sense an attempt to reduce transaction costs and improve the efficiency of collective political outcomes, it is hardly surprising that the end result raises new issues about governance, legitimacy, and power.[48] The Conclusion ends by assessing some of the broader implications of the institutional choices made by the European Union in fostering market integration.

Regulating Europe:
The Political Economy of Market-Building

What Polanyi observed about the nature of the market economy and creation of viable market structures is also true about European efforts to create a single market free of restrictions on the movement of goods, capital, services, and people. The logic of the Treaty of Rome implies that, once individual markets of the member states of the European Union have been integrated, no further intervention in the economy will be either necessary or desirable. In fact, the proper functioning of the market economy hinges on the combination of regulation and competition policy to address the alleged inability of the market place to deal with particular structural problems.[1] Because of market failure, public sector intervention must modify or supplement the operations of the economic system, with different forms of regulation chosen to deal with different market problems.

Government intervention may take the form of licensing, anti-trust provisions, standard-setting, entry rates, or even nationalization. In each case, the aim is to correct imperfections in the market economy. Though there are different types of market failure, the regulatory framework of the European single market is aimed at dealing with these imperfections, through a mixture of policy instruments aimed at increasing the efficiency and equity of market transactions. While the most appropriate policy instrument to tackle income and distribution issues is the tax and benefit system, other market failures are addressed through a variety of rules, norms, and standards aimed at establishing economic security and stability, reducing transaction costs, and responding to increased societal pressures and demands.[2]

Although research has identified the conditions under which markets need intervention, most studies have focused only on the *process* of European integration without considering the *impact* of policy or institutional choices upon the creation and maintenance of the single market. Polanyi's analysis is particularly important for our understanding of the construction of the single market in Europe because he introduces

politics and agency. Although Polanyi was concerned about ameliorat-
ing the effects of market commodification upon society,[3] in many ways
anticipating the need for increased regulation over economic activity, he
did not anticipate efforts by the state to shift regulatory responsibility.
In light of both ideological pressures for liberalization and increased
pressure to reduce public intervention in markets, governments have been
stretched in their capacity to provide regulatory standards for products
and services. In response, many governments, including the European
Union, have harnessed the resources outside the public sector in furtherance
of public policy goals.[4]

Given the twin factors of the internationalization of business activity and liberalization of markets, the continued and exclusive focus on
state intervention seems ill-suited to an environment where states
have lost some degree of regulatory authority over their jurisdictions.
Globalization, regionalization, and the growth of business self-regulation
must be included in our analysis. While the first two have been the
subject of much theoretical and empirical research, the redefinition of
corporate behaviour and activity, involving the relationship between state
and societal actors, has resulted in new forms of regulation and governance that have garnered surprisingly little attention in comparative
political economy. The demand for rules to govern international commerce
has given rise to a variety of sources of supply, and one of the most
significant sources of international governance is the private sector
itself.[5]

Although business organizations assuming governmental functions
are not an entirely new phenomenon,[6] the use of such regulatory frameworks in providing a mix of public, private, and collective goods is increasing at the national, regional, and global level.[7] New technologies and
rapid changes in market conditions present challenges to traditional
regulatory systems, which businesses have responded to by setting down
guidelines, codes, and voluntary standards to ensure a degree of uniformity
in business practices. These arrangements are likely to emerge where there
are mutual advantages in doing so, and where interest heterogeneity is
less pronounced, in order to minimize free-riding and nonconformity
with negotiated agreements. In Europe, this private sector governance
has generated increased interaction between business and governments,
raising interesting questions about the intersection of markets and
governance.[8]

As governments must find new means of providing social protection
while allowing markets to work more efficiently, regulators in all policy
areas are using a wider range of instruments, from market-based agreements and voluntary instruments to contracting out, supervisory bodies,

and regulatory impact analysis.[9] Some studies have examined the ways in which market rules and practices have changed in Europe in specific issue areas.[10] However, the larger questions about the role of governments and markets in delivering a changing mix of public, private, and collective goods and services have not been sufficiently addressed.[11] This book attempts to address these questions by describing and analysing European efforts at international regulatory coordination. How effective are the policy mechanisms chosen by the European Union to create an internal market, and bridge the gap between different regulatory traditions? How has the European Union dealt with the distribution of regulatory competencies between different levels of government? What is the impact and effect of the interplay between the public and private sector in regulating the market, given the fact that different national traditions conceive of public–private authority in different ways, and likewise allow participation in the regulatory process to different constellations of actors? What broader issues relating to legitimacy, accountability, and power are raised by such private sector governance?

The chapters that follow focus on the process and methods by which the European Union has sought to construct an internal market, but also on the effects of the policy instruments chosen to deal with the different regulatory standards hindering cross-border trade. This chapter divides the central theme about how the European Union has constructed a market into four related issues. First, it focuses on the importance of regulation for the European polity, discussing both the meaning and significance of regulation in the European context. Second, it examines theories of economic integration and argues that these have not adequately addressed the importance of the political framework in which markets operate, as their conception of the market does not take account of the diverse set of instruments by which governments set down regulatory requirements, or the self-regulatory bodies to whom governments have delegated regulatory powers. Third, the most prominent theories of regulation are discussed, in order to assess their applicability to developments at the European level. Fourth, the chapter turns to the American experience as a useful comparative example of efforts to reconcile regulation and free trade. The American experience in the nineteenth century saw the rise of the administrative state, focused attention on the balance of power between different institutions and levels, and generated a widespread discussion about the role and effect of regulation in market-making mirroring contemporary European debates.

The regulatory polity

Regulatory issues are crucial to understanding the type of polity that the European Union has become. As Majone notes: with few fiscal resources, the macro-economic presence of the Union is largely confined to monetary policy, and does not include the huge amounts of fiscal expenditure characteristic of member states.[12] Much of the Union's policy activity is focused therefore on regulating the economic behaviour of firms and national governments. Hence, the Community-wide market will be quite different from the mixed economies of the member states, since its redistributive and allocational powers are more limited than its regulatory power. In terms of overcoming member states' opposition to the encroachment of their policy arena, regulatory policies appear to offer the path of least resistance.[13] Regulation is considered likely to be less divisive and controversial than other policies since the winners and losers are less evident than in other areas of policy-making.[14]

Given relative symmetry in state's bargaining power and sufficient time to work out differences, it may be possible for states to agree on a regulatory solution that would broadly distribute the benefits from market integration. This scenario does not, however, account for two important factors. First, regulation does have differential costs and benefits both within and among member states. Member states have different preferences across issues areas, and consequent adaptations in institutions and policies depend on differences in their market economies.[15] Import-competing sectors and firms with low levels of growth and profits are not well positioned to take advantage of liberalization, and are likely to press for protection, while those expanding, profitable, and outward-oriented firms are likely to push for further liberalization. Because of this, member states must be more or less willing to agree to EU regulation, depending on how the resulting burdens are distributed. Second, European member states differ in limited but recognizable ways in their views on the relations between public and private actors, as well as the rules governing market behaviour.[16]

Despite the current dominance of neoliberal discourse, there are systemic differences in how national economies are organized, and member states have chosen distinctive ways of organizing production, investment, and exchange that constitute important varieties of capitalism.[17] Expectations about the purposes of regulation, about who should participate, and about public–private relations are subject to great variation across nations, between different sectors and industries, and over time.[18]

Generally, the types of governance mechanisms—markets, states, firms and associations—vary.

As Streeck argues, *associative regulation* in the German context where organized cooperation among interests plays a dominant role in administering government policies and regulations, underpins the social market economy.[19] By contrast, *strategic regulation* in the French context has focused on modernization,[20] pursuing Fordist type growth, and with the cyclical effects of such a strategy mitigated by Keynesian demand management. Although there have been shifts towards a more disciplined German capitalism, France does so without the dense network of intermediary institutions that exist in Germany.[21] And finally, in Britain, *competitive regulation* characterizes recent efforts to reduce the role of the state and enforce governance using private sector market principles. Despite post-war efforts to manage the economy, the British regulatory approach has been fairly consistent about the role of public power and assertion of the liberal state.[22] As each state, therefore, has its own particular 'mix' of public policies with preferences for one or another interest, and with its own set of rules and domestic laws, different national approaches to the regulation of products and processes are an increasingly visible source of trade conflict among European nation-states.

Thus, in order to manage the complex and often conflicting relationship between trade and domestic policy objectives, the European Union has focused since its inception on removing impediments to trade caused by divergent national regulations. This challenges the capacity of member states to exercise sovereign jurisdictional control within their borders, as regulatory standards, ostensibly designed to regulate commerce and the distribution of goods and services, are now considered some of the most intractable non-tariff barriers to trade.[23] Although these domestic regulations often have legitimate objectives such as product safety, quality, and soundness, as the process of economic integration progresses, disparities in regulation can hinder market access, restrict competition, and create arbitrage pressures.[24] As member states recognize the important indirect effects that domestic regulations can have on business competitiveness, governments have increasingly come under pressure to reduce regulatory burdens, attracting larger shares of mobile factors and production processes.[25] One response to the regulator's dilemma has been to pursue international policy coordination that, at least in theory, reduces this problem and fosters a 'level playing field' on which states can compete.[26]

While realists and liberal institutionalists in international relations have debated the likelihood of effective cooperation among sovereign states, both have treated cooperation as an all-or-nothing proposition.[27] This has led to arguments about why some institutions are better at promoting cooperation than others, and also when problems are amenable to a cooperative solution and when they are not.[28] Institutionalist scholars have pointed out that institutions mitigate problems, providing monitoring and enforcement mechanisms which increase the likelihood of successful cooperation and decrease the temptation to defect.[29] Such delegation to either public or private international organizations is considered an effective means to surmount such problems and reduce transaction costs.[30]

As Majone notes, 'if national regulators were willing and able to take into account the international repercussions of their policy choices; if they had perfect information of one another's intentions; and if the costs of organizing and monitoring policy coordination were negligible, market failures could be managed in a cooperative fashion without the necessity of delegating regulatory powers to a supranational level.'[31] But even with cooperation, there are incentives not to enforce the agreement too strictly, leading to weak and less than credible regulation.[32] Because European governments have heterogeneous preferences, and often disagree over the precise nature of cooperation, its speed and scope, and side payments, the transfer of regulatory powers to supranational institutions can make regulation more credible, and so improve the compliance of regulated firms.[33]

Regulatory authority is thus being reconfigured and reconstituted at the regional level, so that a single market requires not only the removal of constraints, but also the transfer of public authorities' rules and policies to common institutions.[34] The integration of divergent systems and economies requires the constraint of at least some domestic policy instruments, combined with the irrevocable transfer of one or more instruments to the European level. A mere reliance on negative integration (the removal of constraints) without some form of positive integration (transfer of public rules and policies) is not sufficient.[35] Disparities in national laws cannot be solved by mere liberalization, they require harmonization or positive integration to replace existing national laws.

Even where the capacity to condition or regulate market processes is reduced at the national level to enable a single market to emerge, however, the transfer of regulatory competencies in some form to the European level also raises problems of democratic control.[36] Though it is assumed that democracy continues to flourish at the national level, the structural preconditions for democratic self-determination and accountability are noticeably absent at the European level.[37] In fact, the abdication of boundary control in many areas of economic activity within the internal market reduces the range of feasible domestic policy choices and options, and the emphasis on technocratic efficiency in the context of the European regulatory state does not strengthen democratic legitimacy or majoritarian governance.[38] The growing importance of decision-making to the European level—evolving along the lines proposed by Majone—may effectively delegitimate representative governance. While Majone does concede the need to control bureaucratic discretion and enforce greater political accountability of the regulatory process by institutionalizing deliberation and discussion, this presupposes the validity of certain norms, the desirability of certain outcomes, and the assumption that trade-offs between efficiency and equity at the European level can be accommodated.[39]

Regulation and European integration

Although regulation plays a central role in European political economy, the term 'regulation' encompasses a broad array of policies governing economic activity and its consequences.[40] Regulatory policies address firm entry into and exit from particular markets, modes of competition, rates of return, as well as the characteristics of goods being produced, means of production, and the negative externalities that arise from the production process.[41] Such policies have a significant impact on corporate strategy since they can influence investment and production decisions, as well as demand conditions on domestic and international markets.

At the core of regulatory activity is market governance: it involves the design of rules and the creation of institutions for their implementation and strategies for their enforcement. As the defining feature of any system of social organization, regulation can play a central role in structuring relations between the state, societal interests, and economic actors.

Understanding the process by which regulation emerges, how the various organizations interact, what goals the key actors pursue, and how they construct their strategies has produced a rich analytic literature focused primarily on the American context.[42] This has led some policy analysts to describe regulation as a 'peculiarly and appropriately American approach to political economy'.[43] As Skronowek notes with regard to the development of an American national administrative state, 'the leaders of America's reform offensives held up European administrative models as their standard and argued the functional necessity of adopting them, but our governmental transformation followed a logic of its own' mediated by the peculiar structure of the old existing regime and shifts in electoral politics.[44] The resulting American regulatory machine was one characterized by corporate conservatism, professionalism, and the quest for administrative rationality. This came about because the patchwork of business regulations that emerged in the nineteenth century had become a threat to economic development, with a 'weak state' unable to overcome the conflict of interests and institutions that characterized its fledgling industrial economy. The bureaucratic remedy was readily accepted, and resulted in increased government authority over economic regulation, so that the organization of state power coalesced around the establishment of a variety of administrative and regulatory agencies, enveloped in the realm of scientific management and technocracy to insulate itself from the pressures of factionalism.[45]

By contrast, the low visibility of regulatory policy-making in Europe can be attributed in part to the marked differences in institutions and ideologies between Europe and the United States.[46] Historically, nationalization was the functional equivalent of American-style regulation, with nothing analogous to the specialized, single purpose commissions or administrative agencies that characterized American politics.[47] Europe instead chose an interventionist state rather than regulatory state, whereby the mode of governance was public ownership that would enable the state to 'impose a planned structure on key sectors of the economy and at the same time protect the public interest'.[48] The distinction between the American and European context is important as the dominant model in European public administration was parliamentary and/or ministerial accountability and control over public bureaucracies whereas the American public administration model was agency structures characterized by expertise, independence, and specialization.[49]

As a result, the United States instituted independent regulatory agencies as a form of law enforcement and administrative policy-making.[50] Unlike traditional forms of representative government, the agencies were designed to investigate and deliberate within a universe of 'dispassionate expertise'.[51] Because American regulation was justified by the existence of market failure and thus based on the internal logic of economics and the ideology of efficiency, it served as an ideological glue binding together the quasi-legislative, quasi-executive, and quasi-judicial duties of regulators.[52] In certain instances, the market 'failed', requiring corrective policies to generate efficient solutions.[53]

By contrast, the regulatory responses of European governments are often only explicable by reference to the more general aims of an interventionist system. Premised on the notion of saving the market from its own dysfunctional tendencies, governments in the 1950s and 1960s pushed policies which influenced the domestic allocation of resources and income to varying degrees. This intervention, as well as the expansion of the welfare state, assisted the process of European integration as governments were able to compensate and adjust for increased competition and openness of national economies.[54] These policies meant that the economic-regulatory role of the state was difficult to separate from its general welfare activities.[55] Because regulation is embedded in the practices of the interventionist state, few studies have focused on regulation as a distinct mode of European economic policy-making until the seminal work of Majone. Characteristically, European intervention in the economy was based on virtues of Keynesian fine-tuning, indicative planning, and the potentialities of industrial policy. By manipulating macroeconomic variables, applying fiscal and monetary tools to alleviate unemployment, and providing public goods and generous welfare policies, the modes of economic intervention proved to be of long-standing influence.[56]

In more recent years, however, the traditional modes of government intervention have increasingly been questioned. Macroeconomic management in the austere international economic conditions of the 1970s and 1980s was strained, as budget deficits soared and stagflation undermined the policies of economic management pursued by governments. As the fiscal crisis of the state deepened, European government sought new ways of dealing with the crisis. New economic criteria were added to decision-making processes which de-emphasized the need for active government intervention. A firm commitment emerged in Europe to the virtues of the market and a broad shift towards re-evaluating well-established policies such as nationalization, state planning, and subsidies, and policies deemed too intrusive or burdensome. The relationship between the state and the economy underwent dramatic change. In short, increasing reliance was placed on the incentive effects of private ownership and improving economic performance by deregulation, streamlining, and simplifying regulations, and other market-based instruments.[57]

As efforts to scale back the role of the state in the economy have swept across the globe, interest in regulatory policy-making has grown substantially.[58] The attempt to reform regulatory policy-making and deregulate a number of sectors of the economy has paradoxically focused attention on the European regulatory frameworks within which market transactions take place. As Majone points out, 'the skepticism in the ability of the state to act as entrepreneur, planner and direct provider of services did not lead to demands for a return to laissez-faire as the more radical advocates of deregulation and privatization seemed to expect. Instead, there was a demand for better focused and more flexible forms of public intervention. . . .'[59] There has also been a growing awareness, post-deregulation, that policy-makers cannot simply set rules designed to let competition flourish and then stand back. They must also need to intervene to keep markets open.[60] Hence, deregulation does not actually mean the breakdown of rule systems, but only the replacement of one system for another. Similarly, privatization does not constitute the complete adoption of market mechanisms in determining economic outcomes.[61]

In most cases, governments have combined liberalization—the introduction of greater competition in the market—with reregulation or the reformulation of old rules and the creation of new ones. Different institutional settings and market structures shape regulatory reform, and reflect differences in prevailing ideas about the role of governments and institutions in the economy. While these manifestly different models of capitalism enable us to 'contrast regulatory regimes; to compare the embryonic regulatory state with its national rivals; and . . . to pose the question of which model of regulation and of capitalism is being created within the EU,'[62] this assumes that the pattern of reregulation is consistent across sectors. Given that the regulatory scene will be an important battleground for political conflicts about the proper nature and scope of public intervention, the emerging European regulatory regime may actually be a constellation of different interests, ideas, and outcomes.[63]

As Vogel argues, governments may push 'strategic regulation', giving regulatory advantages to domestic firms and using regulation to take away the advantages of foreign firms.[64] Governments may also push 'pro-competitive regulation' by designing regulation to limit the number of new competitors, provide market entry assistance, and add regulations to facilitate the effective operations of markets.[65] They may also engage in 'expansionary regulation' by extending regulations to new areas or by extra-territorial agreements. Finally, governments may opt for 'juridification and codification' to formalize tacit norms, agreements, and practices, or choose to cope with growing market complexity by delegating increased regulatory responsibility to non-governmental actors. Others make a similar point, distinguishing between regulations aimed at the introduction of competition and the creation of markets in terms of regulation of competition and regulation for competition. The first type is a liberal form of intervention which aims to correct 'market failure', while the second has a mercantilist character and aims at 'market creation' by the state.[66]

Although contemporary debates have focused on regulatory reform, deregulation, and efforts to stimulate competition in domestic and international markets through a wide range of market-based instruments, the methods and tools of regulation may change over time, as may the level of governmental involvement, but this is not a zero-sum relationship between states and markets. Self-regulatory arrangements, however, are rarely a substitute for public regulation, and effective private action needs public recognition and oversight as many studies of private governance in national contexts have suggested.[67]

Economic theories of integration and state capacity

The notion of markets as shaped and organized in significant ways by governments is sometimes overshadowed by concern about excessive state intervention in markets and corporate activities. As a result, the formative influence of the state in constructing an internal market and creating the conditions necessary for business success is sometimes underplayed. Traditional economic theories of market integration focus on private economic agents whilst ignoring the capacity of the state to shape market behaviour and outcomes. Emphasis is given to the impact and removal of trade obstacles upon the efficiency and welfare of firms, without acknowledging the institutional properties of economic integration.

The conventional stages of integration outlined by Belassa are widely accepted.[68] Belassa has presented market integration in terms of five consecutive stages, namely, the free trade area, the customs union, the common market, economic policy harmonization, and complete economic union.[69] These stages are problematic analytically; the first three stages refer to classical laissez-faire economies where governments do not intervene in markets, except in a marginal way at the borders, while the latter two stages acknowledge the pervasive, and previously unacknowledged, role of the state as regulator in European economies seeking to harmonize or unify policies.[70]

By employing only a framework in which private economic activity is geared to the larger economic space, such an economic theory of integration does not capture the properties and actual intervention of government in the economy. It is important to recognize that the decision-units in contemporary European economies are both public and private actors, enmeshed in a wide variety of networks and relations. As Jacques Pelkmans argues, the environment that the government creates for commerce and competition is full of restrictions, prohibitions, minimum standards, and controls. In such an environment, private economic decisions can be 'freely' taken but they are actually constrained by the state's power to create, shape, and limit markets.[71]

Although government is widely regarded as responsible for overall economic management, its influence is viewed as limited due to the powerful role of the private sector in economic decision-making.[72]

As Lindblom has pointed out, the decisions of firms on investment, employment, and output have important allocational and distributional implications which influence public policy. Olson posits an economic theory of politics which conceives of the political as primarily an instrument for appropriating shares of resources.[73] The economic performance of national economies is understood in terms of group behaviour, specifically the activities of interest groups. Emphasis is placed on private goals—with private interests able to use or constrain public authority. Institutions and procedures are portrayed as reflecting the resource preferences of private actors, with government actors carrying out the terms of the compromises.

Such analyses emphasize an essentially economistic view of political economy in which markets and economic interests are the leading actors.[74] Seeking 'perfection of the market', the focus is on efforts to liberate the market from obstacles to political exchange, enabling private economic actors to maximize their economic transactions.[75] There is an expectation that once this is achieved, the market will produce the maximum wealth and benefits for its members. But securing and exploiting a comparative advantage depends not only on a firm's ability to undertake market strategies to adapt to the single market, but also on the state's ability to create a suitable market environment. In the struggle to create, maintain, and expand favourable market positions, it is the actions and preferences of firms that are emphasized, with the state merely playing a functional role.[76] This obscures the fact that firms also depend on the state or public authorities to create and enforce a framework for market operations across political boundaries.

Governments act not only as forums for interest group preferences or as 'veto points' for contending interest groups. They can also influence market governance in ways that are not available to other organizational actors. 'Governments maintain not only the legal framework necessary for a market system, but can act as financier, middleman, regulator, advocate and even entrepreneur in a complex economic web where the frontiers between state and market blurred and cross-cutting structures become increasingly intertwined. Even the minimal state is a constant force as the guarantor of the conditions under which market exchanges take place.'[77] It is precisely because governments play an important and even dominant role in shaping the pattern of market development that business attempts to influence policy choices.

In essence, politics shapes the behaviour of firms in the market just as certainly as it shapes the behaviour of institutions operating in a more conventionally recognizable political arena. The political process strongly conditions the outcomes, and market processes are steered,

conditioned, or limited, depending on the political strategies and objectives that have to be achieved. The point is not simply that markets need
states; it is that states possess an independent capacity to shape market
behaviour and outcomes.[78] Governments frequently set out to restructure markets and the institutional arrangements that govern them for
reasons of their own.[79] Likewise, states can choose to lessen their policy role, as demonstrated by the series of cross-national institutional
reforms ranging from privatization of whole industries to the relaxation
of regulatory controls. This retreat does not, however, mean that the
process of market exchange is guided by the invisible hand. It represents
a different process where regulatory change, even if it involves dismantling legal controls, is closely shaped by the ambitions and strategies of
public agencies that act as strategic managers. Regulatory outcomes, in
this view, are not the result of private domination of the regulatory process, but *the products of the political choices exercised by governments.*

Different theories and approaches to regulation: an overview

Since most theories of regulation were developed in the American
context, bridging the gap between the American understanding of
regulation and current developments in European political economy and
public policy is increasingly important for understanding the positive,
descriptive, and normative elements of European governance.[80] Theoretical and empirical work on regulation reflects a variety of perspectives
including those based on public choice, interest group politics, public
interest, and civic republican analysis.[81] These approaches often divide
the subject of regulation in terms of its origins, practice, and consequences.[82] They also tend to be either bureaucratic or legislative in
focus, centring on the behaviour of regulated agencies and their relation
to regulated groups,[83] or upon the electoral process and the influence
and incentives of legislative institutions.[84] Many focus on certain key actors
or stages in the regulatory process, yet derive general explanations of
regulatory behaviour. Most of these studies are primarily concerned
with the American experience, and even those that are comparative or
cross-national in nature take the American experience as their model
or point of departure.[85] However, because of the variation in regulatory
perspectives in terms of their premises and assumptions, and their pre-
dictive ability across different types of decision-making processes, it is
important to provide an overview of the general frameworks that have
gained widespread acceptance.[86]

Public interest

Public interest perspectives assume that the state, acting in the public interest, establishes a legal framework to realize a set of specific regulatory objectives.[87] Those in the public law tradition stress the substantive as well as procedural aspects of regulation, including the content of rules and the criteria for their application. Though the notion of the public interest is vague, it has since evolved to become generally equated with public goods, collective goods, or general welfare. Though initially defined in the nineteenth century to apply to certain types of enterprises as 'affected with a public interest' such as banking, utilities, and railroads, more recently it refers to the need for a strong application of police powers to prevent destabilizing or destructive competition, not only for companies themselves but also for the general public welfare. For seven decades from the mid-nineteenth century, state and federal regulation proliferated in the USA, with some notion of public interest inserted into the legal frameworks of regulatory agencies such as the Federal Communications Commission, Securities and Exchange Commission, and Civil Aeronautics Board.[88] Government regulation thus grew out of a presumed need for a regulatory programme to secure the unfortunate allocative consequences of market failure. This traditional theory of regulation presupposed that, if the objectives of both the regulator and regulated were identical, then the possibility of regulatory failure was removed.

The rationale for such government intervention was based on the premiss that regulators could maximize the benefits to the largest number of individuals. The assumption that regulators are guided by their conception of the public interest was based on the belief that, once the problem is cast in technical terms, regulators can carefully and meticulously consider a response that will produce the maximum aggregate benefit.[89] Expertise was considered to be vital because regulation involved the interpretation of a wide range of scientific and technical knowledge. The theory reflects a benign view of interest group competition, as decisions will be determined not by political consensus and bargaining, but rather a technocratic approach. Freedom from political pressure would increase the ability of administrators to exercise regulatory discretion, and enable regulators to make policy based on public interest concerns rather than political expediency. This resulted in the creation of agencies reflecting the classic dichotomy between public regulation and private activity, which employed traditional command and control adjudication and rule-making powers to achieve their market-corrective goals.[90]

Advocates of the public interest approach have a great deal in common with functionalist theories of integration.[91] In the study of the EU, functionalism gives analytical primacy to social and economic co-operation. It is built on the premiss that functional integration would be pragmatic, technocratic, and flexible, deliberately blurring distinctions between national and international, public and private, and political and non-political.[92] As with the public interest approach, functionalism focuses on the provision of welfare. It assumes that consensual knowledge and common perceptions drive change. Like the public interest approach, functionalists ignore elements of competition and conflict within and between functional agencies, stressing 'problem-solving' rather than political 'bargaining' as the dominant policy style.[93]

However, the public interest perspective encountered significant criticism that it 'represented normative wishes rather than real world phenomena'.[94] The public interest view that it is possible to identify efficient solutions through policy deliberations was deemed largely irrelevant to what was actually happening within regulatory agencies. Such theories, with the provision of public goods as the main policy objective, were rejected by a variety of interest group theories emerging in the 1960s and 1970s that viewed actual regulatory outcomes as reflecting a more redistributive focus. This challenged those who sought to preserve the existing regulatory regime, since the attacks on public interest type regulation carried with it a reform agenda that argued for increased reliance on market rather than regulatory outcomes.[95]

Interest group theories

With the broad re-evaluation of American institutions in the 1950s and 1960s, the role of regulation was challenged by those who wanted greater reliance on market processes. According to these interest group theorists, the existing regulatory system enabled certain interests to use regulatory agencies to serve their own particularistic ends.[96] Rejecting traditional pluralist theory[97] that competition among different interests means that no group has a monopoly of influence, public choice theories began to conceptualize the regulatory process as a form of market place where rational self-interested actors could maximize their utilities. Regulation is thus treated as a commodity which can selectively distribute benefits.[98]

In a seminal article, Stigler shifted the focus from the public interest function by assuming that regulators are rational actors trying to maximize the political benefits from enacting a particular policy.[99] For their part, interest groups pursue regulatory goods, in much the same way as they pursue other goods so that regulatory outcomes are for the benefit of producers, not some broader public welfare.[100] Firms engage in rent-seeking behaviour, viewing regulation as a means to gain income that they would not otherwise enjoy. Although Stigler viewed regulation as analogous to market decision-making, and argued that the regulatory market works to the advantage of organized groups with narrow interests, he recognized that interest groups will face regulatory competition. Ironically, in view of the widespread criticisms about pluralism at the time, Stigler recognized the plurality of the process and the centrality of group behaviour, and acknowledged that no interest group enjoys all regulatory goods due to scarcity and competition for finite resources.

In assuming that government regulatory institutions simply operate to provide a smooth, faithful translation of interests into policy, Stigler did not acknowledge the preferences and interests of public actors. This reinforces a negligible transaction costs view, though political institutions arise precisely because the transactions costs are far from negligible.[101] In responding to these concerns, subsequent research has sought to account for the preferences of other actors.[102] Recognizing that regulatory agencies are not endogenous variables whose behaviour can be strategically manipulated by the firm they regulate, subsequent work by Peltzman, Niskanen, and Becker note that regulatory norms and preferences are themselves one factor among the many that determine regulatory policy and outcomes.[103] Such recognition of bureaucratic preferences has generally assumed that the regulatory agency is an economic actor maximizing its own welfare.

Building on Stigler's demand side model, Peltzman provides a supply side approach by assuming that the regulatory powers of the state can have an impact on the distribution of wealth as well as allocative efficiency. Matching the demand side of the equation, the supply side sought to demonstrate that interest groups can provide the electoral rewards, in the form of votes, to receive certain returns. The regulator, taken as equivalent to an elected politician, arbitrates among competing interest groups.

Like Mancur Olson, Peltzman is proposing a theory of the optimum size of effective political coalitions. Thus, groups with concentrated interests will tend to have more influence than large groups with diffuse interests. In struggles over regulatory outcomes, Olson emphasizes the importance of selective inducements to encourage participation to overcome the pervasive problem of free-riding.[104] Arguing that the commonality of interests is not a sufficient condition for the formation of active interest groups, Olson's conclusion means that the regulatory regime may underproduce collective goods.[105] To offset the problem of collective action, political authority can be delegated to provide public goods. But delegation has its own costs, as a result of the inevitable concern about how to ensure that those to whom authority is delegated actually deliver the regulatory 'goods'. While this has resulted in a substantial literature on regulatory control and oversight (see below), the interest group theories with their notion of 'capture' have exercised a strong influence over the debate about the nature and shape of the regulatory process.

These economic explanations of interest group behaviour in the regulatory process have received substantial criticism. Empirical research in political science has focused on interest group mobilization, in contrast to public choice, which derives interest group preferences deductively on the basis of economic theory, and comes to a different conclusion. As James Q. Wilson points out, 'regulatory capture' does not fit all circumstances.[106] Other studies of legislative behaviour and the effects of regulation also suggest that the economic-based interest group theory's predictions are difficult to reconcile with regulatory performance, such as systematic agency bias in favour of business interests.[107]

Administrative control and oversight

Administrative theories treat regulatory problems as an aspect of control and implementation problems in organizations.[108] These theories use tools derived from game theory, microeconomics, and social choice to assess the degree to which regulatory agencies are responsive, under certain conditions, to efforts at political control of bureaucratic discretion. Many theoretical and empirical studies challenge the implicit assumption by capture theorists that all regulatory contexts are characterized by some basic pattern of group interests. The main thrust of administrative theories is understanding how and to what extent those to whom authority is delegated remain accountable and responsive to public interest constituencies, professional norms, politicians, and oversight committees.[109]

For some, the development of an administrative apparatus based on continuity, professionalism, expertise, and effectiveness meant that implementation was carried out by trusted agents with a high degree of congruence of goals and purpose between political and administrative officials.[110] Legislative oversight mechanisms were sufficient to control regulatory behaviour, and ensure that mechanisms were in place by which voters' concerns are transformed by the political process into policy. This is based on the widely held view that administrative law is a form of 'legitimate' administration that acts as a 'technical executor of a pre-existing and unitary political will'.[111] For others, the need to hold the administrative process accountable and reduce administrative discretion is critical to ensure that democratic processes are more accountable, transparent, and efficient. In the era of the modern administrative state, regulatory statutes have been drafted that vest broad authority in agencies. Administrative discretion has increased as agencies, committees, and bureaucracies have become increasingly prominent in assisting, advising, and interpreting a wide variety of issues related to the implementation of statutory legislation[112] This has led to increasing concern about the growing power of bureaucratic agencies, as the agencies seem to be gaining influence at the expense of the political branches of government and the courts.[113]

Legal scholars have drawn attention to the decisive shift in administrative law toward oversight in the USA by detailing developments in the 1960s and 1970s that expanded opportunities for participation in agency decision-making.[114] This led to an extraordinary wave of reforms, at various levels of government, aimed at increasing bureaucratic responsiveness. Rules of standing were expanded to ease access to regulatory rule-making,[115] along with procedural due process and the requirement that agencies give a 'hard look' at all relevant issues and alternatives. The increasingly frequent substitution of judicial policy-making for administrative and regulatory policy-making, and the increase in judicial oversight were designed to enhance due process and ensure that semi-sovereign bureaucracies review available evidence, engage in reasoned decision-making, and give careful consideration to alternatives.

As Stewart argues, the function of administrative law has shifted from the protection of private autonomy to a surrogate political process that ensures representation for a wide range of affected interests.[116] This has made judicial review a necessary component of the decision-making process to ensure that deliberation and participation prevent the emergence of law that is 'arbitrary and capricious'. Though this has materialized in the United States through such mechanisms as the giving reasons requirement, sunshine laws, and Administrative Procedure Act, the issue has also become increasingly salient in the European context. Community legislation provides for the implementation or adaptation of its provisions, just as national legislation allows governments to adopt statutory instruments. Because of the need to delegate day-to-day policy-making to administrative officials, the concern over the loss of policy coherence or the loss of accountability has generated renewed interest in instruments of regulatory oversight and control at the European level.[117]

In political science, the corresponding interest in the political and legal role of administrative agency regulations resulted in substantial debate

over the effectiveness of political control over the bureaucracy, drawing on principal-agent literature.[118] There are a number of reasons for
principals to delegate to agents, including information asymmetries and
the complexity of policy-making, the need to reduce transaction costs
and shift the blame for no-agreement, and the recognition of regulatory
mismatch and policy failure.[119] Though delegation is designed to produce collective action, often in controversial areas, much of the interest
in regulatory studies has focused on determining the degree of bureaucratic discretion and the extent to which this bureaucratic 'drift' can
be curtailed through various oversight mechanisms. Because of concerns
about the effects of delegation of policy-making, earlier research in organizational behaviour, finance, and business had drawn attention to the
transaction costs involved in enabling an agent to act on behalf of a
principal.[120] This led to considerations about how different institutional
arrangements can structure efficient outcomes and ensure that the agent
is responsive to the principal.[121]

Positing a variety of ex-post and ex-ante oversight procedures, empirical studies have examined their efficacy in controlling bureaucratic
discretion and preventing what is described as slippage and shirking,
i.e. that agents may unintentionally fail to follow their assigned roles or
intentionally act against the wishes of the principal delegating authority.
For the most part rejecting the image of a 'runaway bureaucracy', these
studies have demonstrated that regulatory agencies are responsive,
under certain conditions, to efforts at political control of bureaucratic
discretion.[122] Of course, control can vary depending on the issue and
its saliency,[123] and many oversight mechanisms designed 'to stack the
deck' are themselves costly. These include subsidized interest representation, direct monitoring, legislative veto, and budgetary sanctions, all of
which can defeat the efficiency gains from delegation, reduce flexibility,
and inhibit decision-making.[124] By placing greater emphasis on accountability rather than expertise, many of the new controls are highly coercive and generate new problems reminiscent of older problems.[125]

Legal scholars have been critical of many of the administrative
control and oversight efforts that have preoccupied political scientists.
As the American experience clearly illustrates, efforts to enhance democratic pluralism and ensure fair representation can have unexpected
consequences. Attempts to increase transparency and pluralism in
administrative politics in the United States have often fostered more
cumbersome rule-making procedures.[126] Thus, 'the rule-making process
. . . intended to be quick and informal . . . is now incredibly slow, formal
and judicially supervised. . . . Rule-making has become so tendentious
that the agencies are seeking ways to make policy without making a rule.'[127]

In some cases, not recognized by principal-agent research, this may involve delegation of regulatory policy-making to the private sector. Instead of simply viewing this as 'capture', governments are using business to achieve their regulatory goals. This delegation of regulatory responsibilities has certain advantages. It offers private interest groups greater opportunity to maximize benefits, facilitates faster adaptation to technical changes and economic conditions, and minimize enforcement problems, since the affected parties are involved in the formulation of the rules they must follow.[128] This regulatory design does, however, affect competition within markets, raise accountability and legitimacy problems, and alter the character of governance itself. As we shall see, these issues are central to the construction of a European market.

Beyond capture: private interest governance and the regulatory process

Most accounts of regulation, even those sceptical of the assumptions underlying 'capture theories', have highlighted the question of industry influence.[129] 'Regulatory capture' focuses on situations where the public interest collides with narrower, private interest, reflecting an almost instinctive belief that the role of the 'public' and 'private' can be clearly delineated. As Hancher and Moran note, the very idea of capture is based on the notion that 'private' influence over the regulatory process is illegitimate or detrimental. This does not translate well to the European context. The 'peculiar constitutional imagery' of regulatory capture is very much influenced by the historical, legal, and political experience of the United States.[130]

The subordination of public authority to sectional interests rests on the assumption that private involvement in the regulatory process (in the United States) is perceived as invading the public realm. The spheres of influence of public and private actors are perceived as clearly distinct. The most influential critique of private influence on the regulatory process, Lowi's *The End of Liberalism* is based on the notion that there once existed, and should exist again, a clear demarcation between public and private spheres. In Lowi's view, the basic concept of a public sphere has been undermined, and the interventionist regulatory state, as it currently exists, cannot pursue the ideal of the public interest because it is distorted by the influence of private interests. In denying a legitimate role for private interest, capture theorists dismiss the possibility that private participation may play an important and even necessary part in regulation, if state institutions bring them into the process. By incorporating and using regulated interest groups, thus lessening the demands on a regulatory agency's resources, the relationship between public and private actors is made much more complex.

Capture theory takes a static view of the public–private relationship. Although interest group theories incorporate various explanations about how interests are mediated by state institutions, this ignores the autonomous preferences of state actors. Though there can be little doubt that economic interest groups play a crucial role in lobbying supranational and national actors, this shifts attention to only one pattern of business–government relations.[131] The decisions of European firms on investment, employment, and output do have important allocational and distributional implications which influence public policy.[132] Capture theory extends this, as institutions and procedures tend to be portrayed as reflecting the resource preferences of private actors, and government actors are viewed as carrying out the terms of the reflecting compromises.[133]

The resulting preoccupation with industry influence in studies of European regulation and market integration has diverted attention from other types of organizational relations. Following Coleman, a distinction can be made between conventional lobbying or policy advocacy and the more formalized policy participation role.[134] Based on these distinctions, the range of possible roles of organized interests is much broader than that envisaged by images of capture or lobbying. Two of the most prominent patterns of structured interaction between business and government are corporatism and private interest government.[135]

In a corporatist setting, regulatory policy-making can be characterized by an 'issue network' that brings together both public and private actors who are mutually interdependent. In corporatism, private interest groups work with the state during the policy-making and implementation stage. The network relationship conveys an image of a complex pattern of interorganizational linkages varying across issues and sectors.[136] The dynamics of regulation are thus shaped by the institutionalization of rules and norms based on stable expectations and mutual understandings among the participants.

Private interest government, by contrast, focuses on the delegation and implementation of decisions. Private organizations assuming governmental functions are not a new phenomenon. However, the growth and variety of institutional forms in which private sector governance occurs reflects increased recognition on the part of governments that they can delegate regulatory authority and rule-making to private parties that find it in their own interests to promote transnational cooperation. While the extent to which business can participate in policy-making depends in part on legal and administrative structures and traditions, implicit in this decision-making process is a model of compliance on the part of firms. Business both 'pressures' and is 'pressured'. This questions the conventional wisdom of the capture image, with private interests using or constraining public authority.

Certainly some industry participants have greater influence than others in shaping debates, negotiations, and rules. The patterns of differential access to decision-making has long been a concern in studies of regulation, although scholars have argued that business, labour, and agriculture in the American context have each sought bonds with particular segments of government as public regulation evolved.[137] However, despite the growth of social controls over business and the expansion of public interest groups, there are continued questions about the transparency and accountability of the decision-making processes, as well as the effectiveness of such a regulatory regime in contrast to traditional forms of regulatory policy-making. Although regulatory studies—notably those on administrative oversight and control—are concerned with effective mechanisms to control bureaucratic discretion, the same questions have not yet been addressed with regard to self-regulatory mechanisms and private governance.[138] Subsequent chapters highlight the broader issues of governance raised by market-building efforts in Europe since the contemporary pattern of policy-making binds the public and private sector together in a symbiotic relationship with important implications.

The regulatory landscape, however, is also shaped by its legal framework and the relationship between different governments at the national and supranational level, as well as that of the public and private sector. Far from being uniquely European, an understanding of other market-making efforts provides a good conceptual lens for the current regulatory debates in Europe. While it is commonplace to compare the EU experience with other contemporary regional integration efforts, many of the regulatory trends are found in the earlier American market-building process. Though we need to be sensitive to institutional differences, scholars of European integration have seldom considered the key role played by states, courts, and businesses in both hindering and promoting the American internal market.

Regulating markets in the USA: comparisons across time and space[139]

Historically, the movement from local to regional, national, or international markets has been an important factor in the process of economic development. In considering the American experience in the nineteenth century, the political economy literature has focused on the removal of barriers to trade between nation-states through the historic attack on tariff policies and the advocacy of free trade. However, the most interesting aspect of American market-building and economic development is the removal of internal, interstate barriers to trade, since this comparison across time and space provides useful parallels with European efforts to reconcile regulation and free trade.

As far as state intervention in market processes is concerned, the United States is widely regarded as the prototype of a regulatory state. Business and economic historians of modern American regulation have focused on the strong regulatory response of private corporations and trust formation that emerged in the late nineteenth century.[140] Early regulation was generally termed 'economic' regulation, with a regulatory agency at either the state or federal level regulating the price, entry, exit, and service of a particular industry.[141] 'Social' regulation came later, focusing on a variety of non-economic issues such as employment fairness, safety, health, and the environment, and took the form of taxes and fees, standard-setting, and licensing requirements.[142] The American debate has continued to focus on the role and effects of regulation, and on the present need for regulatory reform. A great deal of this debate has focused on the independent regulatory agencies, with specific interest given to the spate of internal reforms, downsizing, and deregulation efforts affecting sectors such as airline transportation, food and drug approval, surface transportation, and banking.[143]

Although comparisons have been drawn between the semi-autonomous or independent commissions and agencies in the United States and the establishment of European regulatory agencies,[144] the historical precedents for market-building in Europe are better served by comparing the way in which barriers to the free movement of goods and services were addressed in antebellum America.[145] While the institutional development and administrative histories of regulatory agencies have received much scholarly attention,[146] there are interesting and often overlooked parallels with the American market in dealing with obstacles to economic integration. States throughout the antebellum period jealously guarded their prerogatives to create and control economic policy, and advocates of state's rights engaged in many political disputes over economic questions.[147]

Like the United States, the European Union has been confronted by clashes over the 'reserved' powers of states.[148] Interstate disputes, as well as trade barriers under the Confederation, convinced the drafters of the Constitution that it was necessary to regulate interstate commerce to facilitate trade. But in looking at the concept of commerce in nineteenth-century jurisprudence, it is clear that the congressional commercial authority referred to the exchange and movement of goods that had already been produced. Judges and other legal commentators did not argue that local production be directly regulated by national government, due to the limited and delegated nature of federal power.[149] However, this distinction between commerce and production meant that state regulation proliferated in a host of areas, such as inspection laws, licensing, health and quarantine requirements, and occupational taxes because of a narrow reading of the federal governments' commercial authority.[150] The myriad restrictive laws and regulations meant that state and local officials acted virtually unfettered on commercial matters, 'as if they were unaware or at least unconcerned, that the commerce clause might have divested them of powers they had exercised under the Articles of Confederation'.[151]

On closer inspection, this struggle to move from local to national markets in the nineteenth century is an illuminating historical precedent for the European Union.[152] Between 1875 and 1890, business organizations began to challenge state restrictions, and pressed courts for relief.[153] Using law as an instrument to address the legal barriers devised by state governments, business organizations sought to consolidate and expand production, and benefit from the economies of scale envisaged by advocates of the European single market. In many ways, modern business enterprise emerged in response to the growth of the national market. The efforts by large firms to integrate their manufacturing and distribution operations, documented by Alfred Chandler,[154] could only come about if they could promote and induce the courts to adopt a 'free trade' doctrine at the expense of state's rights. A century later, multinational European firms advocated much the same view—supported by economic studies and assessments—about the scale and efficiency benefits of an integrated market (see Chapter 3).

As in Europe, market integration was a long and protracted struggle in the USA.[155] It took some time for the Supreme Court to acknowledge that the rise of mass production had turned communities into a national market requiring government oversight at the federal level.[156] Because the market was profoundly dependent on the legal order, the internal market could only come into being if the law permitted it. How the Court might employ its self-created power of judicial review and oversight and for what purposes remained uncertain.[157] Given that state courts had repeatedly sided with the policies of state governments, recourse through the judicial process was neither inevitable nor necessarily consistent in promoting free trade. The role played by the European Court of Justice as a facilitating mechanism or instrument in fostering a single market is in many ways similar (see Chapter 5).

In both the USA and EU, the role of law is critical in tackling trade barriers and shaping the relationship between different levels of government and between the public and private sector. In the American case, the transformation of the economy with the dramatic growth of communications and transportation networks, and the rise of financial institutions expanding their role in the interregional mobilization of capital, forced the courts to shift from protecting the territorial integrity of states to acting as 'umpire of the nation's free-trade network'.[158] As Chapter 5 illustrates, this was to be repeated by the European Court of Justice in resolving similar disputes and particularly to combat the tendency of state governments to impose unnecessarily restrictive standards, thereby similarly acting as the 'umpire' regarding free trade.

The American case is thus instructive in understanding the market-building process in Europe, and also provides a useful comparative reference about the role of the public and private sector in the economy as documented in subsequent chapters. Beginning with the landmark cases of *Gibbons* v. *Ogden* (1824) and *Brown* v. *Maryland* (1827), the tide began to turn, as the Supreme Court began distinguishing between legitimate and illegitimate trade barriers, and thus determining the division of regulatory competencies in much the same way that the European Court of Justice was later to revisit.

The idea that nationally based business, even without Congressional licence, should engage in equal terms with local merchants and manufacturers led the courts to conclude that valid public policy goals such as consumer protection and public health would have to be achieved by means other than state or local legislation. In the United States, the obvious remedy was either federal regulation or voluntary self-regulation.[159]

As commercial associations, professional and scientific societies, and trade federations sought to address the diversity of local and state standards, the number of new public and private organizations springing up was legion. Extensive debates about the relationship between commercial organizations and the public interest ensured.[160] The emergence of bodies such as the National Bureau of Standards, the United States Public Health Service, American Standards Association, and American Society of Testing and Materials[161] with their emphasis on rationalization and technical expertise, in a sense, laid the foundations for the more familiar regulatory mechanisms—regulatory agencies—of the twentieth century. And yet the relative importance of private actors in the United States in setting standards has not received the same kind of attention, even though it is part and parcel of the growth of the 'regulatory state'.

Moreover, the dramatic expansion of the scope of regulatory power over market relations and practices in the late nineteenth and twentieth century (particularly evident in the post-New Deal period) meant that economic supervision has shifted from the constitutional law arena to the administrative law arena. Although the increased delegation of legislative authority to administrative agencies reflected changing circumstances, and inspired a great deal of commentary about the legitimacy of such a regulatory regime,[162] the political economy of market regulation in terms of production, distribution, trade, and the social implications were originally connected to constitutional law. This changed as concerns about administrative accommodation of interest group politics, so strongly articulated by those that sought to make adjustments to the growing inequality of bargaining power among different interests, became prominent. Even so, these administrative approaches to regulation did not consider the political 'choices' of delegating regulatory responsibilities to the private sector.

Though much less visible, private sector efforts to regulate economic activity complemented public sector activities in integrating local and regional markets in the United States. Industries and trade associations sought to standardize production in order to ease the burdens of doing business on a national scale. Markets were thus integrated by an institutional mix of public and private bodies that established regulatory requirements and standards for a host of industries, trade, and services.[163] While the federal government increased its own regulatory authority over commercial practices, it also used the private sector to achieve its regulatory goals. Many of the standards set by collective agreement in the private sector provided the foundation for federal regulatory requirements, and were often incorporated into law. The industries themselves sought to resolve problems of interstate barriers through negotiation, pre-empting further government intervention. The American government allowed and in some cases encouraged the private sector to perform what is usually considered to be the realm of government activity. Blurring the boundaries between the public and private sector in ways seldom considered in American discussions and debates on regulation.

Constructing a market in the European Union can be better understood in light of the difficulties faced and choices made by the United States a century earlier. While European and American businesses have both used the courts to circumvent trade restrictions, they have themselves been used by the federal government, which has frequently delegated regulatory responsibilities to industry experts involved in private standards bodies, industry and trade associations, and professional societies. The parallels with the American experience are important as they reveal some of the same tensions about delegated power. In the

European case, a great deal of attention has been given to analysing the EU as a 'regulatory state'. While the focus is on the distribution of competencies between the national and supranational level, the varieties of rule-making in Europe include an array of non-state initiatives that shift market governance from the public to the private sector. Although Polanyi is correct in recognizing that the legal order must support market activity, and understood the vital role of the state in constructing and maintaining the market, he did not specify the particular instruments that the state might use in pursuing that goal.

Conclusion

Government regulation of markets cuts across a host of issues and sectors. The wave of regulatory reform across states has focused more attention on reducing the regulatory burden than on the mechanisms of market governance. In spite of the political appeal of deregulation, the growth of the regulatory state at the European level has come to occupy a central role in European research. Paradoxically, free markets require more rules, many of which are increasingly framed at the supranational level, and the process of market creation can transform relations between different interests in both the public and private spheres. Both territorial politics and interest group politics drive a political process that also requires judicial intervention to shape and set the parameters for market access.

While European integration has come to encompass an ever increasing set of policies and directives, free trade has been and still is at the core of the project. Yet the observation by Caporaso that 'European integration charts an incoherent path, is disjointed, and moves forward in fits and starts, and generates intense disagreement over the nature of European institutions will surprise few familiar with the EU or the historical process of market-building with which it is often compared'.[164] The following chapters document these 'fits and starts', and the growth of the regulatory state in terms of some of the same concerns about due process, transparency, accountability, and governance that have characterized regulatory debates in the United States. The construction of both the American and European markets is instructive since they are characterized by competition among different territorial units, and efforts by business to overcome the tremendous legal barriers that hindered cross-border trade. This competition provides an important emphasis on the contested nature of market-making, and the use of resources in both the public and private sector in shaping regulatory out-comes. While many scholars have questioned the democratic implications of the transfer of power in territorial terms, from the national to the supra-national level, but have not questioned the shift from public to private which is at the heart of this analysis.[165]

While the European regulatory process strives for what Majone has described as Madisonian checks and balances, and greater attention is given to bureaucratic control, oversight, and accountability, a more sub-tle feature of this Madisonian system is that the emphasis on expertise is sought in the private sector. The old debates in regulation between technocracy and democracy have resurfaced not only in the public sphere but also in the private sphere. In order to highlight the transformation of governance and system of rule-making for European commerce that has emerged, the following chapters will focus on the development of European regulatory efforts to promote trade liberalization, and deal with the problem of uncoordinated standards that can act as restrictions on free trade.

Removing Barriers to Trade:
Empirical Evidence

Tackling barriers to trade

The foundation of European economic integration is internal trade liberalization. The Treaty of Rome clearly emphasized the creation of a common market, and more specifically the establishment of a customs union for goods, with a limited number of sectoral policies regulated at the European level. As the 1956 Spaak Report makes clear, the EC envisaged a common market along the lines of the United States.[1] This was not the first time the analogy to the American market had been made: the Economic Cooperation Act of 1948 'mindful of the advantages which the United States has enjoyed through the existence of a large domestic market with no internal trade barriers, and believing that similar advantages can accrue to the countries of Europe,' promoted such a goal in post-war economic reconstruction.[2]

By prohibiting the states from erecting barriers to the interstate movement of goods, the USA had encouraged the growth of a national market, but also gave the federal government authority to exercise control and regulation over economic activity.[3] The Spaak Report followed this approach in providing a blueprint for the common market, suggesting that such a market required three primary elements: (1) establishment of normal standards of competition through elimination of protective barriers; (2) curtailment of the effects of state interventions and monopolistic conditions; and (3) countermeasures against distortions including possible harmonization of state legislation.[4]

The size of the American market had fostered the development of large-scale production technologies that were partially responsible for American productivity levels being the highest in the world. Research by Owen also provides support for the industrial logic underlying the instinctive aspiration behind the Community's formation: market size is an important explanatory factor in productivity differences.[5] Using the American experience as a model the EC initially lowered traditional tariffs, starting with the elimination of customs duties and quantitative restrictions in 1958, and introduced a common external tariff in 1968.[6] To avoid large-scale dislocation of member state economies, the EC provided for a transitional period from 1 January 1958 to 1 January 1970, during which the internal tariffs would be gradually eliminated at different stages by individual member states. The net result was a substantial time difference in achieving the elimination of internal tariff barriers between agricultural commodities and industrial products. Total tariff reduction on industrial products was reduced by 80 per cent, while basic duties on agricultural products declined by 65 per cent during the same period. Internal tariff reductions for industrial products were also frequently extended to third countries, if they did not lower a nation's tariff below that of the common external tariff (CET). The extension of tariff reductions to non-members minimized the discriminatory effects of the customs union, particularly in the initial formative period of the EC.[7]

While largely successful, the transition to a common market did not remove all obstacles to expanded trade within the EC. Although EC trade policy was substantially liberalized in the 1960s, a multitude of non-tariff barriers to trade remained, and external non-tariff trade measures were never fully unified. Trade liberalization did help to increase the share of intra-regional trade in terms of total trade, rising from about 40 per cent in 1958 to 60 per cent in 1980. However, these results were affected by factors other than the creation of a common market. In particular, changes in external trade policy and levels of competitiveness vis-à-vis non-EC members enabled the EC to capitalize on intra-EC exports. Enlargements of the EC in 1973 to include Britain, Ireland, and Denmark, in 1981 Greece, and in 1986 Spain and Portugal, also contributed to the increase in intra-EC trade. These new members had a substantial impact on trade flows within the EU, diverting trade with non-EC member states.

Though the Common Market did largely succeed in eliminating tariff barriers, the presence of non-tariff barriers continued to hamper intra-EC trade. As one observer noted, 'the lowering of tariffs has in effect, been like draining a swamp. The lower water level has revealed all the snags and stumps of non-tariff barriers that still have to be cleared away.'[8] The goals of expanding cross-border coverage and internationalization of market scope were hindered by the continued fragmentation of the European market, as firms were constrained by the widespread barriers to entry that prevented them from engaging in cross-border competition. Different national product regulations and standards, quotas, subsidies, discriminatory public purchasing, and licensing seriously impeded market access.

To provide a baseline in assessing the significance of subsequent regulatory strategies, this chapter examines the costs of substantial differences in national regulations, standards, and certification requirements for European business. In an increasingly competitive, global economy, European governments were faced with a double challenge: the proliferation of regulatory obstacles that hamper cross-border trade; and the need to find more efficient ways to protect and promote important public policy goals. Through an examination of the costs of such regulatory-related non-tariff or 'technical' barriers to trade, this chapter emphasizes that the effects of integration vary across industries and countries, depending on the level of concentration, the degree of specialization or differentiation of products, and openness to competition.

In addition to quantitative trade data, the market effects of tackling technical barriers to trade are assessed through surveys of business attitudes towards removing such trade impediments. The concluding section of this chapter discusses the specific nature and effects of standards, regulations, and certification policies which are considered the most prevalent impediments to the free circulation of manufactured products in the European market. In these cases, trade liberalization and regulatory reform can be mutually reinforcing in fostering European objectives to create a single market.

However, the existence of regulatory barriers does not always lead member states to pursue common interests. In certain regions and industries the impact of the single European market could lead to disadvantages. Industries that had been shielded from competition by national rules and regulations could no longer rely on a satisfying strategy of securing a stable market share, as they would be exposed to competitive imports from other European Community member states. Increased competition in the European market threatens the viability of firms accustomed to systems of national protection.

As this chapter and the following detail, the difficulties in pressing for trade liberalization in the 1970s fluctuated with perceptions of trade inequities and a growing conviction that governments should intervene to ensure a level playing field. With national governments seeking more regulatory protection to counter the effects of increased imports and technological competition, trade liberalization and increased market integration were delayed and domestic industries were buffered from import competition.

Through most of the 1970s and early 1980s, Europe experienced a rising trend in trade restrictions. The demand to protect home markets led governments to devise increasingly stringent rules and regulations. Although traditional tariffs were lowered, non-tariff barriers continued

TABLE 3.1 *Share of total imports subject to non-tariff barriers*[a]

Country	1981	1983	1986	Change 1981–6
Belgium/Lux.	12.6	15.4	14.3	1.7
Denmark	6.7	8.0	7.9	1.2
Germany[b]	11.8	13.6	15.4	3.6
France	15.7	18.8	18.6	2.9
Greence	16.2	21.0	20.1	3.9
Ireland	8.2	9.7	9.7	1.5
Italy	17.2	18.7	18.2	1.0
Netherlands	19.9	21.4	21.4	1.5
EC (10)[c]	13.4	15.6	15.8	2.4

[a] Based on non-tariff barriers applied to a constant 1981 trade base. This enables calculations of NTB changes while holding the effects of trade changes constant.
[b] These figures are for the Federal Republic of Germany.
[c] Excludes Spain and Portugal, who joined the EC in 1986.

Source: Adapted from Sam Laird and Alexander Yeats, 'Quantitative Methods for Trade Barrier Analysis', Washington, World Bank. Based on data provided by the UN Conference on Trade and Development (UNCTAD).

to rise, even among such champions of free trade as Germany. Between 1981 and 1986, non-tariff barriers increased by 36 per cent in Germany, 30 per cent in France, and 24 per cent across the European Community as Table 3.1 illustrates. Such policies not only skewed trade balances, but also curbed competition.

European efforts to contain import competition and stabilize industries through more permanent and far-reaching regulation failed to stem the tide, as trade deficits soared. Japanese exports to the EC rose fifteen-fold in the 1970s, from $1.1 billion in 1970 to $17 billion in 1980. Over the same period, US exports to the Community rose fivefold, from $5 billion to $38 billion. Europe was clearly losing ground.[9] This trend was met, in part, by the increase of non-tariff barriers at the national level. Throughout the debates in Europe over these ostensibly domestic policies runs the thread of protectionism, and the concerns about the effects of national responses to international competition upon the internal market.[10]

While Laird and Yeats's statistics are consistent with other assessments of the extensive usage of non-tariff barriers,[11] the range of measures is broad and it is difficult to assess which are the most important in terms of trade impact.[12] Such indices do not provide insights into the restrictiveness of the measures, or the extent to which these quantitative restraints are actually binding on exporters. Though these estimates of non-tariff barriers must be treated with some caution, there is consensus for the proposition that the trade-impeding effect of discriminatory trade practices across Europe was considerable.[13] The problems cut across a wide range of industries, from motor vehicles to computers to consumer electronics and wine and beverages.

Growing recognition of a 'competitiveness gap' also led to strenuous efforts to maintain overall levels of economic activity and provide conditions for viable markets. Although regulated trade had long protected certain agricultural products, steel, textiles, and automobiles, states began curbing competition from imports through voluntary export restraints, quotas, health, and sanitary regulations in many other product areas. While past trade regulation to support or improve the sales base, profitability, and jobs of manufacturing industries had succeeded in promoting national economic growth, the tools of national politics were no longer able to cope with the changes in the international economy. As national oligopolies collapsed, governments stepped in to try to sustain the existing forms of market regulation. When this failed, more interventionist public regulation became unavoidable. These attempts to maintain aggregate levels of economic activity forced states into policies that they could not maintain and undermined trade relations in Europe through the constant emergence and perpetuation of trade disputes.

Rather than continue to use domestic remedies, in the form of denying equivalent access to national markets, attention shifted to European solutions. In particular, policy-makers focused on the *completion* of the European market and the strengthening of European strategies in such areas as technical standards and public procurement to 'improve the existing environment in which companies exist'[14] and guard against market outcomes that relegated Europe to the margins of industrial production and exchange.

The political economy of protection

Many assessments about market integration assume that firms are identical and that if collective goods problems can be overcome, all firms will unanimously advocate a common political position regarding the removal of barriers to trade. Using a simple profit-maximizing model of the firm in perfect competition, the new regulatory strategy focusing on the European market was expected to have three effects: (1) entry and expansion into other markets that were previously highly protected; (2) rationalization of production and sales strategies among existing networks; and (3) the use of the domestic market as a springboard for competition on a pan-European scale.

Yet it is by no means certain that states and firms will accept the implications of removing market entry barriers. As we shall see in subsequent chapters, European policies to liberalize or eliminate distortions in cross-border trade are made in imperfect markets where firms and governments act strategically to affect trade flows and national welfare.[15] Researchers in political economy, international business, and public policy agree that nations use trade policies to act strategically to protect industries threatened by non-domestic competitors.[16] Differences in trade protection and the specificity of trade barriers exist because of differences in the competitive characteristics of firms across member states.

Reactions of firms to efforts at integration may vary according to market structure: the number, size, and organization of firms. Potential advantages from greater economies of scale, improved ratios of fixed to total costs, and the potential widening of markets can be very different for different firms and countries. Although the disciplining effect of increased competition is thought to induce significant improvements in the economic efficiency of industry, significant obstacles to industrial reorganization result from differences in the structural make-up of national political economies in Europe.[17] Different orientations in terms of market scope and production among firms play an important part in the pace of consolidation, reorganization, and rationalization in response to the internal market place. German firms, for example, place more emphasis on vertical integration, training, quality standards, and build-up of long-term market share, whereas French firms have traditionally focused on specific policy instruments, such as preferential taxation, non-tariff barriers, and certain kinds of industrial subsidies, that have led them to focus on maintaining domestic market shares.

Intra-firm differences must also be considered in assessing business strategy and performance. These include competitive positioning, management expertise, and other resources that enable firms to leverage competitive advantage in a single market. Organizational efforts are expressed in and profoundly influenced by different business orientations. While the productivity ethos of the German firm permeates all layers and acts as an integrating mechanism, the predominantly financial orientation of the British, with each unit treated as a separate profit centre, fails to provide a common integrated focus.[18] Such examples highlight the fact that global competition takes place between different systems of cross-border management, varying not only between firms but quite frequently within different parts of the same firm.

While the removal of non-tariff barriers to trade is expected to lower market entry requirements, increase competition, and push firms to engage in dynamic corporate strategies to exploit a unified market, many estimates of direct gains assume perfectly competitive markets and omit adjustment costs.[19.]Rather than follow assumed models of integration, the political economy of protection may encourage different response patterns and consequences depending on the perceived distribution of costs and benefits.[20] As subsequent chapters show, these factors may foster or discourage incentives to engage in collective action to remove non-tariff technical barriers to trade.

This is particularly the case where firms are directly involved in the formation of regulatory goals, leading to bargaining among firms—and perhaps the use of side payments—to reach a unified position. The process of consensus-building can be extremely time-consuming when firms have highly divergent interests. Under these circumstances, even though there may be gains from cooperation, such cooperation is difficult to implement as numerous bargain sets can lead to Pareto-optimal co-operative outcomes.[21] This is not well acknowledged by existing studies of removing barriers to trade, which generally do not focus on problems of collective action and the process of coordinating diverse preferences. Instead, research on specific barriers, implemented at the product level and often targeted towards certain countries, has focused primarily on their type or description.[22] This does not provide a full picture of the trade distorting impact of these measures upon both production and distribution decisions, particularly for internationally oriented firms.[23]

From this perspective, market liberalization is not based on a series of simultaneous interactions among passive agents but dynamic actors who make strategic moves and anticipate change. Strategic behaviour to gain advantages with respect to other firms causes problems of credibility in ensuring that the rules for market access are uniformly accepted by all players.[24] Without reliable monitoring of compliance, to ensure that associated distortions are minimized, and that prohibitive barriers between member states are removed and prevented from recurring, the EU is faced with the possibility that market integration may be asymmetrically implemented across sectors and member states. Before focusing on the problems of credibility and mutual trust to maintain market liberalization, however, we need first to consider the actual extent and costs of market fragmentation in Europe.

Estimating the costs of non-Europe

A great deal of research on regional integration has focused on the value of economic liberalization in promoting trade and welfare.[25] A fully-fledged internal market with participating countries sharing common micro- and macroeconomic policies was perceived by many scholars and policy-makers to offer substantial gains. To gain political support for the regulatory intervention necessary to create a single market, economic evaluations of the impact of the removal of barriers to trade on prod-uct, services, labour, and capital markets were undertaken as part of the European Commission's own 1988 research project, the 'The Costs of Non-Europe' or 'Cecchini Report' after its lead author.[26] Although much of the Cecchini research is now treated with caution, the estimated gains from removing non-tariff barriers to trade were considerable. The estimates were for seven European countries (Britain, France, Germany, Italy, Luxembourg, Belgium, and the Netherlands) accounting for 88 per cent of the EC's GDP. It was assumed that the remaining five countries would realize gains of the same percentage of their GDP.[27] Using both microeconomic analyses of individual sectors, and macroeconomic simulations of the European economy, Cecchini predicted strong welfare gains. A brief overview of both static and dynamic effects will help in understanding the basis of this conclusion.

Static effects

Static effects, in the sense that they represent a one-shot increase in the level of welfare gains, principally affect the price of traded products. For firms, barriers to trade result in duplication of research and development costs, and the loss of manufacturing efficiency as production has to be geared towards different national market requirements. These prob-lems can lead to higher unit costs and unexploited economies of scale, increasing inventory and distribution costs, and the segmentation of product management and marketing.

With the removal of barriers that distort allocative efficiency, the under-lying comparative advantage of the member states becomes increasingly important in determining production profiles and trading patterns. Member countries with relative cost advantages and other factor endow-ments will gain as the removal of barriers to trade decrease transaction costs and lead to increased specialization.[28] Although increased special-ization should benefit all member states, as production is allocated in a more efficient manner, it can also create a division between those that reap benefits from capital intensive industries and those that have advantages in labour intensive industries. This may lead to what Hirschmann des-cribed as the 'polarization' effect of integration, potentially impeding the development of the laggard regions of the Community.[29] Given the 'first-mover advantage' of North European member states in capital intensive

industries, the removal of barriers could perpetuate industrial specialization across the Community,[30] particularly after the expansion of the
Community to include the southern tier of Greece, Portugal, and Spain.

However, according to Neven, the comparative disadvantages facing
these member states may be overstated. Cheap labour and unexploited
opportunities could lead to huge investments in the Southern tier. If they
can exploit their advantages in labour intensive industries, the gains
they make in these areas may help offset the losses in high-tech sectors.
Neven concludes that the main beneficiaries of the removal of trade
barriers are actually likely to be the Southern member states, as their
efforts to 'catch-up' provide them with greater scope for exploiting
scale economies and efficient specialization.[31]

Dynamic effects

Though the Cecchini Report predicted significant static benefits from
removing non-tariff barriers to trade, it joined more recent theoretical
and empirical research in moving beyond traditional analysis of the effects
of market integration.[32] Acknowledging that neither customs union
theory nor theories of perfect competition and constant returns to scale
capture the gains from market integration, Cecchini recognized that
the dynamic effects on market performance are equally significant and
important.[33]

This assumed that the potential gains from completing the single
market, in addition to lower trade costs, would rely on three expected
effects: greater production efficiency achieved through market enlargement, reallocation of resources due to the restructuring of industries,
and the elimination of 'corporate slack' as a result of the pressures of
intensified competition.[34] These predicted growth effects were therefore
dependent on the strategic responses of firms to exploit the opportunities created by market integration, since the 1992 programme changed
many of the rules by which businesses operate. Cecchini assumed that
firms would respond positively to the effects of greater competition and
the removal of market entry restrictions by exploiting economies of scale
and capitalize on market enlargement through rationalizations.

Though the benefits of scale economies can be encouraged by product standardization, the evidence presented by the EC on economies
of scale and rationalization are now considered overly optimistic.[35]
Having sacrificed product diversity for economies of scale, firms may also
become more vulnerable as production of a narrow range of standardized products limits their ability to adjust to continuous technological advances. Alternatively, increased competition may also stimulate

technological innovation and efficient allocation of resources,[36] because the absence of barriers to market entry encourages innovation, as new market entrants have more incentive to promote new processes and products than those with investments in established products and technologies. Thus, intensified competition through the lowering of barriers to market entry could lead to greater contestability of markets.[37] As a result, firms may attempt to improve economic efficiency by adopting business strategies to exploit the real or perceived benefits of broader market access. Mergers and acquisitions across intra-EC borders, the rationalization of production and construction processes, inward investment by non-EC based companies may all increase efficiency and provide the stimulus for competitive behaviour among producers.

Besides these structural changes, there is an increased potential for cost minimization and location arbitrage. With markets no longer segmented, firms can take advantage of price differentials in product markets and exploit differences in taxes, market entry regulations, wage rates, and labour market conditions to locate to the most favourable location. Firms may also concentrate their existing European network, selling off or rationalizing subsidiaries. Since these subsidiaries were often set up as a vehicle to operate within insulated 'national markets', they become less relevant in a more integrated European market.[38]

Chapter 10 addresses these issues at further length, examining how firms have actually responded to changes in market practices, and assessing the impact of efforts to remove non-tariff barriers upon their corporate strategies.[39] This follows the recommendations of Maskus and Wilson that the empirical analysis should include administering firm-level surveys to assess the role of standards, regulation, and conformity assessment barriers in trade dynamics.[40] Here it is important to note that, as the Commission found through its own research, while European business sought a more efficient and transparent market structure, individual sectors varied considerably in their perceptions of market ills and proposed remedies.

Business perceptions

The Commission's survey of over 20,000 businesses in all twelve member states ranked business perceptions regarding the most important barriers to trade in the Community market. The survey ranked technical standards and regulations and administrative barriers as the top priority for the completion of the internal market, followed by frontier formalities, freight transport regulations, value-added tax differences, capital markets control, government procurement restrictions, and implementation of Community law. However, the large volume of complaints made to the Commission by companies about the effects of technical barriers to intra-EC trade indicated that the problem was particularly acute.[41]

The Commission also found significant differences among sectors. Trade in investment goods was more severely disrupted by technical barriers than trade in consumer and intermediate goods. For firms in the engineering and electronic industry, goods transport and medical and office equipment, restrictions imposed by different national regulations and standards result in significant *cost-increasing* barriers to trade. These firms suffered a loss of manufacturing efficiency as production runs had to be adapted to meet different national market entry requirements.

With escalating R&D costs, shortening lead times and product life cycles, European firms perceived that such massive investments could only be recouped by increased standardization. Technological innovation and its application, via product development, design, and engineering, and finally incorporation of process and product technology in the commercial market place, was hampered by market segmentation. Particularly in technologically driven industries, barriers to entry created by diverse standards and regulations hindered economies of scale and efficient production structures as European firms were unable to forge a global unit.

Yet business perspectives were not uniform. Much of the debate about European integration has tended to focus on large firms, especially multinationals with production and distribution facilities in several member states. These firms figured strongly in the Commission's survey of the effects of completing the internal market. Although more than 12,000 firms in the EC have over 500 employees, 15.7 million small and medium enterprises represent the fastest growing element of the European economy. Many small businesses voiced concern about the effects of increased competition and the need for higher-quality standards for contractual purposes in the supply chain.

It is by no means certain, therefore, that the strategic response of firms will be similar. Smaller firms with less than fifty employees considered technical barriers of secondary importance, while companies with more than 1,000 employees ranked technical barriers as a significant obstacle to intra-EC trade. For many small and medium firms that exist profitably at the national or even subnational level, the removal of trade barriers may have a negative effect. Compliance with European regulations may cost them more as a percentage of turnover, while they receive fewer benefits from European rules because they are less likely to engage in cross-border sales.

While 62 per cent of firms surveyed said that the removal of barriers to trade would lower costs, 36 per cent did not expect any changes in their productivity costs. Many firms anticipated that their domestic market share would decline as a result of the immediate direct effects of removing barriers, but expected growth in market shares elsewhere.[42] Of the companies surveyed, 24 per cent expected demand for standardized products to increase. In the larger member states of Britain, France, and Germany, firms expected significant gains from the removal of differing national standards and regulations. Companies in smaller countries often circumvent this problem by adopting the technical standards and specifications applied in the larger countries.[43] The impact of the barriers to trade is thus perceived differently depending on the structural environment in which firms operate. For many firms, the question whether market integration helps them to overcome trade barriers, access relative cost advantages, adapt to structural changes in the industry, and clearly define their core competencies[44] in response to shifts in international competition is taken up in Chapter 10.

Technical barriers to trade and market access

Despite the Commission's comprehensive survey results, assessing the impact on European industry of the removal of barriers to trade is difficult. Business surveys, government reports, and interviews indicate that the problem is widespread.[45] While uncoordinated standards, testing, and regulatory systems produce innumerable trade barriers, their effects tend to be highly industry specific and difficult to generalize, and their very ubiquity added to the perception that the EU market was highly fragmented.[46] The Commission estimated that there were over 100,000 different national regulations and standards in 1985, each a potential impediment to trade.

Because member states valued environmental and consumer protection, they continually introduced new product standards and regulatory requirements that often favoured domestic producers over foreign competitors. These national regulatory measures may present barriers in the form of packaging and labelling requirements, registration or testing procedures, and costs of obtaining proof that the product meets the health, safety, and environmental standards of the importing country. Technical barriers to trade—stemming from differences in standards, regulations, testing, and certification policies—affect business operations directly, in terms of design, production, sales, and marketing strategies.

However, empirically assessing the efficiency gains from removing technical barriers to trade is inherently difficult, since determining the size of the effects requires an in-depth knowledge of the structure of the industry, including the relationship between market demand and price, and the shape of the cost curve.[47] Most studies tend to be either case studies of specific disputes or limited to particular markets and industries.[48] The Commission found that those sectors subject to regulatory standards (chemicals, pharmaceuticals, foodstuffs, and motor vehicles for example) were more heavily dependent on national markets, and concluded that 'technical barriers are effectively discouraging cross-border trade and competition in some sectors'.[49] Firms may simply forgo access to other markets due to the extra costs of having to produce different specifications and design requirements, samples of which must then be tested to see if it meets the importing countries requirements.

With greater adjustment costs for foreign firms and cost-increasing entry barriers, firms may treat countries as separate entities and not base their strategies on the interdependencies between markets.[50] Market liberalization is expected to enable those companies that have a competitive edge in terms of cost advantage to expand their market share. In addition, products may also compete on other factors such as quality and reputation. Those products with a reputation for quality standards may retain their competitive edge despite the disciplining effect of increased competition and the removal of technical barriers to trade.

Because certain domestic firms engage in 'rent-seeking' and divert their energies to maintain trade barriers, they tend to focus on exploiting their captive home markets instead of focusing on dynamic production strategies. In economies sheltered to the pressure of competition, firms may not focus on increasing efficiency through internal reorganization, prefer inward-looking corporate strategies rather than engaging in high value-added activities, and avoid the development of innovative products or new production methods, R&D or quality oriented production processes.[51] Like other forms of trade protection, technical barriers impact the importing country through higher domestic prices, high cost margins, and productive inefficiencies.

Standards, regulations, and testing and certification

The growth of international trade has not surprisingly made impediments created by standards and regulations and the various testing and certification procedures to meet these requirements much more visible. And yet there is much confusion as to what these technical barriers to trade mean in practice. Although often linked together and used interchangeably, they do in fact represent different types of barriers that have become increasingly pervasive in hindering market integration.

Standards

Standard-setting has a long history as public authorities and commercial entities such as merchant guilds sought to regularize weights and measures, products, and coinage. These efforts were intended to reduce problems of fraud and promote product compatibility and exchange, an important goal given the bewildering variety of weights and measures within and between various states and localities.[52] Designed initially to facilitate commerce, economic and business historians have documented the growth of national standards with industrialization, pointing to the linkage between advances in science and technology as well as the growth of the consumer movement to explain the emergence of standardization.[53] Increasingly these national variations in standardization have been at the forefront of trade disputes.[54]

Standards are created and employed across a wide range of different circumstances and they play a different role depending on those circumstances. In principle, standard, are designed to facilitate exchange, guarantee quality, and achieve the provision of public goods. Standards are classified on the basis of one of three purposes: quality, variety reduction, and compatibility.[55] Quality standards satisfy criteria including reliability, durability, and fitness of purpose. Variety reduction standards reduce unnecessary duplication and compatibility standards allow different products or components to work together to insure interoperability.

Standards are usually voluntary agreements that focus on either the design or performance of a specific product, process, or service.[56] Standards can be categorized by two functions. Product standards refer to the characteristics that goods must possess, such as minimum nutrition content, performance requirements, or interoperability of networks. Production and process methods refer to the conditions under which products are made which are broadly production conditions such as working conditions and environmental discharges.[57] Product standards can determine the size and shape of credit cards, film speeds in cameras, the symbols on car dashboards, and the grading systems for screws and threads. Process standards can determine production methods such as life-cycle analysis, risk assessment and impact analysis, and work organization methods.

Much of the research on standards has focused on game theoretic models to explain the conditions under which agreement can be reached, eliciting different views regarding the viability of government or market strategies and solutions.[58] Many of these important standards efforts are considered coordination problems. The potentially negative effects of divergent standards can be mitigated if one standard becomes dominant in the market (*de facto* standards), enabling firms to follow the market leader.[59] Achieving a critical mass of users more quickly than rival standards may be achieved through licensing, early adoption, subsidizing initial users, and forming strategic alliances. Broad market acceptance of a particular standard may enable a single firm to achieve a competitive advantage in the manufacturing process, creating a bandwagon effect as other forms seek to make their products compatible with the industry leader. Alternatively, a firm may wish to market and license its proprietary standard to make sure that it becomes dominant in the market place.[60] Both strategies create a 'lock-in' effect that can reduce competition and make it difficult for new entrants to overcome entrenched standards, even if they have innovative, more technologically advanced products.[61] While solving coordination problems, it can lead to inefficiencies such as the persistence of the Qwerty keyboard, differences in colour television broadcasts, use of metric and imperial weights, and different voltage standards.

Although markets can be effective in setting standards, they are sometimes imperfect, and institutional frameworks are necessary as alternative coordinating mechanisms to resolve collective action problems. Precisely for this reason, standard-setting has increasingly been the result of negotiations among committees of experts (*de jure*). Though formal negotiations in committees can result in a coordinated outcome, there is often disagreement over which of the coordinated outcomes is better. Although each participant may want a common standard, there may be intense disagreements over which particular standard should be chosen.[62] Specific case studies on video recorders, high-definition television, and mobile telephones have highlighted the intense competition surrounding the adoption of an international standard.[63] Policy intervention in setting standards may be needed when there are high public costs of incompatibility, or when specific performance or safety requirements are involved. Though standards committees bring together interested parties, and typically research points to the negotiations and compromises that evolve, there is little discussion of how these standards bodies reach agreement and overcome conflict. Despite the overlapping number of international, regional, and national bodies involved, and the economic impact of their negotiations, there have been few systematic analyses.[64]

While standards are only voluntary requirements, they often assume a quasi-legal status because of their use as references in technical regulations or insurance policies. In certain cases, public contracts may specifically reference national standards so that domestic-produced goods have a significant advantage.[65] Consequently, standards can be critical for a firm's competitiveness, assisting efficiency in production and distribution, and information and technology transfer.[66] For some products, the choice of a particular standard determines not only future technological developments but also international trade flows. In communications and information technologies, with high pre-development costs and short product life cycles, if *de jure* standardization can be accomplished at the pre-competitive stage of research and development, a firm can establish itself as a market leader and effectively shut out alternative products. Examples include the video cassette recorders segment of the consumer electronics industry, where Philips's V2000 (Beta) system gave way to the Japanese Video Home System (VHS), which became the *de facto* world standard. In this context, a firm's standardization policy can become the most important element of its business strategy.

Common standards are often touted as providing significant benefits such as promoting market information and confidence by signalling product quality or compatibility of products or services, reducing costs through simplification of large-scale production processes, and facilitating efficient management and effective commercial decisions if firms adopt quality standards and quality assurance schemes to enhance product reputation.[67] They may also operate by design or by circumstance to restrain competition.[68] Standardization can also cause serious drawbacks, including excessively detailed or unwarranted standardization which may entail high production costs, stifling product innovation and reducing competition and diversity. Dealing with inconsistencies among standards, and particularly when national standards differ substantially in their organization, scope, and underlying legal frameworks, can help mitigate effects of trade barriers, although the choices made concerning standardization are equally salient for both governments and markets.

Health, safety, and environmental regulations

Regulation also has a long history, although the type of regulation and its purpose has varied over time. Though early regulation sought to enforce certain practices regarding usury, primarily for religious rather than economic ends, this was followed by economic regulation concerned with the functioning of markets in terms of price, entry, exit, and service activities, and then by social regulation concerned with safety, health, employment, and a variety of non-economic issues. What is distinctive is that regulations, unlike many standards, are mandatory. Government regulations, whether at state, local, or federal level shape behaviour, and reflect underlying ideological concerns about the proper role of government in regulating market relations. Regulations cover a multitude of issues, including labelling requirements on food packages, warning notices on cigarettes, speed limits on highways, and the requirements for transport of hazardous waste. Many of these regulatory standards are aimed at preventing negative externalities, and are often imposed and enforced by governments.[69] Though these are often expressed as targets, or as certain levels and types of activity that are permissible or impermissible, such increases in protective regulation can be imposed unilaterally or multilaterally.

Although technically and economically complex, regulation has become increasingly controversial and politicized, in part because the scope and intrusiveness of government controls over corporate behaviour has increased. Unlike economic regulations that tended to affect a distinct range of industries, many of the social regulations in the health, safety, and environment area cut across industry lines, and have undermined the distinction between previously regulated and unregulated industries.[70] Although governments do themselves establish standards for a performance or production process, thereby controlling the behaviour of corporations, and other societal interests, many agencies have relied heavily on self-regulation and private enforcement of regulatory goals. Such standards do however depend on state support through some form of legalization to have maximum effect.

While many regulations have laudable public policy goals, like standards, they can create non-tariff barriers by making it more difficult or costly for foreign importers to market their products. Regulatory requirements including stringent import controls, quarantine regulations, licensing and permit requirements may be used to restrict imports.[71] A recent example is the highly publicized dispute over meat safety rules, which threaten millions of dollars worth of exports from non-EU countries. Though designed to control 'mad cow' disease, by banning products manufactured with tallow or animal fat, the dispute has caused significant transatlantic tensions.[72] Trade disputes have also persisted in other areas of food safety, as well as in animal and environmental protection measures[73] highlighting how social regulations have come to occupy an increasingly important place on the trade agenda, driven in part by the rise of public interest in both environmental and consumer issues.[74] Distinguishing between those forms of rent-seeking domestic regulations that were easily identifiable as illegitimate and other forms of restriction on exchange such as regulations on health, safety, and the environment has become increasingly difficult.

While the complexity of regulations and the lack of transparency concerning their application may discourage potential exporters, and are often magnified by procedural delays and other administrative practices that inhibit market access, the discriminatory effects are difficult to determine. Because regulatory statutes may be worded generally, the administrative guidelines and rule-making may be subtle non-tariff barriers since they claim to be introduced for general interest purposes but in fact protect particular interests and provide preferential treatment. More significantly, efforts to address such differences in regulations raise questions about how much harmonization or convergence is needed for an internal market to operate.

Testing and certification

The costs of complying with different product regulations and standards may also impede trade.[75] Conformity assessment involves testing, inspection, and finally certification to determine compliance with both regulations and standards, and raises many of the same trade issues. Although the conformity assessment process is obligatory for regulations, as part of their marketing strategies firms usually also seek confirmation that their product is consistent with designated standards in order to receive certification marks. This provides manufacturers with a readily visible endorsement that the product corresponds to certain health and safety standards.

Differing national regulations and standards lead to the duplication of tests and inspections, and create additional costs for firms that wish to trade in multiple markets. Testing and certification requirements also highlight the differences in regulatory approaches and administrative traditions across Europe. Some member states opt for pre-approval before the product is sold (ex post) while other states opt for oversight after a problem has been detected (ex ante), relying on penalties and self-regulation on the part of the manufacturer.[76] Product approval measures also underscore the obstacles faced by the Community in terms of fostering mutual trust and credibility, as they represent differing approaches to the treatment of scientific evidence, such as safety data and testing information.[77]

The costs of access to different national markets were compounded by the need to obtain additional quality marks or licences. In Germany, for example, authorities insisted that pharmaceutical products from other member states receive not only a marketing authorization but also a special import licence. Even where products did meet different national standards, imports were often retested, due to reservations about the technical competence of inspectorates and certifying bodies in other member states. The problem is compounded by the lack of accreditation or recognition of testing and certification from another member state because the institutional arrangements may differ. While some states may emphasize central government accreditation and control of testing and certification practices, in other states it may be decentralized and left to subnational authorities to enforce compliance, or alternatively left to private sector bodies to engage in self-regulation and monitoring of conformity assessment. Hence the degree of regulatory oversight of testing and certification institutions varies considerably across states and can affect trading opportunities and market access. As the largest potential barrier to trade, conformity assessment is vulnerable to a lack of bureaucratic transparency and susceptible to capture by domestic firms seeking protection. Time delays may be particularly problematic for products with short life cycles, and the cost of uncertainty about market entry requirements can reduce the willingness or firms to compete. The impact of conformity assessment as a protectionist trade restraint is hard to assess, and the effects of these technical barriers to trade are not as directly identifiable as tariffs and quotas, so it is often difficult to determine their overall effect on market structure.

Non-tariff barriers and third countries

Still, even if these non-tariff barriers are addressed in the European context, they will have major trade implications for third countries as well. While non-discrimination is the basic principle governing European policies related to technical regulations and standards from third countries, this does not mean that there are not trade disputes about market access given differences in risk assessment, health and safety objectives, and other societal values.[78] Overall assessments of the relative cost advantage of a single, pan-European market by Cecchini, Emerson, and others were made on the basis of benefits resulting from increased intra-EC trade. However, EU assessments of market integration assume that European firms have the capacity to resist market entrants from non-EC member states. Assuming that barriers to market entry are removed and market integration promotes increased competition, the reduction of trade costs will enhance trading opportunities for non-European firms.[79] The larger pan-European market enables third countries to adopt efficient corporate strategies and reduce transaction costs, which reinforces their competitive position in the European market.[80] Because of the potential trading benefits connected with the removal of technical barriers to trade, third countries have followed developments in Europe extremely closely.[81] Clearly, if technical barriers to trade can be removed, the direction provided by European trade policy measures may have a broader impact on international commercial diplomacy. Thus, the move by the European Union to conclude bilateral mutual recognition agreements of testing and certification as part of its trade agenda provides a powerful incentive for other countries to embrace this model of liberalization.[82] As part of the rapid rise in regional and bilateral trade agreements in the past decade, the negotiations to expand market access through trade facilitation measures, regulatory best practices, and removal of technical barriers to trade created by divergent standards, testing, and conformity assessment system extends deeper into areas of domestic regulations than in the past. The export of the European model of trade liberalization could provide a mechanism to address differences in regulatory policies that are at the forefront of increasingly rancorous trade disputes. Given the new importance of standards in a trade policy context, the impact of European efforts to remove these barriers on external trade relations will be considered briefly in Chapter 10. Though the main emphasis is on the transatlantic impact since this has proved the most important in trade terms, as well as the most politically contentious, developing countries lag behind in their testing, certification, and accreditation capacities to engage in mutual recognition of such practices.[83] Thus the negotiating dynamics and bargaining will be different across different contexts.

Conclusion

This summarizes the three types of technical barriers that can frustrate market access. Assessing the effects of market integration and the removal of barriers to trade has usually focused on the Community as a whole. Despite the increasing internationalization of certain industrial sectors, there are considerable differences in economic organization. Market structures—in terms of the number of firms, the size of these firms, and their organization, affects the process of market integration because it influences the alignment of interests within that industry.

As a result, aggregate assessments of market fragmentation do not adequately account for the differences in market position, which will, in turn, affect policy preferences and corporate strategies. More internationally oriented firms are likely to press for the removal of barriers to trade and undertake corporate strategies to position themselves for a more competitive single market. By contrast, many of the domestic-oriented firms are likely to view the situation differently since these industries have been able to operate in local product markets that are relatively insulated or segmented.

The consequences of change are thus tempered by the effective redistribution between winners and losers. While it is true that the process of removing barriers will foster competition and increase efficiency, we shall see in the following chapters how the spadework necessary to open up markets, to achieve the adoption of common product definitions and the harmonization of standards, is not only unglamorous and bureaucratic but also difficult to implement given varying approaches to the regulation of industrial product markets.

4

Harmonization:
The Slow Strategy Forward

Introduction

From 1958 to 1985, the European Commission sought to address numerous obstacles to trade through an ambitious programme of regulatory harmonization. The Commission sometimes went well beyond what many member states had anticipated by challenging the role of member states in setting their own regulatory standards. The programme was not only a limited success in terms of actual results, but also hurt the image of the Community in ways that could not have been imagined in 1958. In this twenty-seven year period, the EC addressed only a limited number of trade barriers, as it faced political opposition and conflicting goals from member states anxious to ensure that their own domestic industries were not put at a competitive disadvantage.

The Commission was able to achieve some degree of trade liberalization in a few sectors.[1] Generally, however, the experience of the Commission to promote competition between different firms and increase cross-border trade, the cornerstone of a common market, became mired in confusion as it encountered both the complexities of regulation and the contradictory pressures of domestic interests. Nonetheless, the failures of European policy during the 1960s and 1970s provided the building blocks for regulatory reform in the 1980s. The Commission was able to move ahead with new initiatives to promote free trade only after the policy of trying to harmonize different national regulations was widely perceived as a failure.

The difficulties experienced by the Community were not unique given the economic pressure to harmonize diverse standards has been a crucial element of constitutional politics and market-building efforts in the United States. Though a number of Congressional committees were established to deal with standards throughout the late eighteenth and nineteenth centuries, early efforts to establish common standards were in part driven by the anomalies on customs duties, excises, and tariffs across states.[2] Uniformity was the driving force for such efforts since states rights coupled with the local nature of business prevented the establishment of a nationwide standards regime. While Congress provided for various standards in different statutes, public and private efforts at harmonization continued in much the same piecemeal way as early European Community efforts. Though establishment of an independent standards bureau, the National Bureau of Standards and later the National Institute of Standards and Technology in the United States, seemed similar to developments within European member states, the increased number of private organizations involved in standards development at the end of the nineteenth century reflects a more market-oriented than state-oriented approach to harmonization.[3] The United States did engage in some harmonization[4] and found the process equally laborious, and in fact, the federal government had to constantly address the trade impeding effects of divergent regulations and standards in both manufactured goods and agricultural products up until the New Deal era in the 1940s.[5]

The free movement of goods in the Treaty

Harmonization had been presented in 1958 as a remedy for the problems created by differences in national regulatory regimes.[6] According to Carol Cosgrove Twitchett, 'harmonization is the key to the creation and development of the European common market,'[7] and 'involves the adoption of legislation by the Community institutions that is designed to bring about changes in the internal legal systems of the member states'.[8] The aim is not simply to eliminate disparities in national regulatory systems but also to foster convergence through common policy goals. It eliminates or reduces the difficulties that arise from the fact that national legal systems are not only divergent but applicable only within the territory of each nation-state.

While harmonization represented a concerted effort by the Commission to address the proliferation of trade barriers,[9] the possibility that regulatory barriers to trade could impose both economic and social costs was duly recognized in the Treaty.[10] A strong body of political opinion existed within the original Six that the European Community was not merely a useful economic grouping, but also an indispensable basis for political cohesion and consolidation.[11] Their aim was not simply to eliminate disparities between national legal systems, but to ensure that the mechanisms chosen contributed to a well-functioning common market that was free and fair.[12]

Clauses covering the free movement of goods are at the heart of the Community's treaty regime.[13] The fact that the abolition of restrictions to trade covers goods, capital, services, and labour does not mean that the four freedoms were considered in the same way. Given the initial preoccupation with tariffs, and the emphasis in establishing a customs union to promote the free movement of goods, action in the three other areas was extremely limited. Yet all four areas share a unifying thread: the basic structure of the prohibition of trade barriers is coupled with narrowly defined exceptions which would allow member states to depart from the principle of free movement. The free movement of goods, persons, and services are all subject to derogations on the grounds of public health, public policy, and public security. Because the exceptions are broadly worded, they have proved to be highly controversial and it has fallen to the European Court of Justice, as the following chapter illustrates, to apply the aspirations and meaning of the Treaty of Rome to particular circumstances governing free trade versus national exemptions on a case-by-case basis.

The Treaty sets out a number of articles dealing with provisions related to the free movement of goods, although some have been subsequently amended. Articles 12–17 deal with the elimination of customs duties,[14] and Articles 18–29 deal with a common external tariff.[15] Beyond this, Articles 30–6 deal with the elimination of quantitative restrictions between member states.[16] Article 30 contains a general prohibition of restrictions on imports and of all measures 'having equivalent effect to a quantitative restriction'. Article 34 is couched in the same terms, but applies to restrictions on imports. Article 31 obliges member states to refrain from introducing new trade restricting measures, while Article 32 restricts member states from making the existing quotas or measures with equivalent effect more restrictive than necessary. Despite these restrictions, member states are allowed important derogations from the rules of free movement under Article 36. As Article 36 states:

the provision of Articles 30 to 34 shall not preclude prohibitions or restrictions on imports, exports or goods in transit on grounds of public morality, public policy or public security; the protection of health or life of humans, animals and plants; the protection of national treasures possessing artistic, historic or archeological value; or the protection of industrial or commercial property. Such prohibitions or restrictions, shall not, however, constitute a means of arbitrary discrimination or disguised restriction on trade between member states.

Though the Treaty provides for the free movement of goods, Article 36 impinges on this as a negative or dormant commerce clause. Article 36 gives member states certain 'reserved powers' over trade which are

non-discriminatory in intent and apply to both national and imported products. The aims of these regulatory policies are often laudable: member
states can adopt strict health, safety, and consumer protection regulations,
environmental protection and improvement measures, fair trading practices, and the prevention of national treasures from leaving their country
of origin, all of which can protect and often insulate national markets.
Not surprisingly the Community has had difficulty in fashioning its
policy towards legislation that may not necessarily be protectionist in
intent, but has a disparate effect on domestic and imported goods.[17]

Because these derogations under Article 36 run contrary to the basic
objectives of free trade within the common market, the Treaty provides
a solution for this problem through the approximation or harmonization of laws and regulations. This was intended to ensure that these
national rules would not become non-tariff barriers by replacing any
contested national regulations with European ones, with harmonized
regulations dampening the protectionist impulses that often resulted
in vehement complaints amongst member states. Critics of strict and uniform application of harmonization argued that the Community should
be more tolerant of protective measures, since the uniform enforcement
of trade rules through harmonization does not take into account diversity in levels of development, different regulatory practices, and pressures
from foreign competition.[18]

The harmonization of laws was intended to reduce the impact of Article
36 exceptions through the creation of Community-wide regulations for
health, safety, environmental, and other standards. If the Community
standards adequately addressed these issues, then member states rules
and regulations would be pre-empted and cease to act as barriers to trade.
Although harmonization was designed to reduce or abolish inequalities
between national laws where they constituted obstacles to trade, it faced
many difficulties. As Héritier points out, 'European regulatory-policy
making unfolds in the context of the diverse regulatory interests and
traditions of member states.'[19] New initiatives are to a significant extent
characterized by competition among member states, each trying to
shape European regulatory policy in its own image to gain 'first-mover
advantage' rather than be forced to unilaterally adjust their policies.[20]

The legal foundation to address trade barriers

While Article 3 of the Treaty suggests that harmonization was the most
appropriate tool for these purposes, it does not confer direct authority

on the Council or Commission to enact harmonization measures; these measures must be based on more specific provisions of the Treaty.[21] This is because the Community institutions do not have general law-making powers, they can only act in cases where the provisions of the Treaty authorize them to do so. More detailed provisions for harmonization are scattered throughout the Treaty,[22] with Article 100 considered its most important basis. It states that, 'the Council shall, acting unanimously on a proposal from the Commission, issue directives for the approximation of such provisions laid down by law, regulation or administrative action in member states as directly affect the establishment or functioning of the common market.' The Community policy of harmonization differs somewhat from the process of harmonization carried out by other international institutions. Instead of being optional, as in the case of many international efforts to coordinate policies, the legal provisions of the Treaty were subsequently considered by the European Court of Justice as directly effective, and thus directly applicable upon member states. Since national law would have to be modified or adapted to Community law, harmonization was a matter of contention from the outset.

During the Treaty negotiations, the French government feared the possible expansion of harmonization and sought to prevent the possible widening of Community powers. While sympathetic to the unification of law, the French preferred to limit harmonization by insisting that the general provisions of Article 100 could not be used to encroach on national sovereignty, beyond what had been stipulated in the treaty. France's insistence during the Treaty negotiations that some areas should be dealt with by conventions negotiated outside the Treaty framework sheltered a number of areas from European-wide harmonization. German officials also sought to limit the impact of harmonization by excluding issues they felt did not affect other member states, arguing that harmonization was only appropriate for issues that affect the political, economic, and social construction of the common market.[23]

In addition to limiting the regulatory reach of the EU during Treaty negotiations, member states also lessened the impact of harmonization through other means. Harmonization depends on member state compliance, and harmonization measures were adopted in the form of directives which replace a national law, but provide member states with a degree of flexibility in implementing European legislation at the national level. In many cases, national differences in interpretation of harmonization measures led to delays in effective implementation. Harmonization was also plagued by the decision rules of the Community. Article 100 required unanimity among the member states, and harmonization often fell victim to the varying interests and preferences of member states, and the bargaining and horse-trading that often led to lowest common denominator decisions. This helps explain why so few decisions were adopted as member states were able to exercise substantial veto power, a situation reinforced by the Luxembourg Compromise of 1966 resolving the French 'open-chair crisis' boycott of all Council meetings in the autumn of 1965.

On numerous occasions, member states did not implement the agreed-upon directive in the required time frame, as indicated in more detail below. Delaying tactics perpetuated this problem and caused tremendous friction between member states. Although the Community could initiate legal proceedings against recalcitrant member states, there was initially reluctance to make direct challenges.[24] This was reflected in the Commission's initially strict interpretation of Article 100, in part due to the ambiguity of its wording but also because member states had been reluctant to grant extensive regulatory authority to the Commission.[25]

The Commission sought to bolster its regulatory authority by relying on Article 235 as a supplemental power.[26] Though the Article had lain dormant for some time, the Commission opted to expand its usage amid much controversy. Article 235 states that, 'if action by the Community should prove necessary to attain, in the course of the operation of the common market, one of the objectives of the Community and this treaty *has not provided the necessary powers*, the Council shall, acting unanimously on a proposal from the Commission and after consulting the Assembly, take the appropriate measures' (my emphasis added). The Commission seized on this as evidence that it could address a broad range of regulatory issues, even if it could not show that national regulatory policies had a *direct impact* on the common market. Because of the legal uncertainty surrounding the use of Article 235, the Commission relied heavily on its implied powers to push its own regulatory agenda in areas as varied as company law, customs regulations, and protection of the environment.

While the scope of harmonization originally covered market liberalization and free trade, as well as common policies in the transport, agriculture, and commercial policy sectors, the lack of progress in these latter areas played an important role in shifting the focus in new directions. The real turning point in the life of Article 235 came in 1972 when member states agreed that it was 'desirable to make the widest possible use of Article 235 of the EEC Treaty'.[27] Despite strenuous objections from certain member states regarding the legal basis of its action, the Commission justified its activity on economic grounds, arguing that different standards affected the functioning of the market and could lead to non-tariff barriers in the future. The ECJ upheld the validity of Article 235, but only after the Council had shifted its position in 1972 regarding the use of Article 235, by accepting that 'if the Article 100 procedure for harmonization of national legislation does not afford a sufficiently workable solution to the need for Community action, the Council may examine all other relevant treaty clauses to establish an adequate juridical foundation' to foster market integration.[28] Taking advantage of this opportunity represented the culmination of a long learning process for the Commission.

Early efforts at tackling trade barriers

After initially devoting its energies to the abolition of quotas, the Commission announced that it would give closer attention to other trade restrictions. Beginning in 1962, the Community turned its attention to the fiscal and administrative obstacles that hinder free movement in both agricultural and industrial product markets. In 1963, the Commission launched a series of inquiries into the persistence and effect of these non-tariff barriers. The Commission received few submissions from industry and trade federations, and so was unable to gauge the size and scope of the problem. Nevertheless, the Commission relied instead on the experience and reports compiled by other international organizations such as the OEEC, and later the OECD and the United Nations.[29]

From these international organizations, the Commission learned that as direct measures of protectionism had been reduced, disparities in regulations became an easy substitute for the protection of domestic markets. The problem was particularly acute in four areas: foodstuffs, veterinary and phytosanitary standards, pharmaceuticals, and motor vehicles, and tractors. Although other international organizations were coordinating efforts in these areas, these same sectors were later to become the basis for Community action in an extensive effort to tackle barriers to trade.

Harmonization had not initially been a top priority for the Commission. Anxious to make its mark on long-term planning and development, the Commission sought to play a larger role in industrial and economic policy. Given its limited tools under the Treaty to tackle economic policy, the Commission relied primarily on reports and memorandums which national authorities usually chose to ignore. Unable to exercise any leverage over economic policy, the Commission was forced to fall back on harmonization for which it had a clear legal basis in the Treaty. The Commission began increasingly to push harmonization in new areas such as company law, mergers, and fiscal arrangements in order to expand its policy competence.

The bulk of its activity, however, focused on dealing with non-tariff barriers in the agricultural and product market sector. Part of the problem for the Community in coming to grips with these barriers was that discussion was hampered by the lack of precise information on the subject. Firms were often not forthcoming in pinpointing problems for fears that it could lead to trade retaliation and permanently block them from accessing certain markets. The Commission also faced the additional problem of choosing the most appropriate type of harmonization to pursue.[30] The Commission had two alternatives, total or optional harmonization, with very different trade and technology effects. In the case of total harmonization, all products must meet the standards set out in the directive. This extensive regulatory action forced member states to permit goods that complied with the directive to be freely marketed and to prohibit the sale of goods not complying with the directive. In effect, European regulation becomes the exclusive standard by which products can access the domestic market. Alternatively, the Commission could choose optional harmonization. This more flexible regulatory strategy allows for the parallel existence of both Community and national regulations. Optional harmonization allows products that comply with the directive to be sold across the Community, but allows firms that wish to sell their products only on their home market to continue to use national standards. This was particularly attractive for small firms producing solely for domestic markets, since total harmonization would have required them to use new standards without any compensating advantages.[31]

Exercising caution, the Commission began by choosing total harmonization where national laws were quite similar. These early proposals were among the least controversial, since the Commission was trying to set down some important precedents to use later when tackling some of the more difficult trade barriers.[32] Introducing the first package of proposals in 1960, the Commission chose to concentrate on agricultural products. Progress in the field of non-processed foods was impressive; a spillover of political will from the Common Agricultural Policy enabled harmonization of legislation concerning animals, plants, and meat to be achieved with relatively little dissent.[33] It was no coincidence that agricultural market integration, a French priority, proceeded at a faster pace than that of industrial product markets.

Industrial directives adopted during the early 1960s were almost entirely in sectors with marginal trade impacts.[34] Generally, agreement was somewhat easier for horizontal directives which regulated the use of a particular product or practice, than vertical directives which specified detailed design or composition requirements. Even then, the attempt to formulate common standards were far from being totally harmonized; in order to facilitate agreement, the compromises usually left the details of various standards up to the discretion of national regulatory authorities.

At the same time, the Commission's efforts were impeded by the fact that the quantity and scope of national regulations were expanding rapidly.[35] For the Community, the problem was compounded by the absence of any mechanisms to prevent member states from continuing to adopt national regulations. While the Community tackled trade barriers on a case-by-case basis, it had few ways to stop member states from adopting new regulations. Concerned that their work on harmonization was being undermined by national regulatory efforts, the Commission issued a recommendation in 1965 requiring member states to provide prior notification of any new national regulations.[36] This was designed to force member states to take account of current Community efforts to eliminate technical barriers to trade. As the first general effort to tackle the problem, it was hampered by the fact that it needed extensive member state cooperation. The Commission hoped to pre-empt national regulations and prevent new barriers from emerging, as the idea of swapping information about national activities offered new possibilities in dealing with potential barriers to trade. The early General Reports give the impression that the Commission not only underestimated the task facing it, but also faced a number of difficulties in detecting when national measures constituted a 'technical barrier to trade'.[37]

The General Programme for the removal of technical obstacles to trade

By 1968, only a handful of directives addressing the growing issues of non-tariff barriers had been adopted. In March 1968, concerned about the slow progress of harmonization and aware of the limited progress that it had made so far, the Commission proposed a General Programme for the elimination of technical barriers to trade.[38] Adopted by the Council in May 1969, the General Programme set out an ambitious timetable for legislative harmonization that would proceed in three stages and be completed by mid-1971.[39] Only a fraction of technical barriers were however included in the programme, and many products appeared incidental in terms of potential intra-European trade. Some of the more important sectors, including pharmaceuticals and telecommunications, were not included, leaving the impression that the programme simply codified the work-in-progress at the time.

Beyond the basic work-in progress, the General Programme did attempt to address potential barriers to trade through a standstill provision and notification procedure. Building on previous efforts, the General Programme included a provision that member states would have to inform the Commission of all national regulations under consideration if they overlapped with the Commission's own legislative agenda. Member states would be required to refrain from introducing new national regulations for six months to allow the Community to pass its legislation instead, although member states argued for exemptions to the rule for health and safety reasons. This exemption was an unfortunate but costly measure since it enabled member states to circumvent restrictions on introducing new national regulations.

Despite the difficulties in getting member states to consider the trade implications of introducing new regulations, the Commission pressed ahead with the General Programme. They were fortunate in having several methods for removing technical barriers, including some new innovative ones that would become increasingly more important. In addition to the standard tools of total and optional harmonization, the Commission introduced the possibility of mutual recognition of national regulations and reference to standards as two alternative ways of addressing technical barriers to trade. Table 4.1 lists the different ways in which the EU proposed to deal with trade barriers. Significantly, mutual recognition

TABLE 4.1 *Methods to eliminate barriers to trade*

Category	Conditions
Total harmonization	Compliance mandatory Options for local deviations prohibited Counteracts all NTB
Optional harmonization	Compliance optional in local markets Local differentiation preserved For interstate commerce—mandatory compliance
Mutual recognition	Mutual approval of marketing conditions Need high degree of mutual credibility and trust
Reference to standards	Harmonized standards Used as alternative to regulations.

and reference to standards introduced greater regulatory flexibility into the process and opened up the possibility of an approach to regulating markets that relied more on self-regulatory bodies. Commission officials also pressed for the right to update and amend directives to take account of new developments and technological changes. Rather than start the negotiating process afresh, the Commission wanted to be given the right to modify and update existing legislation. The Commission was granted this right to use its regulatory powers to engage in administrative rule-making,[40] although it was subject to oversight by 'comitology' committees composed of national representatives, to ensure that member states retained some control over the legislative process.[41]

In all, the Community was expected to adopt 124 directives under the General Programme over a period of eighteen months. But the actual results were actually quite meagre. Between 1967 and 1972, twenty-four directives were adopted, between 1972 and 1978 thirty-six, and between 1975 and 1978 fifty directives.[42] Given this slow progress, the Commission was forced to modify the programme repeatedly. In the early stages, the deadlines were shifted forward by one year so the final directives would be adopted by the end of 1970, and a separate programme to address trade barriers in the food sector was added.[43] Despite these changes, the schedule for the programme was far too ambitious. Under the original schedule, forty-four directives would be adopted by the end of 1969; instead only a single directive was adopted in this period.

Anxious to make some progress, the Community compromised by establishing prohibitive lists. Based on political rather than scientific or technical considerations, it allowed member states to prohibit certain products and processes at the national level, even though these products may be acceptable in other member states. By allowing states to do this, the outcome was precisely the opposite of what was intended. States could use all sorts of pretences to block imports, making it more difficult for firms to take advantage of a single set of standards. By the time the December 1970 deadline for the General Programme was reached, only nine directives from the original list of 150 had been adopted. A notable milestone was eventually reached in June 1978 when the Commission adopted the hundredth directive of the General Programme to eliminate technical barriers to trade.[44] As a Commission report concluded, 'the free movement of goods within a common market such as the EEC cannot be achieved at a stroke. On the contrary, the experience gained during the 1970s shows that unceasing work was required, day after day, to maintain the status quo in this area.'[45]

Domestic politics and Euro-harmonization

During the 1970s, the Commission faced increasing criticism over its regulatory role. As the General Programme languished, opposition mounted over efforts to regulate what many felt were long-standing national customs, traditions, and practices. The institutional strains of enlargement and the impact of two severe recessions in the 1970s also contributed to the loss of momentum in addressing technical barriers to trade.[46] With Europe plagued by rising inflation, coupled with unemployment and declining growth, the prospects for the liberalization of intra-European trade were muted. The threat to the single market through the *de facto* abandonment of common policies, as nations and national industry federations determined their own unilateral policies vis-à-vis third countries, was matched by impediments to trade between member states that included every conceivable device short of tariffs and quotas.[47]

With national governments seeking individual measures against the economic crisis, the role of the Commission as the exponent of Community interest was being undermined. Pleas for a collective response were tempered by a pragmatic awareness of the difficulty of challenging determined member governments.[48] Although the Commission repeatedly drew attention to the possibilities of a large single market, and attempted to create favourable conditions for fair competition, member states persisted in protecting domestic industries through a plethora of non-tariff barriers and subsidies. In March 1970, the Commission submitted a Memorandum on Industrial Policy, also known as the Colonna Report, to the Council, European Parliament, and Economic and Social Committee.[49] The Report contained a mix of policy proposals for old and new issues, mainly covered by the Treaty. They focused on five main areas: (1) creation of a single market through the elimination of technical barriers to trade; (2) harmonization of legal, financial, and fiscal frameworks to promote transnational activities; (3) promotion of transnational mergers to create Community firms; (4) industrial adaptation; and (5) solidarity in external relations. Although the report emphasized the removal of obstacles to trade for industry to take full advantage of a common market, it did not elaborate on the methods of achieving these goals.

Similarly, a catalogue of measures presented in 1972 to create a 'unified single industrial base' through the promotion of a unified market, the elimination of technical barriers to trade, the harmonization of company law, and the opening up of public sector procurement to all European firms provided only a strategic gloss for a set of initiatives that failed to generate much interest or action. With little consensus among member states, any further ambitions for the Community to play a stronger industrial role were muted. Again the Commission fell back on harmonization only to find that even in this area it was accused of an over-regulatory zeal of 'pursuing harmonization for harmonization's sake'.

Despite this unpromising political and economic climate, the Commission pushed forward with harmonization proposals throughout the decade. While the number of harmonization measures enacted rose slowly after 1970, the long preparatory process, intense negotiations, and difficulties in getting agreement on harmonized standards meant that the results continued to be meagre.[50] In its first and second reports on the situation presented to the European Parliament and European Council in April 1970 and June 1973, respectively, the Commission expressed 'grave concern at the slow process of removing barriers of all kinds'.[51] The Commission advocated revising its programme to address regulations for security, consumer, and environmental protection measures, since these were a large source of obstacles to intra-Community trade.[52] In proposing legislation in these areas, the Commission was anxious to build on growing public concerns. However, the Commission was forced to justify its proposals on strict economic grounds and the potential trade-restricting nature of environmental regulations, even though directives such as the improvement of air and water quality obviously had non-economic implications.[53]

A revised 1973 work programme included a new timetable. The final deadline, after which there would no longer exist any technical obstacles to trade within the Common Market, was set as the end of 1977. Many of the proposals had been outstanding for a considerable period of time.[54] Nevertheless, the Commission was forced to drop such politically sensitive issues as rail, aircraft, and telecommunications equipment, where the potential for economies of scale and competition was greatest. The revised programme included a number of new issues to take account of enlargement and the concerns of the three new states (Denmark, Ireland, and the United Kingdom) to address issues that had not been previously considered of primary importance, and also to act on growing public concern over the environment by pushing for European harmonization in that area.

Not surprisingly, programme deadlines slipped by and criticism mounted regarding efforts to unify the market at the expense of existing national rules. To secure agreement, the Commission made increased use of 'optional' directives which enabled firms to continue to use national standards for products sold in the country that they are produced. While much political capital was expended in trying to reach agreement, criticism continued. It took, for example, fifteen years to reach agreement on mineral water standards and eight years to agree on standards for windscreen wipers.[55] A broad range of similar examples confirmed that harmonization was bound up in trivia and red tape.[56] These 'Euroscandals' were dramatized and often exaggerated in the popular press, and the Commission's efforts to standardize products throughout Europe became the object of derision.[57]

The clearest sign of trouble was in the food sector, where efforts to regulate the composition of foodstuffs clashed with national customs, traditions, and practices.[58] The *Wall Street Journal* captured this sentiment in a startling anecdote:

First some essential background. The Dutch spread jam on bread for breakfast, so they like it smooth. Sugary, too. Most Frenchmen, however, wouldn't touch smooth jam with a barge pole, much less a butter knife. They commonly eat their jam straight from the jar, with a spoon. . . . The negotiators spent years getting the Dutch who want more sugar in their jam and the French who want more fruit, to compromise. But just as that happened, Britain, Europe's largest jam consumer joined the EC—and tossed a spanner into the works.

Its name is marmalade. It seems the low-quality jam in much of Continental Europe was called marmalade, a confusion Britons refused to tolerate. In the end Continental Europe changed their terminology, and low-grade jam simply became jam. After two decades of haggling everyone finally agreed what jam was and what should be in it, and the Eurocrats proudly unveiled a jam standard in 1979. Then the French, who have been eating jam since the thirteenth century and who are extremely picky about it, decided to mediate on the matter for an additional four years or so. It wasn't until 1984 that they got on board. It did not escape the Eurocrats that it had taken twenty-five years to decide on jam, it could take centuries to do the same nit-picking for the many thousands of other products involved in Continental trade.[59]

Industry complained bitterly that, 'the result of the EEC food law harmonization program seems merely to burden us with regulations of unnecessary complexity, without benefiting consumers or manufacturers, or helping trade.'[60] Painstaking efforts to compromise on such issues as the composition of sausages or the noise levels of lawnmowers were seized upon by the media.[61] Despite the fact that these and similar cases represented efforts to insure proper hygiene and quality for foodstuffs, in the case of sausages, and efforts to eliminate the unfair price advantages of poorly insulated lawnmowers in member states that did not regulate noise, they came to symbolize the tremendous amount of time and effort devoted to the ill-fated harmonization process.

For the Commission, it posed a genuine conundrum. The Commission maintained that detailed proposals were often necessary because member states were reluctant to forgo the manipulation of technical standards that protected national industries, but added 'it might be worth questioning some of the scare stories attributed to Brussels—such as the removal of red buses, harmonised Euro-rules for cricket, no more pints of beer, prawn crisps, the square strawberry, whatever. . . . The European Commission has checked all these so-called stories and the vast majority are hearsay, rumour or plain rubbish' (Jacques Santer, Commission President, Address to the Corporation of London, May 1995).

Yet tales of 'barmy European law' often caused considerable domestic irritation or misunderstanding. Nowhere is this more true than the dispute over beer which pitted domestic political and cultural differences against efforts to reduce trade barriers and foster the free movement of goods. German beer producers followed strict rules in producing 'Bier' by using only four ingredients: hops, yeast, water, and malt. This was generally recognized as the world's oldest hygienic law, the *Reinheitsgebot* or beer purity law, originally enacted by the Bavarian Parliament in 1516 as a means of regulating food quality and preventing the adulteration of 'Bier'. Enforcement was fairly unscientific in the Middle Ages; inspectors measured the purity of the beer by pouring it on top of a stool and seeing if it stuck to their leather breeches. However, the regulations were later reissued in modified form by the federal government in 1952.

Regardless of its original intent, German brewers benefited from the purity law as it proved an effective trade barrier and limited competition. In addition, beer delivery and distribution contracts were negotiated for up to twenty years, effectively blocking new competitors from entering the German market. Imports comprised only 3.3 per cent of the market by 1980.[62] Although almost half of the 3,000 breweries worldwide were located in Germany, many were small, local operations that would find it difficult to compete against larger, multinational American, Dutch, and British beer producers.

The Commission's efforts to establish a common standard for beer, known derisively as 'Euro-beer', drew an angry reaction from German breweries, who were under tremendous financial constraints, as stagnant demand and inefficient plant operations had led German banks to reduce their capital investment in the brewing industry. French and Dutch brewers launched a massive advertising campaign in the wake of the Commission's decision to persuade German consumers to switch to new varieties of beer. The German Brewers' Association fought back with a vigorous campaign to discredit foreign beers made with additives and chemicals. The Association promoted its own quality trade mark for 'pure

Bier' to distinguish German beers from their competitors, and two of the largest German supermarkets joined the debate by announcing a boycott on the sale of imported beers that did not conform to German purity laws.[63]

It was not until the European Court of Justice's decision in 1988, discussed in greater detail in the following chapter, that German restrictions on beer imports were finally addressed.[64] Even then, domestic political pressures forced the German government to criticize the judgment as 'an example of the European Commission's growing negligence on honoring the cultural differences of its member states'. The German government also sought to dampen the effect of the decision by ruling that ingredients on foreign beers would have to be listed on every bottle, can, and barrel as a clear reminder that German beer production methods were different, and implicitly superior.

The Euro-beer proposal also sparked a debate in Britain where press reports indicated that the British 'pint' was being abolished in favour of litres—a shift from imperial to metric measures. Although the Commission adamantly argued that it was not making any changes in the British 'pint', it was difficult for the Commission to make its case about tackling trade barriers successfully. So much so that an anonymous paper circulated by a European civil servant pointed out that 'the traditional British hop has nothing to fear from the EEC. Nor have British cooking apples or Scottish whiskey made from peaty water or British yellow-dyed kippers.' Media suggestions that there would be 'no midwives, no Bramley cooking apples, no fresh turkeys, no ice-cream, and no doorstep deliveries of milk and newspapers' created tremendous misinformation about the harmonization process. This was made worse by comments from one national premier that 'there is too much fuss about producing a European loaf, the same kind of chicken, and identical pots of honey and tractor rear-view mirrors.' As *The Economist* commented at the time, 'much nonsense is spoken by European politicians about Brussels busybodies trying madly to standardize European food and drink.'[65]

Vocal campaigns against harmonization were also waged by prospective new members, notably in Norway, which ultimately voted against accession, and Denmark. Fears that achievements in the area of social policy would be whittled down to the lowest common denominator were matched by strong opposition to the impact of harmonization on national identity. As small states, Norway and Denmark felt that with virtually one stroke of its pen, 'Brussels' could push for a uniform approach to market integration and social standards. Not only did enlargement increase the number of different regulatory traditions that needed reconciling, but the political attitudes to harmonization in Denmark and Britain ranged from sceptical to stridently hostile.[66]

In spite of the lack of enthusiasm from the new members, the Commission pushed ahead with its efforts to draw attention to the increasing number of trade barriers through such soft law mechanisms as warnings, appeals, communications, resolutions, and declarations non-stop throughout the 1970s. The Commission reported to the European Council and European Parliament in 1973 that 'the situation is regarded as more and more intolerable and anachronistic in a Community moving towards economic union'.[67] In a vain hope of generating more support, the Commission maintained an increasing number of contacts with national bureaucracies, and continually met with national officials to discuss individual cases of trade restrictions. In many cases, however, the Commission was forced to take legal action against member states for not implementing legislation designed to deal with trade restrictions. Acting on the fifty or more complaints it received every year, the Commission found that the problem was often the reluctance or unwillingness of member states to implement directives. One hundred cases of non-implementation were reported in 1973 alone. By the end of 1974, only one of the thirty directives which dealt with industrial products had been properly applied in all member states. The growing non-compliance hampered Community efforts to tackle trade barriers. The Commission argued:

we must not lose sight of the great advantages offered by the harmonization of national technical regulations. Harmonization in production at the European level will facilitate long homogeneous runs. It is also the only way to avoid an overdependence on norms or regulations developed by non-member states, for it will allow the Community to effectively wield influence at the international level.[68]

Deeply concerned by such reactions to harmonization, the Commission stressed that its approach was actually much more pragmatic.[69] The Commission carefully responded to these and other criticisms, especially from new members, by curbing its harmonization plans in some areas and withdrawing some of the more unpopular proposals.[70] Faced with criticisms that its efforts interfered with national idiosyncrasies, traditions, and habits, the Commission was forced to acknowledge that the benefits from the harmonization process 'hit the wall of diminishing returns'.[71] As Table 4.2 illustrates, 150 directives dealing with technical barriers were adopted between March 1968 and January 1985, making only a minor dent on the many thousands of barriers that continued to exist across Europe.

TABLE 4.2 *Technical harmonization (industrial products), 1969–1982*

	Directives adopted by Commission[a]	Commission proposals	Directives adopted by Council	Proposals pending 31 Dec. 1983
1969–72	0	—	35	—
1973	1	12	11	34
1974	2	33	14	59
1975	1	15	12	65
1976	4	13	22	55
1977	1	6	17	51
1978	5	11	11	46
1979	7	7	11	42
1980	1	25	10	58
1981	5	6	6	57
1982	14	4	7	58
TOTAL	41	132	156	525

[a] The Commission has been granted limited regulatory power to adapt directives to technical progress.

Source: Commission of the European Communities.

Assessing problems in market harmonization

The story of harmonization provides ample evidence that the regulatory policy chosen by the Community failed to adequately address the issue of trade barriers. We have already seen a number of indications as to what went wrong, and why reform was needed.

First, the decision rule of unanimity on single market issues made it extremely difficult to get agreement amongst member states. Since Community measures for harmonizing trade require the Council to act unanimously under Article 100, individual member states could exercise veto power. In the absence of unanimous agreement, the result was a continuation of the status quo ante.[72] Second, harmonization is largely a technical matter on which governments usually accept the advice of their experts, whose influence can be quite considerable. Proposals for harmonization are drafted by working committees within the Commission. These committees draw freely upon experts from both national government administrations as well as professional associations, trade associations, and individual firms.[73] Although this stage of the policy process is usually informal, with preliminary studies undertaken by working committees to supplement the Commission's efforts and bolster their expertise on specific issues, the process is time-consuming. At this stage, difficulties may also arise because harmonization often deals with issues that cut across several national bureaucracies or departments. Coordinating national responses can take considerable time, and often the lack of coordination at the national level can result in compromises that are subsequently challenged or rejected at later stages of the consultation or negotiating process.[74]

Although much has been made of the influence of interest groups in shaping the policy process, the attitudes of interest groups in the early years of the Community was more reactive than active. As Morgan noted, 'interest groups are more concerned with the actual and potential impact of harmonization legislation on their constituents than with the chance to play an active if consultative role in suggesting objectives or strategies through their contacts with the Commission.'[75] Even without extensive pressure group activity, what Majone and Schneider term the 'copinage technocratique' often required a lengthy period of negotiation, taking on average four years of negotiation before a proposal addressing a technical barrier to trade was proposed to the Council. Even then, the protracted negotiations over technical details give no guarantee that positions will not change within the Council's working groups, in deference to political and economic ramifications.[76]

Moreover, such a protracted process placed a huge burden on the Commission's resources, and efforts to address the constantly increasing number of regulatory barriers were compounded by rapid changes in technology and production methods that can render negotiated directives obsolete by the time they are adopted. The relative disinterest on the part of national politicians was also understandable, as they gained little credit by trying to explain the value of harmonized measures. Although political initiatives to break the deadlock on a few long-standing proposals did occur, it was rare for governments, individually or collectively, to give a high priority to harmonization issues.

Third, as with so many aspects of Community legislation, the task was made more difficult by the relatively limited restrictions placed on domestic regulatory practices. Although the Community pressed for a standstill agreement to prevent member states from introducing new regulation in areas where European regulatory policy was under consideration, this had a limited effect. The agreement was not legally binding, since member states had added an explanatory footnote that it constituted only a 'gentlemen's agreement'. Consequently, efforts to stem the tide of new national regulations were extremely ineffective. As Macmillan observed, 'in fact the agreement never worked satisfactorily because it was a gentleman's agreement, because the time-frame given to the Community institutions was far too short, and because it excluded national standards from the agreement'[77] Thus, the task of dealing with technical barriers was due to implementation problems. Dependent on member states to implement its harmonization policy, the Community faced an uphill struggle in making member states comply with the legislative requirements.[78] Frequently, the Commission was forced to take legal action to force member states to implement directives.

Fourth, the institutional strains of enlargement made the Commission increasingly cautious. Faced not only with the accession of new member states hostile to harmonization, the new Commission led by François-Xavier Malfatti (1973–7) was markedly different from its predecessors, and particularly the more dynamic Commission of Walter Hallstein (1958–67). As a result of enlargement, the Commission was reorganized to reallocate portfolios to new members. The Directorate General for the Internal Market and Harmonization of Laws (DG XIV) which had been established in 1967 was abolished. This made it more difficult to pursue harmonization as different departments dealt with different sectors.[79] Prior to 1973, harmonization in most areas, with the exception of agriculture and transportation, was dealt with in DG XIV. The break-up of this directorate led to transfer of some harmonization measures to DG XI (Internal Market) with DG XII covering harmonization issues related to Research, Science and Education, and DG XV covering harmonization issues related to Financial Institutions and Taxation. This arrangement proved disastrous, as it increased coordination problems, caused considerable delays, and signalled that harmonization was a lower priority for the new Commission.

Fifth, in addition to these institutional constraints, the onset of economic recession in 1973 contributed to the loss of momentum in removing technical barriers to trade. Declining economic conditions meant that member states sought to protect their industries against recession through increased protectionism and intervention. As the previous chapter discussed, European economies languished in the 1970s, and many European firms focused on retaining national market share, unable to benefit from the possibilities of a large common market due to outdated management structures and inadequate financial resources.[80]

And finally, often overlooked in terms of arguments in favour of shifting policy gears was that the harmonization approach was rigid, inflexible, and increasingly outmoded given changes in economic production. The shift in employment from industry to services, as well as changes in the factors of production in the 1970s made the extraordinary regulatory effort of the Commission seem inappropriate in the changing economic environment. As companies shifted from economies of scale to increased flexibility, the production revolution was shifting from cost advantages based on limited product variety to greater variety at lower costs.[81] Hence, efforts to standardize were at odds with increasing efforts to shift toward more flexible production.[82] Although economies of scale created competitive advantages for large firms, the shift in emphasis towards more specialized, niche products, especially among small firms, seemed less well suited to harmonization. Firms facing greater product variation, more intense competition, and shorter lead times and product cycles felt that harmonization often created new barriers by hindering technological innovation. In some cases, the pressures to remain responsive to local markets was in sharp opposition to harmonization and uniformity since the willingness to exploit a single market required the ability to continuously adapt to market developments.

Conclusion

In retrospect, it is easy to view the failure of harmonization as somehow inevitable. However, initial support for harmonization from the original six members indicates that they intended to deal with the problems of market fragmentation by giving extensive regulatory authority to the European level. The zeal with which the Commission pursued its policy of harmonization led to accusations that its regulatory policy was inflexible and burdensome, since it did not take into consideration existing national rules, regardless of their merits.[83] As the Commission accumulated evidence of the increasing effect of non-tariff barriers, they encountered difficulties in successfully dealing with them, and became increasingly frustrated with the reluctance of member states to enact and implement legislation. Faced with the onset of economic recession and enlargement, the odds against getting collective agreement among member states diminished rapidly. The Commission also demonstrated a great deal of anxiety about a regulatory strategy that was subject to intense political and media scrutiny. This forced the Commission to reassess its strategy in an effort to find a better way of dealing with the proliferation of non-tariff barriers.

The changing pattern of European policy highlights the contradictory pressures noted at the beginning of this chapter: the construction of the market involves a combination of liberalization and reregulation. Yet there is a difference in substance in terms of what the Community was trying to achieve which explains the apparent contradictory policies. The Community recognized that it was removing regulatory restrictions, reducing market entry barriers, and seeking to enhance competition, but it was also regulating market behaviour to ensure common standards.[84]

The regulatory strategy of harmonization proved ineffectual because it was viewed as increasingly inappropriate at addressing the widespread effects of non-tariff barriers. This policy reflected what Stephen Breyer characterizes as *a regulatory mismatch*, where the instruments chosen are ill-suited to dealing with the problem.[85] In this case, the mismatch occurred because the regulatory style chosen was inappropriate, and could only be corrected by a more appropriate match-up between policy approaches and problems.

This does not tell us how the EU managed to drop its old regulatory regime and shift its policy to make better progress in removing barriers to trade. As the next chapter demonstrates in more detail, the shift in policy depends heavily on the role of law. The Community was able to do this because the European Court of Justice legitimated a new regulatory strategy, providing the Commission with the rationale to address non-tariff barriers in new ways. By promoting an interstate market place and removing discriminatory barriers, 'legal rules' foster an environment in which firms could operate more easily. In the struggle to create, maintain, and expand favourable market structures, the role of law has been crucial in the European context. Because political action on behalf of broad markets was slow and uneven under harmonization, judicial decisions had a decisive impact.[86] This is not unlike the United States, where trade barriers have been removed most frequently by judicial decisions rather than reciprocal state statutes and congressional pre-emption.[87] This is not to suggest that the critical role that the judiciary came to play in delimiting states' authority on interstate commerce was inevitable (in either the US or European context).[88] Nor is it to suggest that the law has been consistent in deciding that the European interest in fostering economic unity should take precedence over member states' interests in exercising their essential powers of regulation.

Case law concerning trade barriers is constantly reviewed, indicating that the territorial balance of power is not judicially fixed, and over time the ECJ has modified its position in assessing the degree to which the European level can restrict a member state's regulatory activities. Market integration in Europe can be viewed as a dynamic mode of governance, in which the different institutional elements are constantly evolving. The crucial impact of judicial decisions upon the relationship between the Community and member states in promoting or hindering an integrated economy is discussed in the following chapter.

5

The Intersection of Law and Markets

The emergence of free trade

The previous chapter demonstrates the difficulties experienced in achieving the harmonization of various 'interests' through political negotiations. This problem did not go unnoticed by the European Court of Justice (ECJ), which has often used its judicial power for the purposes of fostering an integrated economy.[1] Like its American counterpart in the nineteenth century, the ECJ has functioned as a strong centralizing institution, particularly in the area of trade and commerce.[2] Though inter-state barriers can be removed by reciprocal state statutes and congressional pre-emption statutes, the most frequent means of addressing trade barriers within the American market has been judicial decisions.

Writing in 1968, with reference to the US Supreme Court, Shapiro noted that 'it is the Court that has constantly defined and redefined such concepts as "control of the market," "share of the market" and, most crucially, "market" itself in order to shift federal policy to meet new problems and new economic theories'.[3] Shapiro's statement is equally relevant to the European context where judicial interpretation of statutes, regulations, and derogation clauses has given the ECJ substantial leeway in shaping market practices. In doing so, a large measure of the credit for creating a regional market belongs to the ECJ. It has consistently viewed Treaty provisions concerning the free movement of goods as not only prohibiting protectionism, but as a means of establishing a single, unified market.[4]

The Treaty of Rome is much more explicit in terms of its treaty provisions aimed at prohibiting impediments to intra-Community trade than the US Commerce Clause, although the Supreme Court has used its brevity and ambiguity to fashion the economic relationship between different constituent units. Like its American counterpart, the ECJ played a corresponding role in the creation of an integrated economy, by balancing the necessity of breaking down trade barriers among states with the recognition of local diversity and needs.[5] In performing this balancing act, the ECJ has looked primarily at the aims of legislation to ascertain whether it serves a protectionist policy or whether it promotes a legitimate national or local interest.[6] This approach to defining trade restrictions has been extremely important, and the overriding interest of the ECJ in ensuring that both member states and businesses did not circumvent the law meant that certain practices were subject to intense judicial scrutiny.[7]

Because markets are profoundly dependent on the legal order that shapes intergovernmental relations and the relationships between business and government, the legal framework that has evolved over the past forty years in Europe deserves careful attention. Like its American counterpart, the ECJ was aware that its actions were regularizing the market and establishing the parameters within which states could exercise their autonomy. Though there is considerable debate among economic historians in the USA about the impact of tariffs upon industrial development,[8] greater attention is now paid to the internal trade restrictions and subsequent legal shifts that laid the foundation for a national market.[9] Focusing instead on the struggle to achieve 'internal free trade', recent scholarship on American economic development has shown that early case law did not deprive states of all power to introduce obstacles to the free movement of goods throughout the nation.[10] State governments retained ample authority to devise more subtle forms of protection through such measures as inspection laws, occupational licensing, and public health statutes.[11] Until the last quarter of the nineteenth century, appellate courts regularly sustained such state statutes and regulations. Only through challenges by big business, anxious to create a single national market, did the Court respond to the changing structure of business enterprises.[12] Until the late nineteenth century, the American legal system recognized and gave preference to the broad commercial activities of state governments.

Regional interests forestalled congressional action under the Commerce Clause[13] throughout the nineteenth century in the United States, with interventions on the part of states playing a key role in determining the scope and nature of interregional trade.[14] Hampered by interstate licensing and marketing restrictions, inspections and quarantine laws, discriminatory taxation, and other barriers to trade,[15] large corporations sued with increasingly frequency throughout the nineteenth century.[16]

Beginning with the landmark cases of *Gibbons* v. *Ogden* (1824) and *Brown* v. *Maryland* (1827), the Supreme Court stepped into the fray and focused on commercial transactions, distinguishing between two types of commerce: manufacturing production and interstate commerce.[17] In doing so, the Court was distinguishing between what was a legitimate object of federal regulation, and what was not. Efforts within the European Community to achieve an analogous common market have strong similarities with the American experience.[18] However, this chapter will also show that the European single market was established with much more interference upon the sovereign powers of states than in the United States.

Disagreement over the regulation of commerce, and what constitutes a legitimate or illegitimate restriction on trade are at the heart of the Community system. Like the United States, seemingly arcane issues relating to the sale of products opened up an avenue for the ECJ to determine what is permissible or impermissible under the treaties. In both nineteenth-century America and in twentieth-century Europe, a largely unarticulated premiss has evolved: when legislative institutions remain silent in removing market barriers, the courts rely on the power of judicial review to supply the necessary voice.[19]

Supreme Court Justice Potter Stewart perceptively summarized this common role:

it is of course an open question whether the central political institutions of the two systems might, in the absence of judicial review, have summoned the will to curb protectionist policies adopted by the states. Yet, even if one supposes that they might have done so, it is difficult to imagine that they could have effectively coped with the myriad local enactments that, though perhaps of minuscule effect when viewed individually, constitute in the aggregate a serious impediment to the maintenance of a common market.[20]

Though a fully outlined comparative case study of market-building cannot be presented here, it is striking that both the Supreme Court and the ECJ recognized review of state commercial regulations as an essential judicial function. In doing so, both have had an enduring influence on economic growth and free trade. Without the ECJ's wide interpretation of free trade, the Community would have remained completely subservient to the member states as regards both the adoption and implementation of policies, and it is likely that the obligations set out in the treaties would have remained a dead letter. In articulating the historical priorities of the Community, the ECJ ensured that national mercantilistic interests did not undermine the legal obligations of the treaty.[21] As many of its subsequent decisions illustrate, the ECJ has succeeded in allocating to itself and the Commission the task of reconciling the demands of integration with the pursuit of legitimate regulatory objectives.[22] The ECJ has sought to provide the boundaries and scope of regulatory competence, by expanding and institutionalizing Community control in relation to the free movement of goods.

This chapter provides a brief overview of the impact of judicial activity in Europe in regularizing a common market. Why did the ECJ intervene so forcefully in issues surrounding the free movement of goods? How did the ECJ determine what constituted an unlawful trade barrier? Has the ECJ been consistent in its interpretation of free trade? What has been the impact of law in fostering market integration? The answers to these questions highlight the degree to which case law has played a pivotal role in fostering economic integration.

Summary of existing legal analysis

Over the past two decades, legal scholars have demonstrated the critical importance of law in understanding the advances of economic integration.[23] Rather than focus on political bargaining and negotiation, pioneering studies by Weiler, Stein, Scheingold, and Cappelletti have illustrated how the ECJ played a critical role in interpreting the objectives and attainment of the common market by conferring upon the treaties legal principles which unmistakingly enhanced its own authority.[24] Other scholars have subsequently provided a wide range of evidence supporting the argument that the ECJ has played a major entrepreneurial, activist role over the past two decades in tackling barriers to trade.[25]

Although the Court has given special emphasis to the common market imperative, it was the 'constitutionalization' of the Treaty which ultimately enhanced European governance and created a regime which conferred judicially enforceable obligations and rights on public and private institutions within the Community.[26] As Weiler notes, the doctrine of direct effect and supremacy are at the core of the constitutional contract.[27] The landmark cases that applied these legal principles have thus created a 'legal' community which has been critical in fostering an 'economic' and 'political community'. Legal integration has clearly resulted in a system of judicial decision-making that has had a pervasive, albeit increasingly recognized effect, on Community politics.[28] The legal regime has played a crucial role in constituting the present-day Community, and in declaring that the Treaty of Rome is a constitutional instrument with enforceable rights and obligation on citizens and states played a central role in market-making. As Shapiro acknowledges, 'much of the actual legal doctrine created by the Court in these decades was relatively modest and set few limits, either substantive or procedural on the organs of national and Community government. Bold establishment but modest application of the tenets of judicial review seems to be the pattern of the Court'.[29]

The establishment of these legal principles was of great importance in enhancing both the legitimacy and effectiveness of the ECJ in promoting market integration. The constitutionalization process was driven by the relationship between private litigants, national judges, and the ECJ under the preliminary reference procedure (Article 177).[30] National courts were encouraged not only to ask the ECJ for a correct interpretation of European law but to set aside incompatible national policies.[31] The effectiveness of the Community legal regime depended on the willingness of national courts to refer disputes to the European Court. From a maximum of seven cases per year from 1952 to 1966, the number of references for a preliminary ruling rose steadily to 23 cases in 1967, 40 in 1972, and 119 in 1978.[32] Without the doctrines of direct effect and supremacy, it is unlikely that national courts would have sought out preliminary references from the ECJ. This linkage has been strengthened by lower courts that have been willing to use the Community legal system to bypass the national judicial system. By doing so, national courts (including lower courts) enhanced their own powers of judicial review of existing national legislation.[33]

At both the national and European levels, courts were slowly developing a legal framework that would be of crucial importance for economic development and interstate commerce. Equally important in demarcating the regulatory boundaries between different levels of government was the legal doctrine of pre-emption.[34] Pre-emption is necessary to determine whether and to what extent the conferral of legislative authority on the federal government in certain areas precludes the states from acting.[35] The extent to which states possess residual powers to provide for the health, safety, and general welfare of their constituents is obviously crucial for commercial transactions. Like its American counterpart, the case law of the ECJ has on occasion affirmed the validity of certain state regulations affecting interstate commerce, resulting in a complex legal system that has used different formulas, objectives, and strategies over time to preserve the interests of states (see below).[36]

Though the ECJ has relied on rather specific treaty provisions aimed at removing restrictions to trade (Articles 30–6), it has been willing to adjust its decisions and practices in light of changing or particular circumstances. Although the ECJ generally follows its previous decisions, it is not bound by them. The ECJ can—and does—depart from past practice, illustrating both its flexibility and its recognition of the political environment in which it operates.

The ECJ's free trade jurisprudence was surprisingly limited until the mid-1970s despite the increasing significance and impact of non-tariff barriers on intra-Community trade.[37] There were only six judgments on the impact of quantitative restrictions on trade in the 1960s and only fifteen between 1970 and 1975.[38] It was not until after the deadline for the establishment of the 'common market' had passed in 1970 that the ECJ assumed such a prominent role in deciding the merits of state legislative action concerning free trade.[39] The Court had rarely intervened in cases involving free movement of goods, preferring to allow the Commission to pursue its policies of harmonization. Once the deadline passed, the Court was much more willing to critically examine member states laws and practices hindering cross-border trade. Even then, the development of case law relating to Articles 30–6 was initially slow, considering the scope and variety of non-tariff barriers.[40] The Commission noted that case law in this area was regrettably sparse, an astonishing fact given the strong treaty language on prohibitions on quantitative restrictions and other measures that could render many national measures and practices unlawful.

This situation changed dramatically after several landmark judgments, beginning with the *Dassonville* case in 1974, followed by *Cassis* in 1979, and then *Keck* in 1993. Since that time, as empirical research by Kilroy confirms, the ECJ has heard more cases involving the free movement of goods than any other area.[41]

Interpreting the treaty basis concerning free trade

Since the legal foundations and authority on which the commitment to market integration was based varies in terms of their specificity and intent, the treaties have elicited different interpretations as to their meaning and goals. While some legal scholars have advocated an expansive role for Community institutions whenever necessary for the establishment, functioning, and development of the common market,[42] other legal analysts have advocated a more restrictive application, viewing the common market as an extended customs union, allowing a wide latitude for national authority.[43] This has meant that the construction of the market has been intrinsically connected to the boundaries established by the ECJ. The ECJ has found itself obligated to define particular cases on which the treaties offer only general guidance between lawful and unlawful trade barriers.

Establishing the doctrine of quantitative restrictions

The growth of restrictive trade barriers did not go unnoticed by either the Commission or the Court. The reaction to import restrictions which were prohibited under Article 30 resulted in some early, often confusing, legislative efforts by the Commission to clamp down on quantitative restrictions or 'measures which have equivalent effect to a quantitative restriction'. Part of the problem was due to the fact that measures initially dealing with restraints upon trade were primarily considered to be quotas. Because of the initial concern with tariffs, quotas, and customs duties, the Commission focused on the applicability of Article 30 towards numerical restrictions to trade. The term 'quantitative restriction' comes from GATT Article XI, which generally prohibits 'quotas, import licenses, or other measures' subject to various exceptions. Given this rather clear sense of 'quantitative restriction', the notion of 'measures having an equivalent effect' to a quantitative restriction—which was not a GATT term—was expected to have a similarly narrow meaning.[44]

The Commission set out to define the concept of 'measures having an equivalent effect' through a series of legislative initiatives in the mid-1960s.[45] Legislative action was designed to detail those measures that were prohibited under Article 30. However, this assumed that the Commission was able to determine the actual intent of the member states in terms of the discriminatory effects of specific national regulations. This meant that the Commission would engage in what legal scholars term proportionality criteria, or a balancing standard for assessing the effect of national measures on intra-Community trade, weighing the particularistic interests of the state against that of the regional effort to promote free trade. The Commission was thus taking on the complicated task of determining whether a regulation was reasonable and justified in terms of the goals it was trying to achieve.

This is not unlike developments in the United States, where judges invoked 'indirect-direct' tests under the Commerce Clause to distinguish between laws and contracts in restraint of trade and those not in restraint of trade.[46] In the American context, this balancing technique had enabled judges to draw lines between what constitutes a trade restriction and what does not, often with inconsistent results.[47] Since it is 'not always a simple matter even to discern whether a state stature impinging on commerce is discriminatory', the outcome of many cases in the American context tends to 'reflect satisfactory compromises between states and federal interests'.[48] Given the uncertainty surrounding many of the conclusions reached under the American Commerce Clause, it is not surprising that the same concerns were expressed about the Commission's analogous efforts to foster an integrated economy through balancing states rights and Community goals.

The Commission asserted its view on the matter in response to written questions from the European Parliament in 1967.[49] Concerned that national authorities and private enterprises needed to know what was meant by the concept 'of measures having an equivalent effect', which had been expressed in terms as broad as they were ill-defined, the Parliamentary questions brought a cautious response from the Commission. The Commission set out a twofold distinction of 'measures having an effect to a quantitative restriction' under Article 30. At this point, the Commission was in a state of uncertainty, since it did little more than provide a series of examples that it felt were covered by the Article. The Commission considered overtly discriminatory measures as subject to scrutiny under Article 30, and also presumed that 'indistinctly applicable' measures were compatible. The presumption that 'indistinctly applicable' measures were compatible was highly controversial.[50] In the first of a series of Parliamentary questions beginning in the 1960s, the Commission was asked about decrees and regulations that applied to both domestic products and imports. In many cases, the national authorities were unable to show any convincing reasons for the measures which indirectly placed higher burdens on imported products to meet domestic requirements.[51]

Legal scholars have been divided as to the way in which the Treaty should be interpreted.[52] According to Slot, a restrictive interpretation of Article 30 covering only measures that discriminate between domestically and imported goods means that many technical barriers to trade cannot be considered unlawful as they apply indiscriminately to both imported and domestic goods. He argues that: 'The consequence of this view gives a rather large room for maneuver to member states, given the fact that most trading rules concern the production, marketing and use of such products and as such are applicable without distinction between imported and domestic products.'[53]

Critics of this narrow view of Article 30 argue that all state measures with the effect of restricting trade, in so far as they are not regulated by other treaty provisions, are prohibited. If discrimination was construed broadly, then more restrictive requirements for foreign goods were contrary to interstate commerce and illegal under Article 30. While legal scholars debated the degree to which non-tariff barriers were prohibited under Article 30, the Commission found itself unable to clearly specify what constituted 'measures having an equivalent effect'. In its annual report of 1968, the Commission was forced to concede that defining the applicability of Article 30 was an extremely sensitive issue, since a great variety of national provisions and practices would be affected if they expanded their scrutiny of barriers to trade.

Clearly the situation was untenable. Slot notes that the different interpretations of Article 30 meant that interstate trade barriers could be the result of:

- regulations that were discriminatory or retaliatory against out-of-state competition;
- regulations which applied equally to domestic and non-domestic firms, but in practice burden out-of-state companies, because they make market access more difficult and costly placing an undue burden on out-of-state companies;
- regulations which appear non-discriminatory but have a discriminatory effect, and so constitute a trade barrier.[54]

The limits that Article 30 could impose upon member states would play a major role in circumscribing their regulatory role. However, the Commission did not undertake primary responsibility for working out the negative implications and burdens of national trade measures, perhaps for fear of a backlash from member state governments. In a further effort to provide some guidance for those trying to engage in cross-border trade, the Commission outlined its interpretation of 'measures having equivalent effect' in a 1970 directive.[55] This provided further details about the variety of measures affecting Community trade that were impermissible as they violated Article 30. It imposed more restrictions on national regulatory practices which were discriminatory in intent, as well as expanding the notion of discrimination to those practices that did not actually discriminate between domestic and foreign goods directly, but nevertheless made it difficult for foreign products to gain market access.[56] This was clearly aimed at addressing the thorny issue of the numerous trade measures that were considered more restrictive than necessary and could be dealt with in ways that were less of a hindrance to interstate trade. Such a focus on trying to find the least restrictive means of regulating trade (using the concept of proportionality) was to have significant repercussions later in tackling barriers to trade.

Despite the proposed directives regarding equivalent effect, the Commission was constrained in its efforts to tackle national restrictions by member state interpretations of the actual intent of the legislation. The member states would not admit to adopting legislation that was deliberately protectionist in intent, and most of the cases that the Commission examined passed the test of proportionality. The Commission recognized the careful balance that needed to be maintained between the rights of member states to regulate and the rights to restrict these efforts. Although the treaties obligate member states to dismantle their trade barriers, Article 36 permit them to enact legislative restrictions to trade and commerce if they further certain legitimate policy goals and promote the common good. Since Article 36 provides derogations that set limits to the applicability of Article 30, member states were free to maintain such restrictions for a number of specifically enumerated purposes. Member states were more than willing to use this 'loophole' to justify their actions.

The Court steps in

As the Commission struggled to determine the relationship between Article 30 and Article 36, firms sought relief in the courts. This has strong parallels with the strategy pursued by big business in United States a century earlier. Faced with increasing difficulty in accessing different national markets, many firms argued that the Commission's efforts were insufficient in addressing the rising problem of non-tariff barriers. And since Article 30 was directly applicable at the end of 1970 when the common market was supposed to come into effect,[57] the ECJ emerged as an alternative avenue to challenge the legitimacy of state action.[58]

The ECJ began hearing cases with increasing frequency after 1970. Underlying all of the early trade-related cases was the conflict over quantitative restrictions, and the extent to which state legislation can hinder or restrict commercial imports from entering domestic markets.[59] The *Sekt-Weinbrand* case of 1975 provides a striking example of this tension. In *Sekt-Weinbrand*, the ECJ concluded that it was not permissible to use these generic terms solely for domestic products.[60] While the ECJ found little difficulty in determining that overt restrictions which discriminate directly against goods from another member state are contrary to Article 30, the more vexed issue still concerned 'indistinctly applicable measures'. The ECJ initially side-stepped this issue.[61] Those measures which applied to both domestic products and imports alike, but still had the effect of restricting trade prove particularly troublesome. These covered a range of measures, including pricing, technical, economic, or other public policy provisions used to improve the terms of trade, protect national markets and provide domestic manufacturers with a comparative advantage.

The Dassonville *formula*

The ECJ crystallized all of the earlier political and legal attempts to deal with non-tariff barriers in its 1974 *Dassonville* judgment, which provided a definition of 'measures having an equivalent effect' under Article 30.[62] The ECJ then applied the same *Dassonville* formula concerning measures that restrict trade to agricultural products in its *Charmasson* judgment.[63] Before discussing the implications of *Dassonville* in more detail, it is helpful to review the background of the case.

Dassonville revolved around a 1934 Belgian law that required importers not only to produce a certificate of origin for certain types of hard liquor, but to ensure that the certificate came from the country of origin. The defendants, Dassonville, were parallel importers who in 1970 had imported into Belgium various quantities of Scotch whisky from France. Although Dassonville had a certificate from France indicating the origins of the whisky, the firm was prosecuted as the certificate was not from the country of origin. The ECJ was asked to rule if the Belgian law violated Article 30 and imposed a 'measure having equivalent effect to a quantitative restriction'.

The ECJ found that once goods were permitted on the market, their movements across member states should not be impeded, and extended the scope of Article 30 to conclude that 'all trading rules enacted by member states which are capable of hindering, *directly or indirectly, actually or potentially*, intra-Community trade are to be considered as measures having equivalent effect to a quantitative restriction'. Although the ECJ could have treated the measure as a narrow quota-related restriction, it chose not to. Instead, the ECJ chose a broad definition of what constituted a trade restriction. This meant that it was not necessary to show that a measure actually restricts imports, only that it has the potential to do so.

Despite the wide ambit given to Article 30, the ECJ softened its rule by recognizing that

in the absence of a Community system guaranteeing for consumers the authenticity of a product's designation of origin, if a member state *takes measures to prevent unfair practices* in this connection, it is however subject to the condition that these measures be *reasonable* and that the means of proof required should not act as a hindrance to trade between member states and should, in consequence be accessible to all community nationals. (Author's emphasis)

Because the *Dassonville* case did not fit this criterion, and since the requirement of a certificate of authenticity was more difficult to obtain for Belgian importers, the Belgian law constituted an unreasonable restriction upon trade.

Although the ECJ seemed to give this seemingly innocuous phrase in Article 30 an extraordinarily expansive interpretation, the *Dassonville* formula was not new. The Commission had given a somewhat similar interpretation in 1970.[64] In addition, the ECJ itself had used the argument in a different way in its earlier judgments of *Grundig*[65] and *Consten* under Article 85 covering competition issues.[66] This is not surprising as both Articles concern the free movement of goods, and the principle was used in *Dassonville* to judge the legality of interventions in the market, whether from public or private actors.[67]

Since *Dassonville* settled the question as to whether Article 30 applied to 'indistinctly applicable measures', the ECJ has struck down a variety of measures including excessive verification of imports,[68] the fixing of prices that places imports at a competitive disadvantage,[69] and restrictions on door-to door sales.[70] Time and again, the ECJ has argued that it is not necessary to show that a measure actually restricted exports, only that it *potentially* does.[71] Even if the measure is temporary or in place for an interim period, if it has an 'appreciable effect' on imports then it violates Article 30.[72]

Although the ECJ has used a broad-based effect approach, this does not mean that all domestic regulatory measures are invalid.[73] The ECJ concluded that Article 30 does not cover obstacles to trade governed by other provisions of the Treaty. As the ECJ stated clearly in the *Meroni* case,[74] customs duties, state aids, and internal taxation fell outside the scope and scrutiny of Article 30. However, the Court was willing to look at measures at local, state, or regional level, thereby opening all levels of regulatory activity to judicial scrutiny.[75] By bringing a range of measures within the scope of Community purview, 'the Court simultaneously asserted its own authority to review national regulatory measures, while legitimating the Commission's role in the harmonization of national laws'.[76]

As Amstrong notes, the ECJ's approach does present a potential danger of the emergence of 'regulatory gaps'.[77] It has actively struck down many national measures, but by 'pre-empting' national regulatory competencies in many areas of health, safety, and environmental regulations, the ECJ's judgment is predicated on the ability of other Community actors being able to adopt common rules that both establish legitimate objectives and ensure the free movement of goods. But as Chapter 4 described, if these other Community institutions are unable, due to political and institutional constraints, to reconcile the imperative of regulation and free trade through harmonization, the resulting regulatory gaps can affect the governance of the market.[78]

The Cassis *formula*

The ECJ was not unaware of the problems posed by such regulatory gaps. In what has surely become its best-known case, *Cassis de Dijon*, the ECJ allowed certain national measures which actually or potentially restrict trade to continue as long as they were necessary to pursue specific national requirements, which were carefully defined in *Cassis* and subsequent judgments (see below).

Few cases have inspired such animated debate as *Cassis*, based on the importation of blackcurrant liqueur.[79] Both legal and political analysts have argued about the ramifications of the judgment for market integration.[80] Legal debate and analysis has focused around the degree of discretion that courts and member states should have in the realm of Article 30.[81] They have frequently drawn attention to the practical limitations of case-law guarantees in creating a single market, and have pointed to the impact of *Cassis* in creating a feasible policy solution to the problems encountered by harmonization. By introducing the principle of mutual acceptance of goods so that member states should accept the product standards of the other member states, except in well-defined circumstances, the perceived need for harmonization was reassessed. The result of such a 'least restrictive trade principle' was to concentrate systematic harmonization in those areas in which national laws, regulations, and practices were not equivalent, and thus constituted barriers to trade.

Although it is widely (and somewhat mistakenly[82]) held that the *Cassis* judgment introduced the principle of 'mutual recognition or mutual equivalence',[83] this did not mean that harmonization was irrelevant. For the ECJ, mutual recognition was appropriate only where there was already a degree of regulatory convergence between member states. As explained in more detail below, *Cassis* did not, as some commentators have argued, render harmonization obsolete due to the mutual recognition of standards and regulations. Rather, it was a landmark judgment consolidating earlier jurisprudence in a new form. *Cassis* shifted the burden of proof to those seeking to show that the measure restricting trade was justified, in essence making it the responsibility of states (national, local, or subnational) to show that their regulation was not simply disguised protectionism and more restrictive than necessary.[84]

The facts of *Cassis* are as follows. In 1979, the Court was asked for a preliminary ruling (under Article 177) by the Finanzgericht of Hesse, Germany, to consider action pending between Rewe Zentral AG and the Bundesmonopolverwaltung für Branntwein (Federal Monopoly Administration for Spirits) on the interpretation of Articles 30 and 37 in relation to the German law on the monopoly of spirits. Because there existed a statutory provision fixing a minimum alcoholic content for products marketed in Germany, Rewe, a cooperative importing goods, applied for authorization in 1976 from the Federal Monopoly to import from France into Germany certain spirits, including Cassis de Dijon. The Federal Monopoly informed Rewe that the authorization was not necessary under existing law. However, the import/export firm could not import Cassis since wine-spirits needed a minimum alcoholic content of

32 per cent to be marketed in Germany, and Cassis had an alcoholic content of only 15–20 per cent.[85]

Rewe brought suit, charging that the German regulation constituted a non-tariff barrier to trade, particularly as Commission proceedings against Germany had recently resulted in an amendment to regulation on minimum alcohol content.[86] The ECJ dismissed questions concerning Article 37, since the case did not concern an exclusive monopoly. Instead, it focused its attention on the relevance of Article 30, whether legislation fixing a minimum alcohol content prevented other member states from marketing in Germany, and constituted a measure having equivalent effect to a quantitative restriction.[87] This was not the first time the ECJ had addressed this question, since the *Dassonville* judgment had focused on interference with trade rather than discrimination against imports. The ECJ had previously also held that non-discriminatory provisions fell within its purview, so the questions raised in *Cassis* did not involve a radical departure but rather clarification on a point of law.[88]

The German government defended its regulations on the basis of protecting the consumer against unfair commercial practices. The German government argued that in the absence of harmonization, the margin of discretion for setting standards was the responsibility of member states.[89] Further arguing that domestic manufacturers would be at a comparative disadvantage if the same rules did not apply to foreign products, the German government stressed the risk that member states would be forced to lower their standards in order to protect the competitiveness of their industries. Noting that their regulation on alcoholic content applied equally to both domestic and imported goods, the German government strenuously argued that the measure did not fall within the scope of Article 30.

The ECJ ultimately rejected all of the German government's arguments related to the case, noting that the protection of the consumer could be achieved by less restrictive measures. The Court concluded that 'the requirements relating to the minimum alcohol beverage content do not serve a purpose which is in the general interest and such as to take precedence over the requirements of free movement of goods which constitutes one of the fundamental rules of the treaty'.[90] In the most frequently cited passage of the ruling, the ECJ argued that 'there is no valid reason why, provided that they have been lawfully produced and marketed in one of the Member States, alcoholic beverages should not be introduced into any other member state.'[91]

This ruling transformed the traditional obligations of free trade, and assumed that the burden of proof to show non-discrimination fell on the German government. The ECJ thus reversed the argument it had used for liberalization to that point, shifting the focus away from the question of the legitimacy of a state's domestic regulatory measure to a comparison of regulatory measures across member states.[92] In *Cassis*, the ECJ presumed that national standards were sufficiently equivalent to be mutually recognized and acceptable.[93] This relieved the regulatory burden of the Community, since harmonization would now only be necessary where national regulations were not equivalent.

Although the notion of equivalence of regulations across states was the most widely publicized dimension of the ruling, the ECJ included an additional layer of jurisprudence that opened up a 'regulatory space' for legitimate national measures which may survive judicial scrutiny. It outlined these measures by stating:

Obstacles to movement within the Community resulting from disparities between the national laws relating to the marketing of products in question must be accepted in so far as those provisions may be recognized as being necessary in order to satisfy mandatory requirements relating in *particular to the effectiveness of fiscal supervision, the protection of public health, the fairness of commercial transactions and the defense of the consumer.*[94] (Author's emphasis)

This is the key passage in the *Cassis* judgment.[95] Derogations (from free trade) for the purposes of public health, fair competition, and consumer protection are possible under Article 30. However, the ECJ makes clear that these exceptions may be extended, as indeed it has in other cases to include the protection of the environment and the protection of national culture (see below).[96] Clearly, it was willing to entertain exceptions—but they had to be convinced of the value of the measure.

The ECJ has extended the number of exceptions beyond that of Article 36, by recognizing that additional policy objectives may be exempt from free trade principles. Though it did not invoke Article 36 in its judgment, since it did not have the power to add exceptions to the existing treaty; instead, the ECJ interpreted Article 30 in such a way as to give it more leeway and discretion in assessing the degree to which national restrictions to trade were allowable. *Cassis* rationalized some of the earlier cases by applying a *rule of reason*.[97] American scholars often term this a 'balancing standard' where state regulation affecting interstate commerce will be upheld if (*a*) the regulation is related to a legitimate state end; and (*b*) the regulatory burden imposed on interstate commerce, and the resulting discriminatory effects, are outweighed by the state's interest in enforcing the regulation.[98]

After *Cassis*, the ECJ judged national regulations not just in terms of their effect upon trade but whether they were the most effective and appropriate means.[99] The ECJ's criteria included:

- *causality*: where there is a direct cause and effect link between the rule in question and the mandatory requirement to be satisfied.
- *proportionality*: the rules are appropriate and not excessive to the requirement to be satisfied. In other words, the rules should be proportionate to the objective.
- *substitution*: there is no alternative solution which would allow a member state to achieve its purpose or goal and create the least disturbance to interstate trade or commerce.[100]

As applied in *Cassis*, the ECJ found that the German regulations failed on all three counts. The regulations served particularistic interests and thus did not achieve their stated objectives or causality. The rules failed the proportionality test on the grounds that there were no means for importers to establish that their product did not threaten the public interest. And finally, the German law could have chosen a least restrictive alternative or substitute (for example labelling of products for alcoholic content) which met its policy objectives of protecting public health and informing the consumer.

By adding exceptions to Article 30 under which member states could retain legitimate national regulations, *Cassis* also represented a movement away from the very wide definition under *Dassonville*. The Court was seeking to judge, evaluate, and balance the effect of a measure on interstate trade against the responsibility of a member state to impose certain mandatory or necessary requirements. As Kommers and Waelbrock conclude, the justices of the ECJ were probably aware of the

meandering course of American commerce clause jurisprudence, with its frequent swings between the poles of centralization and decentralization. Thanks to the US experience, the European judges were able to take shortcuts. This explains how merely a few years after the first case involving Article 30 was submitted to them, they were able to adopt a balancing test very similar to the one used in Pike v Church (in the US) and managed to avoid the vagaries of police powers, indirect-direct which plagued US justices over the years.[101]

But that does not mean that the jurisprudence of the ECJ has been completely consistent or is always bound by previous decisions.[102] As critics of the ECJ have pointed out,[103] there are conflicting arguments regarding what is permitted or prohibited under Article 30, with some of the same questions raised in discussion of the 'reserved powers' of the states in the American system also being relevant in the European context. The following two sections clearly illustrate the substantial impact that choices made by the ECJ have on the governance of the European market, as well as on the relationship between the member states and the Union.

The post-*Cassis* environment: regulating the market or the state?

Following the *Cassis* judgment, the ECJ has continued to clarify the complicated body of case law on Articles 30–6 in its effort to safeguard the creation of a Community-wide market. As a result of its efforts to reconcile regulation and free trade, the ECJ has in effect transformed Article 30 into an economic due process clause measuring the reasonableness of public intervention in the market. The ECJ has been careful to acknowledge the regulation of local economic life (known in the United States as 'police powers') when there is no Community legislation or harmonization efforts in place. Yet in all instances, the ECJ has reserved the power to review these measures in so far as they may affect interstate commerce.[104] Clearly, the ECJ is determined not to relinquish any of its powers of judicial review.

In a series of cases following the *Cassis* judgment, the ECJ has dealt with the validity of a number of member states laws restricting the sale of foodstuffs.[105] The rulings in these cases concerning pasta, dairy products, and bread have closely followed the *Dassonville–Cassis* formula by reviewing the purpose, reasonableness, and application of the regulation.[106] In each case, the ECJ has assessed whether member state measures are the 'least restrictive means' to achieve stated regulatory objectives.[107] These rulings are important because they highlight the tension between local regulations and traditions and Community-wide market access.

The ECJ has found that prohibitions concerning the sale of pasta not made specifically from durum wheat, prohibitions against the marketing of products as vinegar unless made with wine, and restrictions on the content of bread to exclude imported brioches were not proportionate to their objectives and could not be justified on health grounds. In the pasta case, Italian restrictions were rejected on the grounds that they constituted a barrier to imports from other states, and, returning to an old theme, the ECJ maintained that it was possible for labelling and content regulations to provide the consumer with adequate information about 'pasta'.[108] The restrictive effects of Italian regulations concerning vinegar were also struck down because they rendered the sale of products from other states more difficult and thus constituted a barrier to trade. Similarly, the Dutch 'bread order' or *Broodbesluitt* was found to discriminate against bread imports. Despite Dutch claims about regulating public health, the Court struck down the legislation citing past decisions that freedom of trade was a *right* not dependent on the discretionary powers of member states.[109]

The use of such national interest or public health arguments was also rejected in two other notable cases. Belgian regulations requiring margarine to be sold only in cube-shaped containers to prevent confusion with butter which was sold in round containers was successfully challenged. The ECJ also decided the famed *Rheinheitsgebot* judgments against Germany and Greece regarding 'beer purity' regulations that precluded the sale of any product as 'beer' which was not brewed with specific ingredients. Here the ECJ insisted that the measure unreasonably placed importers at a competitive disadvantage.

The rejection of such a wide range of national measures under the purview of Article 30 also encroached upon many national traditions and practices, generating a significant amount of protest from many affected domestic constituencies.[110] The increasing number of market-enhancing rulings clearly marked the determination of the ECJ to promote European law-making and realize the possibilities of a regional market. However, the ECJ has not dismissed the validity of some member state regulatory concerns.

Shifting ground: exceptions or aberrations to interstate trade?

While developing a more expansive definition of free trade and its determination to uphold the single market, the ECJ has also acknowledged circumstances where the *Cassis–Dassonville* formula is not admissible. In certain cases, the ECJ has found local policies to be legitimate and accepted certain derogations or exceptions to free trade that go beyond its *Cassis* doctrine. The acceptance of certain regulatory practices as justifiable, for both health and safety and socio-economic reasons, has led to some concern of a shift in jurisprudence away from the all-encompassing jurisdiction of Article 30. However, market values have never occupied the whole range of public policy, and the ECJ has accepted that they must be balanced with important social concerns.

In both *Eyssen*[111] and *Sandoz*,[112] the ECJ upheld prohibitions on the addition of nisin in cheese, and on the addition of vitamins to food products. Though the cases seemed similar to *Cassis*, the ECJ accepted the argument that the scientific evidence regarding their inclusion in products was inconclusive, and so member states had the right to regulate in the absence of common rules or harmonization. In view of the uncertainties inherent in, and differing interpretations, of scientific assessment, the ECJ has had to better define the doctrines established in *Cassis* in determining when and if national regulations are equivalent.

For example, the Court gave a clear definition of equivalence in the 'woodworking case' concerning regulatory differences between France and Germany over the safety of woodworking machines.[113] Because of differences in safety training of machine operators, the ECJ ruled that a French regulation restricting German imports was valid, since it is for member states to decide the level of protection that they intend to provide, given due regard for the requirements of free movement of goods. Hence the French regulation was a legitimate policy choice despite its inherent trade-restricting effect.[114] This formulation was again articulated in an environmental case involving recycling bottles in Denmark.[115] The ECJ recognized an environmental protection argument as a legitimate reason for imposing restrictions on trade, even though the measure was disproportionately unfair to non-domestic producers, who faced higher costs in returning bottles for recycling to their country of origin.[116] The ECJ's willingness to accept unilateral measures, even those creating potential barriers to trade, can be interpreted as making further Community harmonization necessary 'as a further bulwark against market balkanization and the possible abuse of powers by member states'.[117] The ECJ was keen to push member states and the Commission to make more progress in harmonizing standards in some areas, which would enable it to avoid potentially controversial decisions.

As Dashwood notes, the ECJ has become sensitive to the danger that the *Cassis* doctrine may approach the bounds of national tolerance.[118] In a number of cases, the ECJ's approach is also at variance with *Dassonville*, and it has paid increasing attention to the socio-economic policy choices of member states, even if this adds a third layer of reasoning beyond the rule of reason and Article 36 arguments. The most criticized judgments are that of *Oebel*[119] concerning night-work and *Blesgen* concerning alcohol (again). In both cases, the ECJ concluded that the regulations were for specific social goals and did not fall within or contravene Article 30. The *Oebel* case concerned a ban on night-time deliveries which was alleged to contravene Article 30, since it obstructed the delivery of bakery products in Germany. The ECJ disagreed, reasoning that the ban on night-work was to protect workers and constituted a legitimate socio-economic objective. Similarly, the ECJ accepted the Belgian argument in *Blesgen* that the sales ban of alcohol in public premises did not negatively affect imports, and was justified on the social grounds of public health and safety concerns regarding alcohol consumption. While these measures raised fears that the ECJ was reducing the scope of Article 30,[120] several other cases suggest an attempt to assess whether socio-economic objectives are acceptable, and in doing so to look at the circumstances in which goods are sold to see if there is a genuine intra-Community effect on trade.

In *Cinématique*, the ECJ scrutinized the French law prohibiting the sale or hire of video films for one year to enable significant returns for the film industry and thus protect a culturally important sector. Because the measure applied without distinction to both imported and domestic videos, the ECJ decided that it was for member states to determine the need for such a restriction. The French law was upheld on the basis of a legitimate socio-cultural objective. The ECJ made clear that the problem was not the French regulation *per se* but the disparities between different national regulations concerning the conditions for release of cinematographic work in member states.

Distinguishing when a measure has a sufficient impact on trade to merit judicial review is also increasingly difficult as many of the cases involve normative regulatory goals. This became apparent in the Sunday trading cases, where the ECJ was asked to hear challenges to national laws prohibiting or limiting Sunday trading.[121] These cases raised the problem of determining the effect of such measures, which did not involve specific products or individual targets but a general mode of trading. Because these national regulations often involved long-standing trading acts for social or religious reasons, the ECJ was asked to determine a balance, not between two conflicting trade interests, but between community free trade and national moral, social, and cultural norms.

The ECJ initially left it to the national courts to decide on whether Sunday trading regulations were justified restrictions upon trade. The ECJ cited the *Oebel* case, rather than *Cassis* or the Article 36 derogations, in deciding that the measures governing Sunday trading reflected socio-cultural choices that were matters for member states. This led to inconsistency among the national courts, who were left to determine the appropriateness of such policies in the context of Community-wide trade.[122] The ECJ was thus forced to step in and determine the issue itself, and decide if another exception to Article 30 based on social, moral, and cultural grounds was permissible if there were no existing community regulations in place. The ECJ did not apply the *Cassis* formula (balancing method) since it doubted whether it could 'measure' the free trade economic premises of the community against valued national social, cultural, and moral considerations.

Gormley argues that the key to understanding these cases is the increased effort by the ECJ to reduce challenges to national regulations having only an incidental or speculative affect on intra-community trade.[123] While he concludes that the ECJ has not been terribly sympathetic to attempts to invoke Community freedoms in national situations and circumstances, it has been forced to examine many of these sensitive issues since it has consistently advocated a broad definition of free trade under Article 30. Although the ECJ recognizes that member states have regulatory competence in areas where there is no community legislation, it has not left member states with unfettered powers and discretion, fearing that to do so could undermine (actually or potentially, directly or indirectly) free trade.

By supervising the action of member states, the ECJ 'protects the community interest, even against the wishes of member states, and that it did not accept a right of the collective members—or the majority of them—to give an interpretation of the community treaty.' [124] In some respects this follows the precedent of the US Supreme Court in *McCullough* v. *Maryland*. The ECJ sought the right to establish jurisdiction over an area, and then whether or not it wanted to take the case, particularly where the result could lead to a controversial or sweeping ruling.[125]

After *Cassis*, the ECJ refrained from imposing mutual recognition by judicial fiat. Broadly applied, mutual recognition would eliminate countless barriers to trade, with the result that member states could not demand conformity with domestic rules as a condition of entry to the national market. This would reduce member state regulatory sovereignty. However, the Court was much more cautious, determining on a case-by-case basis the 'equivalence' of national regulations, and whether states' rights could be curtailed under Article 30. This was clearly aimed at pushing member states to coordinate or harmonize their national policies, and reduce the need to keep challenging the legality of national laws. The prospect of a largely case law-based guarantee of a single market has practical limitations, not least of which is the need to continually assess the equivalence of national regulations, which would take place on a case-by-case, piecemeal basis.[126] There is also the possibility of cases at variance with the expansive definition of free trade under *Dassonville–Cassis*, potentially leading to the imposition of judicially created limitations on trade.

As both the American and European experiences illustrate, the legal foundations of market-making may not always be consistent, reflecting a willingness to shift course, revisit member state prerogatives, and narrow or widen the scope of the regulatory power of governments. Given that the ECJ faced so many legal challenges to member state regulations, in some cases it may simply have chosen to push the problem back onto the political branches in determining whether sensitive national measures constitute a trade barrier, to be resolved through political agreement on common regulatory standards. As Joliet concludes, 'each community institution must act within the limits of its powers. Harmonization of the laws of member states is a function that belongs to the legislature and not to the Court.'[127]

The Keck *formula*

Subject to a great deal of legal scrutiny and criticism regarding its efforts to balance various policy objectives[128] the ECJ further modified its position in *Keck*.[129] While it was understood that the ECJ could decide whether there should be regulation, and if so, who had the power to regulate, it faced increasingly difficult cases involving 'jurisdictional line-drawing'.[130] The Court seemed to be drawing fine lines between deciding when Article 30 was relevant, and whether regulations had a sufficient impact or effect upon the single market to warrant review regarding what was permitted and what was prohibited under Article 30.[131]

Given its willingness to expand what constituted a trade restriction in its *Dassonville–Cassis* jurisprudence, the Court was faced with a growing number of cases for preliminary review. *Keck* was intended to clarify and refine a long list of cases concerning measures that 'directly or indirectly, actually or potentially' hindered Community trade. Despite the Court's intention to provide greater guidance in this area, *Keck* generated much commentary and criticism because 'it harbors substantial ambiguity concerning its precision and scope' with regard to free trade.[132]

The facts of *Keck* are as follows. Keck and Mithouard, managers of two French supermarkets, had violated French law prohibiting resale of products below their purchase price (resale at a loss).[133] The plaintiffs (Keck and Mithouard) argued that although it applied equally to domestic and imported goods, the French law was unnecessarily restrictive and did not protect any imperative requirements such as consumer protection, public health, and fair trading (as set out in the *Cassis* formula). Although Article 30 was not actually mentioned by the national court, the ECJ dismissed the claim that the French law was incompatible with Article 85, which refers to the free movement of persons, services, capital, and the establishment of free competition. Instead, it assessed the French government's contention that the case did not come under Article 30 because the measure did not constitute an effect equivalent to a quantitative restriction.[134]

Following its earlier judgments, and notably those concerning the Sunday trading laws,[135] the ECJ adopted a more reserved approach towards national rules, that, like the Sunday trading laws, were not intended to regulate intra-community trade. The ECJ considered whether these regulations were 'indirect, direct or purely speculative' in effect.

Recognizing the *Dassonville–Cassis* formula, the ECJ agreed that the French 'resale at a loss' provision may potentially prohibit trade between member states. However, the central question was whether the possibility that this may occur made the French regulation 'equivalent to a quantitative restriction' under Article 30. Because of the increased tendency of traders to invoke Article 30 as a means of challenging any policy that hindered their commercial freedom, the ECJ took this opportunity to review its *Cassis–Dassonville* formulations. Article 30 had become 'the last refuge for litigants in distress' with the result that 'the case law is not only plentiful; it is overgrown.'[136]

Anxious to reduce the number of cases in this area, the ECJ made an important refinement to its earlier rulings:

> *contrary to what has previously been decided*, the application to products from member states of national provisions restricting or prohibiting *certain selling arrangements* is not such as to hinder, directly or indirectly, actually or potentially, trade between member states within the meaning of the Dassonville judgment . . . provided that those rules apply to all affected traders operating within the national territory and provided that they operate in the same manner, in law, and in fact, the marketing of domestic products and of those of member states. (my emphases)

Although the ECJ appeared to have backtracked from its ritualistic invoking of Article 30, *Keck* was not a complete renunciation of previous case law.[137] While *Keck* did seem to exempt a number of cases from the ambit of Article 30, reducing the scope of judicial scrutiny, the Court was careful to restrict its application to 'selling arrangements'.[138] While this has caused some question as to what constitutes a 'selling arrangement', the Court has been careful to concede that its ruling was based on the fact that *overall* access to the market was not more restrictive for imports than domestic products. In a sense, the Court was shifting the burden of proof onto the trader that member states 'selling arrangements' actually impact interstate trade, apply to cross-border trade, and deserve scrutiny of their legal justification under Article 36 or *Cassis* 'mandatory requirements.'[139]

In any event, the ECJ's approach in *Keck* is not entirely novel or new.[140] The balancing of various factors is inevitable since as 'integration progresses, the "stakes" of Article 30 cases have concomitantly increased: disputed member state restrictions now lie in intensely contested regulatory spheres, with particularly high value being attached to local control.'[141] In its judgment, the ECJ was clearly responding to the shift in political environment towards integration, and *Keck* may also be viewed as a response to the shift back to member states under the principle of subsidiarity, where member states are given more leeway in determining their policy objectives, particularly in areas that have limited effect upon intra-Community trade. This shift is echoed by subsequent cases where the ECJ has used the 'selling arrangements' formula to exempt a number of issues from judicial scrutiny under Article 30, including national measures prohibiting Sunday trading,[142] and provisions regarding mandatory closing hours, pharmaceutical advertising, and restrictions on television advertising of certain products.[143]

The ECJ may be trying to improve its legitimacy in the eyes of its various constituencies, lest it risk a revolt against perceived judicial activism. Conscious of the effects that its judgments have on domestic politics, the ECJ may be seeking a balance between different jurisdictions. Though Chalmers has indicated that its recent rulings represent a retreat by the ECJ in internal market regulation, it still leaves open the possibility for political action to integrate markets.[144] By leaving it to the Commission to determine when national measures constitute a trade restriction, the ECJ encourages the possibility that harmonization could mitigate the effects of derogations and state strategies undermining the single market.

The example of the USA is instructive in demonstrating that the Court's use of judicial review in breaking down state barriers is not immutable, and responds to changes in the political environment. In the late eighteenth and early nineteenth centuries, the American states were left with much of the responsibility associated with governments including public safety, education, welfare, economic development, and control of business activity. This ebbed and flowed in the twentieth century, as the Supreme Court reflected on the legitimacy and extent of federal legislation in regulating local commerce, and the degree to which states can or should perform certain regulatory functions.[145] The articulation of a free trade agenda by the ECJ, albeit with some efforts to balance local needs with broader integrative goals, does not constitute the emergence of a radically new approach to integration. In this light, the ECJ is simply ruling on the economic relationship between regulation and the market, and the political relationship between member states and the Union.

The intersection of law, regulation, and markets

As this chapter has demonstrated, the role of law has been critical in sustaining a market economy by playing a central role in the integration of an economy fragmented by the traditions and interests of member states. Without the role of law, the single market cannot function. Even while tackling the mercantilist traditions of member states and constructing a more centralized economic order, the ECJ has also been concerned about preserving regional and local diversity. It has fashioned a legal regime to resolve interstate disputes through its carving out of the doctrines of supremacy and direct effect.

Like the United States, the European Union has been confronted by clashes over the 'reserved' powers of constituent states. Law is important in shaping boundaries, and resolving conflict between central and local units of government. This is not to suggest that the critical role that the judiciary came to play in delimiting states' authority on interstate commerce was inevitable.[146] Nor is it to suggest that the ECJ has been entirely consistent in deciding that the federal interest in fostering economic unity should take precedence over states' interests in exercising their essential powers of regulation.[147] The re-evaluation of precedents in the EU and US cases in the field of interstate commerce indicates that the territorial balance of power is not judicially fixed; courts can shift positions in assessing the degree to which the federal level can restrict states regulatory activities.

As Beer[148] and Sbragia[149] have argued, governments have institutional self-interests that they seek to defend vis-à-vis other governments. Market integration in Europe is thus a dynamic mode of governance in which institutional elements are constantly evolving; the relevance of judicial decisions upon the relationship between states in promoting or hindering an integrated economy is critical. Thus, the decision to 'review national regulations, and if so, according to what criteria, implies choices regarding the division of competencies between the member states and the Union'.[150] The ECJ thus chooses how it shapes both states and markets, since its judgments determine not only the 'constitutional limits to state or public intervention in the market' but also the level of government at which regulation is most appropriate or legitimate.

The basis upon which cases regarding free trade and interstate commerce were decided was intimately tied up with conceptions about the nature of the market, the member state–community relationship, and the role of regulation in the economy. Both governments and firms sought to use the law to maximize their interests and to enhance their market position. Their activism has led to a series of ECJ judgments that set the foundations for the advancement of a single market, discussed in more detail in the next chapter since it opened up new avenues for regulatory reform.

Conclusion: laying the groundwork for regulatory reform

As this chapter illustrates, law has rendered important support to market processes.[151] In dealing with the discriminatory effects of regulatory barriers to trade, the European Court of Justice has played an active role in *negative* integration, by invalidating discriminatory national rules. Through negative integration, the EU has an extremely powerful set of legal tools for removing national barriers to the free movement of goods, and for intervening against national policies that could be construed as distortions to free market competition. But European law is not limited to market liberalization, since the Court has provided the window of opportunity for the Community to foster *positive* integration through the creation of a new regulatory regime—using the private sector to integrate and regulate markets. Market-correcting regulations are negotiated not only to improve allocative efficiency and competitiveness, but also to enhance other non-market values such as safety, quality, and health. These political efforts to foster integration are discussed in Chapters 6 and 7.

The Court has in essence both liberated the market and transformed the way in which markets are regulated. This resulted in a fundamental retooling of the regulatory functions of the Community to complement harmonization: more emphasis was placed on mutual recognition, and a new strategy of delegating regulatory responsibility to private standards bodies was designed to shift the burden of market integration away from the politicking of Community institutions. The idea underpinning regulatory reform was to shift the issue of market-building from intergovernmental bargaining to include a host of other public and private players to set the rules. This symbiotic relationship enables public sector officials to use private sector resources to achieve their goals of fostering common rules for a single market. This dependence, as later chapters illustrate, comes with its own problems and difficulties. However, it is the pivotal role of the judiciary that facilitates such new strategies and options which is described in more detail in the next chapter.

6

Regulatory Reform Strategies and the Single Market Programme

The decisions of the ECJ created the potential for institutional innovation.[1] The idea of mutual recognition, originally formulated as a circumscribed doctrine by the ECJ, was swiftly seized upon by European policy-makers as part of a new strategy to promote market access. The Commission endeavoured to extend the ideas implicit in the legal doctrine into a new coherent policy option. Criticized for what seemed a fragmentary presentation of proposals without due regard to the overall economic and political objectives of the single market, the Commission issued its own political interpretation of *Cassis*.[2] This quasi-legal or soft law communication spelt out the implications of the law,[3] and provided the Commission with an opportunity to act as a policy entrepreneur in promoting the single market programme.[4]

In its brief, the Commission built on the ECJ's guidelines to argue that '*any* product imported from another member state must in principle be admitted to the territory of the importing member state. . . . If it has been lawfully produced, and conforms to the rules and processes of manufacture that are customarily and traditionally accepted in the exporting country . . .' The Commission thus not only extracted from *Cassis* a general principle of mutual recognition or equivalence of European standards in agricultural and industrial products, but also drew a much broader free trade principle than the ECJ itself had concluded.

The Commission argued that member states could not take an exclusively national viewpoint, since many national regulations were broadly equivalent. With this degree of regulatory convergence across member states, most products would no longer need complete total harmonization. However, the Commission recognized that even if member states agreed to such regulatory equivalence, this would not address the barriers created by national standards bodies. The Commission argued that

these national standards were not designed deliberately in order to create obstacles but are generally meant to serve worthy aims: rationalization of production, improvement of product quality, protection of workers, users and the environment . . . the way they are drawn up and the fact that only the national industry is actively involved in their preparation gives the national manufacturer a two-fold advantage over their competitors: they can be sure that in the preparation of these standards due consideration will be given to their views and manufacturing processes; they are aware of the intended pattern of development and modification in advance of their competitors, and therefore have time to prepare for it.[5]

To address the trading-impeding effects of both standards and regulations, the Commission advocated greater coordination among national standards bodies, based on the strategy of mutual recognition or equivalence being pursued in the regulatory field. This broad interpretation given of the *Cassis* doctrine generated intense political and legal controversy.[6] Member states were immediately hostile to the Commission's position, as it limited powers reserved to them in the absence of Community regulations. In their efforts to check the Commission's assertiveness, member states also repeated the argument advanced by Germany during the *Cassis* judgment, that mutual recognition would result in unfair competition, reduce consumer protection, and lead to a downward regulatory spiral towards the lowest common denominator. Fearing that stricter national rules would be under pressure, placing domestic producers at a competitive disadvantage, member states were concerned that they would be forced to relax their product regulations to protect the competitiveness of their industry.[7]

The Commission's position was also challenged by the Consumer Consultative Council (CCC).[8] The CCC expressed concern that the Commission's interpretation reversed the judicial reasoning and generalized too much from *Cassis*, since the Commission's stipulation that barriers to trade were unlawful was contrary to the ECJ's judgment that merely considered whether, in particular cases, certain barriers to trade were justified *de jure* or *de facto*.[9] Noting that the Court has viewed each restriction on a case-by-case basis, the CCC argued that the new policy promoted the unconditional liberalization of trade at the expense of consumer protection. Harmonization was still crucial in those areas where economic and industrial groups stood to gain from a single market. Faced with such opposition, but also receiving support from industry and trade associations that were increasingly dissatisfied with excessive harmonization, the Commission continued to push for a reappraisal of the harmonization approach.[10]

This chapter examines the changes in the Community's regulatory strategy that built upon the ECJ's reasoning in *Cassis*, and came into being as part of the single market programme.[11] The Commission took advantage of the trend among member states to champion the liberalization of markets, renew efforts to stem the rise of protectionist barriers to trade, and enhance international competitiveness through market integration, so that regulatory reform found a receptive audience during a timely window of opportunity.[12] It offers a good illustration of how the removal of restrictions on market access and the addition of regulations governing market behaviour operate concurrently. And equally important, the combination of bold liberalization with market surveillance and regulatory supervision, though differing in substance and jurisdiction from its predecessor, further diffused authority both territorially and functionally.

Although the origins and development of the single market programme have received significant attention in the literature, the regulatory strategies and policies aimed at tackling technical barriers to trade have not received similar focus.[13] Before examining the new regulatory strategies in more detail, the chapter provides a brief account of the political and institutional reforms that resulted in the inclusion of these new strategies in the Commission's White Paper on the Internal Market to place the reforms in context.

The state of the Internal Market: political and institutional reform

After encountering much resistance to a more liberal interpretation of the *Cassis* doctrine, the Commission appealed for positive action and vigilance on the part of member states. Though there had been a continuous stream of studies, resolutions, and declarations to improve the functioning of its institutions and make the single market a reality, it was difficult to push measures from paper into practice.[14] The treatment of products from third countries in directives on technical barriers, the need for an information procedures on technical standards, and the simplification of cross-border formalities attracted the most attention in meetings related to the single market. With over thirty proposals pending in these areas, they were considered priorities to increase competitiveness.[15] Many proposals were blocked by disagreement over the treatment of products from third countries and the necessary certification requirements.[16] Work on technical barriers had ground to a halt as there was no consensus about the relationship between the internal market and the common commercial policy.

Member states defending free trade at all costs were pitted against those wishing to link the opening of the internal market with its closing to third countries. As a result, no progress was made on other key proposals, such as the stronger system of notification and information for standards and regulations to control the rapid advance of national standards and regulations (see below). Though there had been some initial willingness to provide the Commission with a mandate to study member states practices that distorted competition and trade, the reticence to follow through led the *Financial Times* to conclude that, 'in their conduct of internal community affairs, EEC governments tend to resemble the biblical evangelists celebrated in the southern states of America, whose private lives fell sadly short of the standards they preached.'[17]

Sessions of the Council of Ministers in February and March 1983 were devoted to the internal market. Progress was achieved on two directives on access for third country products, and the exchange of information procedure, overcoming six years of blockage from France, Italy, and later Greece.[18] Despite consistent reluctance by some member states to pursue greater liberalization, joined with the fear of greater import penetration, calls from European industrialists aided the Commission's efforts to mobilize support for addressing technical barriers to trade.[19] The American Chamber of Commerce in Brussels (AMCHAM) found widespread complaints among American companies about industry standards, border formalities and export licences, identifying France and Italy as operating the worst trade barriers.[20] The European Confederation of National Employers' Associations, UNICE, also articulated the concerns of many trade associations about the effects of non-tariff barriers. And the most influential effort came from some of Europe's leading multinational companies who added their considerable pressure and influence for European solutions through the formation of the high-profile European Roundtable for Industrialists (ERT) in 1983 to focus government attention on the completion of the internal market.[21]

According to their own calculations, member states resorted to at least twenty-three different practices to protect their national markets. Anxious to publicize the scope of the problem, European Commissioner Narjes, responsible for the internal market portfolio, forwarded a list of the most problematic barriers. In communiqués sent to the member states, the Commission noted that they were investigating over 400 cases of such barriers, a quadrupling of cases in just four years.[22] The issue was made more contentious by the circulation of an inventory of non-tariff barriers by the French.[23] Tired of being depicted as the most outrageously protectionist sinner, the French government produced a fascinating no-holds barred overview of the problem that was circulated confidentially around the Commission. Targeting Germany as the most difficult market to penetrate, the 'protectionist racket' depicted by the French made member states increasingly sensitive to being targeted as blocking efforts at removing trade obstacles.

It is against this background that repeated efforts were made within the Commission, Parliament, and Council to promote European integration as a means of economic revival.[24] The Council created an Internal Market Council to consider many of the problems reflected in the communiqués. The initial failure to achieve concrete results was partly due to the existence of too many unresolved problems. However, major steps were taken that broke the *immobilisme* that had stifled further integration: agreement was reached on the long-running dispute over Britain's contribution to the Community budget and a committee was set up to focus on the reform of the institutional and decision-making structure of the Community.[25] While these two actions were important in enabling the Community to turn its attention towards promoting market integration, the agreement at the 1985 intergovernmental conference to 'study the institutional conditions under which the internal market could be achieved within the time limit' proved critical for the market integration process.[26] In 1983, the Spinelli Report had drawn attention to the need to link national regulations and institutional reform, followed by the draft Treaty on European Union in 1984, which focused on the need for institutional reform, calling for increased Parliamentary powers and greater use of qualified majority voting. On the basis of proposals received from the intergovernmental conference, the treaty reforms were brought together in the Single European Act (SEA).[27] The SEA endorsed the single market and altered the decision-making rule for single market measures (with exceptions such as taxation) from unanimity to qualified majority voting. This linked institutional reform with substantive goals, and made it more difficult for recalcitrant member states to simply veto legislative action, as had been the case under harmonization.

The White Paper: a programme for action

The mandate given to the Commission in March 1985, to provide a comprehensive package of proposals to complete the internal market, was the culmination of earlier Commission studies undertaken between 1981 and 1984. The programme was written quickly under the direction of Lord Cockfield, the Commissioner in charge of the internal market, and presented to the European Council meeting in Milan in June 1985. The White Paper, entitled *Completing the Internal Market*, contained a comprehensive assessment of the remaining obstacles to trade, grouped together in three major categories: physical, technical, and fiscal barriers.[28] Non-tariff barriers included such practices as technical specification of products, the use of different health and safety standards, environmental regulations, quality controls, restrictive procurement and transportation practices, and differences in indirect taxation.

The White Paper provided a unifying document for a disparate series of measures. Though many of the issues had been on the agenda in the form of draft directives and regulations for a number of years, the White Paper provided a comprehensible and readable package of proposals with a clear timetable for implementation. The Commission expected that the proposals would be adopted within one or two years by the Council, and member states would be allowed two years to implement the new directives and regulations into their own national frameworks.[29] While this was ambitious, given past policy achievements under harmonization, the Commission hoped that the timetable proposed for initial agreements would then create the momentum for the potentially more difficult and controversial measures.[30]

Though the passing of the deadline did not mean the completion of the single market with proposed measures such as company harmonization and corporate taxation still on the drawing board, the strategy went beyond formal agreement on legislation. And yet legislatively, it was considered most successful in dealing with market distortions and obstacles related to technical barriers. The free movement of goods had a central place in the philosophy of the White Paper, as two-thirds of the proposals were concerned with so-called technical barriers to trade. More importantly, the White Paper built upon the fundamental principles laid down in the case law of the ECJ, and pushed for a reappraisal of the strategies to achieve market integration.[31] While the new strategy focused primarily on technical barriers, the conceptual framework of market liberalization was applied to all areas. The White Paper explained that the traditional dichotomy between goods and services was now obsolete, and technical barriers were the same problem for industry whether in the goods or services sector.[32] By treating services as essentially financial products, the new strategy for liberalization was to be the same.[33]

The White Paper also applied the mutual recognition principle that the Commission had advocated in its communication following the *Cassis* decision. The proposal advocated minimal coordination of rules based on the principle of mutual recognition of national laws. As the White Paper noted:

this does not mean that there should be the same rules everywhere . . . subject to certain important constraints, the general principle should be approved that if a product is lawfully manufactured and marketed in one member state, there is no reason why it should not be sold freely throughout the Community. Indeed, the objectives of national legislation, such as the protection of human health and life and of the environment, are more often than not identical. It follows that the rules and controls developed to achieve these objectives, essentially come down to the same thing. . . . What is true of goods, is also true for services and people.[34]

The generalization and extension of legal rulings would mean that the perceived need for widespread and systematic harmonization could be reassessed. Since so few results had been achieved under harmonization, the Commission was essentially advocating that more attention be focused on areas in which differences in national laws, practices, and regulations created—in the eyes of member states—justifiable barriers to trade. While not giving up its own interventionist role, this functional and technocratic approach to market integration provided the opening needed for the Commission to introduce a more efficient means of addressing technical barriers to trade.

New regulatory strategies for market integration

Bolstered by the need to provide 'less regulation and more freedom of choice for business',[35] the Community successfully pushed its new regulatory strategy to address the trade problems due to the innumerable standards, regulations, and product approval practices that companies encountered across Europe. The favoured strategy worked on three fronts: (1) to proactively prevent new technical barriers to trade from arising; (2) to harmonize regulatory differences through 'reference to standards' accompanied by the promotion and development of European standards and mutual recognition; and (3) to provide market surveillance mechanisms to ensure compliance. The Commission was aware, however, that these reforms could not by themselves stem the flow of new barriers. With this in mind, the Commission sought advice and assistance from national public authorities, standardization bodies, industries, and trade associations in their efforts to put forward a new plan of action.[36]

Regulatory pre-emption and mutual information

A crucial feature of the Commission's efforts to address trade barriers was the adoption of the Mutual Information Directive in 1983.[37] Given the pace and scope of national activity, the Commission was concerned that European efforts could be undermined by new national standards and regulations. To prevent such problems for hindering the internal market process, the Mutual Information Directive was designed to function as an 'early warning' mechanism.[38] Rather than wait until new regulations and standards were adopted, the legislation sought to increase transparency and cooperation between the Commission and Member States in preventing new technical barriers to trade. This meant that member states and national standards bodies were required to notify other interested parties if they were to introduce new standards or regulations. This was backed by a 'standstill' policy whenever the Commission believed that the proposed national legislation would generate new barriers. What was interesting about this information exchange procedure was that it applied to both standards and regulations, thereby exercising some form on obligation of both public and private institutions.

The Commission had pursued this path because of the widespread failure on the part of member states to provide notification under the Gentlemen's Agreement agreed upon in 1969.[39] The Mutual Information Directive allowed the Commission to assess the potential restrictive effects of national action upon the operation of the single market, initiate infringement procedures against member states for failing to comply with the Mutual Information Directive, and request member states to refrain from continuing their activities pending Community action, strengthening the collective oversight functions of the Community institutions. The scope of the Mutual Information Directive was widened by two amendments to increase coverage from manufactured goods to agricultural products, including foodstuffs and medicinal products.[40] The Commission has also proposed to extend coverage to include so-called information society services.[41]

During the three-month standstill period, the Commission, member states, or national standards bodies may react to a draft work-in-progress. If no action is taken, the national standards bodies or national authority can proceed as normal. If objections are raised, then the national standards or national public authorities must take account of any comments, including detailed opinions requesting amendments to draft proposals, and intentions by the Commission to pre-empt national policy through European regulation. This means that member states must suspend their own work for a limited period.[42]

Yet as Commissioner Narjes concluded: 'there is widespread failure to observe the notification obligations and numerous infringements thereof . . . [It] is already apparent that far more technical regulations are adopted and published in the official gazettes of the member states than are notified to the Commission under directive 83/189.'[43] Other commentators agreed that member states and national standards bodies were slow to comply with the Mutual Information Directive.[44] To enhance compliance, the Commission urged the European standards bodies to improve their obligations to provide information on pending national standards.[45] Responding to concerns that national standards activity was not diminishing, despite efforts to establish European standards, the European standards bodies undertook internal reforms to ensure that each national member responded to the Mutual Information Directive by providing early notification, and suspending activities pending responses from other members. However, early notification remained a significant problem as national standards bodies continued to inform European institutions at the final public screening stage, after much of the work has already been completed.[46] Increased concern that national standards continued to proliferate led the Commission to note that vigilant and continuous monitoring was necessary in view of the high proportion of specific national initiatives, and the continued allocation of resources to the national rather than European level.[47]

The compliance situation in the regulatory sector was just as problematic. Member states continued to notify the Commission of pending regulatory activity in a number of sectors, but the problems were due to the content of regulations. This was particularly acute in the agricultural sector, where the desire to protect the geographical origin of identifiable agricultural or food products led some member states to establish 'certified designations of origin' that constituted barriers to free movement.[48] Since this amounted to a 'blockade' of member state legislation, it required a degree of political sensitivity to reach some form of compromise.[49] To avoid singling out any one member state, the Commission often conducted 'group' meetings with several national authorities to exchange views, discuss problems, and search for acceptable solutions.

The Commission typically responded to over half of the national regulations notified, with particular concern for the compatibility of draft national regulations with European law. Generally the Commission began with additional requests for further clarification, and used the opportunity to remind the notifying member state of possible infringement proceedings or earlier notifications if related to an alleged breach of trade. The most prominent problem with draft regulations was the absence of provisions respecting the principle of mutual recognition.[50] Marking requirements, language requirements, specific ingredients or materials, limits on usage of certain products, and certain marketing and approval arrangements often had to be revised.

While the Commission sought to resolve problems through informal means, pre-empting subsequent legal challenges, it did have recourse to judicial action to push states into modifying their regulations in compliance with Community law.[51] Though judicial remedies can take time, the importance of complying with the Mutual Information Directive increased with the decision of the European Court to make notifications of draft technical regulations directly effective.[52] As a 'pre-emptive' mechanism, however, the policy has something of a mixed record, since it was clear that the process of drawing up an inventory of problems was a formidable task. However, the mechanism does provide an important tool in preventing further impediments to the single market, and has led to subsequent measures (decision 3052/95/EU) aimed at providing information on national measures that derogate from the principle of free movement because of the imposition of product withdrawals, general bans, and product modifications by specific member states.[53]

Shaping the regulatory agenda: the Low Voltage Directive

While the Commission sought to stem the tide of national regulations through exchange of information and standstill procedures, there was also the need to find a New Approach to dealing with existing technical barriers. A strategy to alleviate the burden of total harmonization was first advocated as early as 1968. An innovative draft directive using a 'reference to standards' technique (*renvoi aux normes*) had been supported by both the European Parliament and Economic and Social Committee as an alternative to the traditional method of approximation of laws.[54] The Low Voltage Directive adopted in 1973 was an important first step in shifting the regulatory burden from the public to the private sector.[55]

Though rarely acknowledged in assessments of the single market, the Low Voltage Directive provided important lessons about the difficulties of promoting European standards. It was the first instance of the application of mutual recognition and reference to standards in traded goods, albeit in a limited area, long before mutual recognition and standardization were given prominence by the single market programme. A 1982 Communication to the Council and Parliament on the role and application of the Low Voltage Directive made clear that the Commission intended to apply this model to other sectors.[56]

The importance of the reference to standards technique was not completely understood at the time. The Low Voltage Directive provided a short outline of vaguely formulated safety goals, leaving the ultimate decision of whether the policies adopted were safe to the courts. Also, the legislative reference to safety standards established by the private sector was not uniquely European. It was a common practice in some of the member states as well as the United States, where regulators relied heavily on industry to establish voluntary rules. These rules were often incorporated into national legislation, provided that they survived judicial review regarding fair procedures and appropriate notice and comment procedures.[57]

In the case of the Low Voltage Directive, general safety requirements were provided by designated non-governmental actors. European standards bodies were asked to provide appropriate European standards meeting the necessary regulatory requirements. Though the directive covered only products in the electrical and electro-technical sector, it opened up those markets considerably. By delegating responsibility for the detailed rules governing market access to the European standards bodies, the policy was a welcome relief for manufacturers, though not without its critics. During the 1970s, it had taken twenty-seven meetings among member state representatives to reach agreement, as caution regarding the prospect of forgoing regulatory control led to protracted negotiations. The loss of sovereign control was a key concern; once foreign firms met these European-wide standards, member states were obligated to admit them without further scrutiny.

Even though it seemed purely a technical and politically insignificant measure, the potential impact of the Low Voltage Directive led to intense negotiations with the then applicant countries, Ireland, Denmark, and Britain. Consulted only at the final stages of the draft proposal, these three states demanded a number of modifications. The most significant was the postponement of the date of implementation until 1978 for Denmark, five years after the directive had been adopted. Further difficulties were encountered, as only Ireland among the nine member states was able to implement the directive within the designated eighteenth-month time frame.

In view of problems encountered, the Commission began legal action for non-compliance against eight member states. Only Italy refused to implement the directive, citing the dissolution of the Italian Parliament in its inability to adopt an implementing law. The Italian government further defended its non-compliance by stating that the directive was already covered by existing Italian law. Unconvinced, the Commission charged the Italians with 'not having brought into force, within the proscribed period, the laws, regulations and administrative provisions necessary to comply with the Council Directive 73/23/EC'. In *Commission* v. *Italy*, the ECJ ruled against Italian objections to harmonized standards agreed in European standards bodies, composed of national standards bodies from both the European Community and from the non-member states of the European Free Trade Association (EFTA).[58] Though the ECJ clearly viewed the establishment of safety standards by a private organization as an equivalent means by which to establish economic integration, legal scholars have consistently voiced concerns about such delegation of decision-making power.[59]

These and other concerns focused attention not only on whether organizations principally performing private and commercial activities can adequately act in the public interest, but also whether the reference to standards technique constituted an invalid delegation of powers. Though delegation of regulatory policy was to become a central foundation of the Community's strategy to reduce technical barriers, the criticisms that the Commission had gone far beyond its implementing powers by transferring the production of technical standards to private organizations was not invalidated by the ECJ.[60] The ECJ was willing to allow private actors to provide certain regulatory functions, as long as oversight mechanisms were in place to make sure they met legal requirements.

Although the ECJ assumed that commonly agreed-upon European standards met safety requirements, in practice governments sought to retain their authority through a final review over proposals for standards in which their individual interest was often comparatively minor.[61] Member states were quick to exploit the escape clause in the Low Voltage Directive, which allowed them to do so.[62] Although designed to allow member states to prohibit the import of certain products, if there were no harmonized standards or legitimate safety concerns, member states continued to raise objections and deliberately refuse products with broadly equivalent standards.[63]

Despite the reluctance of governments to accept the regulatory simplicity of the directive, it received considerable support from both the national and European standards bodies who felt that it placed them in a better position to coordinate different national requirements.[64] Continued recourse by member states to the escape clause protecting domestic markets ultimately forced the Commission to seek judicial intervention. In *Frankovitch* v. *Cremoni*, the ECJ responded to complaints about restrictions on the importation of electrical equipment that had complied with safety standards in Germany and Belgium. Although the Italian authorities refused the imports on the grounds that they did not meet the standards established by the Italian Standards Institute (UNI), the Commission argued that the refusal to do so constituted a discriminatory trade restriction. Acknowledging that not all European standards were harmonized in the electrical sector, despite efforts under the Low Voltage Directive, the ECJ applied the principle of direct effect and struck down the prohibition that the sale of goods from one member state must meet national requirements of the importing country. In spite of opposition from the Italian, British, and French governments, the ECJ ruled that products meeting minimum regulatory requirements must be accepted even if the safety standards were achieved by different means. The ECJ also dismissed arguments by national authorities that no attempt was made to ensure reciprocal market access for non-European imports, ruling that the recognition that standards were mutually equivalent extended to non-European states, provided they met the provisions in the directive. Although there was still the problem in ensuring that adequate European standards were available, the practice of reference to standards in the Low Voltage Directive provided an important lesson and opportunity for a more flexible general regulatory strategy.

Anxious to avoid criticism that the mandatory safety requirements of the Low Voltage Directive were inoperable without European standards, the Commission was careful in its generalization of the reference to standards technique as a regulatory model. Unwilling to countenance excessive interference by member states, the Commission set out to avoid such problems by making sure that the regulatory model adopted outlined the essential safety requirements precisely, creating legally binding obligations on member states that could be directly implemented.[65] Even if European standards were not available, there would be provision for manufacturers to meet the regulatory requirements by other means, making it unnecessary and, the Commission hoped, illegal for member states to impose additional obligations and hinder the free circulation of goods.[66]

The New Approach

In January 1985, the Commission announced a more detailed proposal of technical harmonization and standards.[67] This followed the Commission's 'Conclusions on Standardization', that had received overwhelming support during the European Summit at Fountainbleau in 1984, and gave the green light for the policy of mutual equivalence and reference to standards to be codified.[68] The proposal was officially presented by the Commission in its White Paper of 1985, and this New Approach together with a draft 'model directive' was adopted by the Council in May 1985.[69] The model directive set down various requirements for inclusion in the 'New Approach'.[70] These provisions included the scope of the directives, which as a general rule were to be based on total harmonization, and could only be placed on the market if they did not endanger the safety of persons, domestic animals, or goods, and respected the essential requirements such as protection of health and environment. In addition, the model directive set out a general clause outlining the responsibilities of member states, and emphasizing that the essential safety requirements must be clear and unambiguous to avoid the criticisms levied against the Low Voltage Directive.

The model directive included a free movement clause, requiring member states to accept products throughout the internal market that have conformed to the necessary regulatory requirements. The directive also provided for several means of conformity or compliance, either through conforming with European standards, or, in the absence of available European standards, through independent third party verification. A safeguard procedure was also included allowing member states to withdraw a product from the market, on the basis of concerns about the safety of the product. To prevent protectionism and abuse, member states were required to inform the Commission of their actions, triggering a thorough review of the situation. Given the possibility that questions about implementation were likely in view of the broad scope of the directive, a standing committee was created to address these issues. The technique used in the model directive, and subsequently applied to the New Approach, provides for a sliding reference technique that allows flexibility in determining which standard is appropriate to meet the necessary regulatory requirements. However, it was quite clear that the New Approach would be applied to broad sectors rather than individual products, and focus on areas that had not yet been addressed.[71]

To put the model directive into practice under the New Approach, the Commission strategy was based on a sharing of regulatory functions between the public and private sector. Private standards bodies would act as 'proxies' for government in the regulatory process.[72] The New Approach aimed at the acceleration of regulatory decision-making was based on two guiding principles: (1) where possible, there was to be mutual recognition of regulations and standards, as well as the means of conformity with them; and (2) where necessary, the harmonization of technical regulations would be undertaken by reference to European standards.[73] In essence, the Community was seeking an efficient means to organize regulatory responsibilities, while maintaining mechanisms to uphold the public interest.

The new policy meant that Community regulation was restricted to defining the essential health and safety requirements, mandatory for all member states.[74] The standards bodies were now responsible for taking state of the art practices into account in defining the technical standards to meet the essential regulatory requirements. These technical standards were to remain voluntary non-binding agreements, allowing firms a choice in accepting European standards as meeting their necessary regulatory obligations. If firms preferred to pursue their own means of demonstrating conformity to the legislative requirements, they were allowed to do so. This provided firms with a degree of flexibility, particularly in areas of rapid innovation and change, although it was assumed that meeting designated European standards would be the easiest route for compliance. While public authorities must allow the free circulation of products that conform with the safety requirements of the New Approach directives, even though this implies a loss of regulatory control, it did not mean deregulation since oversight is exercised by placing liability for the products in circulation upon the producer or importer, committing them to place a marking on each product[75] that assumes this obligation.

The New Approach did not formally do away with harmonization, but restricted it to essential safety requirements. While the New Approach was far from being a vast exercise in deregulation,[76] it did represent a fundamental shift in philosophy that began with the Low Voltage Directive. Instead of requiring individual directives for each product, the New Approach enabled the adoption of broad legislative frameworks covering numerous products or services. This resulted in a number of sectors of considerable economic importance being subject to regulatory delegation, requiring a substantial number of European standards meeting the technical requirements of the European directives. The New Approach represented an important regulatory innovation, since it shifted attention from detailed technical specifications in European legislation, based on the distinction that can be made between performance and design standards.[77] Replacing detailed design standards that establish specific technical requirements, the use of performance standards allowed for different national engineering traditions and concepts that were broadly equivalent, so that the product harmonization did not favour one technology or approach over another.

The delegation of such rule-making authority to private law bodies outside the institutional framework established by the consolidated treaties was a contractual relationship.[78] Prior to the legislative adoption of a New Approach directive, the Commission was required to issue a call for tender for requests for European standards. If the European standards bodies agree to provide such services, a contractual agreement between the two parties is negotiated, although 'no Community legal act even lays down an obligation on these parties to accept these requests'.[79] Through such a process, the Community sought to address the potential problems of inviting private European standards bodies to perform functions that it had traditionally undertaken.

The Commission also closely monitored the operations of the European standards bodies to ensure that standardization does not deviate from the overall regulatory objectives of the Community.[80] In using private European standards bodies for public purposes, the Commission recognized the need for mechanisms to define the institutional relationship between standardization and legislation. A series of negotiations between the Commission and Standards Bodies sought to clarify the situation to avoid any semblance of 'regulatory capture', given the overwhelming number of producers involved in standardization.[81] This included a number of ex-ante and ex-post mechanisms aimed at ensuring compliance with legislative goals. For example, the Commission can impose budgetary sanctions when the European standards bodies fail to meet agreed deadlines, and use technical experts and committees to monitor the output of the European standards bodies to determine whether the standards produced match their expectations, values, or goals. This verification procedure and threat of rejecting European standards is seldom used, although it remains one way of addressing legal concerns that the delegation is not unconditional.[82]

Member state governments also examined the draft standards closely, given the implications for their own regulatory activities. The Commission sought to assuage their concerns by ensuring that it would monitor the activities of the European standards bodies to ensure consistency between standards and regulatory requirements.[83] Although this was not a veto procedure by the Commission, some draft standards were subsequently returned to the deliberating committees within the European standards bodies for further refinement.[84]

The memorandum of understanding and guidelines for cooperation between the European standards bodies and the Commission also set out terms and conditions allowing for standardization mandates though which the European standards bodies would be paid for their work. The development of European standards under the mandates was to follow the same procedures as any other regulatory effort, although the Commission reserved the right to prepare European standards without delegating them to CEN, CENELEC, and later ETSI.

While the New Approach drew a clear distinction between standards and regulation, the separation of the two also presented problems in ensuring that European standards were accepted on the part of member states. Unlike the Low Voltage Directive, which conferred the task of defining basic safety requirements upon the European standardization bodies, the New Approach was not nearly as ambitious.[85] This would have inevitably reopened long-standing debates, calling into question the results secured through standardization, with exactly the same drawbacks and delays that had led to the failures under harmonization. To provide further assurance that standards were legally sound and presumed to conform with European regulatory requirements, the Commission agreed to publish references to European standards in the *Official Journal of the European Communities*, both as a means of conferring legitimacy on them and establishing that they have satisfied legislative intent.

Promotion of the reference to standards approach was aided by the adoption of similar strategies at the domestic level in some member states.[86] In Britain, France, and Germany, regulatory policy had already made use of the private sector in assisting with regulatory compliance. European governments have increased the interaction between governments and standards bodies throughout the 1970s and 1980s. In Germany, most industrial standards had proceeded under a voluntary basis by the Deutsches Institut für Normung (DIN), and relations were further institutionalized in 1975 through a contract designating DIN as the principal standard-setting institution.[87] Similarly, in Britain the government signed a memorandum of understanding with the British Standards Institute in 1982, making the latter the leading national standards body responsible for assisting the government in referencing standards in national legislation. And finally, in France, standards set by the Association Française de Normalisation (AFNOR) located under the Ministry of Industry, found its role in standard-setting enhanced in 1984.[88]

Though both Britain and Germany claimed parentage of the New Approach, since they both used standards for regulatory purposes on a 'deemed to satisfy basis', the assignment of legislative and regulatory powers in the domestic context was less controversial.[89] In principle the domestic and European strategies are similar, but the delegation to private bodies has very different implications at the national and European levels. In the national context, the legal status of each standard is integrated into the legislative process, without much debate about the effects of delegation or the concerns about oversight mechanisms. In the Community context, legal ratification would require ratification of European standards by the Commission through a regulatory-type committee procedure that would have created significant procedural hurdles.[90] Thus, European standards remain voluntary, and do not have the same statutory power as those used as substitute regulations at the national level.

The Global Approach

Even with the harmonization or mutual recognition of European standards and regulations, trade barriers would remain if divergent testing, certification, or product approval practices were not addressed.[91] In many ways, the process by which products were tested and certified was more problematic than reconciling health and safety standards.[92] Because each member state had its own system of certification and trade marks, tests were often carried out by national institutes according to national policies and practices. Where such certification was mandatory, member states generally recognized only their own national marks.[93] This proved costly not only for producers, and particularly for small and medium companies, but also enabled states to effectively screen out foreign competitors.

Recognizing the need to address the issue, the Commission canvassed opinion on testing and certification issues at a special conference in 1988.[94] The idea for holding a conference to develop a strategic and coherent policy in this area had been proposed by Lord Cockfield, the European Commissioner responsible for the single market in 1986.[95] Interest in the issue was widespread and the conference attracted over 800 participants from both the public and private sector. The sheer number of participants surprised the Commission, which was forced to establish working groups to consider different issues and proposals. Despite general consensus that something needed to be done to coordinate the various organizations, agencies, and institutions in this area, there were deep divisions over whether this should be mandatory or voluntary, reflecting differences in national regulatory regimes. British firms were increasingly focusing on self-certification, quality assurance programmes, and manufacturer liability while German firms were pressing for regulatory compliance through involvement of third parties for approval, inspection, and certification, rather than trusting manufacturers' self-monitoring capacities.[96]

As with standardization, concerns regarding the delegation of such tasks from public to private authorities were also raised. Member states recognized that, without some degree of mutual recognition of tests and certificates, manufacturers would be faced with continuous roadblocks.[97] The principle, under mutual recognition, that checks be performed in the country of origin and not subject to double oversight meant that public authorities in the host country must accept that products from another member state had gone through adequate testing and approval procedures. This was in turn based on the principle of mutual trust and credibility between the different authorities of the member states, assuming that the capacity, effectiveness, and expertise of each member state's regulatory and monitoring framework was comparable or equivalent.[98]

The solution, agreed upon in only six months, represented a compromise between the two regulatory systems of Britain and Germany. In July 1989, the Commission introduced an innovative proposal to deal with the problem. The Global Approach to Testing and Certification was aimed at coordinating the different procedures and practices across Europe.[99] While emphasizing the need for harmonized rules on testing and certification, the directive allowed a degree of regulatory flexibility, providing companies with several options to demonstrate that they had complied with the necessary regulatory requirements. The Global Approach recognized that there were different risks associated with different products, with some products such as medical devices requiring more stringent testing and certification procedures. Accordingly, manufacturers were given a clear choice in demonstrating conformity through different modules. These options or 'modules' would be specifically referenced in each New Approach directive, so that there would be no confusion regarding the obligations upon manufacturers in meeting the necessary requirements for market access.[100] While manufacturer's self-certification or self-regulation was expected to be the rule, signalling a more flexible approach, more comprehensive testing and certification would be required if the product posed significant risks.

The Global Approach modules ranged from manufacturers self-certification (the preferred British approach) to full quality assurance and independent verification by an appropriate body.[101] Self-certification meant that companies perform their own internal evaluation, keep documentation in case of random inspection, and assume liability for their actions. More stringent requirements necessitated independent testing and surveillance by a recognized body (known as a notified body) that is accredited or recognized as competent by national authorities. The options or modules are aimed at providing sufficient flexibility for product innovation and design, while ensuring that testing and certification procedures carried out by either manufacturers or independent bodies are subject to common rules, criteria, and standards so that products would be guaranteed European-wide market access.

While a great deal of emphasis was placed on manufacturer's self-declaration, placing liability for non-compliance or unsafe products upon importers or producers, this did not mean the complete absence of regulatory intervention.[102] Notified bodies play a crucial role in the implementation of the Global Approach. Member states were to choose these bodies, either public or private, that were to independently verify and certify high-risk products. Public authorities were thus responsible for ensuring the competence of these independent assessors (notified bodies), and to continue to monitor them. Under the requirements of the Global Approach, both producers and certification bodies were required to meet certain criteria or standards (EN 29000 and EN 45000) and hence provide some form of proof that they were accredited to European standards.[103]

The solution—like that of standardization under the New Approach —involved the transfer of some regulatory responsibilities to either producers or third party testing and certification bodies with contractual responsibility to ensure that products conformed to regulatory requirements.[104] These independent accredited bodies had to be notified to other member states and the European Commission, in part to establish some form of trust and credibility that the oversight functions are similar, and to alleviate the concerns by member states sensitive to the political consequences of transferring such responsibilities outside their jurisdictional boundaries. Although both the European Parliament and Economic and Social Committee agreed that recasting the regulatory framework was crucial in tackling the 'dangers of inconsistency, and excessive bureaucracy and uncertainty for manufacturers', there were continued concerns about the multitude of testing and certification systems in areas not covered by European regulations.[105] The Commission envisaged that 'one-stop' accreditation would lead to 'one-stop' certification, through mutual recognition agreements in both the public and private sector.

To address this goal, the Global Approach provides for the setting-up of a new organization, the European Organization for Testing and Certification (EOTC) to foster mutual recognition agreements, which is discussed in greater detail in the following chapter. EOTC would encourage mutual recognition agreements between national bodies to supplement the work of the European standardization process in the area of conformity assessment. Though mutual recognition agreements had existed in certain sectors, under the auspices of CENELEC, the Commission hoped to expand the number of mutual recognition agreements in order to build confidence among private and public testing and certification bodies in a number of sectors.[106] Although on paper the policy represented the final building block of the single market regulatory regime, it proved very difficult to implement in practice, since it required the build-up of mutual confidence and trust. Efforts to coordinate activities affect lucrative national testing and certification bodies which face pressures of increased competition through mutual recognition agreements.

The politics of conformity assessment is not only confined to the internal market since the global approach has external implications.[107] Non-EU manufacturers must use notified bodies in the EU to test and certify their product. Though in principle there is no formal discrimination, it may entail higher costs for those companies based outside the EU. Again, it was the USA that sought to influence the process by requesting notified bodies be located in the USA, that some testing practices be subcontracted to American bodies, and that increased reliance by placed on self-certification. The high-level focus given to these issues by trade negotiators on both sides is examined in more detail in Chapter 10 as it demonstrates the export effects of the European regulatory regime.

At the time, no mention was made of conformity assessment activities in the international standards bodies (particularly ISO and IEC), GATT/WTO, and OECD which addressed some of the same problems multilaterally.[108] As a result, companies had to keep abreast of activities at both the regional and international level as it affected their production, marketing, and distribution.

Conferring final approval: European certification marks

European firms feared that, in addition to reform of the testing and certification process, simplification and coordination of the various national testing and certification marks would be needed to resolve potential market entry problems. For the Community, any reform in this area was difficult as the European standards bodies had already tried to establish some form of European mark of conformity. Their efforts had been unsuccessful as national standards bodies were reluctant to lose this lucrative source of revenue by allowing conformity marks to be harmonized at the European level. Also, the widely recognized national marks were still considered valuable tools of identification of quality and reliability.[109] In many cases, however, national marks tightly regulated trading activity and created problems for companies exporting to multiple markets.

To address the issue, the Community proposed a visible and easily identifiable mark of conformity—the CE mark—to signal that certain products had satisfied European regulatory requirements of the New Approach and the Global Approach. Perceived as a kind of passport to prevent heavy-handed inspection and certification checks at community borders, the policy initially faced opposition stemming from inconsistencies in how the European marking system was to work. Because different New Approach directives had different marking requirements, the Commission was forced to revise its policies to ensure consistency across products.

The question as to whether the European CE mark replaced existing national marks was also problematic. Providing a European symbol for products to circulate community-wide would obviously detract from national marks that touted the quality of the product. The Commission argued that, because the CE mark was simply an informational mark, designed primarily to prevent customs officials and traders from imposing new checks, national marks could be retained for business marketing and commercial means. Companies were now required to affix the CE mark to their product, while choosing which national mark was most beneficial for meeting customer requirements. Many complained that this simply added another regulatory burden with limited value, as they still found it necessary to seek national certification marks to do business in more than one national market.

The CE mark was a means of demonstrating legal conformity to essential regulatory requirements under the New Approach. It was not, however, intended to be a badge of quality or environmental soundness, and hence differed from the well-known commercial marks such as the German Punktmark, the American UL label, and the British kitemark. Though strongly criticized by the national standards bodies as providing no real value-added, the Commission regarded the CE mark regulation as the last piece of the new regulatory system. Unlike aspects of the New Approach and Global Aapproach that divided regulatory responsibilities between the public and private sector, the policing and enforcement of the CE mark was left to public authorities. The Commission was not capable of monitoring the use (and abuse) of the CE mark, so that task fell to national inspectors and customs officials.[110]

Market surveillance is thus delegated to member states to ensure compliance with this new approach. Member states must nominate or establish authorities to be responsible for policing the market. Though the CE mark is designed to demonstrate regulatory conformity, the EU requires in some circumstances further regulatory action. In case of product recalls, safety hazards, and accidents, there is in place a monitoring system that provides safeguard clauses to suspend free movement until further public legitimation.[111] The 'shadow of hierarchy' is ever present even under such private governance regimes, and the European Community has sought to design appropriate devices for the monitoring of compliance. However sizeable the discrepancies in regulatory style between member states, the performance of governance functions by standards bodies represents one way to include those participants that have a stake in reconciling regulation and free trade.

Conclusion

The search to improve the effectiveness of the European regulatory system resulted in several innovations to accelerate the reduction of technical barriers to trade in the single market. The mismatch between regulatory style and outcome had produced a new effort to tackle both potential and actual barriers to trade, and had focused on a dual strategy of addressing incongruent regulations, standards, and testing and certification practices. The regulatory pattern that emerged corresponds to the conditions outlined in Chapter 2. While mutual recognition promoted *pro-competitive regulation* aimed at facilitating the effective operation of markets, and enhancing competition among different regulatory systems, the new approach followed *juridical regulation* in the sense of codifying standards into legal norms.

The result of such action meant that binding essential requirements requiring some degree of regulatory action have been coupled with voluntary technical standards, leading to a regulatory decision-making process that further blurs the boundaries between the public and private sector along the lines of *associative regulation*. This regulatory strategy seems much more interventionist than that of the United States, where the public and private sector have remained much more distinct. The United States is characterized by a fourfold standards system that includes state, local, federal, and private entities. Though the United States also practises the reference to standards technique,[112] borrowing standards from the private sector for public use, there has been a long-standing tradition of private sector governance. While private standards organizations have certainly proliferated in the USA, there is much less attention given to the use of standards for industrial policy and competitiveness purposes. By contrast, the strategic use of standards in the EU through government-guided efforts, as well as the increased centralization of activities at the regional level in the testing and certification area indeed accentuated the differences in institutional arrangements between more 'state'-directed versus 'market'-oriented policy styles. In essence, the European policy followed a *strategic regulatory* pattern as denoted in Chapter 2. It is this distinction more than any other that underlines the differences between US and European market-building and regulatory efforts.

Although the new regulatory strategies enabled the Community to delegate certain responsibilities to the private sector, using the private sector to achieve its own political objectives also entailed certain risks. The autonomous nature of the European standards bodies led to fears that such private decision-making would dilute the public interest, and to perceptions of regulatory capture. This has fostered increased attention on monitoring and oversight functions. Though aimed at ensuring that the private standards bodies are responsive to public goals and objectives, the delegation of regulatory authority from the public to the private sector also raised increased concerns about market governance, accountability, and legitimacy. The reference to standards technique and delegation of powers to the European standards organizations has also brought attention to problems of liability and political responsibility created by such a mixture of public and private rule-making.

While the issue reflects the assumption underpinning regulation that the public interest can only be served by public law-making, the substitution of private rule-making is not without some safeguards and constraints. As the following chapters make clear, the Community sought to ensure that mechanisms and procedures were in place to make the process subject to some form of governance and oversight. Part of that governance is exercise by competition among market players, anxious to shape negotiations over standards and gain first-mover advantage. It is also exercised by regulatory authorities themselves through ex-ante and ex-post procedures that are discussed in more detail in Chapters 7 and 8.

The preoccupation with the legal implications of delegation has masked the actual institutional procedures and operating norms underpinning standardization. By focusing so much on the legal aspects of the policy, and the overall adoption of New Approach directives, the regulatory strategies are assessed only in terms of the legislative process without looking at the overall market-building efforts in terms of effectiveness and implementation. Translating the political objectives into some form of agreement is crucial in understanding to what degree the new regulatory strategy has been successful in completing the single market. While the adoption of the New Approach was a hard fought victory for the Commission, how the strategy has fared in practice cannot be understood without an examination of the actual European standardization process.

Setting European standards:
Politics, Rules, and Norms

The use of new regulatory strategies to foster coordination among divergent national policies institutionalized the participation of private and semi-private organizations in the policy-making process. Aimed at overcoming the problems that had plagued harmonization, the new policies were a critical part of a two-pronged regulatory strategy that took account of an increasing number of societal interests and preferences in fostering market integration. The resulting, institutionally intertwined system brought new rules, bargaining processes, and players to the pre-existing strategy, which had focused on intergovernmental relations. Most assessments of the Community's New Approach considered it a decisive step towards the effective dismantling of technical barriers to trade.[1] In Previdi's words, 'the setting up of a true internal market . . . was founded on an approach that innovatively reorganized the responsibilities and role assignments of the various economic and institutional actors involved in managing regulatory policy.'[2]

Given their importance in the development of a new regulatory strategy for completing the internal market, it is important to understand the histories, organizational structures, and operating environments of these private or semi-private standard-setting organizations. No single organization encompasses all aspects of standard-setting. A host of public and private institutions exist at the international level include the International Standards Organization (ISO), International Telecommunications Union (ITU), International Electrotechnical Commission (IEC), and Codex Alimentarius sponsored by the World Health Organization (WHO) and Food and Agricultural Organization (FAO). At the regional level, the most prominent European standards bodies are the European Telecommunications Standards Institute (ETSI), Comité Européen en Normalisation (CEN), and Comité Européen en Normalisation Électrotechnique (CENELEC). Other regional organizations patterned after the European bodies add to the fragmentation and institutional density of regional level standardization. These include COPANT (the

Pan American Standards Commission) comprising eighteen members, PASC (Pacific Asia Standards Congress) that links APEC members and the Asia-Pacific Economic Cooperation Forum, and ARSO (African Regional Organization for Standardization), composed of thirteen member states.[3]

Though several studies of the organizational rules and institutional framework surrounding standardization have been published,[4] less attention has been given to the operating environment and bargaining that may foster coordination and cooperation.[5] In the European case, those studies which discuss the standards bodies assume that delegation to private actors produces required policy outcomes. As Genschel points out, however, the organizational fragmentation and multitude of standard-setting organizations raises questions about the efficiency and efficacy of such forms of market governance.[6] The multiplicity of organizations and interests involved in setting standards—whether at the national, regional or local level—makes more difficult any assessment of the impact and effectiveness of these institutions in tackling barriers to trade. Agreement must be reached within different standards organizations, and also between different standards organizations.

The status of standards bodies varies across EU member states from quasi-governmental institutions to private, non-government, independent organizations. Their legal status is often extraordinarily complex.[7] Though many standards are voluntary agreements set by private standards organizations, standards can often become mandatory through incorporation into law as statutory or administrative regulations. Some states rely more heavily on these private institutions to meet their regulatory requirements, with the relationship between public and private authorities often codified, institutionalized, or contractual in nature. Although this is a common technique, the use of private bodies in the regulatory process has not been without debate.[8] Because their status and role is often difficult to define, except in legal terms, the national and regional standards bodies tend to be seen as 'technical' rather than political actors in regulation and regulatory policy-making. Consequently, they are often not studied in the same way as conventional political institutions.[9]

As Shapiro argues, however, information and technical decisions do not lie in the cradle of scientific harmony above and beyond the clash of interests and political struggles.[10] Though discussions are defined by functional areas, with different sets of interests and constituencies mobilized by different issues, the technical becomes political when it becomes policy relevant.[11] Divergent notions of safety, risk assessment, and the unwillingness of participants to accept different national concepts and administrative practices raises numerous difficulties for those involved in standard-setting.[12] The strategic bargaining and negotiations within standards committees is obviously important to understand the role of standardization in market integration, and is considered in more detail in subsequent chapters.

This chapter provides a brief overview of the development and operation of European standards bodies. It does so by outlining the institutional components of these bodies involved in standardization, and their operating norms and practices. This institutional framework is critical to assessing the impact and effectiveness of such delegation to private bodies, examined in detail in Chapters 8 and 9.

History and origins of the European standards bodies

Though European standards bodies became more visible after the shift in regulatory strategy by the Commission in the mid-1980s, the two principal European standards bodies are not new. CENELCOM (later known as CENELEC) and CEN were created in 1959 and 1961, respectively. CENELEC is the Comité Européen de la Normalisation Électrotechnique, concerned with standards for electrical and electro-technical products. CEN is the Comité Européen de la Normalisation, concerned with standards in all other product areas, with the exception of telecommunications. A separate standards body, ETSI (European Telecommunications Standards Institute) was created in 1988 to set telecommunications and information technology standards. Due to its different structure, organization, and history, ETSI is dealt with separately from the two traditional standards bodies. The existence of separate organizations for different standards activities stems from the early standardization activities in the electrical and electro-technical sector and the domination of state monopolies in setting telecommunications standards, which has resulted in separate organizations at the national, regional, and international levels.

CEN and CENELEC have continuously resisted pressures to merge at the European level, and have served as territorial organizations representing the national standards bodies of each of the members of the European Community as well as those of the European Free Trade Area (EFTA). Over time, each has also increased its membership. Currently, CEN has nineteen full members (EU, EFTA, and the Czech Republic), fourteen affiliate members, primarily from Southern, Central, and Eastern Europe,[13] and six associate members representing broad European interests.

The latter include the European Trade Union Federation (ETUC/TUTB) for health and safety issues, the European Construction Industry Federation (FIEC), the European Confederation of Medical Devices Association (EUCOMED), the European Chemical Industry (CEFIC), the European Office of Crafts, Trade and Small and Medium Enterprises for Standardization (NORMAPHME), and the European Association for Cooperation of Consumer Representation in Standardization (ANEC). CENELEC has eighteen members, seven affiliate members from Central and East European states, and formal cooperative arrangements with seventeen European industry associations.

During the 1950s and 1960s, CENELCOM (the predecessor of CENELEC) was concerned with the coordination of standards only within common market countries. The formation in 1960 of a second organization, CENEL, focused on implementing international standards at the regional level and caused considerable confusion about the locus of standardization activities in Europe since it include both the six Common Market countries involved in CENELECOM and the EFTA members. The different roles of each body reflected in part the different natures of the EFTA and Community trading regimes. By 1973, this divergence had receded as the two institutions merged prior to the first enlargement of the Community, resulting in CENELEC becoming the primary institution responsible for standards in the electrical sector. In some cases, member states have actually created national standards institutes to ensure adequate representation at the European level.[14] Together with the creation of associate membership for countries seeking to join the Community, the European standards bodies have become an increasingly important influence in shaping the rules for market access in both East and West European markets.[15] This influence was, however, several decades in the making.

Recognized as non-profit technical institutions under Belgian law, the relocation of CEN and CENELEC from Paris to Brussels in 1975[16] did not enhance their visibility or role in Community policy-making. Though routinely invited in the 1960s and 1970s to discuss their activities with the Commission, they were never viewed as a potentially important or useful resource in plans for the removal of technical barriers to trade. Given their low profile, the meetings and activities of the two European standards bodies received little attention, except from national standards bodies. Most businesses preferred to participate in standardization at the national level, as they viewed the European standards bodies as weak organizations that were unable to provide the significant membership benefits and selective incentives of the national standards bodies.[17]

Despite the broad and often incompatible array of national standards existing across Europe, firms had no intention of addressing the cumbersome task of coordination at the European level. Many multinational firms were set up as nationally federated companies to focus on domestic markets. In exporting their services or products to other European member states, subsidiaries were established complete with their own production and marketing departments to circumvent any potential trade barriers. Rationalization across product lines and divisions was minimal as company strategy focused on localization rather than globalization. European management gave little attention to European standards, with the possible exception of Britain and Germany, and seldom recognized their importance upon corporate strategy. With production spread out across different member states, firms focused on particular sets of standards, technologies, processes, and products, usually for their various 'domestic' markets.

As the old agenda of serving domestic and international markets separately receded, however, firms began to reconsider supporting European standardization efforts. This was driven in part by technological developments. Those in high-tech sectors found that the only way to amortize massive investments was through regional sales, as national markets were too small a revenue base to recoup investment costs. Anxious to reduce their lag in innovative technologies, high-tech firms became the most visible proponents of European standardization.[18]

This is in contrast to the occasional efforts to use the expertise within the European standards bodies in the 1960s and 1970s, which had produced few tangible results. In response to questions from the European Parliament, about alternative means to achieve harmonization in Europe, the Commission acknowledged that there were significant disadvantages. Among the many criticisms, the Commission commented that the European standards bodies were not only extraordinarily slow, but also failed to pay adequate attention to requests from the Commission.[19] Much to its surprise, the Commission found it difficult to generate support for the European standardization bodies among firms.[20]

Throughout this period, CEN and CENELEC's roles and intentions were unclear, and their members questioned the future direction of each organization. This indecision and lack of direction was a source of intense discussion among non-European participants engaged in international standardization.[21] Many feared that European standardization would detract from international efforts and result in new trade barriers at the European level. After much discussion between various national standards bodies in Europe, it was agreed that the two regional bodies would not compete with international standards activities, or undermine the existing linkages between national and international standardization. The ambitions of the Commission in using the European standards bodies were thus effectively thwarted by the rather timid role that CEN and CENELEC pursued in their relations with other standard-setting bodies at the national and international level.

Renewed efforts in the 1980s to push the European standards bodies to produce more standards were marred by two factors in particular. First, deference to international standard-setting continued to hinder activity at the European level, as international standards were often lowest common denominator agreements accommodating the heterogeneous set of interests involved. Since international standards were often less stringent than European regulatory standards, there were also concerns of lax regulations and a 'race to the bottom' if they were accepted as the norm in Europe. Second, European states were frequently allowed to add additional regulatory requirements, enabling them to shield their own industries from competition and deviate from international norms.[22] Until the Community placed standardization at the centre of its single market programme, the European standards bodies were hampered in their efforts to create linkages between European and international standards, and European and national standards. Both national and international standards bodies jealously guarded their roles, and were reluctant to accept an expansion of the regional-level activities. However, the launch of the single market programme in the mid-1980s generated renewed interest in these regional coordinating mechanisms to deal with the trade-impeding effects of diverse regulations and standards.

The structure and operation of the European standards bodies

Although the European standards bodies provide the framework within which negotiations take place, they do not actually set standards. They are 'peak associations' bringing together over 25,000 participants at the European level. While they are formally independent, they have established close ties through memorandums of understanding and contractual obligations with the European Commission.[23] The standards bodies receive political mandates from the Commission indicating the type of work that the EU specifically needs to meet the requirements of the New Approach directives.[24] In some cases, they are required to work together to avoid duplication; in other areas they receive exclusive mandates. Since the organizational structure and rules of both CEN and CENELEC are almost identical, they are discussed together here, with any significant differences highlighted.

Despite the increase in work from the Commission, the European standards bodies remain firmly linked to the national standards bodies, and constantly emphasize their independence and activities beyond that related to the single market. Although CEN and CENELEC are financed by their member organizations, the national standards bodies, and the European Community and EFTA, the national standards bodies are the only institutions involved in the governance of European standardization. Figure 7.1 illustrates the institutional framework of the European standards bodies.

General Assembly

The governing body of both CEN and CENELEC is a General Assembly in which officials from the national committees of each of the

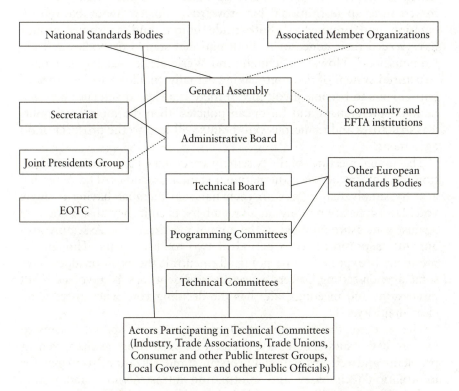

FIG 7.1 Institutional structure of the European standards bodies

eighteen member countries are represented.[25] It has the full power of decision within the standards organizations. The structure of the Assembly
ensures that the national standards bodies are involved in all major policy issues at the management level. Because of its territorially based
representation in governing decisions, the General Assembly reinforces
the image of nationally vested interests. Each national standards body
has one permanent member of the General Assembly to express its
opinions and interests. Associate and affiliate members may participate
in the activities of the General Assembly, but they do not have voting
rights or decision-making powers.[26] Other organizations such as the
International Standards Organization and International Electrotechnical
Commission are given observer status.

The General Assembly debates the overall policy goals and direction
of standardization and acts as a forum for taking crucial policy decisions about long-term strategy. It largely determines who will be heard
and shapes how each of the European standards bodies defines its overall mission. This role has been criticized by both the European Trade
Union Confederation (ETUC) and European Consumer Lobby (BEUC)
for creating an institutional bias towards industry-favourable representation and preferences. Both trade unions and consumer groups
have voiced their concerns to both national standards bodies and the
Commission.[27] However, Schmidt and Werle argue that the nationally
structured system of decision-making actually enables a wider range of
participants to become involved.[28] If there is a clear divergence between
national preferences and European policies, then the multi-level political structures and numerous veto points will lead to the prospect of no
agreement.

The annual meetings of the Assembly are designed to act as a coordination mechanism between the national standards bodies. The Assembly
acts by simply majority, with each national member having a single
vote. Decisions are binding on all members, even if they abstain or vote
against a measure adopted in the annual meetings. The Assembly also
appoints a president for a period of two to three years. Though the
president is expected to be politically neutral, the position does have
some agenda-setting powers, since the president may be involved in all
discussions and meetings, and has the deciding vote when there is no
clear majority.

The work of the Assembly is supplemented with special forums to
explore new issues. These have focused on such issues as management
problems and reforms within European standardization, strategies for
information technology and information infrastructures, and testing
and certification policies. Though they are dominated by representatives

from the national and European standards bodies, they attract a number of trade associations, government ministries, and large multinationals.[29] Aimed at drawing attention and publicizing the importance of standards, testing, and certification for European business and other societal interests, they are widely viewed as public forums for the exchange of ideas amongst interested parties, including the Commission.

Administrative Board and Secretariat

An Administrative Board and Central Secretariat carry out much of the day-to-day planning in CEN and CENELEC. The Administrative Board acts as a corporate body to oversee the work of the standards bodies and coordinate action taken by all other bodies within the standards organizations. The Administrative Board currently has eight members, appointed for a fixed term. Each member of the Administrative Board is allowed one vote, and decisions are taken by a simply majority of those present.[30] Though the General Assembly must approve any changes in working methods or procedures in European standardization, the Administrative Board and Central Secretariat have clearly grown in significance over the last decade.

The Administrative Board handles most administrative matters, with the daily management of the European standards bodies carried out by the smaller Central Secretariat, headed by the Secretary-General appointed by the General Assembly. The activities of the Secretary-General are set out in the statutes, internal rules, and adopted decisions of the standards bodies. While secondment from the national standards bodies to the European level was not initially a high priority, the surge in activity at the European level has made appointments to the Central Secretariat increasingly important.

Although the Central Secretariat was established for purely administrative purposes, it has become increasingly important in its liaison function with both the Commission and Third Countries. Beyond this coordinating role, the Central Secretariat has been faced with increasing numbers of inquiries regarding European standardization, and has consequently created separate units to deal with public relations and third countries. In interviews, several CEN and CENELEC staff felt that many of these inquiries could be handled through a particular trade federation, especially given the lack of specificity of some of the requests. Since the Central Secretariat provides information about the activities of European standard-setting, however, it is the focal point for many general inquiries and complaints from firms and governments regarding specific standards and practices. To address criticism that its activities were not transparent, the Central Secretariat has provided ongoing reviews of developments to various trade federations and business associations from outside Europe. These were also designed to show that European-wide standards were not protectionist, but designed as a means of improving European-wide market access.[31]

Technical Board

The Technical Board (TB) coordinates the work of hundreds of committees that actually set standards for different products and services. This includes advising on all matters relating to the standards bodies, overall coordination and long-range planning of standards work, monitoring the progress of standards work, imposing standstill obligations on the activities of other standards bodies to prevent duplication, and organizing technical liaison with other international organizations.[32] The Technical Board also acts as an information source for other standards bodies, the Commission, and other actors. It also performs a number of oversight roles, including monitoring the various standards committees and handling appeals by participants dissatisfied with outcomes in their various technical committees. To ensure coordination between national and international activity, the Technical Board includes both the president and permanent representatives or delegates from the national level. Assistance to the Technical Board is provided by the Central Secretariat, which generally convenes the meetings to discuss issues or problems, though on occasion the meetings are convened by a request from two or more member states.[33] However, the Technical Board is independent of the Central Secretariat and designed to provide overall technical advice and input. It is also responsible for setting up committees and working groups to establish specific standards.

Setting standards: the work of committees

As noted above, much of the actual negotiations take place in committees established by the European standards bodies. The groundwork for negotiations is carried out by interested parties nominated by their national standards bodies to participate in specific committees. Currently there are over 25,000 participants involved in over 2,000 committees at the European level. While establishing standards for products and processes as diverse as electrical equipment and plugs, environmental management, transportation networks, telecommunications equipment, biotechnology, and food-processing can seem relatively mundane and technical in nature, potential outcomes are highly controversial and invoke contentious debates. In general, however, participant accounts of such committees typically emphasize compromise, teamwork, and sharing information, rather than how these bodies deal with conflicts.[34]

Despite the consensual nature of the process, standards have significant distributional impacts and questions of distributional equity cannot be settled solely on technical principles.[35] Because they determine acceptable levels of risk and cost, the choices between proposed standards are also made on the basis of political and socio-economic criteria.[36] Committees setting standards draw on scientific and technical considerations, but do so through what Majone calls 'an intrinsic vagueness' that offers strategic advantages to the regulated, both at the level of standard-setting and in the process of implementation.[37]

The committees provide a forum for those with considerable knowledge in a particular field to work together.[38] With limited resources, the European standards bodies are dependent on these technical committees to produce agreement on appropriate standards. The committees are assigned the task of framing the issues, guided by formal organizational mandates and specific decision-making rules that apply equally to all committees and participants. Because the selection of participants is determined by national standards bodies, the national representation on technical committees can vary across member states.

The committees can include representation from trade unions, consumer groups, local governments, national government officials, as well as individual firms and trade associations. National standards bodies may normally appoint three delegates per committee. Although this can result in as many as thirty to forty members per committee, not all members play an active role. Because of the time and resources needed to really influence the process, some committee members rarely participate in policy debates.

Participation is organized by expertise, which usually means that certain firms (or occasionally governments) play a key agenda-setting role. Thus, it is important to distinguish between what Grant calls the costs and benefits of passive membership and the costs and benefits of active participation. As Salter notes, 'the standards community is characterized by policy participation not policy advocacy. . . . Significant barriers are erected against the type of intermittent or partial commitment that would be appropriate from small or medium sized manufacturers, newly industrializing countries or from users of the technology and standards.'[39]

Pushing standards is often the work of a few firms willing to commit resources and time. Because the process is designed to air all opinions and objections, the structure and rules governing participant inputs are extremely important. The basic principle of decision-making at the national, regional, and international level is consensus—a vote is only taken as a measure of last resort. This requires constant discussion and argument 'either until an agreement is found or absolutely incompatible positions have been cleared (and the standardization issue dropped). . . . and after all arguments on each item have been exchanged, at the very end of the process, all committee members are asked whether everyone can accept the result or—the other way round—whether there is someone who still opposes it fundamentally.'[40] Achieving consensus can be difficult as differences in outlook and interest have to be bridged, with negotiations that are often time-consuming, costly, and protracted.[41] Under these conditions, the likelihood of success within standards committees depends in large measure on the intensity of conflict and the organizational clout of those expressing opposition.[42] Agreement is made more difficult by the fact that it is not an iterative game, in which vested interests that lose or follow at this stage can win or lead later. Once a standard is locked in, it is extremely difficult to change.[43]

Since many participants seek to gain first-mover advantage, by defining the problem and setting the agenda,[44] one of the most important features of the committee stage is the designation of a committee secretariat. The secretariat is often given to a national standards body that may be chairing the same committee at the international level. Where there are no corresponding committees, the decision is made by mutual agreement among the national standards bodies. On occasion, other organizations such as professional associations, quasi-governmental agencies, or non-profit institutions may serve as secretariats. These actors tend to exhibit narrower concerns, and develop highly specialized standards for specific industries or sectors. For example, the Joint Aviation Authority (JAA), focusing on airline safety and equipment standards, and the European Workshop for Open System (EWOS), focusing on open systems for the computer industry, have been responsible for coordinating work within specific secretariats.

Opinion is divided as to the importance of chairing the committees.[45] While some see the position of the secretariat as neutral, the number of secretariats held by different member states was politically controversial in the 1980s. Within the various standards committees, it is generally British, German, and French firms that play the dominant role in the process, acting as a 'first mover' by pushing their own national standards forward for adoption at the European level.[46] Though the apparent dominance of German firms has been a source of political tension, Eichener concludes that the differences in the abilities of member states to participate effectively in committee work may reflect a considered decision.[47] Many participants from states with low levels of regulation 'frequently prefer to listen to discussions in order to obtain early information on future regulation, rather than actively contribute to its definition.'[48] This does not lessen the need to mobilize support from less active participants, who can engage in tactics of delay and thus exercise considerable leverage in extracting concessions.

The lack of a scheduled time frame can also result in gridlock or obstructionism. Standardizers rarely go into the process with a specific time horizon. It is not unusual to see working groups and committees negotiate for ten to twenty years. For example, negotiations for earth-moving machinery began in 1968, and the technical committees have successfully produced more than a hundred standards at both the European and international level, while more than twenty years of negotiations over common plugs and electrical voltages have resulted in ongoing deadlock. Though many observers have commented on the rising number of European standards over the past decade,[49] this does not take account of the politics of non-decision-making, where highly contested issues do not even reach the agenda-setting stages. Nor does it account for the effect of market structure on influencing the incentives of producers to reach agreement. Those involved in high-technological sectors are less likely to agree on voluntary standards, since agreement on which standard to adopt is itself a competitive decision.[50] Many of the firms in high-technology industries prefer pre-competitive collaboration through business consortia due to the slow pace of standardization activities. This has led to a host of organizations competing with the traditional committee-based framework of standardization, and also raised considerable anti-trust (such as abuse of a dominant position) concerns.

Committee work does have structured practices and oversight. Written progress reports are prepared annually to present to the Technical Boards that oversee the work of the myriad of committees involved.[51] However, the oversight process is made increasingly difficult by the growth of subcommittees and working groups to handle different aspects of the negotiations. Committee secretariats often divide up work programmes on standardization, and delegate responsibility for specific issues to different working groups and subcommittees that tend to attract a small number of interested participants. Technical bodies working within the standards institutions expanded dramatically in the late 1980s and early 1990s. From 1985 to 1995, the number of technical bodies in CEN increased from 60 to 490, and in CENELEC from 38 to 170.

This growth increases fragmentation and coordination problems within committees, as they must deal with different networks working on very specialized problems.[52] Firms routinely exploit the multiplicity of points of access to push their proposals, given the sheer number of committees working on standards issues in different organizations.[53] This means that if firms are unsuccessful in one committee forum, they can seek to push their preferred standards options elsewhere. The European Standards bodies attempt to prevent such 'committee shopping' within their own organizations by allocating work items to specific committees.

The initiation of work at the European level imposes a standstill on any standards work that is proceeding at the national level, providing another constraint to firm opportunism.[54] Members are required not to take any action which could prejudice the intended harmonization, nor publish or revise any national standards when European standards are in preparation.[55] Although this is designed to prevent unnecessary duplication, the national standards bodies often ignore the provisions requiring notification of work programmes to the European standards bodies as required by the Mutual Information Directive described in Chapter 6. Despite their misgivings regarding the notification process, however, the national standards bodies have been working towards better implementation.[56] Increasingly national standards bodies are pushing work programmes at the regional level, recognizing that this provides the best opportunity to push forward a specific national standard and gain considerable commercial advantage by shaping the European standards agenda.

The establishment of the European Telecommunications Standards Institute

In telecommunications, unlike many other sectors, standards were traditionally set by state-owned national post, telegraph, and telephone authorities. National regulations established mandatory standards for networks and equipment, and required any piece of equipment to receive 'type approval' or certification from a national post, telegraph, and telephone authority. This resulted in relatively insulated national markets with distinct services and incompatible equipment.

New technologies and services have pushed telecommunications from monopolies towards liberalization in the provision of networks, services, and equipment. Pressures at the European level to push forward with an industrial strategy also shaped the direction of telecommunications and information technology through collaborative research and development, standards, and market liberalization.[57] These developments were prompted by intense concern that nationally segmented markets would impede innovation and discourage cross-border development in comparison to the changes underway in the USA and Japan.[58] With the advent of new technologies in microelectronics and data-processing, the Commission also felt it necessary to promote greater coordination and compatibility to enhance European competitiveness.[59]

Encouraged by a sharp increase in informal ad hoc arrangements between firms in electronics and information technology, the Commission became more convinced that direct participation by firms in shaping the European regulatory environment was the most efficient and effective way of achieving a unified market. To promote industry collaboration, the Commission encouraged collaborative efforts in a number of high-technology areas, and particularly to enhance European competitiveness in communications and information technologies which had been hampered by major differences in national technical standards. Toward this end, the Commission prompted CEN and CENELEC into creating a European Workshop for Open Systems (EWOS) in 1987.[60]

Although affiliated with the European standards bodies, EWOS comprised representative trade federations and business consortia in the information technology sector to draft standards for open systems. Organizations such as COSINE (the Cooperation for Open Systems Interconnection Networking in Europe), ECMA (European Computer Manufacturers' Association), and SPAG (Standards Promotion and Application Group) were all directly involved. Additional efforts to develop programmes in pre-competitive technology and research and development were part of the Commission's efforts to directly enlist firms to work together on European standards. The ESPRIT (European Strategic Programme for Research and Development in Information Technology), RACE (Research and Development in Advanced Communications Technologies in Europe), and EUREKA (European Strategic Programme for Research and Development) were also viewed as critical alternatives in promoting European standardization and industrial collaboration.[61]

Supported by manufacturers of telecommunications equipment and users and providers of telecommunications services, the Commission found ready allies in its effort to push Community-level cooperation. With the additional pressures of deregulation and liberalization, the national telecoms systems were under tremendous pressure to change. The Community signed a memorandum of understanding with the European Conference of Post and Telecommunications (CEPT) in 1984—not unlike that with CEN and CENELEC—to produce common standards, testing, and certification procedures for telecommunications equipment (known as type approval) which would ease connection and access to public networks. However, CEPT was slow in promoting collective action, and the Commission was increasingly frustrated with the existing system, fearing that CEPT was ill-equipped to cope with the growing demands for standardization.

After a fact-finding mission on the telecommunications sector in the United States in 1986, the Commission proposed the creation of a single standards body devoted entirely to telecommunications. Commission officials had been particularly impressed by the commitment of American firms to telecommunications standard-setting and efforts to link telecommunications with various information technologies. The Commission similarly wished to push for a more flexible and modern organization in the European telecommunications sector.[62] This move was supported by manufacturers of telecommunications equipment, private service providers and users, many of whom had interests that were different from those of public network operators (PTTs) and telecommunications administrations and felt that their interests were inadequately represented in the existing standard-setting bodies.

The circumvention of the existing European standards system was clearly on the Commission's agenda as it proposed a new standards body in a consultative Green Paper on telecommunications in 1987.[63] This document proposed the complete restructuring of the institutional arrangements for standards in telecommunications, and the creation of a permanent and independent European Telecommunications Standards Institute (ETSI). This was a clear challenge to the status quo. Until the 1970s, standards-setting in telecommunications was monopolized by the CCITT (Consultative Committee on International Telephone and Telegraphy, now known as the ITU-T), which was part of the International Telecommunications Union (ITU) and CEPT.[64] Both CCITT and CEPT had been established to deal with numerous technical, operational, and tariff questions, and had become the focal point for standards regarding telephony. The Commission proposed an alternative institutional framework for standardization to bypass what 'in the past did little more than arrange for interfaces at national borders and rules for revenue sharing'.[65] While conflict emerged over the respective roles of CEPT and ETSI in Europe, the Commission was also anxious to play a central coordinating role in defining priorities for both the two other European standards bodies, CEN and CENELEC.

CEPT, CEN, and CENELEC were opposed to the creation of a new organization, fearing that this would undercut their own role in setting standards. However, the creation of ETSI as a separate and autonomous standards body was approved by national telecommunications

ministers in 1988.[66] To signal a genuine break from the national, territorially based structure of standardization, ETSI was set up along
radically different organizational lines. Not only was ETSI located in
France—to signify its distance from the other organizations—it allowed
direct access for interested parties including postal and telecommunications authorities, operators of public networks, manufacturers, and
other users. ETSI consequently bypassed the national standards structure, bringing its 'own unique brand of standards-making to the European
scene'.[67] As Besen notes, however, a more heterogeneous membership may
actually make collective agreement more difficult, as the risk of deadlock
and stalemate may increase with more diverse interests and members.

The structure and operation of the European Telecommunications Standards Institute

ETSI is composed of a General Assembly, Secretariat, Technical Assembly,
Technical Committees, and Project Teams.[68] Its members are drawn
from the twenty-one countries represented in CEPT as well as additional
members from Austria, Cyprus, Malta, Norway, Sweden, and Turkey.
The 212 initial members included 27 national administrations, 27 public network operators, 131 manufacturers, 21 user associations and
private service providers, and 6 research bodies. This has now expanded
to include 647 members from 49 countries. Though keen to promote
broader representation than that of CEN and CENELEC, ETSI also functioned in part on a territorial basis. Some start-up costs were paid by
the Commission, but financing was based along national lines with administrations paying on the basis of GDP and telecommunications-related
turnover.

Reflecting Commission concern about the pace of decision-making
mechanisms and rules of access within the traditional standards bodies,
ETSI's operating rules and norms also differed from those of CEN
and CENELEC. Instead of endless negotiations to achieve consensus,
ETSI's voting procedures were designed to be more flexible and prevent
minorities from blocking agreement. Proposed standards could be
adopted by 70 per cent of the weighted vote, and be rejected only by a
blocking minority of over 30 per cent of those members voting. This effectively prevented minority interests from exercising the same kind of veto
power that they possessed in other standards organizations. CEN and
CENELEC argued in reply that the search for consensus was crucial if
standards were to be used in the market.

Differences in voting rules can also have important implications for jurisdiction. In areas with considerable overlap in standards activities, the initial choice of standards body may influence both the pace of standardization and the type of standard adopted. ETSI is different from the two other European standards bodies in this regard. Rather than agreeing to a standard and allowing what CEN and CENELEC term 'deviations' to accommodate divergent preferences, ETSI will not permit several 'options'. Since this is more restrictive, considerable resources are likely to be expended in resolving conflicts among competing standards.[69] Firms can expect very large returns if they prevail in such negotiations, but face higher risks if the standard adopted is not their preferred one.[70] Thus, the competitive and cooperative dynamics are different in the various institutional environments. This is particularly true as many of the negotiations within ETSI deal with pre-competitive standards, and collaboration begins earlier in areas of high technology to avoid having one particular technology from being 'stranded' and incompatible with others.

To protect their respective 'turfs', the existing standards bodies demanded greater clarity about the areas that would be assigned to ETSI. Though they expressed concern about limited resources and the duplication of activities, CEN and CENELEC had themselves fought to establish their own identities, independent of the international standards bodies. To facilitate coordination, a joint presidents group was established to link the activities of the three standards bodies at the administrative and management level. This was supplemented by the creation in 1985 of an Information Technology Steering Committee (ISITC), a joint group that deals with issues of information technology to make sure that ETSI is able to work with the existing standards bodies in areas of mutual interest. With these issues ironed out, and a permanent directorate to deal with day-to-day activities, ETSI became operational in March 1988. Standard-setting within CEPT was now transferred to the ETSI.

The bulk of ETSI's work takes place in committees and working groups along the same lines as the other standards bodies. ETSI has been given a large number of mandates in both information technology and telecommunications, covering a number of critical areas. Beginning with the directive on telecommunications terminal equipment,[71] which was aimed at certifying that pieces of equipment meet relevant standards and are thus accepted by all member states, ETSI has been involved in developing over 200 standards for a range of services including open systems, electronic data interchange, mobile satellite terminals, voice telephony, and advanced manufacturing technology. Standardization and mutual recognition in these areas were key elements of the Commission's strategy to foster market liberalization, which also enhanced the institutional profile of ETSI vis-à-vis the other two European standards bodies.

The creation of the European Organization for Testing and Certification

The emphasis on European standards overlooked the absence of any institutional means to coordinate the hundreds of testing and certification bodies across Europe. Although the Commission had adopted the Global Approach to testing and certification in 1989, policy in this area languished far behind that of standardization. While committees within CEN, CENELEC, and ETSI were creating new standards for the single market, firms were still faced with numerous obstacles generated by divergent testing, certification, and product approval practices in member states. Estimates indicated that there were over 1,000 certification agencies and over 10,000 testing bodies in Europe. Many had become dominant in certain domestic sectors and were concerned about the effects of competition on their long-term survival.

Persistent complaints about the costs of multiple product approvals led the Commission to propose a new institutional framework for testing and certification.[72] As illustrated in the previous chapter, the Commission's policy to coordinate testing, certification, and inspection practices met with widespread interest. Because the lack of confidence in testing and certification practices of another member state was a major stumbling block, the Global Approach urged the application of common ground rules established by a central coordinating body. Though the Global Approach was designed to offer flexibility by allowing different practices and procedures, depending on levels of risk and safety and public health concerns, the Commission sought to institutionalize and regulate testing and certification practices through accreditation of such agencies.

The Commission pushed for both public and private sector involvement in this effort. The private sector was asked to coordinate their activities by promoting common standards for testing and certification. This would facilitate and enhance the acceptability of testing and certification practices across markets through common criteria and objectives. Paralleling the work in the standards bodies, the Commission hoped to use the private sector to work towards removing barriers to trade. In 1990, the Commission created the European Organization for Testing and Certification (EOTC).[73] Through a memorandum of understanding between the Commission, EFTA, CEN, and CENELEC, EOTC was designed primarily to do two things: (1) coordinate testing and certification practices to prevent firms from having to undergo multiple market entry and approval requirements, and (2) develop a common European framework to encourage mutual confidence and trust in member countries regulatory and self-regulatory testing and certification practices. Unlike traditional regulatory agencies, the EOTC's role is to delegate to national regulatory agencies or private testing and accreditation agencies, so that it relies on them to apply similar standards. The inspection of manufacturing facilities and the certification of reviewers of applications will thus proceed according to agreed-upon standards (EN 4–5000 series) established by CEN, CENELEC, and ETSI. EOTC's role was seen as critical in encouraging producers, consumers, users, and testing and certification bodies to work together to tackle the remaining barriers in this area. While the EOTC was envisaged as a private organization, its working methods were designed to enhance transparency and openness in much the same way that ETSI had broadened the number of participants involved in setting telecommunications standards.

Industry was expected to take the lead and identify areas where coordination was vital for the single market. Unlike the traditional standards bodies but similar to ETSI, the EOTC was not supposed to be based along national territorial lines, open to all recognized interests in this area as well as participants from outside the EU and EFTA. Like the standards bodies, however, EOTC was designed to act as the coordinator or umbrella organization.[74] It quickly set up its institutional framework and operations in Brussels, with substantial input and participation from standards organizations in sixteen European states and twelve pan-European standards, consumer, and industry associations. Initial efforts at coordination focused on testing and certification practices in information technology, electrical products, and environmental issues.

Not all of these efforts at cross-border cooperation among testing and certification agencies were new. Many were long-standing agreements that simply became institutionalized and formalized within EOTC. A growing number of sectors were encouraged to deal with the problems created by divergent testing and certification systems, with EOTC acting as a forum for negotiations among various different interests. Many of the smaller agencies had cornered the market in specific sectors and were concerned about the effects of regulatory competition. This led to debates within EOTC about the possible anti-trust implications of reduced competition as agencies began to search for cross-border linkages and consolidation. Anxious to ensure a level playing field in this area, the Commission supported the creation of harmonized standards and criteria for testing and certification agencies as a means of improving quality and promoting transparency in testing and certification operations.

EOTC had been established via Commission funding, in part to ensure its independence from the existing European standards bodies. While the bulk of initial finances to set up the EOTC came from the Community, the Commission expected that over time EOTC would rely on a combination of revenues from user groups, national standards bodies, and testing and certification agencies. Since both CEN and CENELEC had invested time and resources in promoting testing and certification issues, going as far as developing their own quality marks (such as CENCER, HAR, and CCA), they viewed the EOTC as something of a competitor, particularly as it raised the prospect of shifting future revenues to another institutional body. With considerable reluctance in 1991, both CEN and CENELEC signed a memorandum of association with the Commission and EFTA, establishing the legal basis for the EOTC.

The European Organization for Testing and Certification

Although similar in function to the European standards bodies in terms of their coordinating function, the EOTC has a different structure. The EOTC Council is composed of fifteen members from various national and industrial interests, acting as the coordinating mechanism for the committees working within the EOTC framework and also as a liaison with various standards bodies. The Council also has the responsibility of sanctioning agreements proposed for mutual recognition of testing and certification in different sectors or industries. Specialized committees provide the necessary expertise in considering the broad range of sectors interested in establishing mutual recognition of testing and certification practices to common standards. Sectoral committees have been established for promoting mutual recognition and agreement in product areas such as gas, health, and information technology, as well as for horizontal issues such as quality assurance and testing methods that cut across different industries.[75] To ensure some form of national representation and input from the national standards bodies, the sectoral committees comprise national representatives and industry participants involved in the testing and certification process. The latter work together in agreement groups where most of the details over common acceptance of tests and certificates are drawn up. Certification organizations from at least three participating states must agree that there is sufficient interest to establish an agreement group.

The EOTC offered several political and economic benefits to the Commission's efforts to promote the single market. Not only did it address persistent complaints from industry, but it also allowed the Commission to delegate the problem onto the private sector. In doing so, the Commission expected that many of the agreements reached through industry bargaining and negotiation could be easily transferred to the public sector. This would effectively outflank those member states attempting to block market access in numerous regulated sectors. The EOTC was widely viewed by members of the standards community as yet another example of Community efforts to circumvent traditional channels, providing a means for the Commission to use the resources of the private sector as it did not have the level of resources or administrative capacity to do so itself.[76]

With the increased responsibilities of CEN and CENELEC, and the creation of ETSI and EOTC, the overall structure of reform envisioned by that Commission had shifted regulatory responsibilities for market governance from the public to the private sector. How this new system translated those regulatory objectives into practice is discussed below.

How standards are developed

Demands for European standards come from one of three sources: (1) national standards bodies may submit a request; (2) CEN, CENELEC and ETSI, the EC, or EFTA can suggest areas where European standardization is critically important; and (3) scientific bodies, professional associations, and commercial organizations can request specific areas for European standardization. Several types of standards can be adopted by the European standards bodies, reflecting differences in the degree to which convergence on appropriate standards has been reached. Standards can be classified as harmonized documents (HD), European standards (EN), or European pre-standards (ENV).

The primary difference between European standards and harmonized documents is the degree to which they are binding on national standards bodies. A European standard is regionally recognized, requiring all national standards bodies to implement or transpose this standard in identical fashion at the national level. This requires the withdrawal of any conflicting national standard. Harmonized documents require member state bodies to implement the standard and withdraw any competing national standard. Member states may, however, issue a national standard that falls within the scope of the harmonized document, provided that it is equivalent in technical content. This reflects the similar difference between Community regulations and directives, where in exceptional cases national standards may deviate from the requirements of the harmonized document in order to accommodate specific circumstances (such as Arctic weather conditions in Finland or Sweden). These deviations, known as B Deviations under CEN/CENELEC rules, are due to particular technical requirements whereas A deviations are due to different national and administrative provisions. Harmonized documents are designed to ensure sufficient equivalence and not radically alter many national practices. In practice, this has been difficult to achieve as many national standards have been difficult to compare. Many also referred to other national standards, causing additional entry barriers for foreign competitors.

Given the unsuitability of using harmonized documents as a means to ensure a uniform system of standardization throughout the single market, the European standards bodies have stressed their preference for collective agreement on European standards (ES). These European standards require all member organizations to implement or transpose the standard in the required time frame. The European standards bodies may also choose to adopt European pre-standards (ENV) as prospective standards in areas where there is rapid technological change and innovation. These aim to provide guidance for manufacturers, and tend to focus on compatibility and intellectual property issues rather than health and safety requirements. European pre-standards have become increasingly important within the ETSI. A specific category of Eurocodes has also been established for the Iron, Steel, and Construction sector. These are technical guidance documents that supplement European standards and provide information on how to interpret many of the performance standards developed in these areas.

After the request for a new standard has been made, it is examined within the European standards bodies by the Technical Boards. Their judgment is based on whether the request responds to problems identified by industry or other bodies, involves adapting an existing standard for technological progress, or comprises part of the Commission's programme under the New Approach. If approved, relevant technical committees are formed and required to solicit existing drafts or documents. Usually, these drafts are from one of three sources: international standards bodies, national standards bodies, or specialized trade federations.[77] If work is already being undertaken at the international level, the committees will use this as the basis for their own work. If there

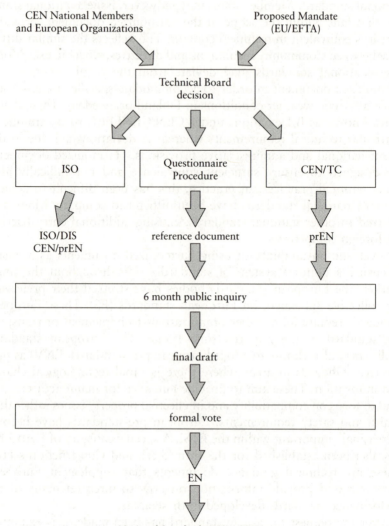

CEN National Members
and European Organizations

Proposed Mandate
(EU/EFTA)

Technical Board
decision

| ISO | Questionnaire Procedure | CEN/TC |

ISO/DIS
CEN/prEN

reference document

prEN

6 month public inquiry

final draft

formal vote

EN

National Standards (NS)—EN . . .

Fɪɢ 7.2 The standards process

are no international standards under discussion or available, the committees will circulate a preliminary questionnaire to determine whether
sufficient interest in the topic exists.

The draft stage allows a preview of the degree of consensus and agreement among different national standards bodies. Though the national
standards bodies are supposed to follow what goes on in other national

standards bodies, they rarely do. Hence, the draft stage and preliminary questionnaire sent out by the Technical Board often alerts them to potential allies and opponents. The preliminary inquiry may provide a basis for a working draft, as national standards bodies are given three months to provide detailed information on any existing national standards work-in-progress. If trade associations or other organizations have provided the draft document, then they must negotiate with the European standards bodies to ensure that they follow the internal rules and procedures for European standardization.

In all three cases, draft standards are circulated for comments among committee members. This encourages debate and allows all members to voice their opinions on specific aspects of the proposal. It also allows those with significant expertise and resources to exercise considerable influence in promoting favoured solutions. According to Salter, 'Outsiders, even major users of the standards and technologies, have little influence except if they themselves become standards developers, and in effect, join the standards community on its terms.'[78] The relationship between insiders and outsiders is made more complicated by the role of observers. Representatives from the Commission, EFTA, and other international standards organizations may request observer status to follow the negotiations. Though they cannot vote on the actual proposed standard, it does allow other organizations to monitor the ongoing work programme of European standardization. However, this is an exceedingly difficult job given scarce resources and the number of committees, subcommittees, and working groups that are negotiating at any one time. Because the Commission cannot effectively monitor all activities, it frequently uses outside experts to monitor standardization activities and ensure that their interests are adequately represented.

Once the relevant technical committee reaches agreement on a draft, national standards bodies are given six months to circulate the draft for discussion and public comment. Many participants are constrained by the fact that, even after they reach agreement within regional committees, they are required to get approval from the national level. Under the voting procedures and rules of European standardization, the agreement reached at the European level must be ratified at the domestic level.[79] Thus what happens at one level may influence strategies and outcomes at other levels. Domestic policies are not exogenous, and the ability to manoeuvre at the European level may be constrained by what is domestically acceptable in each member state.[80]

Because those debating approval at the national level must reach a single opinion to accept or reject a negotiated European standard, opposition must be unusually strong, organized, and widespread to prevail. Although Putnam contends that side payments or compensatory measures can facilitate agreement in such a negotiating environment, this may be difficult and costly to orchestrate when any deviation from the negotiated standard perpetuates market fragmentation and barriers to trade.[81] Many domestic firms and societal interests do not participate in draft discussions and negotiations at the regional level, but they can wreak havoc on carefully crafted compromises by forcing their national standards body to vote against the proposed European standard. Perhaps the example best known to policy-makers, and certainly most visible to the general public, is German and British opposition to common electrical standards and plugs for appliances.[82] Despite negotiations spanning eighteen years, their opposition on the grounds of safety and cost blocked the deal, much to the consternation of both the Commission and other national standards bodies.

Once national positions are reached, a vote is taken at the European level based on a complicated weighting system that still allows blocking minorities to prevail. In CEN and CENELEC, voting is weighted among the national standards bodies, with the four standards bodies in France, Britain, Italy, and Germany each receiving ten votes, Spain votes eight Belgium, Greece, Netherlands, Portugal, Sweden, and Switzerland receiving five votes, Ireland, Norway, Denmark, Finland, and Austria three votes, Luxembourg two, and Iceland one vote.[83] With a combined total of ninety-six votes, the draft standards need to meet the following four requirements to be adopted: (*a*) simple majority (no abstentions); (*b*) at least 25 votes in favour; (*c*) no more than 22 votes against; and (*d*) no more than three national standards bodies against. If a proposed standard fails to meet these requirements, a second vote is taken excluding non-EU members. If a majority of EU members approve on the second count, the standard is adopted and all national standards bodies must implement the European standard regardless of their individual positions.

National standards must be replaced by those agreed at the European level. Any differences in assessment or technique at the national level are no longer acceptable. While non-EU members who strongly oppose the standard do not have to adopt the agreement, those who voted in favour of it are obligated to implement it. This allows for the possibility that certain non-EU states could retain their national standards and use them as a protective barrier to trade. In practice, however, this is difficult to sustain as the EFTA markets are very small and face tremendous pressure to adopt any agreed standards which enable their own firms to benefit from enhanced market access.

Little regard was given to the rules and operation of European standardization until the mid-1980s when the Commission delegated considerable regulatory responsibility to them and took a closer interest in their internal processes (see below and Chapter 6). Though the standards bodies have established close ties with the Commission, they are formally independent organizations that have fought to maintain their autonomy. Their workload and visibility have increased as a result of the political mandates from the Commission under the New Approach. However, both sides have complained about the financial obligations and administrative costs of meeting the large number of requested European standards. Though these costs are partially compensated by annual contributions from national standards bodies, the national standards bodies have continued to request an increase in EFTA and EU contributions due to the increased workload resulting from their use of private standards bodies for regulatory functions.

The national standards bodies complained bitterly about their own increased contributions, as they have seen a significant transfer of funds from the national to European level.[84] Their major criticism was that the Commission's financial support for specific mandates to meet legislative requirements did not take into account the resources and time contributed by firms and trade associations. From the perspective of the national standards bodies, the revenue from the Commission supported operations at the European level without filtering down to them. Even though a great deal of preliminary work may take place at the national level, and national standards bodies are responsible for the implementation of European standards, they received no financial remuneration for their increased workload. This situation was also a source of frustration for many industrial federations.[85] These federations faced increased costs in participating at the European level, while their members continued to contribute substantial fees to the national standards bodies. It is not surprising that the national standards bodies— and increasingly many companies—have found fault with European standardization.

Negotiating dynamics

The interrelationships between institutions, processes, and actors make the standard-setting process extraordinarily difficult to assess.[86] How nationally based experts render opinions, form alliances and coalitions, and portray their national interests without undermining their own individual or company interests is understudied. We have few assessments of how firms actually bargain, negotiate, and react to developments in European standardization. Specific case studies on high-definition television, video recorders, and mobile telephones have highlighted the intense competition surrounding the adoption of an international standard.[87] Also, a considerable literature using game theory may help to describe the choices facing firms in a standards contest.[88]

This work focuses on the coordination problems in reaching agreement, either through negotiation in committees, alliance formation, or market competition.[89] In some cases, attracting a critical mass of users more quickly than rival standards can also be achieved through licensing, early adoption, subsidizing initial users, and forming strategic alliances. While markets can be effective in setting standards, they are sometimes imperfect, and institutional frameworks are necessary as alternative coordinating mechanisms to resolve collective action problems.

Because consensus is the general decision rule in standards organizations, the result is a 'battle of the sexes' problem where important benefits are dependent on the ability to cooperate, but cooperation is dependent on resolving conflict over the solution chosen. Thus, if two parties are already using a different standard, they may prefer coordination on their own standard so as to avoid the costs of converting, but since the choice of a standard may strongly advantage one party over another, the policy preferences of key actors are influenced by the distributional consequences involved.[90] The general problem of the committees negotiating can be understood on the basis of collective decision logic as suggested by Arrow: if all the participants do not have the same preference function, no satisfactory outcome will be found.[91] In other words, given a divergence of interests, getting agreement on a standard may be more likely if their preferences converge together. If not, the end result may be deadlock, as different preferences and interests reduce the likelihood of agreement or promote a tendency towards lowest common denominator agreements.

While economists have sought to determine conditions under which cooperative behaviour takes place, theoretical models also look at the strategic impact of standards on competition, market share, and business policy.[92] These models typically assume that economic position will be enhanced by being a first mover and forcing other firms to adjust. While this image of decision-making views outcomes as determined by relative power and strategic rationality, this instrumental view is largely indifferent to the decision-making constraints posed by bounded rationality, information costs, and the way in which organizational culture may affect the ease or ability of those involved to pursue a particular strategy. As a result, communicative rationality is at least as important as instrumental rationality in understanding the dynamics of standardization processes.[93] Problem-solving, consensus formation, and the patterns of mutual trust and credibility become important. Each standard is by no means the best possible solution from a given set of alternatives, but rather reflects the complexity of the environment and the behaviour of players to decipher and order the environment in a way that results in some form of coordination.[94] The outcome of the standardization process depends partly on the pay-off structure but also on the organizational dynamics, norms, and synergies within the organization.

Organizational culture and operating norms

Though the operations and structure of each of the standards institutions are slightly different, and they differ in technical orientation and composition, the operating norms are similar. The problem-solving nature of the standard-setting process is influenced by a set of cognitive and normative factors that interact with formal rules of decision and strategic bargains described above.[95] Decision behaviour is seen as driven by a logic of appropriateness; reflecting historical, symbolic, and normative orders.[96]

Many European firms readily acknowledge that they engage in both cooperation and competition within the multitude of committees that characterize standard-setting. They are also keenly aware that technical expertise is crucial for problem-solving at this stage of the process.[97] Influence depends on putting forward an idea, such as best available technology or integrated pollution control, around which preferences can converge due to the persuasiveness and credibility of the proposal. In contrast to the assumption of comprehensive rationality and perfect information, those involved in setting standards follow more closely the organizational traits of bounded rationality identified by Simon. Technical standardization usually involves much cognitive uncertainty concerning appropriate solutions, given differences in risk assessment, scientific uncertainty, and goals of regulation, so that building a consensus also depends upon reputation, expertise, and credibility.[98] A belief in the integrity and competence of other participants is often critical in reaching some form of agreement.[99] This explains why arguments about the feasibility of proposals occupy such a central position in the initial policy deliberations.[100] As Héritier observes in her work on environmental policy-making, 'participants know that their relationship is not merely a temporary one, but meant to be durable. They therefore think twice before ruthlessly seeking to maximize their individual interest.'[101]

Participants in the process are anxious to reduce their adjustment costs by having their own domestic regulatory policies and practices adopted at the European level. Under the norms of standard-setting, however, those that refuse to adjust their position are often considered 'outsiders' in the policy process and relegated to the margins of standards organizations. 'Members' exerting maximum influence are those directly integrated into the network where decisions are made.[102] Unfamiliarity with the norms of a network can reduce bargaining power and leverage as a set of mutual expectations governs the relationship among those involved in standardization.[103] Consequently, the environment in which actors are embedded and the networks of relations among standards participants are considered important factors in fostering cooperative agreements. As Eichener and Majone note, committee work is characterized by a *copinage technocratique*—that is, actors on the technical level share more common interests than political actors.[104]

Expertise is a general rule for effective work in committees dealing with such technical issues. In such a context, analysis and deliberation are important for collectively identifying advantageous solutions. Though many players are seeking to promote their own goals, they must justify their positions by appealing to the merits of the case. Shaping the debate and influencing a particular outcome depends on such factors as persuasion and evidence.[105] Before these committees start working together, fundamental conflicts have to be settled and basic agreements and group specific norms have to be found.

Since most committees have to contend with one or more negative votes, alternative proposals and objections are considered carefully. Having often worked together for a number of years, members of a committee are extremely reluctant to force decisions on reluctant members and are extremely sensitive to technical objections.[106] Though this has led to constant complaints from the Commission regarding excessive delays, many participants are reluctant to ride roughshod over minority interests, since this would result in standards that are not universally accepted.[107] If agreement is unobtainable, even after extensive discussion and consultation, then the process is suspended indefinitely.[108] For those involved it may be economically inefficient to spend extended periods of time and resources in trying to reconcile divergent preferences. It becomes difficult for those involved to move negotiations forward without compromising their own specific preferences and 'the only way that they could do that would be to sacrifice their (distributive) interests'.[109]

The norms of the process make it easier to block alternatives, since all actors have a general interest to push forward bargaining and are taken more seriously if they raise legitimate concerns. Limits are observed, however, as members who consistently block proposed solutions will lose credibility and be taken less seriously in future discussions. Although this means that delaying tactics and obstructionism can provide bargaining leverage, it does not necessarily guarantee that the veto player will win the day. Maintaining standing within the community is also a key factor in getting agreement, and obstructionism (especially if it is viewed as politically rather than technically motivated) does risk the possibility that another technical committee or standards body will set the agenda.

The prospect that another committee (at the regional or even international level) may move forward often pushes reluctant committee members into some form of negotiated agreement. This was certainly the case in videotex standards where competing standards from France (Antiope), Canada (Telidon), and Britain (Prestel) emerged at the international level. The conflict between Britain and France was finally settled in the (former) European standards organization, CEPT, by including both standards in the European standard. The agreement was pushed in part by the prospect that Canada and subsequently the USA would get a head start in international negotiations. This would have been a costly prospect for both European states given their substantial domestic commitments.[110] And in the case of GSM standards, the standards for mobile telephone networks, both the International Telecommunications Union and the European Telecommunications Standards Institute were involved in the standard adoption strategy. GSM was originally an initiative of the telecoms monopolies organized in CEPT, and received strong support from the Commission interested in proposing initiative on standardization, telecoms, and joint R & D in the context of the single market programme.[111] While industry and governments in Europe support one particular standard, called UMTS, which ETSI opted for in 1998, the ITU has been faced with a multitude of standards proposed by the USA, Asia, and Europe. While most of the world has adopted variants of the European designated GSM, including the Japanese mobile phone giant, NTT/Nippon, the United States has comparatively few GSM networks and has a mixture of several other standards.[112]

The GSM standard supported by a Council recommendation (87/371) to ensure EU-wide acceptance was designed to prevent the problems caused by incompatibility that existed with the first generation analogue mobile network systems. The effort by European companies to push through their singular standard irked many American negotiators and industry leaders such as Qualcomm that insisted the ITU must accept multiple standards. The American position was weakened by the prominence of several American suppliers of GSM equipment, including joint development between Alcatel of France and Motorola of the USA, and Ericsson of Sweden and Lucent Technologies in the US. Given that Motorola owned a majority of the GSM patents, and had agreed cross-licensing in Europe, this allowed ETSI to pursue an open, non-proprietary standard, enabling the Europeans to accomplish both a competitive market for such networks, and major progress on standardization while the ITU lagged behind in part due to heterogeneous preferences that made it difficult to promote its own leadership role proactively.[113]

Despite these competitive pressures and institutional competition, participants are quite conscious of what they frequently refer to as 'due process'. Anxious not to ride roughshod over minority interests, there are both organizational norms and procedural mechanisms to prevent this from happening. Committee members may find that at some stage they prefer a different outcome to that which is on offer. At the same time, they may prefer coordination (a standardized outcome) to the alternative of diversity and fragmentation, even while disagreeing with the proposed solution.[114] Such disagreements are common, and may be due to different participants planning to serve different segments of the market, disparities in experience and use of particular standards, or genuinely held opinions as to which is the best for the entire industry in the long run.[115] Yet choices have to be made and this may lead to a lock-in effect which is why there is often resistance to certain market developments.

Participants who believe that committee negotiations are unfair have a number of options. They can directly appeal to the Technical Board to hear their grievances. Alternatively, they can rely on the fact that they often have multiple memberships. Not only can participants threaten to push an alternative standard in another committee, institution, or arena, but they can lobby against the disputed standard at the national level. Since interests are aggregated twice—at both the regional and national level—the principle of nationally organized votes transforms standardization into, at a minimum, a two-level game. The impact of such an institutional setting, with its multiple veto points and consensus decision rules, was not sufficiently understood by the Commission when it sought to overhaul European standardization and meet the demands of the single market programme.

Conclusion: interlocking politics

All of the elements of the new regulatory strategy were now in place. The European Commission delegated a degree of regulatory authority to the European standards bodies to enable them to collectively agree on common rules for the single market. The institutional framework for market coordination was now far more complicated than that under harmonization, as the Commission began both to use existing institutions and to create new ones. Standards bodies had taken over a significant amount of responsibility for meeting the objectives of the single market. This was premissed on the assumption that the standards bodies would be able to collectively agree on common standards. This redirection of regulatory activity brought in more players but also increased the number of vested interests, raising the risk of deadlock and stalemate. The following chapter illustrates this point in more detail.

These new regulatory instruments resulted in a system of interlocking politics that engaged various institutions and interests at both the national and regional level, as well as public and private actors. Manœuvring within certain legal and market constraints, the standard-setting bodies and those participating in them were given a central role in shaping the policy-making process. This view of regulatory politics requires us to consider the politics among firms (and other interest groups) as well as more conventional intergovernmental politics. The distribution of regulatory competencies has become more convoluted and complex, and standard-setting has become ever more critical in European efforts to reconcile regulation and free trade. As the following chapter illustrates, many of the difficulties encountered under harmonization resurfaced within the European standards bodies. Dealing with both interest heterogeneity and collective action dilemmas had been transferred from the Community to the private sector organizations.

Case Studies in Standards Negotiations[1]

Introduction

After the adoption of its new regulatory strategies, the Commission sought to publicize the new policy and explain to various trade associations, industry federations, and individual companies that their activities should now focus at the European level. In the first fifteen years of the new regulatory approach, from 1985 to 2000, the Community adopted twenty-two New Approach directives covering a range of industries (see Table 8.1). Unlike the detailed harmonization directives of the past,

TABLE 8.1 *Standardization activities related to the New Approach*

Directive references	Areas	Mandated	Ratified	Under approval	Under development
90/384/EEC	Non-automatic weighting instruments	1	1	—	—
87/404/EEC	Simple pressure vessels	47	38	5	4
88/378/EEC	Safety of toys	10	6	1	3
89/392/EEC	Safety of machinery	894	214	370	310
89/686/EEC	Personal protective equipment	300	159	47	94
90/385/EEC ⎱ 93/42/EEC ⎰	Medical devices, including active implantable medical devices	248	127	60	61
90/396/EEC	Gas appliances	91	45	32	14
93/15/EEC	Explosive for civil uses	51	0	0	51
94/9/EEC	Potentially explosive atmospheres	50	5	8	37
94/25/EEC	Recreational craft	49	15	11	23
95/16/EEC	Lifts (elevators)	17	4	3	10
94/62/EU	Packaging and packaging waste	21	0	0	21
89/336/EEC	Electromagnetic compatibility	128	79	11	38
92/75/EEC	Energy labelling	5	3	1	1
91/263/EEC	Telecommunication terminal equipment	30	25	—	5
93/97/EEC	Satellite earth equipment	8	5	—	3
89/106/EEC	Construction products	(Overall program under development)			
97/23/EEC	Pressure equipment	771	280	250	241
COM/96/0643	In vitro diagnostic medical devices	22	0	4	18
COM/97/0034	Railways equipment	104	12	28	64
COM/93/322	Precious metals	8	0	2	6

Source: 'Efficiency and Accountability in European Standardisation under the New Approach', Report from the Commission to the Council and the European Parliament (COM/98/291), Commission of the European Communities, May 1998.

these New Approach directives were horizontal systems of governance rather than individualistic, product specific systems of regulatory control. Firms that had been only marginally affected by European regulations found that many of the New Approach directives would have an impact on their decisions about market entry, production methods, product attributes, and transactions between firms. The new regulatory strategy actually increased the responsibilities of firms in the standardization process, since they were now given a mandate to adopt the necessary standards for the operation and actualization of the single market. Though this did not preclude the involvement of other interests in standard-setting, in practice the lack of institutional capabilities and resources meant that firms were not likely to encounter substantial political resistance from unions or consumer groups.

More than a decade later, however, the standardization process is again the subject of increasing criticism, and the Commission remains deeply dissatisfied with progress achieved. The regulatory strategy which had appeared to solve the Commission's problems by delegating negotiations onto other institutions proved to be just as prone to endless bargaining and inaction as the harmonization process that it replaced. Though some argue that it has been an unmitigated success,[2] this reflects a focus on the legislative adoption of directives rather than on levels of compliance, implementation, and legitimization of European standardization.[3] While agreement on common standards has certainly been reached in a number of areas (see Table 8.2) as the pace of standardization has picked up markedly over the past decade, the perceived failures of this policy are rooted in the fact that

the issue of technical barriers to trade is complex. A barrier to one company, industry or country may provide advantages to another. All efforts to remove barriers to trade meet resistance from those who feel threatened. This explains

TABLE 8.2 *Aggregate summary of standardization activities related to the New Approach (as of June 1997)*

	Mandated	Ratified	Pending approval	In preparation
CEN	2,182	633	847	702
CENELEC	231	103	33	95
ETSI	143	86	29	28
Public Procurement	349	92	172	85
TOTAL	2,905	914	1,081	910

Source: European Commission, 'Economic Reform: Report on the Functioning of Community Product and Capital Markets', COM 1999 10 Final, 21 Jan. 1999.

the halting and uneven approach to removing such barriers. Results are not achieved by dictate, but by negotiation which involves a search for consensus and consent.[4]

As Foray concludes, 'the interplay of reputation, credibility, and the ability to generate a coalition of common interests is an important determinant of standards setting process.'[5] In other words, standard-setting resembles the type of political coalition formation akin to that of the legislative process.

In an assessment of legislative decision-making that is equally applicable to standard-setting, Shepsle and Weingast point out that committees are not only transaction cost-economizing agents, but also specialized factors of production. They serve as specialized bodies of experts that collect and use information in order to enhance their competitive advantage and/or promote certain social outcomes. In standard-setting, with its procedural rules of consensus, the threshold of decision-making is high and the preferences of participants are often firmly established, with participants sometimes locked into a 'joint decision trap'.[6]

While the Commission should have anticipated such difficulties, since the few occasions it had used the reference to standards approach in the 1960s and 1970s had produced few timely results, standardization is further complicated by the fact that European standards bodies are also working to accelerate agreement on anticipatory standards, developed in advance of products and services to be marketed, to avoid more difficult negotiations when interests are firmly entrenched.[7] While traditional standardization focused on coordinating products already existing in the market place, in cases where firms already have entrenched interests, the problem has become one of getting agreement among different and often alternative international political systems, technological rules, and regulatory practices.[8] This new environment also includes anticipatory standards where no particular standards had been chosen and intellectual property issues are the major issues of contention.[9]

This chapter assesses the new regulatory strategy through four detailed case studies. The cases of toys, machines, construction products, and medical devices highlight both the technical and the political difficulties encountered by the New Approach. Each case study considers trends in trade and production, the legislative proposals and history, reactions from interested parties, and the resulting regulatory and standards programmes that reflect new efforts to address many long-standing barriers to trade. Each of these cases was targeted by the Commission because trade barriers were preventing significant cross-border trade. The standards bodies have achieved variable results in addressing those barriers.[10]

While standardization has been remarkable successful in the toy sector and medical device sector, it has been much more problematic in construction products and machinery. The cases also demonstrate how European standards bodies have sometimes sought to deflect criticism regarding their own slow progress by criticizing the activities of the European Commission.

Case 1: the toy directive

In 1985 the Commission proposed a directive addressing the need for common safety requirements to allow for the free circulation of toys. As one of the two earliest New Approach directives, it was considered a key test for the operation of the new policy. The measure was finally approved by EU trade ministers in May 1988 and was expected to become operational in 1990. The toy directive would ban dangerous toys that caused about 20,000 accidents every year within the Community. In addition, the toy directive established common guidelines to ensure that toys using chemicals or electricity did not endanger children.[11] The legislation applied to both imported toys as well as those originating within the Community.

From the consumer's perspective, the most noticeable difference in purchasing toys was the introduction of a distinct symbol of compliance known as the 'CE' mark. This identified toys that the manufacturer had declared were complying with the essential safety requirements of the toy directive.[12] Although the member states were generally favourably disposed to the proposal, and agreed that the establishment of a single market for toys necessitated common standards, the issue proved a tough test of the Community's New Approach.

Trends in production and trade

Although the sector was not large, the toy industry had an annual turnover of 5 billion ECU within the EU. The sector comprised about 2,500, mainly small companies employing about 85,000 people. Germany, France, and Italy accounted for 26, 23, and 18 per cent respectively of the market, and actively supported negotiations to ease cross-border trade. However, harmonization was considered far too difficult; in 1955, the toy industry marketed approximately 5,000 types of toys, and by 1979 this had risen to over 60,000. The extraordinary increase in production raised concerns about the safety of regulations cross-nationally. The sector also increased in importance in terms of production and trade. From its origins as a marginal, seasonal, and purely local market, the toy sector increased dramatically as income levels and other factors increased European consumption patterns.

Although 85 per cent of the toys sold in Europe are manufactured there, the EU imports twice as many toys as it exports, mainly from South East Asia. Small and medium-sized companies have frequently complained about the economic impact of these imports. The European Federation of Toy Industries (FEFJ), representing national associations and small manufacturers, argued that the SMEs would be put at a competitive advantage vis-à-vis foreign imports because many foreign manufactures did not meet the high EU standards. In response to such concerns, the Council adopted a 'code of good conduct' in June 1992 to combat imitation toys manufactured in Asia. Asian newspapers ran a number of stories about the EU toy standards and the need to comply in order to avoid hefty fines.[13]

The trend towards shifting production to South East Asia only amplified concerns among European manufacturers about compliance. European companies tend to specialize in traditional toys with longer product life cycles, and many such as the Danish Lego company, German Playmobil, British Spears and Waddington, and French Monneret benefit from high brand recognition. They were concerned with problems of piracy and copyright over their designs, trade marks, and models. The larger companies also recognized that common standards would ease their own market access, since widely different practices existed across Europe: Portugal and Luxembourg had no regulatory requirements for toy safety, Germany had stringent legally binding requirements, and Belgium had voluntary standards.[14] Austria, Germany, and Finland adopted general safety requirements for toys as part of their consumer policy framework, whereas Ireland, Britain, Switzerland, and subsequently Germany moved towards more specific regulations covering a number of hazards related specifically to toys.[15] The Commission's own assessment of the problem indicated that there were considerable barriers to trade in the toy sector, and cited the difficulties that Italian toys had in accessing the German market as an example.[16] According to one national trade association, the most pressing issue was proof of compliance, since testing and certification practices varied widely across Europe.[17]

Legislative history

The Commission had tried to establish uniform toy safety standards since the mid-1970s, succeeding after a decade of wrangling before agreement was finally reached in 1988. Initial discussions were carried out with toy experts, manufacturers, and consumer organizations in 1976. After two years of discussion, the Commission had hoped to introduce a proposal to the Council in mid-1978. The draft directive was expected to cover general aspects of toy safety, with some more detailed information on mechanical properties and flammability on which there was considerable agreement. Additional legislative proposals were expected later on toxicity and other associated risks.

To achieve compliance with these proposals, the Commission relied on the work undertaken in CEN, which had already reached agreement on issues related to standards for inflammability, and the mechanical and physical properties of toys. On other aspects of toy safety, however, CEN had been unable to resolve differences, and the question of acceptable levels of toxicity was hotly debated. No clear scientific consensus on permitted levels and absorption effects had emerged, frustrating the Commission's own efforts to come to some form of agreement on acceptable substances.[18] CEN's inability to reach agreement forced the Commission to propose its own solutions in the form of a list of toxic substances that were permissible in toys. This created considerable delay, as the Commission needed advice from its own expert committee on toxicology, and the Commission was not able to table a proposal for Council consideration until 3 July 1980.

The proposal was extremely complex, with over eighty pages of technical annexes. It covered general safety aims, technical standards, and procedures for consumer associations to request safety assessment by relevant authorities. Market surveillance by consumer organizations was strongly supported by the Consumers' Consultative Committee within the Commission. However, the proposal drew sharp criticism from trade associations, who felt that the industry was already 'over-legislated and in danger of being strangled by restrictions'.[19]

After consideration within the Consumer Affairs Council, the directive was submitted to the European Parliament and Economic and Social Committee, where it encountered further difficulties. While the draft directive was given to the Economic and Monetary Affairs Committee, the Environment Committee was also asked to consider the proposal since it contained important health and safety issues. Frustrated over the detailed provisions of the proposal, the Economic and Monetary Affairs Committee wrote to Étienne Davignon,[20] the European Commissioner in charge of the internal market portfolio, and other Commission officials,[21] expressing opposition to the draft proposal and refusing to consider it. In the view of the Committee, 'it [was] not difficult to imagine what the newspapers [would] say about such proposals, and the sort of amendments the anti-marketeers [would] table in the plenary.' The Parliament also repeatedly criticized the proposed directive,[22] and insisted that the Economic and Monetary Affairs Committee Working Group on Technical Barriers to Trade meet with Commission officials and other experts to resolve the impasse.

In these informal meetings, the Working Party questioned CEN about its own work programme concerning toy safety, and particularly why these standards had not accompanied the Commission's proposals. Representatives from CEN noted that they were not consulted in the early stages of the proposal, although they were quick to acknowledge that cooperation had subsequently increased. However, CEN officials had difficulty in defining CEN's role, as the Commission's proposals were extremely detailed, and the division between statutory provisions and voluntary standards was not clear cut. Although two toy standards had been adopted in 1975, CEN faced problems in adopting standards to meet the present proposal. Certain national delegations (which CEN did not explicitly name) opposed the European standards as they contradicted national regulations in force in their own countries.[23] The result was widely varying perceptions about levels of safety among experts within the technical committees. Given this, CEN was not willing to make a political decision for the convenience of achieving a European compromise that would ultimately not be acceptable to all. CEN officials felt that the Commission's efforts in the toy sector undermined their own work. They felt in particular that the Commission's reference to standards reduced their flexibility, since the standard became binding on all member states and limited CEN's ability to make necessary adaptations over time.

The Commission regarded the situation differently. It was not up to Community legislation to adapt to European norms, but rather for the European standards bodies to adapt to directives drawn up by the Community. The Commission had waited patiently for the standards bodies to draw up toy standards, but when these were not accepted by all member states, the Commission decided to take the matter into its own hands.

In July 1981, the Economic and Monetary Committee recommended that the tabled proposal be rejected. The committee suggested that the Commission resubmit a simplified proposal with general framework principles, and then submit separate directives to deal with specific safety problems. The Commission reacted by abruptly suspending its draft proposal in October 1981 to re-examine its merits. Two years later, following intensive discussion and review, the Commission submitted a revised proposal which comprised three separate directives that made reference to European standards. The Parliament was still not satisfied, arguing that the legislation was still too cumbersome. The disagreement and continued deadlock stemmed over the inclusion of standards in the directive. The Commission continued with its inclusion of mandatory standards in the draft proposal, while the Parliament, joined by the Economic and Social Committee, felt that there was a need for non-mandatory standards and a greater responsibility on the part of manufacturers to assume responsibility for safety by using European standards.

The deadlock continued until October 1984, after the European Parliamentary elections, when the Economic and Monetary Affairs Committee lobbied for the proposal to be resubmitted. The toy directive then languished for ten months, until Lord Cockfield, who had succeeded Étienne Davignon as European Commissioner responsible for the internal market portfolio, indicated in September 1985 that it would not be possible to revise the proposal any further. Cockfield initially rejected the possibility that toy safety could be considered under the new simplified approach to technical harmonization and standards. After continued months of indecision, the Commission withdrew the proposal in October 1986.[24] Then, in a surprise turnaround, the Commission agreed to propose a toy directive under the New Approach. The Commission also proposed tougher surveillance over toy manufacturing and more stringent certification procedures for toys.[25] This represented a victory for the European Parliament, since it had lobbied for amendments to ensure maximum uniformity in approval and inspection systems.

Although welcoming the fact that the Parliament no longer had to cope with overwhelming technical details, several members were concerned that the European standards were not of a sufficiently high level with regard to safety issues.[26] Several members proposed amendments to ensure consumer representation on the technical committees responsible for drafting the toy standards. Despite the acceptance of most of the Parliamentary amendments, several members continued to express opposition.

On 8 March 1988, during the second Parliamentary reading, an amendment by several Danish representatives proposed rejection of the entire toy directive on the grounds that individual member states could not impose stricter rules than those outlined in the legislation.[27] The Danish Parliamentarians were particularly concerned that too much authority was being delegated to the European standards bodies, who they believed to be dominated by toy manufacturers. Bolstered by opposition from the Danish Environmental Administration, the Danish Parliamentary members were able to secure several concessions, including provisions that Denmark could retain its own stricter safety rules on toys that it had adopted from the United States and Sweden. After this, the Commission was unwilling to accept any further amendments and vigorously defended the division of responsibilities between the European Standards bodies and the Community. The toy directive was finally approved and scheduled to come into force on 1 January 1990 with the necessary European standards to accompany the legislation.[28] The economic reach of the directive was expanded in 1994, when the EEA Joint Committee decided to extend the toy directive to the five EFTA countries.

Reactions and response

Almost before the ink was dry, many companies and consumer groups expressed their concern about the toy legislation.[29] Additional problems surfaced at the implementation and enforcement stage. In most member states, toy safety had been regulated using national standards before the adoption of the European directive. Many companies were thus familiar with different national requirements and safety marks. The Commission also encountered problems in pushing member states to meet their legal obligations, with infringement proceedings started against Greece in 1991 for incorrect implementation of the directive. Though adopted relatively quickly compared to previous harmonization efforts, the toy directive did not come into effect as planned in 1990. Two years later, Luxembourg became the last member state to implement the directive in February 1992.[30]

Opposition to the legislation continued to grow. The European Consumer Safety Organization (BEUC) complained that the toy directive did not guarantee safe toys since manufacturers were free to affix the CE mark themselves. Several national consumer associations, including the National Swedish Board for Consumer Policies and the Consumer Association of Ireland, carried out their own checks and found a number of toys that they considered unsafe still on the market.[31] Though the directive required manufacturers to keep detailed information about how they had verified compliance, the head of the toy safety committee of the Toy Manufacturers in Europe, Poul Muller, emphasized that it was critical for national authorities to conduct spot checks.[32] The Commission had published a list of EU-approved bodies that could independently test compliance of toys with EU rules, but there was considerable confusion about what this meant.[33] Many firms preferred to conduct their own in-house tests, and then kept information on file about their compliance with the appropriate European standards.

Firms continued to complain about the costs of compliance. A British company found itself charged with violating the European toy directive for including ordinary pipe-cleaners in its modelling kits. Based on in-house research it contested the claim that its kits were unsafe, and sought compensation for lost sales. The trading standards officials appealed the decision and won their case. The company then had to recall tens of thousands of kits despite the fact that it had sold 260 million without incident.[34] This case only added to complaints about burdensome regulations and red tape, and highlighted the difficulties of effectively coordinating agreement on appropriate standards for market access. The director of the British Toy and Hobby Association, David Hawtin complained that 'people agree to do things at a very high levels in Brussels but that understanding doesn't necessarily filter down.'[35]

The German authorities added a new wrinkle to implementation by insisting that German food laws apply to toys. All manner of toys were subject to toxological tests designed to ensure that plastics used for cooking containers, which are also contained in toys, meet German specifications. David Hawtin complained that, 'the small toy manufacturer in Cornwall and Devon who complies with the toy safety directive frankly doesn't expect any problems. . . . Imagine his surprise when he is told to comply with German food laws.'[36] Germany was unmoved by these complaints and began seeking to have its standards adopted Europe wide. This could only lead to protracted negotiations within the European standards bodies, underlining remaining national differences in practices and approaches to toy safety.

Setting standards for toys

The toy directive sets out the essential requirements, and provides manufacturers with two methods of compliance with the regulation. European standards are the easiest way to prove that the product meets the required regulatory guidelines, although manufacturers have the option of submitting their products for testing and approval to an independent body that evaluates the company's own standards.[37]

The groundwork for toy standards had already been laid out in the European standards bodies, since they had been working in this area since the mid-1980s, but obstacles remained before agreement could be reached. Although the European Federation of Toy Manufacturers had worked on draft proposals to forward to the European standards bodies for consideration, these needed to be revised after the toy directive was passed. The process was difficult as anomalies were carried over from the earlier efforts at harmonization, and the toy directive still contained parts of earlier drafts dealing with technical aspects that should have been incorporated into a standard. The technical details in the legislation also contained certain errors, probably stemming from the lack of technical expertise on the part of the negotiators or from a political decision to reach an acceptable compromise, further complicating the task of the European standards bodies.[38]

The Danes were given the secretariat for toys, and proceeded to canvass opinion on the necessary work to be achieved. For toys, six standards were viewed as necessary under the mandate given to CEN by the Commission, with some liaison work with CENELEC necessary in areas where electrical and electronic toys were involved. The toy standard has six parts: EN 71-1 (1988) Safety of Toys Mechanical and Physical Properties; EN 71-2 Flammability; EN 71-3 Migration of Certain Elements; EN 71-4 (1990) Experimental Sets for Chemistry and Related Activities; EN 71-5 (1993) Chemical Toys other than Experimental Sets; and EN 71-6 Graphical Symbols for Age Warning Labels. The toy directive would also have to comply with the low voltage and electromagnetic compatibility directives for toys with electrical or electronic components.

Negotiations in the technical committee moved along quickly at first. Agreement was reached on the standards for mechanical and physical properties of toys, despite German opposition against the proposed standard. This reflected German concerns not only that the new requirements would increase the regulatory burden in their domestic markets, but also that German firms would find themselves at a comparative disadvantage if testing, certification, and product approval practices varied across Europe. They opposed the British emphasis on quality assurance practices that did not actually test product quality, but merely demonstrated that a company was following certain documented practices.

This was not the only issue that caused problems. Progress on toy safety was further jeopardized when the British, German, Austrian, and Belgian delegations announced that they would veto any additional proposals related to the chemical properties of toys. Such strong disagreements are rare, and somewhat surprising since the British and German opposition to one of the six toy standards masked the fact that they, along with the Dutch and French, had been the most active participants in the technical committee. Though they had ample opportunity to voice opposition in the negotiating stage, they did so at the voting stage as well. Because the standard failed to overcome opposition among all members, a second vote was taken with just Community member states. Despite British and German opposition, their veto was overridden and the specific toy standard that was part of the six standards necessary to meet European regulatory requirements came into force. However, the EFTA member states were under no obligation to accept the agreement, and Austria's earlier opposition meant that they were not obligated to adopt a European standard they deemed unacceptable. The final Toy Safety Directive (TC 52) as completed by the CEN Technical Committee, and all six standards have been ratified including the CENELEC Technical Committee for Toy Safety (TC 61) finalizing work on standards for electrical toys, although they will all be subject to constant updating and revision.

Impact and effectiveness[39]

The standards necessary to comply with the toy directive are in force. In assessing the impact and effectiveness of the toy standard, often considered a successful example of the New Approach, it is clear that problems still remain. However, these relate less to the standards themselves than to the mutual recognition of testing and certification of toys. There are some concerns about the equivalence of product approval procedures across Europe. In a survey conducted for the Commission, the Adkins Consultancy Group found that trade associations, importers, and manufacturers still perceived differences in market surveillance and control within member states. The ANEC (European Association for Cooperation of Consumer representation in Standardization) confirmed this, by noting that industry remains concerned about the speed and number of defective product withdrawals.

Despite the existence of both essential requirements and standards, trade barriers remain. Some complaints relate specifically to the interpretation of the European standard, while other problems relate to broader social and environmental issues such as the restrictions on television advertising for children's products,[40] and recycling provisions that impose additional burdens on exporters.[41] Several complaints have been raised against the controversial Toubon Law, for example, which requires that packages containing toys be relabelled with a description in French before sale on the French market.

Many remaining obstacles are non-regulatory in nature, reflecting business preferences. Several companies noted that German retailers require additional tests beyond the simple acceptance of the CE mark, and do not accept mutual recognition of essential requirements. For many firms, the biggest obstacles are not in complying with the European standards but in getting acceptance of testing and certification across borders. Several companies complained about delays in accepting their certificates, differences between testing bodies, and insistence on having the product tested in the country of export, since this adds additional cost to the manufacturer.

The impact on corporate strategy also varies. Many large companies indicated that they produced products for the entire European market. For larger manufacturers, brand reputation and quality image are paramount, and the toy directive did not have an immediate impact on their production or corporate strategies.[42] Smaller firms view the situation differently.[43] In many cases, they have invested in improving their plant operations to comply with the directive, and have found compliance with testing and product approval procedures more expensive than in the past. Most companies prefer to test their own product to European standards, rather than seek independent approval. Hence, the availability of European standards is crucial.

Case 2: the machinery directive

In July 1986, the Commission presented its first working paper on co-ordinating machine regulations across Europe. At the beginning of the 1980s, many of the existing machine safety regulations in European states had their origins in regulations written some 150 years before, in the early years of the Industrial Revolution.[44] These regulations were often drafted in a very prescriptive way and tended to deal with specific safety hazards, according to the social and political pressures of the time. This approach proved inflexible in accommodating modern integrated machinery, with its increasing complexity of risk factors. Since it was estimated that the required directive would have to cover over 40,000 different types of machine products, tackling the widespread differences in safety, risk, and technological practices in the machine sector was considered one of the most challenging areas for regulatory coordination.

Trends in production and trade

Given the size of the machine market and its technological importance for many European industries, the machine directive was considered one of the most important New Approach directives. Although estimates of the effects of removing barriers to trade varied, the machine sector constituted about 47 per cent of intra-EC trade throughout the 1980s. In its preparatory drafts, the Community estimated that about half of engineering production fell within the scope of the machinery directive.

The interests of thousands of small and medium companies that supply the European machine market and of a handful of multinational firms, such as IBM, Siemens, and Nixdorf, that supply firms with the computers that control the machinery were at stake.

The continued vitality of the European machine tool industry, in the face of intense competition from Japan and the United States, indicated that, despite existing trade distortions, the industry enjoyed buoyant economic conditions with a strong and dynamic regional demand. The state of the machine tool sector is closely tied to the general condition of manufacturing industry. As machine tools are capital goods used by other manufacturing industries, they are subject to the fluctuating demands stemming from cycles of investment.[45] After a deep recession in the 1980s, worldwide demand increased, with an upsurge in investment throughout the 1990s. This masks, however, the different competitive positions of the national machine tool industries, as the British share of machine exports has fallen dramatically and Germany has been able to maintain at least a third of world exports.[46]

The machine tool sector is concentrated in five member states: Germany, Italy, Britain, France, and Spain, which account collectively for 97 per cent of EC production. Half of the output is generated in Germany. The industry is extremely fragmented, with approximately 1,400 small and medium firms, most of which employ less than fifty employees. Italy and France have a particularly high concentration of small firms, although both Italy and Germany also have a higher concentration of larger companies.[47] Many of these companies tend to be private or family owned, and have been more resistant to European efforts to standardize products than larger specialist companies having greater resources and investment, and more likely to benefit from reduced unit costs with increased standardization.[48]

Product harmonization in the machine sector is subject to tremendous product differentiation.[49] The introduction of computer technology and numerical control in the 1980s has transformed the sector. Demand for conventional machine tools is declining, as many firms have turned to the new technologies to increase flexibility and multiple product options. The focus on niche markets and customized machine tools has meant that companies are concerned about the effects of standardization upon product variety and differentiation. The machine tool sector is represented by CECIMO (Comité Européen de Cooperation des Industries de la Machine Outile) in Brussels, although a variety of national trade and European trade associations, such as the European Committee of Woodworking Machinery Manufacturers (EUMABOIS), represent specific segments of the industry. Industries that had conveyed opinions to the trade associations about barriers to trade have long underscored problems with respect to different standards, testing, and certification requirements, as well as export restrictions and licences.[50]

Legislative history

The Commission has sought to address barriers to trade in the machine sector since the 1960s. Some success had been achieved, with legislation passed in 1971 on noise levels for specific industrial machines, and in 1975 on harmonizing lifting and mechanical machinery.[51] This was followed by efforts to deal with trade impediments created by differences in the agricultural and mobile machine sector,[52] largely in response to complaints that French firms were imposing unnecessary restrictions via standards that provided domestic manufacturers with an unfair advantage.[53]

Further progress in the machine sector was extremely slow, with negotiations on specific products often lasting many years. For example, discussions over fork-lift trucks dragged on for ten years because the British government would not approve the directive until all the technical annexes and appendices had been discussed. Because the Community initially chose optional harmonization rather than adopting uniform European standards, machine products manufactured to local standards could continue to be sold on domestic markets, which in effect continued to insulate many markets from competition. Many of these old approach directives were extremely narrow in scope, extraordinarily detailed, and had to be constantly updated to adapt to technological progress.

Until the mid-1980s, the establishment of European-wide regulations for the machine sector had a relatively low political profile. The decision to apply the New Approach to the machine sector shifted attention from negotiating over technical details to that of basic safety requirements. Machine standards were politically sensitive because machine safety laws were usually the concern of labour and social affairs ministries, who were reluctant to lose their policy role if the issue was redefined as an internal market issue.

In preparing their proposal, the Commission's internal market directorate general (DG III) recognized this sensitivity, and invited representatives and experts to four preparatory meetings between 1985 and 1987. Among those participating in the preliminary discussions were the European Machine Tool Association (CECIMO), Orgalime, the European Trade Union Federation (ETUC), the European Standards bodies, CEN and CENELEC, and the EC's Advisory Committee on Safety, Hygiene, and Health at work.[54]

The machine directive was also viewed as extremely important by many in the Commission because it represented part of the social dimension of the single market. In particular, the machine directive was considered one of the driving forces to prevent states from pushing for a reduced regulatory burden in response to pressures from states with more lax standards. The Commission proposal included technical annexes with innovative risk assessment proposals, drafted by a British Labour Inspector who had been unable to promote the same proposals at the national level.[55] The issue was important enough for the Commission to convene two discussion meetings in November 1987.[56]

It was clear from the start that the scope of the proposed directive satisfied no one, since it remained incomplete. Though the draft proposal stated that machines should be designed safely, it did not outline the conditions under which machines should be operated or used for safety purposes. This shortcoming enabled France to argue before the European Court of Justice in the 'woodworking case' detailed in Chapter 5 that it could continue to impose restrictive national safety standards since national equivalence of health and safety objectives were not guaranteed.[57] The ECJ agreed, noting that, in the absence of common European standards, a member state could insist on imposing its national safety rules, and thus restrict the importation of machines, if there were legitimate safety concerns.

Faced with this decision, the European Commission Directorate General for Social Affairs (DG V) began work on five related proposals: workers safety, use of machines in factories, protective equipment, exposure to visual display units, and protection of workers against back injuries.[58] Companies protested that the machine directive was now reverting back to the old approach by imposing increased regulatory requirements, while trade unions lobbied strongly for the maintenance of worker protection. During several long meetings in late 1985 between the Commission, the European Trade Union Federation, and CECIMO and Orgalime, the two trade associations representing the machine industry, the trade union strongly promoted workers health and safety issues and found a sympathetic audience in DG V. This discussion crystallized into a revealing power struggle between departments within the Commission, manufacturers, and trade unions—even before the proposal was forwarded to the national level. Inadequate policy coordination between DG III, with its focus on the internal market, and DG V, with its focus on health and safety issues, was rooted in the very different aims and views of the Commissioners in charge of each policy area.[59] DG III

Commissioner Lord Cockfield had a reputation as a tough crusader for free trade. Manuel Marin, the Spanish Socialist Commissioner in charge of social affairs, viewed the issue very differently. Rather than cooperate, the two directorates duplicated each other's work and appealed to different constituencies to support their views. The sensitivity of the issue was highlighted when DG III took the unusual step of sending out drafts to all the member states before putting the issue on the table for a full meeting of the Commission. This effort to pre-empt the debate forced Commission President Delors to attempt to broker agreement on the issue during two discussions in November 1987.

Marin refused to yield, and blocked any further discussion on the machinery proposal until DG V had finished its own proposal on worker safety. The draft proposals were then passed on to the working groups within the Council to iron out the disagreements. Germany, holder of the EU presidency at the time, was forced to abandon further discussions on the machinery proposal because of internal disputes within its own national ministries. Although the German Federal Ministry of Labour and Social Affairs took the lead on the machinery directive, discussions took place in the Internal Market Council where the Federal Ministry of Economics participated. The two German ministries strongly disagreed on the directive. The Labour Ministry wanted the safety requirements in the proposal to be mandatory, while the Economics Ministry was far more concerned about the effects on trade liberalization. Though the Labour Ministry supported the broad scope of the directive, they were opposed by German trade unions, occupational injury insurance companies, and testing and certification agencies, who all wanted assurances that the proposed machine law would not undermine German regulations.

Pressured by these domestic interests, the Labour Ministry insisted on participating in the Council working groups dealing with the machine directive. This did little to resolve the internal conflicts. By March 1988, new disagreements emerged within the working group between the German and Danish government and the British government over testing and certification issues. Both Germany and Denmark wanted national authorities to issue safety certificates for machines, while the British government felt that manufacturers could self-certify their products in accordance with the regulatory requirements. Germany further opposed any efforts to continue to accept each other's national standards until European standards where available. Though not opposed to efforts to remove the obstacles to trade in machinery, Germany voted against the proposals put forward. As the largest machinery manufacture in Europe, Germany stood to gain from market liberalization. Yet it refused to accept the proposal, which was viewed as deficient in protecting German workers from unreliable imported machines. This negative vote was largely a political gesture to the Labour Ministry and its constituents since it was clear that a majority within the Council would override German opposition.[60]

Germany's opposition to the proposal also meant that it could maintain its higher standards during the transitional period in which European standards were not available.[61] Several other member states saw German objections as protecting German machine makers, who did not want to open the floodgates to cheaper imports. To address German concerns about quality, the British proposed the creation of a specialist committee to decide whether national standards were equivalent and acceptable. Though this was designed to alleviate some of the workload of the European standards bodies, British efforts to resolve the issue actually backfired as subsequent meetings of national officials raised further practical problems with the machine directive. Supported by British industry, British officials argued that the essential safety requirements were so restrictive that companies would not be able to innovate.

British firms complained that national authorities would have wide discretion to establish tougher safety rules within the interim period when European standards were not available. This position received little sympathy from Germany. The sharp disagreement between the two sides led officials in Bonn and London to continue to rewrite the directive in ways that did not match.[62] While this battle continued, the working group in DG V responsible for the five worker safety directives applicable to machine products had not even met. After a considerable delay, their draft proposals were given to the European Parliament and Economic and Social Committee for comment.[63] The Economic and Social Committee expressed concern about the lack of inclusion of certain machines in the directive. In response, the Commission proposed to modify its proposal to include woodworking machines. This was welcomed by the ESC, which judged the high protection level and innovative health and safety at work proposals positively.[64]

The European Parliament also welcomed efforts to remove barriers to trade in the machine sector. However, Socialist members voiced criticism about the haste in which the proposal had been drafted. In their view, European standardization ensured that companies were well represented, but did not provide the necessary guarantees that other social partners would have sufficient access. Although the European Parliament had appropriated money in the budget for trade union participation in standardization, opposition centred around the need for more opportunities for participation by social partners at all stages of the standard-setting process.[65] While this concern was accepted by the Commission, the Parliament was unable to persuade the Commission to impose more stringent testing and certification procedures upon firms.[66] After accepting some changes and modifying the proposal, the Commission submitted an amended machine directive to the industry ministers, where the proposal was agreed in a mammoth Council session in June 1989. The directive first entered into force in December 1992, with a transitional period of three years. Several amendments have since been made to the machine directive, which has been extended to include machinery for lifting people and to safety components sold separately.[67] To bring clarity to these and other amendments, the Commission proposed and the Parliament, Council, and Economic and Social Committee agreed in June 1998 that the directive should be consolidated to avoid any further confusion.[68]

Reactions and response

The machine directive generated considerable concern among different constituencies. Trade union groups were opposed to changes perceived as offering lower levels of protection, and also resented their loss of influence in domestic regulatory policy.[69] German unions were extremely vocal about their reduced role, as the Berufsgenossenschaften and the bipartite occupational injury insurance body would lose comprehensive regulatory powers. These concerns were coupled with complaints from many firms that the prescriptive nature of such outdated national regulations hampered the development of new modes of production. Orgalime, responding to feedback from its business constituency, also complained that the proposals emanating from DG V were unclear. Orgalime was concerned initially about whether worker safety was to be the responsibility of the machine tool makers or the employee operating the machinery. Some machine tool makers felt that the directive only added further confusion to the number of directives that they already complied with. The existence of the Low Voltage Directive, electromagnetic compatibility, and machine directive meant that some firms were required to ensure that they complied with all three in order to put their product on the market. This was not an easy issue to address, and subsequently drew complaints from CEN regarding the need for coordination among the various directives. Recognizing that the issue needed ironing out, CEN and CENELEC held a conference in 1996 to explain some of the overlap, and also to explain their efforts to simplify the approval process for firms.

In many cases, the complaints were about testing and certification changes. Many firms were faced with additional changes not only in standards but also in product approval practices, as in the past they had been able to comply with national safety standards through independent third party testing. While this was still an option in some cases, due to their hazardous nature the concept of mandatory testing for some classes of machinery was relatively new, and firms were concerned that the capacity and expertise to meet the new requirements would lag behind demand. Many companies reported that they had sought advice from national trade associations and national standards bodies to clarify legal aspects of the directive. This included the issue of second-hand machinery, a substantial part of the trade in machine products. The initial ambivalence and uncertainty over this issue—which was also raised by American trade negotiators—was finally resolved when it was included in the machine directive.

Setting machine standards

The machine directive covers over 50,000 different types of machines, with a wide range of mechanical engineering products obligated to meet the general essential requirements. Some classes of machinery have additional regulatory requirements—notably in the area of testing and certification—which reflect their particular hazardous nature.[70] Under European law, machines are 'an assembly of linked parts or components, at least one of which moves, with the appropriate actuators, control and power circuits, jointed together for a specific application, in particular for processing, treatment, moving or packaging of a material'. The term 'machinery' also covers an assembly of machines, arranged and controlled so that they function as an integrated whole.[71] This ensures that computer aided machinery (CAD) is also covered by the directive. All machines fitting this broad description are affected, with a few exceptions such as construction site hoists, firearms, and agricultural tractors.[72]

As with other New Approach directives, the machine directive is extremely broad, and lists hazards rather than classifying machines into types. Where those hazards exist, the machine manufacturer must take action to reduce or eliminate the risks. The machine directive is highly innovative since it makes the effective prevention of hazards obligatory. Instead of providing well-defined machine or workplace related risks, the directive was much more encompassing, since it acknowledged that the working environment has become more complex so that risks may occur in many different circumstances.[73] Flexible manufacturing systems, automation, and other technological innovations pose more hazards than the traditional single machine operation, leading traditional mechanistic approaches to safety to be viewed as increasingly inappropriate. This meant that the European standards bodies would have to come up with a work programme to meet the innovative essential requirements outlined in the directive. Although the European standard is a voluntary means of compliance, the language of the legislation means that the manufacturers must take account of technical development, placing a considerable burden on them that, in designing their machinery, they must take account of the current state of the art. Because the standards in this field are expected to be constantly changing as a result of economic and social developments and field experience, the European standards bodies must constantly review and modify their work.

Though it deals with a complex and rapidly changing sector, the machine directive is a remarkably simple regulation, emphasizing hazards, design, and operation of machinery. Most provisions are as general as they are brief. However, the most significant provisions require that the principle of safety be integrated into all aspects of the production process. The risk assessment philosophy, designed to include future technological developments, has led to concern within the machine industry that the directive is uncertain and ambiguous. Several firms have expressed concern about the product liability problems that could be raised due to the lack of specificity of the directive. Because industry tends to focus on setting standards to meet specific targets, firms involved in the development of European standards also feared that it would be impossible to ensure that their machinery was risk free.

CEN set up a programme committee to focus on 'safety of machines' in October 1986, but the standards bodies had already begun work on machine safety in 1985, at the same time that the Commission was developing its own directive. Both CEN and CENELEC were given mandates, with the latter responsible for electrical safety and safety of particular products such as household appliances. The sheer size of the task was reflected in the creation of some forty technical committees and 240 working groups involved in the programme.[74] Most of the technical committees were made up of a relatively small number of representatives, including firms, trade unions, and a number of health and safety institutes.[75] German firms dominated many of the machine committees, not unsurprising given the size and importance of the sector domestically. While British and French representatives also played a visible role, Italy as the second largest machine manufacturer in Europe was poorly represented, and Spain, Portugal, and Greece played even lower profiles.[76] Firms such as Siemens, Nokia, AEC, Norsk, Renault, Peugeot, Volvo, and ICI were actively involved, in part because they had the resources to be so.

Machine standards include both vertical standards covering the safety of specific machines (such as lasers, welding, portable hand tools, and woodworking machines) and horizontal standards covering basic safety principles focusing on risk assessment, safety devices, and information on a wide variety of safety issues such as ergonomics, noise, and control of dust and fumes in the workplace. The programme for machine standards sets out a hierarchy of standards: *A standards* provided the basic safety philosophy for all types of machines; *B1 standards* provided information for designer needs such as measurement of noise levels, safety distances, and surface temperatures; *B2 standards* were for safety-related devices that could be used across a wide range of machines such as interlocking devices, and two-handed controls; and *C standards* covered specific requirements for a particular machine type or group of machines.[77] The hierarchy sought to eliminate the need to reinvent the wheel for each set of standards, since basic safety concepts covered by A standards were given priority. This scheme had the additional advantage that, if no C standards existed, then firms could get most of their guidance and requirements from those developed earlier as A and B standards.

Agreement on basic safety standards proved easier than that of other specific product standards, largely because basic safety issues affected all companies and did not promote one companies technology over another. Beginning in 1991, three standards—EN 292, EN 1050, and EN 414—on basic concepts of safety of machinery had been adopted. Other standards were not adopted so quickly, forcing the Commission to postpone entry into force of the machine directive until 1995 and allow member states to continue to market machines that do not comply with the national standards in the importing country. With 700 standards still needed (150 A and B and the remainder C) a standards deficit clearly existed.[78] By mid-1998, some 78 had been completed, another 300 were at the inquiry stage, and the rest were in the initial development stage.[79] More recently, the CEN Annual Report indicates that as of June 1999, 221 standards were ratified, 342 under inquiry, and 137 further standards were needed to complete the overall programme.[80] While concern developed within the Community about the slow progress being achieved, the initial EN 292 safety standard had been transferred to the international level for consideration as a global standard. Consequently, European efforts in coordinating basic safety concepts produced a potentially valuable spillover effect beyond the Community market as other states adopted similar versions of the European standard. Attempts were made to export the B and C standards to the international level as well, in an effort to provide European firms with even greater market reach and a first-mover advantage in regulatory design.[81]

Impact and effectiveness

The Parliament reacted strongly to the backlog of European standard-ization in the machine sector. In informal meetings in 1991, members of the European Parliament had sought assurances that the Commission would not change the deadlines for implementation. They feared that in the absence of European standards, manufacturers could market machines that did not comply with the national standards in effect in the importing country, and a manufacturer using lower standards could continue to sell machines if the directive was postponed. In 1992 the Commission decided to seek postponement of the machine directive until 1995. The Parliament was outraged, and pointedly argued that the Commission was 'bowing to the forces of neo-protectionism' and that this reflected the 'dyed-in-the wool protectionist' tendencies re-emerging in the Commission.[82] In response to this criticism, European Commis-sioner Bangemann emphasized that the Commission's efforts had been trying 'through money and words of encouragement to get the stand-ards bodies to speed up their efforts'.[83] Unable to negotiate the technical agreements themselves, the Commission bore the brunt of the criticism for the slow pace of European standardization, even though they had hoped that shifting some of the regulatory burden elsewhere would ease trade liberalization efforts. Despite member criticisms, the Parliament did agree to extend the implementation deadline for machine safety, but this only increased the uncertainty of many firms in interpreting the EC essential requirements in their own production process.[84] Many larger companies such as Bosch and Black & Decker that had shifted produc-tion to low-cost assembly plants in Asia were aware that they would have to meet European standards, and saw developments in Europe in the context of their global market strategies.[85] For many companies in this sector, there was also the expectation that this would buffer them from competition, especially from cheap machinery that had flooded the market from China, since higher standards would mean that they could compete on quality rather than price.

Case 3: medical devices

In the early 1980s, the Commission began discussions as part of its effort to harmonize different national regulatory practices to allow for the free circulation of medical devices. Harmonization of electro-medical devices had resulted in the adoption of one directive in 1984.[86] Despite being a key economic sector, cross-border trade was hampered by the technical specifications and design of electromagnetic equipment, and by the administrative procedures for examinations, tests, inspections, and authorizations required for the marketing, use, and implantation of such products.[87] Because of the degree of risk posed by medical implants and devices, member states actively regulated such products to protect patients against potential risks.

Although national regulations often form part of the more general provisions applicable to medical equipment and pharmaceuticals, Commission surveys found that many problems stemmed from the rapid rate of innovation, which rendered many traditional regulations obsolete by the time they were adopted.[88] Part of the problem was the differences between national systems with regard to labelling, authorization, or registration procedures and production control which meant that approaches to ensuring patient safety also differed across national boundaries.[89] Some systems attach importance to the inspection of equipment before it is placed on the market through extensive product approval and certification procedures, while others allow firms to verify product safety through the use of good manufacturing practices (GMPs). Firms complained that conformity assessment also varied greatly: the German type approval, French *homologation*, Italian type-testing, and British Quality Assurance meant that associated costs and delays made cross-border trade difficult.

Although these national approaches are based on different concepts of safety,[90] the Commission felt that more coordination was needed, and proposed a series of directives to address barriers to trade and various safety aspects in the medical devices sector. The end result was three directives, the Medical Device Directive (MDD),[91] the Active Implantable Medical Device Directive (AIMD)[92], and the In Vitro Diagnostic Medical Devices Directive.[93] As with the first directive, the AIMD entered into force in June 1993, and allowed a transition period of two years for firms to make the necessary adjustments and meet European standards. Although narrow in scope, it provided the model on which the Commission built its later proposals. However, agreement on three separate directives should not belie the often heated political negotiations and extensive expert advice that surrounded their adoption, or the large number of standards that are necessary for the legislation to operate effectively. Nor should the adoption of the directives be separated from many of the public purchasing, reimbursements, and insurance practices in the medical and healthcare sector that continue to favour domestic producers over importers.[94]

Trends in production and trade

Estimates of worldwide production of medical devices indicate that the sector is growing in economic and technological importance. As of 1996, medical devices had an annual turnover of about 80 billion ECU ($90 billion).[95] Japan and the United States account for 18 per cent and 52 per cent of worldwide sales, respectively, while the EU accounts for 26 per cent of worldwide sales, with Germany being the largest producer in Europe. France, Italy, Britain, Belgium, and the Netherlands also have sizeable industries. Some 50 per cent of the EU market is supplied by the member state producers,[96] who employ about 240,000 people. Research is a critical factor in the performance of the sector, accounting for about 5 per cent of annual turnover.

An estimated 85,000 medical devices are available on the market.[97] In vitro devices account for about 16–18 per cent of the market, with EU member states accounting for a world market share of about 38 per cent, and an annual turnover of about 4.6 billion ECU.[98] This subsector comprises about 400 medium-sized firms, with research-based activity employing about 20 per cent of those in the medical devices field.

A range of European and national industrial federations and professional associations have a considerable interest in the medical devices legislation.[99] These include active European trade federations such as the European Diagnostic Manufacturers' Association (EDMA), European Confederation of Medical Suppliers' Association (EUCOMED), European Proprietary Medicines Manufacturers' Association (AEGSP), and the Coordination Committee of the Radiological and Electromedical Industries (COCIR) among others. A number of professional associations such as the EC Dental Liaison Committee and Pharmaceutical Group of the EC are also interested in the directive, although the Commission has been careful to point out the differences between the regulations for medical devices and medicinal products.[100]

In a survey commissioned by the Directorate General for the Internal Market, the Commission found that the sector was highly competitive with a great deal of emphasis on product innovation, niche markets, and cutting edge biomedical and technological research. The industry uses technologies from a variety of industries, and tends to be dominated by five multinationals (GE, Philips, Siemens, HP, and Toshiba).[101] It is also highly dependent on other industries for technology and raw materials, and tends to be sensitive to evaluation and performance by users (hospitals, researchers, patients). The growing number of start-up firms tend to depend on a single product line, and because of their limited financial resources and distribution networks are often merged or purchased by larger manufacturing companies.[102]

Legislative history

Although the Commission began working on electromedical devices in the early 1980s, it relied on existing international standards, which were accepted by CENELEC, as meeting the general safety requirements for all electromedical equipment.[103] Although the directive listed a number of devices that were covered, the new programme regulating medical devices was much more comprehensive, and reflected considerable preparatory work on harmonizing the marketing and use of medical equipment.[104] The Commission began by surveying the existing situation in the member states to find some common guidelines for action. Recognizing that there was enough support for some form of regulatory coordination, the Commission began with the collaboration of a wide range of experts, including representatives of CEN and CENELEC, manufacturers, government officials, users, trade associations, and professional groups to draft a number of working papers on the topic.

The Commission's first difficulty was in defining exactly what was meant by medical devices.[105] This caused some confusion amongst those participating, and the Commission found that it continually has to differentiate between medicinal products and medical devices.[106] Once some degree of agreement had been reached, the Commission began categorizing medical devices according to the level of risk, the nature of the device (active and non-active), and the type of industry to which they belonged. This was aimed at sorting out how to draft comprehensive essential safety requirements that covered all types of equipment and circumstances. The Commission initially sought to produce four directives on active implantable electromedical devices (such as pacemakers), active non-implantable medical devices (such as X-ray equipment), non-active medical devices (such as contact lenses), and in vitro diagnostics (such as laboratory instruments).[107] Although the Commission prepared two separate directives in 1990 on active and non-active medical devices, it then changed its approach and chose to draft a single comprehensive directive to reduce any potential problems of misunderstanding.[108]

The Commission's efforts were complicated by the number of directorates with an interest or stake in the issue. Although DG III (Internal Market) took the lead, the broad-ranging nature of the issue meant it had to be coordinated within the Commission. DG V (Social Policy) was involved because of public health and disability issues, DG XI (Environment, Nuclear Safety) because of radiation protection, DG XII (research and development) because of medical research, and DG XIII (General Telecommunication) due to telematics networks and resources applied to health issues. The Commission relied on two standing EU committees for drafting the proposal: the 83/189 Committee that served to coordinate all standards and technical issues and the Medical Devices Committee. While the standing committees sought to broker agreement among themselves regarding key provisions or amendments to the draft directives, many of the meetings involved negotiators from various ministries or departments of health, Commission officials, and national experts who often sought opinions from representatives from the major European trade associations. Representatives of DG III continued to brief other actors such as the Scientific Committee on Medicinal Products and Medical Devices (DG XXIV) on legislation concerning medical devices when scientific and technical questions arose.[109] Because of the complexity of the issue, the Commission, aided by expert groups, issued a number of non-binding documents known as MEDDEVs, seeking to clarify problems and uncertainties regarding the implementation of the medical device directives. Although MEDDEVs have no legal force, they represent a common understanding of necessary action regarding implementation as well as procedures for market surveillance and product recall.[110] They are written by and for all interested parties, and are not dissimilar to the Eurocodes in the construction products sector (see below).

In drafting proposals, the Commission followed a similar pattern in all three New Approach directives. The directives addressed legal definitions of medical devices, essential requirements, the role of standards, and conformity assessment procedures.[111] Each time, the Commission faced a number of ethical questions and concerns, as well as political pressure to strengthen the oversight mechanisms of national authorities in the wake of several much publicized crises such as the blood scandal in France and the BSE scare in Britain. Because 'medical devices' involves three directives, the legislative history of the latest one, in vitro diagnostics, is used here as a case study to illustrate the political dynamics surrounding its adoption.

Unlike other medical devices, in vitro devices are used outside the body for medical examination of samples taken from the patient. They are important for diagnosing illnesses, checking progress on a source of treatment, and other medical applications such as pregnancy tests, HIV, hepatitis, and glucose tests. Given the critical importance attached to reliability, performance, and precision of these devices, as well as the protection of public safety and health, the Commission proceeded cautiously, beginning with a survey in 1991 to compare and analyse member state legislation, and assess the different regulatory requirements. The Commission found that Britain, Spain, Italy, and the Netherlands have no legislation on in vitro devices, except for a few selected products. France had introduced new registration procedures to check on the performance of many of these medical devices, and Belgium was in the process of introducing more stringent legislation. In Germany, the devices were governed by stringent regulations, with additional monitoring and authorization procedures for some products.[112]

Due to different political strategies and conflicts, the directive took eight years of negotiation before adoption in December 1998. Having gone through several drafts starting in 1990, the rising concern over health and safety standards and consumer protection generated a tougher regulatory policy. At the heart of the controversy was the regulation of the use of human or animal tissue and derivatives in medical devices that had pitted the Council, Commission, and European Parliament against one another.[113] After four years of hearings and consultations, the Commission put forward its proposal in April 1995, and received opinions from the Economic and Social Committee in October 1995 and the European Parliament in March 1996.[114] While the ESC was generally positive about the draft proposal, there were some concerns about the product approval procedures covering a wide range of devices and different circumstances and conditions.[115] Because of the serious implications of inaccurate analyses, the Committee sought to monitor the market and protect the public interest by introducing a Medical Device Vigilance System, whereby manufacturers notify public authorities of any malfunctioning products.[116] The Parliament was much more critical and put forward fifty amendments to the original proposal. In addition to strengthening market surveillance, as the ESC suggested, the Parliament sought further clarification on the scope of medical devices. The Parliament proposed the inclusion of therapeutic or homoeopathic measures in the draft and, more controversially, expansion of the directive to include devices manufactured using human tissues. While accepting a substantial number of the amendments, the Commission was also conscious of potential divisions within the member states. Failure to agree on the use of human tissue delayed the adoption and consideration of the IVD directive further. The Commission subsequently chose not to address the Parliament demand on medical devices of human origin.[117]

The Commission's reluctance also reflected the divisions within the Council on a number of key issues related to the proposed directive. Although political agreement was reached by qualified majority, the French and Austrian delegations vigorously opposed the compromise package.[118] The French representatives drew attention to a number of health and safety aspects which they felt were not resolved by the draft directive, and asked for further debate on more stringent measures for those medical devices that posed a threat to human health.[119] The Council agreed to extend the scope of the medical device directive to cover certain products obtained from cells or tissues of human origin, so that the

Commission was able to notify the Parliament that it would now address one of its major concerns, though this would be done separately from the in vitro directive under current consideration. While the Council had reached agreement on three of the four main elements of the proposal, namely certification, market surveillance, and the structure of competent notified bodies that would exercise surveillance, the French wanted stricter public health provisions.[120] Their opposition enabled France to maintain mandatory testing for devices where human tissues were used in the testing procedures. The progress of the proposal was slowed down considerably by this issue, with the French position largely based on an AIDS-related blood scandal that put political pressure on many health officials and politicians in France to move slowly and ensure stringent precautions.[121] The Council finally approved a common position for the directive in March of 1998. Member states will have to enforce the new directive by June 2000, with a transition period until 2005.

Reactions and response

Although the Community had passed major pieces of legislation regulating medical devices, many small companies had taken no action as they do not regard their products as medical devices.[122] However, the European trade federations, EUCOMED, EDMA, COCIR, and EUROM, had been actively coordinating their activities and working on joint position papers which they circulated for discussion to both European and international regulatory authorities.[123] Their staffs also sought to publicize the forthcoming legislative developments through newsletters, conferences, and guides directed towards their membership. To address questions raised by implementation of the directives, the major trade associations also set up formal policy-setting forums to discuss questions related to health care, trade, and technical and regulatory issues under the rubric of the European Medical Devices Industry group. Because efforts to increase regulatory oversight from traditional self-regulation demonstrate the political will to raise standards (race to the top) in this area, companies have increased notification requirements for new products and design or product changes.

Furthermore, under the new medical vigilance system, companies must report any incidents to regulatory authorities (or similar notified bodies) in order to take corrective action for product recall or replacement. This raises the standards higher than the general product safety directive, and increases cross-national coordination and information exchange as well as ex-post regulatory oversight. Companies have expressed concern about the new implementation measures and the differences in accreditation and certification practices across the EU. The major disagreements centre on definitions of risk. The industry believes that the legislation is in place to regulate products whereas some notified bodies believe that the directive is broader and regulates practices as well.

In addition to the industry response, regulatory authorities had to institute changes to their surveillance systems. In some systems such as Britain, the directives required a shift from voluntary control to statutory control over the industry.[124] In others such as the Nordic Countries, ten years' experience of cooperation among competent regulatory authorities on medical devices created a network of confidence-building measures between users, manufactures, and health care providers that other member states were trying to emulate.[125] And in Germany and France with statutory control over industry, the regulation of medical devices has initiated less domestic change and adaptation. In the French case, the state has imposed its regulatory reach on accreditation, certification, and medical vigilance invoking a precautionary principle in the interest of public health, causing considerable anxiety among European and American industry about the administrative guidelines and approval process beyond that already in the IVD directive.[126] In Germany, both federal and land governments were involved with federal agencies and land authorities establishing accreditation of notified bodies, as well as an institute for notification and vigilance[127] that typifies the associative regulatory model characteristic of the German state.

The directive rejected the US Food and Drug Agency (FDA) approach as too rigid and resource intensive. Because fewer resources are devoted to pre-market approval of medical devices under the New Approach, many manufacturers have been in favour of the new legislation as European governments are able to approve advanced medical devices more than three times faster than the FDA. This has meant that many multinational firms are pursuing a Europe-first marketing strategy, despite the Food and Drug Modernization Act in 1997 that sought to allow some third party organizations to review regulatory requirements in the USA. Medical device manufacturers were also concerned that a harmonized regulatory system could result in additional health and safety reviews through national reimbursement systems. Several governments, including France, Sweden, and to a lesser extent Britain and Spain, have introduced government-funded technology assessment bodies, which adds another hurdle for firms to overcome as governments focus on cost-cutting measures to drive down prices. Because the EU directive focuses on safety and risk issues, it does not examine the cost-effectiveness of the product. Medical firms are anxious that national governments do not use cost containment measures and reimbursement systems to prevent new technologies from entering the market and shield domestic industries from foreign competition.

Setting standards for medical devices

All medical devices are now subject to mandatory European safety requirements aimed at protecting users and third parties against the risks posed by physical and chemical properties of the devices. While recognizing that manufacturers must perform a risk analysis, the directives recognized that there were different risks associated with various products, and outlined three different means by which medical devices had to conform: Class I were low risk medical devices; Class II were intermediate risk; and Class III were high-risk medical devices.[128] Manufacturing firms were now subject to traceability requirements ensuring that those firms stating that their product met European standards could be contacted and questioned about their production practices. The Medical Devices Vigilance System was outlined in guidelines published by the Commission, explaining its purposes, the types of incidents to be reported, and the procedures to be taken by public authorities. In many ways, the directives harnessed the resources outside the public sector in furtherance of public policy goals.

To meet the requirements of the directive, the European standards bodies, CEN and CENELEC, were given three standardization mandates for medical devices.[129] Although the two standards bodies had been working on the issue in anticipation of the mandate, the request was extremely ambitious, since medical devices covered a broad range of products, incorporating many different levels and technologies. To meet the requirements, negotiations between the Commission and European standards bodies resulted in three types of standards activity: (*a*) basic standards or 'horizontal standards' covering common requirements for a broad range of products; (*b*) Level 2 or 'family standards' covering related medical products; and (*c*) product standards for specific medical devices. The standards encompassed a range of issues from risk analysis, surgical implants, laser systems, contraceptive devices, to radiation safety.[130] Standard-setting involved a huge number of participants in over twenty technical committees and thirty-eight working groups. The mandate assumed that the work would be completed according to an ambitious timetable, with the horizontal and family standards targeted for adoption in July 1995, and the more individualized standards realized between July 1996 and July 1998.

Despite the two-year transition period for active implantable medical devices and three-year transition period for other medical devices, firms expressed concern over the lack of priority given to mandated European standards within the European standards bodies. Increasingly behind schedule, the standards programme for medical devices necessitated stop-gap measures and further transition periods so that firms could continue to use national standards until the European standards were available. Although about thirty standards had been published by mid-1996, a significant number of standards remained on the table. By mid-1998, EUCOMED estimated that the status of the CEN health care programme had resulted in 158 harmonized standards, with 32 agreed upon, and 316 non-harmonized standards still at the negotiating stage, with 133 agreed upon. The backlog was likely to continue with the adoption of the in vitro directive, although many firms felt that the groundwork had already been laid and many of the existing standards could also be applied to the newly adopted legislation. So far, three standards have been adopted, six are under inquiry, and ten remain in the early development stages for the IVD directive.[131] The active implantable devices directive is almost complete with thirty-two standards adopted, three under inquiry, and seven at the preliminary stages. There has clearly been a surge in standards in this area, although some blame the hold-ups on the relationship between CEN and CENELEC, as many standards cut across both bodies and required coordination between different committees.[132] Several trade associations expressed concern about the lack of European participation in international standards, fearing that new barriers would occur if the European standards were significantly different from international ones.

Impact and effectiveness

While many firms believed that the medical devices directives did reduce or eliminate regulatory barriers, many chose not to complain about continuing problems they faced, since many of the medical devices were purchased by governments directly or indirectly through national health care systems. Companies were concerned that reported problems would negatively impact their ability to bid for government contracts.[133] While proper implementation of the directives had been slow in many member states, legal action taken against Belgium for non-implementation of the AIMD directive provided the necessary signal to member states to act quickly.[134]

Other restrictions remained that hampered cross-border trade in the medical device sector. In particular, practices that fell outside the scope of the directive such as labelling requirements in Italy and France (in case the product contained human tissue) meant that firms incurred additional costs. Spanish requirements for medical device registration within thirty days of market placement constituted an additional and unnecessary requirement that the Commission addressed through infringement procedures. Other barriers relate to tender requirements and health care provisions, which reflect the problems still inherent in public procurement practices in most member states. Because medical devices are often purchased by hospitals and local health authorities, firms are required to bid for contracts. Complaints about practices in France, Britain, and Germany regarding the need to provide additional information are also viewed as contrary to the practice of mutual recognition and free trade.[135] This is in part due to the concern that certain notified bodies in Greece and Portugal, for example, are not sufficiently rigorous in their product approval.

Non-European manufacturers and trade associations have also been concerned that the European Commission is developing new performance specifications for certain products rather than relying on international standards. As a result, the impact of European standardization efforts in medical devices have gone beyond the single market. The Community has entered into negotiations concerning mutual recognition of conformity assessment or product approval practices with the United States, Canada, Switzerland, New Zealand, Australia, and Japan in a number of areas including medical devices.[136] In implementing confidence-building measures such as organizing seminars, and comparative evaluation of compliance practices between the EU and other states, the EU is hoping to expand its efforts at trade liberalization. In the USA, pressures to accept European testing and certification practices were initially resisted by the FDA.[137] However, new legislation to overhaul the way the FDA carries out checks on drugs and medical devices has followed the European pattern of using third party, private testing and certification bodies.[138]

Because medical devices have been oriented towards global markets for many years, there has also been pressure for international harmonization and a Global Harmonization Task Force was established in 1992.[139] Though the task force comprises representatives of regulatory authorities and industry in the triad countries of Japan, the USA, and Western Europe, the Commission has chaired the task force since 1992. The focus is on promoting greater regulatory convergence, and the task force closely follows the development of international and European standards related to medical devices.[140] In 1996, another task force began focusing on medical device vigilance, with many representatives from European industry associations actively involved.[141] Thus, European regulation of medical devices has become an importance reference point for international harmonization efforts.[142] With seven global medical devices conferences already held, the effort to promote regulatory convergence demonstrates considerable interest in the standardization strategies adopted as part of the single market programme.

Case 4: construction products

As one of the largest industrial sectors in the Community, the construction products industry was obviously an important target for trade liberalization. The Commission had suggested the inclusion of the 'construction plant and equipment' sector in the supplementary programme of 1973 to the General Programme of 1969. As discussed in Chapter 4, the General Programme was aimed at eliminating technical barriers to trade in industrial products. The issue was also brought to the Commission's attention by the Committee for European Construction Equipment, which highlighted the problems of regulating the building industry.[143] The variety of national safety tests reflected different national characteristics and traditions that often hindered cross-border trade. Differences in the provisions adopted on methods for testing, calculating, or classification, as well as marketing and control characteristics, created significant barriers to trade.

Faced with a 'hodgepodge of standards' that in some states meant safety applied to all buildings, while in others only to public buildings or just to hotels, the Commission proposed to harmonize the various national regulations in force.[144] Construction products also cut across other legislative areas, since construction site machinery and tools were often covered by regulations governing machinery.[145]

Trends in production and trade

When the Community first began addressing barriers to trade in the construction industry in the 1970s, the industry provided jobs for over 7 million employees. This represented about 18 per cent of total employment in manufacturing. The bulk of construction materials and products are used mainly in the building and civil engineering sector, with a large percentage used within Europe itself: 100 per cent of bricks, tiles, cement, and ceramic tiles; 70 per cent of the plate glass; 60 per cent of wood products; 25 per cent of plastics; and 10 per cent of aluminum.[146]

Construction and civil engineering accounted for 15 per cent of EU GDP and 60 per cent of gross capital formation in the late 1970s.[147] The sector is also crucial in producing investment goods, generating 58 per cent of gross fixed capital formation, and is one of the most important supply sectors to public purchasers in Europe. In 1996, works contracts represented almost 30 per cent of advertised opportunities across the EU. The value of cross-border trade is still relatively low compared to the total value of the construction market in Europe.[148]

By the late 1980s, the construction sector had expanded significantly, employing over 14 million people in over 1.8 million firms. Most companies were small, with fewer than twenty employees, and primarily active in regional markets. While construction products still accounted for 10 per cent of the EU's GDP, the Commission's efforts were designed to breathe life into an ailing building industry characterized by local markets, cyclical conditions, and substantial barriers to trade. An estimated 14 million workers in service enterprises, the public service, marketing, and in all manner of ancillary industries were indirectly dependent on the construction industry.

The Commission also thought that efforts to harmonize building codes and products would be a key factor in exporting to third countries. Given the contraction in demand in the Community as a result of cutbacks in public spending, the building industry was increasingly searching for contracts elsewhere. Because it faced strong competition from Japanese, Korean, and American firms, common regulations on building materials, as well as other issues such as technical standards, export credits, and public contracts, were a key factor in improving the competitiveness of European industry in third country markets.[149]

The situation was similar in the USA with its myriad building regulations, standards, and codes at the national, state, and local levels. If harmonization could be achieved in Europe, this would mean that the Community construction market would be more integrated than that of the USA.

Legislative history

The Commission began working on harmonizing construction standards in the early 1970s. After substantial input from various industry associations and experts, the Commission categorized the technical barriers into three types of existing national regulations: road traffic safety; safety at work; and protection of the environment from airborne noise. The Commission acknowledged that the negotiations would be difficult and that only 'by dint of considerable effort' would the deadlines laid down in the General Programme of 1973 for eliminating technical barriers be met.[150] The Commission was required to provide the Council with a general directive outlining the procedures to be followed in the construction sector, and then a special directive on permissible noise levels by January 1975.

The construction sector cut across several Commission directorates general, including DG III (Internal Market) and DG XI (Environment). Noise levels for construction products were deal with by DG XI, based on the Community programme of action on the environment of 1973. Because environmental concerns were also increasing in importance at the domestic level, the Commission faced the additional problem that many states were beginning to legislate on permissible sound levels, raising the prospect of additional barriers to market entry. In February 1974, for example, the French government notified the Commission of draft legislation on permissible sound levels for construction equipment such as pneumatic drills. Five months later, the German government also notified the Commission of its own legislative efforts to limit the noise levels of pneumatic drills.[151]

In the face of these national regulations, the Commission found it difficult to press on with its own programme in the construction sector. It finally proposed a general framework for harmonizing the laws, regulations, and administrative provisions for construction products in November 1978. The proposals drew on past experience with harmonization in other sectors, and took the view that it would be inappropriate to try to harmonize all products on a systematic basis.[152] The Commission instead drew up a list of products requiring urgent action, giving priority to those products where the advantages of liberalization were greatest. These included ceramic tiles, concrete walls, thermal insulation material, plywood, sewage systems, and cement, indicating that the directive covered structural products, timber products, plastic and synthetic products, and products to equip buildings. By drawing up such a framework directive the Commission hoped to simplify harmonization procedures, which also reflected the views of the European Parliament and some member states.[153] This required that the Council transfer competence to the Commission for subsequent implementing of the construction products legislation under Article 155. Without waiting for approval of the framework directive, the Commission had begun working on standards for certain products including cement, glass, ceramics, and fire resistance for building materials.

After a year of discussions, and taking into account the opinions of the European Parliament and ESC, which sought further clarification on implementation procedures, the Commission made several amendments to the construction products directive.[154] This proposal encountered further political problems, as several member states were unwilling to delegate authority to the Commission to issue specific directives as part of the general framework directive.[155] The Commission complained that 'if the Council still cannot bring itself to delegate to a large extent the technical details of a matter such as the harmonization of building materials, it would be proving that the Community is unable to make any real and prompt contributions to the solution of economic problems.' [156]

In addressing specific questions from the Parliament regarding backlogs in tackling specific barriers, the Commission noted that 'a Community in which ten foreign ministers tried to adopt specific directives on nail plates personally would reap public ridicule and deprive the Commission of a part of its executive function, and moreover be announcing the bankruptcy of the necessary technical harmonization measures.'[157] The Council nevertheless continued to deny the Commission greater discretion, with disagreement centring on whether the proposed Committee for Implementing Directives should adopt a specific construction products directive by majority vote or unanimity. Italy, Belgium, and Britain were against a majority vote, and the latter generally opposed the idea of delegation and extensive harmonization .

The impasse over delegation left the Commission unable to promote European standards or 'Eurocodes' for the construction industry.[158] The Eurocodes were designed to replace the various rules in force in member states. Commissioner Davignon was extremely critical of the construction industry for not placing enough pressure on member states to pursue harmonization of construction techniques, and for showing insufficient interest in the preparation of Eurocodes.[159] In a speech to the International European Construction Federation in 1980, Davignon questioned whether the industry actually wanted common codes for buildings and common standards for building products.

Unable to move forward quickly, the Commission began the slow process of regulating on a piecemeal basis, focusing first on noise levels for construction machinery, and emphasizing environmental rather than internal market objectives in this sector. As part of the framework directive for construction products, the construction machinery directives covered such machines as hydraulic machinery, shovels, diggers, and loaders.[160] Although referencing the directive on construction products and equipment, first proposed in 1974 but not yet adopted, the Commission was now taking an alternative tack. The effort to reach acceptable limits on noise levels within the context of protection of the environment followed a similar pattern, with the general machine directive taking account of state of the art technology and the need for industrial adaptation.[161] Though some disagreement arose between the Economic and Monetary Affairs Committee and the Committee on the Environment, Public Health, and Consumer Protection within the Parliament, the directive on construction machinery quickly moved forward. Fifteen directives were adopted during a mammoth 1984 Council session, including six covering construction plants and equipment, as well as more specific directives on noise levels for a host of construction-related products.[162] The Commission also reached agreement on four Eurocodes aimed at providing a basis for common rules, and promoting a degree of harmonization in the construction products sector.[163] These had been drafted between 1978 and 1983 by the Commission's coordinating group on Construction and Engineering, aided by work that was being done in the international and national standards bodies.[164]

Because progress on developing standards or Eurocodes was extremely slow, the Commission signalled that it would include construction products as part of the New Approach. In many ways, the framework directive was well suited to this more flexible regulatory approach. During the negotiations leading to the construction products directive, however, national delegates involved in the Standing Committee on Construction Products were unable to reach agreement.[165] This led to the drafting of six interpretive documents outlining certain technical criteria and specifications for construction products. In many ways, this made construction products unique among the New Approach directives. Instead of establishing essential requirements to be applied to construction products, the directive applied not to construction products *per se*, but to the final product of the construction action, i.e. the work as a whole. This came under substantial criticism from many in the construction industry who felt that 'totally comprehensive rules to cover as subjective a process as judgment are not practical'.[166]

The national representatives were unable to draft the specifications themselves, and were obligated to coordinate their work with standardization experts. Because the European standards bodies were obligated to wait for these interpretive documents, the mandate given to CEN and CENELEC was more circumscribed and problematic than in other sectors. Dependent on this work first being carried out within the Commission, the European standards bodies were thus hampered in starting negotiations on harmonized standards. When the construction products directive was finally adopted in 1989, the relationship between regulatory goals and the necessary standards was still murky. In 1993, the Commission and CEN signed mandates requesting 205 standards for the construction products directive to come into full operation. A

revised mandate given to CEN in 1995 contained only a few construction product requests. Mandates for forty product families of construction products were finally given to CEN in 1997, with five other
mandates given to CEN and the European Organization for Technical
Approval, which is responsible for standards for innovative products.
Any construction product meeting the requirements of a harmonized
European standard or a European Technical Approval (ETA) can now
circulate freely.[167]

Reaction and response

Although the construction products directive is more than ten years old,
many in the construction products industry have complained that there
is still not a single construction product with the CE mark available
on the market.[168] Opinion is divided across the industry on the strategic
importance of harmonization of construction products regulations. As
much of the construction industry is concerned with local markets, many
small and medium firms feel that efforts to create common standards
and certification practices are unnecessary. Given uncertainty about the
effects of such regulatory changes on both products and construction
processes, the directive has been subject to a great deal of criticism from
the European Construction Industry Federation (FIEC).

Problems with the construction products directive have been
attributed to the fact that the original directive was designed to facilitate free circulation for a host of products that are never sold across
national borders.[169] Firms have also complained that the essential
requirements of the directive have been interpreted so broadly that they
go beyond the health and safety objectives which comprise the basic
principles of the New Approach. Because the construction products directive embraces a larger number of products than originally anticipated,
the size and complexity of the number of standards necessary has
increased the burden on the European standards bodies.

Member states have shown little enthusiasm in recognizing the regulations of other member states as equivalent. As a result, almost all
construction products and processes have necessitated some form of
harmonization. In a number of cases, FIEC has protested the need for
certain mandates on the grounds that no barriers exist inhibiting the
sale of certain products (e.g. concrete), and that the end result would
actually raise construction costs. Differences in national practices and
traditions regarding health and safety objectives has meant that the
construction products directive has been the subject of repeated objections by member states.[170] This has also contributed to the slow pace at

which standardization mandates have been given to CEN and the European Organization for Technical Approval. Industry has also complained about the certification process, arguing that its reliance on existing international or European quality management systems is unnecessarily repetitive and bureaucratic, and that more attention needs to be paid to the integration of quality and environment standards and certification practices.[171]

Setting standards for construction products

The directive on construction products covers any product produced with a view to its incorporation in a permanent manner in construction works.[172] Products may only be placed on the market if they are fit for their intended use. Works in which construction products are incorporated must satisfy the essential requirements with regard to mechanical strength and stability, fire safety, hygiene, health and the environment, safety in use, protection against noise, and energy-saving features. Contrary to other New Approach directives, the essential requirements do not focus on construction products *per se* but on the final product or works as a whole.[173] To meet these requirements, the directive outlined the need for interpretive documents to link the legal provisions with the necessary standards.[174] These were expected to be published in 1991 and the delay in publication until 1994 hampered implementation of the directive. The extent and complexity of the interpretive documents is a matter of concern for those involved in standardization.

Construction firms were expected to meet certain standards, mainly through self-certification, unless the products were required to meet more stringent building codes which entailed independent verification in order to assess and monitor production. Although the European standards bodies complained that they had not been initially consulted early on in the process regarding the relationship between the interpretive guidelines and standards, the standards bodies began working on a massive programme of standards for construction after the directive was adopted. Both CEN and the European Organization for Technical Approval were expected to receive about forty mandates for approximately 1,500 performance-related standards in the construction area. Due to considerable delays within the Standing Committee on Construction within the European Commission, few mandates have actually been given, and much of the work has actually proceeded on the basis of provisional mandates. Although there are currently forty-three committees working on construction-related products, with the bulk of the secretariats held by the British, French, German, and Italian standards bodies, the work so far has focused on fire safety, heat-insulating products, windows, doors, and related building hardware.[175]

Many member states were unwilling to agree on standardization mandates without the inclusion of significant elements of their national regulations. Consequently, drawing up a contractual agreement with the European standards bodies took much longer than would have been the case if the Commission had chosen to adopt individual directives for different groups of construction products.[176] Usually New Approach standardization mandates referred to nothing other than essential requirements. The construction products directive seemed to be creeping back towards the old approach, as legislation was premissed on the assumption that particular construction products (such as doors, cement, fibreboard) had already been harmonized, and assumed a common approach to risk assessment, scientific testing methods, and other factors. It was taken for granted that much of the activity of the European standards bodies would be to establish specification for: (i) mechanical resistance and stability; (ii) safety in case of fire; (iii) hygiene, health, and the environment; (iv) safety in use; (v) protection against noise; and (vi) energy economy and heat retention outlined in the interpretive documents.[177] This has proved more difficult than anticipated as the European Commission, aided by technical committees on construction products composed of representatives from the member states, has continued to add detailed regulatory requirements to the standards mandates. This has delayed the implementation of the directive considerably as those involved in drawing up the interpretive documents and mandates for standardization proposed listing 'desirable' characteristics for products rather than strictly necessary ones.[178] Member states had thus gone beyond what was strictly necessary, and in doing so delayed the process of implementation.

Impact and effectiveness

At the beginning of 1994, the Atkins Consultancy Group stressed the importance of the building sector for European competitiveness. In their view, 'there is a danger of failing to grasp the opportunities and allowing the markets in Europe and the quality of construction to decline. There is still much to be done to make the industry stronger and to remove some of the weaknesses and to improve the environment in Europe.'[179] The Commission found this a very difficult challenge to meet.

Under Article 23 of the construction products directive, the Commission was required to report on the operation of the legislation at the end of 1993, and submit amendments where necessary. The mandate for construction products had promoted a veritable frenzy of standard-making.[180] Construction products alone required no fewer than 2,000 standards. Some of those involved feared that the scale of the work required was leading to a decline in the quality of standards being written. Of particular concern was the fact that the construction products directive attracted far more criticism than any of the other New Approach directives. The Molitor Group, established to deal with administrative and legislative simplification, criticized the legislation for construction products on the grounds that the drafting of mandates for harmonized standards had taken too long and slowed the progress of European standardization. More importantly, the directive did not allow firms to meet standards for individual products but instead required them to meet European standards for entire construction projects, leaving many companies unsure about compliance. Though firms could opt for European technical approvals and recognized national technical specifications while waiting for European standards, this has only served to increase confusion about the relationship between standards and regulations. In a sharp critique of this policy, the Molitor Group concluded that the New Approach did not work in the construction products sector, and needed further simplification. However, industry was opposed to any further changes in the construction products directive, fearing that this would prejudice progress already made.[181]

The Commission's own 1996 report on the construction products directive argued that the process was slow because the scope of the directive was very broad, and the technical aspects were not perceived in the same way by member states. The report also emphasized progress that had been made, while recognizing that another five years would pass before European standards were ready for most products.[182] After consulting with member states and the European standards bodies about the perceived difficulties, the Commission proposed a number of reforms including more mutual recognition of product testing and revised drafting of mandates to ensure greater flexibility. Acknowledging that the construction products legislation was not as effective as it should be, the Commission placed substantial blame upon the member states for drawing up detailed implementation rules, and the standards bodies for not putting in place a long-term programme to develop harmonized standards.

Despite being in force for several years, the construction products directive remains one of the most problematic in terms of implementation and effectiveness. With a backlog of needed standards, the Commission proposed to include construction products as part of its simplifying measures related to the single market initiative (SLIM).[183] Relying on national representatives, and users of the legislation (notably firms and consumers), the Commission included construction products in the first phase of SLIM, and later extended this to include another problematic New Approach directive, electromagnetic compatibility. These steps mirror American company complaints that the EU needs 'to simplify, simplify' as its standardization objectives have proven difficult to attain and led to increased uncertainty among many firms wanting to export to Europe.[184] This view was echoed by the European Parliament in a critical 1997 report, which stated that the Parliament 'does not share the Commission's opinion that the results so far achieved have been "positive"'. The Parliament also noted that the Commission waited for five years before considering the problem, 'which leaves a great deal to be desired'.[185] The report found that by mid-1997, eight years after the directive was adopted, standardization mandates had been drawn up for only seventeen product families (of at least forty) for requirements relating to safety in case of fire, hygiene, health and the environment, safety in use, protection against noise, energy economy, heat retention, mechanical resistance, and stability. However, the Parliament concurred with both the Commission and the standards bodies that the delay was primarily due to the member states' obstructive policy in the Standing Committee on Construction, and their unwillingness to put national provisions to the test.[186]

The common thread: overcoming coordination problems and negotiating agreement

The four case studies broadly illustrate the conditions under which standardization may be successful. Collective action problems are endemic to international politics. However, the evolution of cooperation is a fragile mechanism. Although standards institutions rather than the market can provide focal points for agreement, the institutional context has produced varying degrees of success in the four cases. Despite significant legislative progress in a number of areas, the standardization process did not match the Commission's expectations. Under pressure to meet deadlines for the single market programme, the Commission began to push for regulatory reform. The Commission feared that problems or deadlocks in agreeing on a single standard made it much more difficult to realize the economic benefits of market integration, and that the investment, production, and technological benefits related to the single market would not materialize.

These economic expectations and political interests were out of sync with the technical work of standardization. The result was an unproductive interchange between the Commission and the standards bodies over regulatory strategies and objectives, culminating in a push for significant reform of the European standards bodies throughout the 1990s. The regulatory reform efforts and the problems that this revealed with the Commission's choice of regulatory strategy to meet the demands for market integration are discussed in more detail in the next chapter. Market-building has become extraordinarily contested, as efforts to shift the blame for the non-completion of the single market reflected the political pressures facing all the actors involved.

The cases in this chapter illustrate the complex interplay of interests that make agreement on tackling trade barriers difficult to achieve. Based on an interrelationship of institutions, processes, and actors, the standard-setting process is also extraordinarily difficult to assess.[187] As Antonelli concludes, each standard is by no means the best possible solution from a given set of alternatives, but rather reflects the complexity of the environment and the behaviour of players to decipher and order the environment to produce some form of coordination.[188] The outcome of the standardization process depends partly on the pay-off structure but also on the organizational dynamics, norms, and synergies within the standards bodies. The case studies in this chapter have shown that when multiple interests are involved, coordinating costs rise and the free-rider problem can be significant.[189] Recognizing that by the time the committee is convened, participants often have vested interests that may be incompatible or well entrenched, committees, like markets, may also be imperfect coordinating mechanisms.[190] Despite efforts to promote trade liberalization by delegating to private standards bodies, the shift in regulatory strategy did not fully achieve the required policy outcomes.

Market Management:
Assessing and Evaluating the Standards Process

Facing the challenges of governing the market, the European Union was forced to confront not only the design of legislation but also its implementation and evaluation.[1] Not all of the difficulties involved in standardization were anticipated at the design stage of legislation, and the European institutions were forced to move forward with initiatives ranging from increased consultation to legislative simplification in an attempt to meet the political challenges and commitments of the single market. An effective regulatory regime meant that the issue of standardization was now front and central in the minds of policy-makers concerned about the efficiency and efficacy of the single market.

This chapter focuses on the internal politicking that surrounded standardization. It starts by examining the efforts to promote regulatory reform of the standards bodies, and the critical reactions to such proposals. By looking at the problems encountered with the regulatory strategy, we can see them as part of the broader set of initiatives dealt with later on in the chapter about the functioning of the single market, triggered by a critical rethinking of European regulation by a host of interest groups and member governments in the wake of the Maastricht Treaty.

The standards debate

Faced with a challenge in meeting legal deadlines, the Commission chose to make public its concerns about the slow pace of standardization,[2] issuing a consultative Green Paper on *Development of European Standards* in October 1990[3] and soliciting comments from the general public. Though 'Green Papers' and 'White Papers' are often used as a means of consultation to stimulate debate, the Green Paper on standardization produced more than 300 submissions, mostly from businesses and trade federations, with national and international standards bodies, consumers, and trade unions also offering their opinions. Not surprisingly, the national, European, and international standards bodies were upset by the nature and tone of the Green Paper that attributed the blame for poor performance in meeting regulatory objectives largely to them.

This dispute continued throughout the 1990s, as the Commission followed up with a number of memos, internal documents, and meetings with the European standards bodies to rectify what it perceived to be as problems with the design, operation, and structure of European standardization. However, the Commission chose to push ideas and promote suggestions to improve the efficiency, accountability, and transparency of the standardization process, largely avoiding an evaluation of the efficacy of its own policies.[4] Much of the evaluation done by the Commission focused initially on financial-budgetary concerns and political deadlines, and sought to treat the problem as one emanating from the lack of political will and administrative capacity on the part of the European standards bodies. The tendency to ignore the Commission's own management problems and implementation failures, in part because the costs of regulatory policies are borne by both member states and firms, meant that questions about improving overall regulatory performance were not initially addressed.

As the standards bodies were quasi-private or semi-private institutions, which they consistently stressed, they were not always pleased with interference in their internal operations. Nonetheless, the Commission sought a number of ex-post and ex-ante measures to 'stack the deck' and mitigate the effects of delegation. These include the oversight mechanisms, rewards and sanctions, and administrative procedures discussed below. While these mechanisms are aimed at ensuring regulatory compliance with stated goals, and to prevent what the administrative theorists discussed in Chapter 2 define as agency slippage and shirking, they are not without cost. The overall effect was strained relations between Commission and standards bodies, despite appearances that the public and private sector were working well together.[5]

The reform debate in Europe provided an interesting parallel to developments in the USA, where efforts to reform standardization along the lines of the more centralized European model were based on perceptions of a close relationship between national and European public and private agencies.[6] While these reform proposals toward a more state-oriented approach were controversial within the American business community, and were ultimately rejected in favour of a market-oriented approach, developments within the European regulatory regime suggested that the relationship in Europe was much less harmonious than the Americans perceived. Achieving its regulatory objectives was proving to be more difficult than the Community had envisaged when it shifted regulatory strategy in the mid-1980s. This had significant political effects, as many deadlines for implementation were missed or postponed. As detailed in Chapter 10, the problem is not simply the institutional development and administrative reform of European policy-making, but also the impact on firm policies and strategies. Uncertainty in the market can undermine any benefits generated from reconciling regulation and free trade.

The Green Paper on standardization

The Commission's Green Paper on the *Development of European Standards: Action for Faster Technological Integration in Europe*, sparked a major debate on the goals and institutional arrangements surrounding standardization in Europe. It had been preceded in 1989 by an internal memorandum from the Commission, also distributed to some national standards bodies. The memorandum laid out some of the reappearing concerns on the Commission's agenda: effectiveness, transparency, and accountability.[7] Not entirely satisfied with the current system of European standardization, the memo forcefully pointed to the political as well as technical importance of the task at hand. The Commission was anxious to draw attention to the need for better coordination, transparency, and planning to enhance the coherence and legitimacy of the existing structures.[8] The proposals reiterated the Commission's threat that, if the European standards bodies were not up to the task at hand, the Commission could always create a new standards body. The Commission had inter-institutional support for this option, as a European Parliament resolution of October 1980 urged the Commission and Council to consider the desirability of setting up a 'Community standards institution'.[9]

The Commission Green Paper raised concerns about the lag in European standards to meet the demands of the single market programme, and offered a number of suggestions to improve the standard-setting process in Europe. The Commission acknowledged that it had three explicit purposes in drafting the Green Paper. First, to draw the attention of producers and users of industrial products, in both the public and private sectors to the strategic significance of standards for the single market. Second, to accelerate the delivery of European standards. Third, to generate debate about producing a satisfactory regulatory framework to promote stability and increased dynamism within European standardization.

The Commission went on to argue that 'the distance between today's great achievements and tomorrow's goal is still great'.[10] And the lag between need and output reflected, in part, a lack of 'flexibility' on the part of CEN and CENELEC. Specifically, the Commission criticized CEN and CENELEC for:

- excessive concern with reaching consensus in the adoption of standards; despite provisions for the adoption of weighted majority voting, it was infrequently used and considerable delays and gridlock were common;
- infrequent use of project teams to draft standards, instead relying on a collegiate system dependent on full consideration of all national views;
- cumbersome procedures for public inquiry, examination of comments, and voting on draft standards, all of which delayed the delivery of standards, especially in new technologies that were continually evolving;
- requiring that European standards be transposed as national standards in each member country before they can be used caused tremendous delays and confusion for business;
- inadequate dissemination of information on work being undertaken at the national level despite the existence of procedures to that effect (Directive 83/189/EC); and
- failing to make information on European standards activity available in a clear and comprehensive fashion to industry.[11]

The remainder of the document focused on institutional and procedural reforms to improve the efficiency and accountability, coordination and structure, and membership and cooperation of the standardization process. Other issues addressed including financing, testing, and certification and intellectual property rights. As it turned out, the most controversial proposals challenged the autonomy of the European standard-setting bodies. Given the broad nature of the document, the focus here is on those proposals that generated the greatest discussion among interested parties.

Efficiency and accountability

Stressing that standardization needed to be more efficient and accountable, the Commission argued that current working methods were not capable of delivering the large number of standards needed before the 1 January 1993 single market deadline.[12] Noting that on average it took CEN about three years to produce a draft standard at the European level, another year for public inquiry leading finally to the voting and adoption of a standard, and at least six months to implement the standard in all member states, the Commission expressed concern about the practical aspects of getting work done and the mechanisms by which agreements were negotiated. The Commission maintained that if CEN and CENELEC were more willing to follow the example of ETSI and use both project teams and majority voting, the time frame for European standardization could be lessened considerably. Though consensus was an admirable goal, the Commission argued that this resulted in gridlock and often brought the standardization process to a standstill.

The Commission was clearly unhappy with the territorial representation of standardization, and suggested a move away from this model by using alternative avenues such as outside consultants and industry-based associations to draft preliminary standards. These could on occasion replace the technical committees of CEN and CENELEC, and thus circumvent national standards bodies. However, this proposal generated concern about the points of access for consumer and other interested groups who may not have the necessary resources to participate at the European level.[13] Yet the Commission remained steadfast that consumer groups, trade unions, and other parties would be better able to channel their views if they could directly participate at the European level rather than have their 'voice' filtered through national channels.

Coordination and structure

The recommendations for improved coordination and procedural changes constituted an overhaul of the existing standardization system. The result was a series of radical proposals aimed at fostering a new regulatory style and mode of operation. The Commission pointed to the institutional divergence between CEN/CENELEC and ETSI. Despite efforts on the part of ETSI to bring its rules and structures into line with CEN and CENELEC, many differences remained, including the direct representation of all interested parties in standards work rather than the system of national representations. In the Commission's view, this gap was clearly untenable since it created the prospect of jurisdictional competition, while the Commission was interested in improving co-ordination between the three bodies. The Commission warned against the potential pitfall of jurisdictional competition, in part, by referring to the American system with its multiple and often overlapping system of over 400 standards bodies.

To prevent such competition, the Commission proposed a 'European Standardization System' which would clarify the division of labour between national and European level, and accelerate the production of European standardization.[14] The proposals combined regulatory reform with significant institutional change. By creating a single standardization structure, the Commission proposed a four-tier process. First, a European Standardization Council that would be responsible for overall policy direction. This would be composed of representatives of European industry and social groups, as well as the European Commission, EFTA Secretariat, and European standardization bodies. Second, a European Standardization Board would serve an executive function in managing and coordinating standardization activities. This would be composed of representatives from the European standardization bodies and the secretary of the Standardization Council. Third, the European standardization bodies would be fully responsible for standardization in their field or sector. This would provide the necessary autonomy to finance, prepare, and adopt European standards, subject to compliance with the general rules of the European standardization system. Fourth, the national standardization bodies would have a much diminished role, working largely on behalf of the European standards bodies. They would canvass opinion on draft standards, hold public inquiries, and provide information on their national activities to ensure that they were not undertaking work that was best performed at the European level.

Cast as a careful balance between decentralization and regional co-ordination, the proposed reforms were clearly aimed at reducing the role and potential political interference of the national standards bodies. Although noting that national standardization still had an important role to play, the Commission was clearly setting out its bargaining position and sending a strong signal that the status quo was no longer acceptable.[15]

Membership and international cooperation

The Commission recognized the growing importance of standardization for strategic trade policy. Strongly supportive of technical cooperation with Central and Eastern Europe and the growing number of requests for assistance from other regions such as the Mediterranean and South America, the Commission duly noted that these efforts should build on similar arrangements developed with ASEAN, India, and the Andean pact countries.[16] Providing information on current and future European standardization efforts and financial assistance for the training of industry and standardization experts in these regions could only enhance the profile and use of European standards, and create substantial 'lock-in' effects. At the same time, the Commission was concerned that resources be concentrated on the production of standards for the internal market. Consequently, the Commission recommended postponement of membership in the European standard bodies for the Central and East European countries, as this would only increase the difficulties facing the current members in reaching agreement on complex technical issues.[17] As a compromise measure, the Commission suggested associate member status, which would provide the CEECs with access but not real influence.[18] While recognizing the interest of non-European countries in gaining access to European debates, the Commission felt that the extent of participation should be determined by the standards bodies themselves. The Commission also suggested that efforts to influence European standardization would best be achieved at the international level through enhanced participation in international standardization activities.

This was clearly a reference to the United States' demands for a seat at the table in European standardization.[19] Though this had been refused, despite high-level intervention by American policy-makers, the Commission fiercely resisted any effort to further accommodate third country concerns, focusing instead on the principle of non-discrimination with regard to mutual recognition and standards.[20] The Commission did suggest that representatives from international bodies such as ISO and IEC be given observer status within the various technical committees, but this was common practice because of mutual interests in certain sectors and work programmes.

Although it was national standards bodies that participated directly in international standards organizations such as the Consultative Committee for International Telegraph and Telephony (CCITT), International Standards Organization (ISO), and International Electrotechnical Commission (IEC), the European standards bodies—particularly CEN and CENELEC—had established regular discussions with their international counterparts in 1989 and 1990 as their work programme increased and a growing number of European standards were being adopted.[21] The Commission felt that international standardization bodies should address some of the work proposed at the European level in areas not related to European legislation.[22] It went on to suggest that: 'if international standardization bodies can respond by accelerating work on projects which are of high priority to Europe, with a view to delivering results within the timetable set by European requirements, European level standardization can be avoided.' Despite this offer, however, most of the 123 international members were not inclined to see international standards as secondary to European ones.[23]

Concluding comments

The reforms proposed by the Commission would inevitably threaten vested interests and generate widespread resistance. To strengthen its position, the Commission closed the Green Paper by raising the sensitive issue of financial contributions. Noting that the Commission and EFTA provided 70 per cent of CEN's operating budget, and about 55 per cent of CENELEC's, the Commission advised the standards bodies that this could not go on indefinitely and that they should seek alternative revenue sources for their long-term sustainability. The Commission suggested that this could be achieved in two ways. First, a portion of the revenues from the sale of European standards could be redirected from the national to the European level. Second, industry should provide greater financial support to European standardization, in addition to or in place of current support at the national level.

Underlying the Commission's proposals was the unstated goal that efforts at the European level to create a framework for standards, testing, and certification not be undermined at the national level. The Commission recommended that the standards bodies coordinate more closely so that barriers created by different testing and certification practices did not mar their efforts. Despite having little formal authority in many of these areas, the Commission had a keen interest in promoting a common conformity mark for the entire European market. This would relieve manufacturers of the need to invest time and resources in obtaining certification or conformity marks in several national markets.

The Commission had a major stake in the standardization process, and was particularly concerned about the effects of the single market lagging behind its scheduled deadlines. Though at the forefront of policy innovation and launching new regulatory efforts to foster integration, the Commission's policy formulation role was being displaced by increased difficulty in ensuring effective implementation and converting new ideas into practice. Without significant changes, the situation would only worsen and send a negative signal to other markets.

The Green Paper ended with a statement that it was intended to 'provoke a wide-ranging discussion with a view to generating agreement on how to take the next steps on the development of European standardization'.[24] It is unclear whether the Commission expected the volume of subsequent and often extremely critical responses. The problems identified by the Commission generated proposals designed to address the problems of delegation. These included ex-post and ex-ante mechanisms to increase their oversight and pressure on the European standards bodies, and mitigate the effects of delegation by:

- Shifting the blame for the problems in achieving the single market deadlines onto the European standards bodies.
- Exercising pressure to reform and reorganize existing procedures and practices to motivate and circumvent the traditional standards bodies.

- Imposing budgetary sanctions when the European standards bodies fail to meet deadlines. If the contract is incomplete, then the Commission withholds payment and seeks to ensure that there is no misrepresentation of their abilities to reach agreement within the scheduled deadlines.
- Exercising oversight through verification or promulgation to ensure that standards are appropriate and suitable to meet regulatory 'essential requirements'. The threat of rejecting agreed upon standards within comitology committees is akin to a 'fire alarm' rather than 'police patrol' approach to monitoring delegated authority.

Faced with these criticisms, trade associations, standards bodies, and individual firms put forward a variety of opinions. These focused on administrative and managerial problems within the Commission, the Commission's misunderstanding of the nature and goals of standardization, and the changes necessary within European standardization.

Industry responses to EU proposals

European industries were most concerned about the Commission's radical proposals for a new system for European standardization. Many believed that modifying the structure of the three European standards bodies would jeopardize progress at a critical stage in European standard-setting, unnecessarily diverting attention to root and branch reform at the expense of actual standard-setting.[25] As the Institute of Directors commented, 'the idea of a European Standardization Council is an irrelevant luxury that should be discarded.'[26]

Acknowledging the need for coordination of new standards activities across industrial sectors, many trade associations argued that this could be done by the presidents of the three European standards bodies. Close liaison between CEN, CENELEC, and ETSI could address the need for greater coherence to prevent overlapping or damaging contradictions among the different sectors, and provide an increased role for firms in the major programmatic and planning stages.[27] Most large firms and trade associations supported common rules to be applied across all three standards bodies, emphasizing the need for closer coordination to avoid duplication of activities and expending scarce resources.[28]

However, the Commission's drive to expedite the current process through substantial procedural reforms met with mixed reviews. Many firms felt that CEN and CENELEC had used the associated bodies, such as the European Committee for Iron and Steel Standardization

(ECISS), Association Européene des Constructeurs de Matériel Aerospatial (AECMA), and the European Workshop on Open Systems (EWOS), for a variety of tasks. These European sector committees were already considered important in providing input to both European and international activities. While AECMA supported a model of standardization that was not centrally structured nor closely tied to national patterns, many other trade associations such as Orgalime and UNICE feared that the proliferation of associated standards bodies could increase fragmentation and make coordination among the various bodies more difficult.[29]

More contentious were the proposed changes in voting, with the suggestion that more use should be made of weighted majority voting being clearly unpopular. Many firms stressed that standards were successfully developed and used because every effort was made within the working groups and technical committees to achieve consensus. Majority voting was considered a last resort and not a routine option by most companies. The European Roundtable of Industrialists (ERT), UNICE, and the European Centre of Public Enterprises (CEEP) emphatically supported the notion of consensus. CEEP feared that standards adopted by qualified majority would enable large companies to promote the standards they favoured, at the expense of small businesses and marginal competitors.[30]

Many firms felt that CEN and CENELEC had already altered their internal regulations under earlier pressures from the Community, and permitted qualified majority voting on draft European standards. Because standards were traditionally voluntary in nature, except for European regulatory requirements such as public purchasing and new approach directives, many firms were reluctant to sanction such changes. Standardization was not a governmental process, in spite of what the Commission believed, and should not be subject to the same kind of decision-making rules.

Hundreds of trade associations and firms agreed that the Commission's goal of encouraging companies to invest in future markets by releasing the necessary experts and resources to draft standards reflected a misunderstanding about the nature of standardization. Trade associations argued that participation must be voluntary on the part of the companies involved, and that the Commission grossly underestimated the support given by industry to standard-setting.[31] Several firms pointedly remarked that they usually selected standardization projects which were vital to their overall corporate strategies and competitiveness, whether these were national, European, or international.

European industry also supported national standards bodies through membership dues, and argued that their financial commitment was already heavy enough, and in no way alleviated by the funds that the Commission paid directly to the European standards bodies. Many firms considered the Commission's suggestion that they make even more financial contributions unwarranted optimism, again reflecting a poor understanding of the standardization process. One after another, trade associations opposed any radical restructuring that would bypass the national standards bodies, on the grounds that it would adversely affect the ability of small and medium enterprises (SMEs) to participate through national channels.[32] Several sectors dominated by SMEs, such as machines and toys, were directly impacted by the single market programme, and firms expressed concern about the course that these reforms would take. Many did not possess the resources needed to influence standardization on the European level, in contrast to multinationals that can invest considerable resources into a particular standard, internalizing a direct and positive return on that investment.

The same situation faced trade unions and labour groups. However, the Commission did provide direct support to weaker interest organizations such as the European Trade Union Federation (ETUC) in the hope of ensuring a more balanced representation of interests. This has helped to alleviate the collective action problem with respect to the advocacy of general interests which are even more extensive at the European level than within the member states.[33] However, this subsidization created a firestorm of protest from some industries. Although there was general support for encouraging increased participation from consumer and trade union groups at the European level, subsidization was widely considered inappropriate. Critics argued that, as with SMEs, trade unions, consumer groups, and public authorities could make their views known at the national level.

Reactions from the national standards bodies

If the Commission found only limited support for its proposals from industry and trade associations, then it should not have been surprised by the reaction from national standards bodies. In most cases, they registered vehement protests against the proposed structural reorganization and the creation of European standards that were no longer exclusively implemented and sold by national standards bodies. While proposals to speed up and improve the efficiency and accountability of the standards process generated significant commentary, the national standards bodies shared a common concern that structural reform would distract from the ongoing delivery of European standards. They knew well that the proposed changes would cripple their operations and reduce their influence in the standards process. In separate submissions, the national standards bodies outlined their valuable role in channelling the interests of all interested parties into the process.[34] They argued that this prevented even greater fragmentation, duplication, and intersectoral conflict.

To promote these arguments, the national standards bodies launched an all-out effort to stave off the threat of reduced influence. Arguing that over 25,000 participants were involved in developing European standards, the British Standards Institute (BSI) felt that they provided an important channel to exercise different views and opinions.[35] Officials of the German standards body (DIN) were quick to point out that a broad array of interests are represented at the national level, including producing industries, service industries such as banking and insurance, consumer, trade unions, scientific organizations, state and federal governments, and state-owned enterprises.[36] This opposed the notion that the standardization process was prone to 'industry capture'.

Although there were clearly vested interests at the national level that did not wish to see the influence of national standards bodies decline, the proposed institutional reorganization was not the only cause for concern. The idea of a single European standard, having an independent status, generated significant opposition from the national standards bodies because it would mean losing not only control over the implementation process, but also revenue from the sales of European standards. This was an extremely sensitive issue, as national standards bodies derived more than 50 per cent of their income from the sale of national and European standards.[37]

As for the overall objectives of the Green Paper, the national standards bodies were in broad agreement and sympathetic to the need to highlight the significance of European standardization, just not at their expense. Like the industrial groups, however, the national standards bodies questioned the Commission's understanding of the standardization process. In particular, several of the standards bodies considered that the Green Paper focused almost exclusively on the role of standards in support of Community directives, ignoring the large number of standards driven by market pressures not regulatory mandates.

BSI and DIN argued that it was not so much standards as different national testing and certification practices that must be addressed if barriers are to be removed. Reliable and mutually accepted testing and certification procedures were crucial to the acceptance of any standards. Differences in this area threatened to undermine the operation of the single market, even after relevant standards had been adopted. Noting that industry had also attached enormous importance to this problem, which received only peripheral attention from the Commission in the Green Paper, the standards bodies were eager to shift the blame elsewhere.

In their view, the Commission had asked CEN and CENELEC to deliver large numbers of standards within a short time frame, while failing to remove some of the obstacles to progress under its own control. Several national standards bodies also felt that the Commission was operating under unrealistic guidelines. As one standards official noted, 'standards are being rushed through. They are poorly drafted and open to misinterpretation'.[38] Standard-writing is always a time-consuming activity, a fact that the Commission seems to have overlooked, or 'chose to ignore' according to one standards official, when defining the deadlines for entry into force of European legislation.[39] Even if procedures were introduced to accelerate standard-setting, it would continue to be a long-drawn-out process to ensure adequate representation and high-quality standards.

Reactions from the European standards bodies

The European standards bodies responded individually and collectively to the Commission's proposals, displaying striking differences in their approach to the debate about European standardization. The Commission had clearly taken into consideration many of the suggestions provided by ETSI in earlier informal contacts.[40] CEN and CENELEC, by contrast, were put on the defensive as many of the criticisms were aimed at their management and operating methods, which were considered the root cause of the 'standards deficit'.

CEN and CENELEC believed they were being unfairly criticized since they had made considerable and successful efforts to establish European standards, while respecting the particularities of various market sectors.[41] They also felt that the focus on internal market priorities excluded consideration of virtually all other issues. For the European standards bodies, this focus created artificial pressures that could be ruinous to a system based upon consensus and market needs.[42]

While stressing their openness to practical improvements, they were quick to point out that European standardization was not homogeneous and uniform changes ignored the fact that the standards bodies were at different stages of development, served different market sectors, and had different international partners. Both CENELEC and ETSI stressed that most of the work programme in their particular sectors was well on target, due to collaboration and support from interested parties. Not surprisingly, CEN was anxious to deal with the complaints, approaching the issue primarily as one of redefining their management and operating procedures, rather than root and branch reform.

CEN and CENELEC did acknowledge that they could improve overall efficiency and use of resources, and provide a better work business orientation for their work programme. Both admitted there was an obvious need to improve their credibility through limited reforms of internal processes and procedures, but they stopped short of endorsing many of the proposals 'for fear of increased bureaucracy and increased costs'. In a stinging critique, the standards bodies pointed to the meagre accomplishments of three decades of harmonization. They argued that this should have provided the Commission with a better awareness of the different priorities that reinforced barriers to trade, as well as the special characteristics of national policies and regulations that influenced the patterns of production and distribution in domestic markets.

The European standards bodies were not uniformly unsympathetic to the Commission's concerns, suggesting some tension between the three. ETSI was much more receptive to the Commission's proposals, and 'wholeheartedly welcomed the Green Paper as a guide for future developments for European standardization'.[43] Given that the Commission had used ETSI as the model for many of its ideas, it was not surprising that ETSI was prepared to accept many of the proposals and conditions. The Green Paper clearly reflected many of the Commission's strategic priorities and views about how telecommunications and information technology standards could be coordinated to enhance the competitive position of European firms.

Although each had submitted individual commentaries, the European standards bodies quickly sought to smooth over their differences. Discussions among the three led to a common position that, if they were to maintain their credibility, they had to deal with and recognize that effective European standardization could only be achieved by closer cooperation and coordination. By May 1991, the three standards bodies had come to sufficient collective agreement to engage in extensive discussions with then Internal Market Commissioner Martin Bangemann.[44] Bangemann sought to reach some form of agreement 'on the objective of serving the needs of the European economy in the best possible way'.[45] Yet it is evident that the three bodies continued to differ on some issues due to their histories, membership, and sectoral portfolios.

Regulatory oversight of European standardization

The ensuing debate produced a number of initiatives by both the European standards bodies and the Commission, with the starting point being a 1992 follow-up Commission report identifying areas of broad support for the aims of the Green Paper. However, the report also acknowledged considerable disagreement over the means to improve the standardization process.[46] Forced to back-pedal from its radical reform proposals, the Commission acknowledged that the current set-up should remain in place for the foreseeable future. This was a major victory for the standards bodies, as the Commission conceded that it was partially at fault. The Commission could not simply request certain essential regulatory requirements and expect the European standard bodies to understand and interpret the rationale for the legislation, unless they were provided with clear guidelines or programming mandates to orient their work.

Concerned that companies still focused on national standards,[47] measures were taken to raise the profile of European standardization. These included better notification of national standards work to the European level to improve coordination, continued mandates and funding from the Commission to reorient work towards the European level, and improvement in the administration and working procedures of CEN and CENELEC. Perhaps most importantly, CEN and CENELEC agreed to make more use of qualified majority voting to speed up the process and prevent significant delays. After staving off a major threat to their institutional position, they readily assented to a number of incremental reforms to appear more responsive to the problems encountered in meeting single market deadlines. These changes included shorter public inquiry periods, more project team work, and increased efforts at long-range planning to meet contractual obligations. As part of this process, the standards bodies recognized the need for greater oversight and monitoring of work-in-progress to anticipate problems that may occur in different committees and threaten to derail progress toward agreement.

The end result was something of a compromise. The Commission had focused attention on what it perceived as a problem in making the single market operational. While not prevailing in some areas, steps were made to tackle bottlenecks. In the end, the Commission was able to push a resolution onto the 1992 Council agenda emphasizing the strategic importance of standardization, encouraging the use of European standards as an instrument of economic and industrial policy, and advocating broader use of standards in Community policy-making.[48]

The controversy that surrounded the Green Paper seemed to quietly die down as both the Commission and European standards bodies addressed the difficulties they faced in meeting the demands of their constituents. The Commission maintained a keen interest in European standardization, working to improve the situation as part of its broader assessment of regulatory policy.[49] This strategy reflects in part the increased consultation between the European standards bodies and the Commission at earlier stages of the legislative process, which has helped to iron out problems over both technical content and regulatory jurisdiction.[50]

Though much less than other projects, the standardization policy of the European Community has remained the subject of regular review and evaluation. Not only has the Commission done so through a series of internal assessments such as working papers and internal memorandums,[51] but the need for continuous evaluation has been underlined by the European Parliament and Council.[52] This ex-post monitoring of the effectiveness of Community legislation has produced some encouraging results. One important indicator is the dramatic increase in the production of European standards, with CEN producing over 250 standards per year after 1992, and CENELEC producing over 250 standards per year after 1993.

The potential for meeting deadlines is enhanced by increased speed. Since 1993 ETSI has reduced the average development time for individual standards from forty-five to twenty-eight months, and CENELEC also reduced its development time to between twenty-four and forty-eight months. While CEN still requires on average seventy-five months, this is a substantial improvement from the average of 135 months that CEN needed to agree on European standards in 1991. After more than a decade of interaction with the standards bodies, the Commission has come to recognize the variation across organizations and sectors in meeting regulatory requirements, and acknowledged that the number of standards needed for the many New Approach directives puts different pressures on industry. For example, the machinery and pressure equipment sectors required over 700 standards, the medical device sector about 200, and the construction sector over 1,500.

Alongside these acknowledgements is the recognition that the nature of the standards process differs between the three bodies. ETSI is mainly concerned with proprietary technologies and intellectual property rights, working to develop coordination at the pre-standardization stage. By contrast, CENELEC relies heavily on international standards and can thus avoid duplication and delays, while CEN is concerned with many standards in new areas such as ergonomics, food irradiation, and environmental management which makes their development process more innovative as well as more time-consuming in reaching common agreement.

Although the results achieved are encouraging, continuing concern about standardization also reflects efforts to broaden the use of standards in certain areas of public policy, such as public procurement. Because the Commission was clearly anxious to promote further programmes of standardization in this area[53] as well as request standards for other economically important sectors such as transportation, biotechnology, and energy, it was crucial to improve the functioning and overall coherence of its regulatory system.[54] Beginning in 1992, the effort to push for European standards for public contracts and information technology and communications, in areas such as open network provisions, integrated services digital networks, and satellites, was intended to increase competition and promote interoperability of products and services. For the Commission the expansion into new areas has been both a way of responding to criticisms about excessive European regulation and a means of promoting standards as an alternative instrument to Community regulation.

But as the traditional distinction between manufacturers, operators, and service providers is becoming increasingly blurred, the need for service standards rather than product standards raises questions about the capacity of the standards bodies to meet these new demands. The fact that professional services such as accountancy and insurance often undertake standardization activities through their relevant international federations raises concerns about institutional competition and overlap. Yet with the growth of the service economy, the Commission may request further standardization including banking, insurance and finance, tourism, hospitality, travel, and health care services. It has also sought to use the mutual information directive to address such information sectors as online professional services and interactive entertainment, which the Commission feared could increasingly be regulated at the national level, resulting in further fragmentation of the single market.[55] There has been some resistance from Germany about the expansion into service standardization at the European level, whereas Britain and France[56] are more supportive of service standards.[57]

Recognizing these challenges, a 1995 Commission staff working paper on 'The Progress of European Standardization' acknowledged that standards bodies have adapted to some of the changes in the European technological and regulatory environment, but also cautioned that 'there is nonetheless room for improvement'.[58] Though conceding that standard-setting is a consensus-based process and not simply a 'rubber stamping' routine, the Commission has maintained its earlier concerns about the structure and activities of European standardization. These concerns were expressed in a circumspect manner, with the Commission noting only that 'the onus will be on European industry, it if wants the harmonized standards, to provide sufficient resources to finish the job.'[59] In a separate statement, however, the Commission more forcefully argued that further reform is needed since 'the present standardization system cannot meet all the requirements of the market, whilst in other areas the system is sometimes challenged for reasons of representativity and accountability.'[60]

A number of trade associations and national government agencies voiced similar concerns. The Danish Agency for Trade and Industry highlighted not only the lack of standards in some areas but also the lengthy development time before standards were adopted.[61] Coupled with complaints that testing and certification bodies responsible for confirming that standards are met frequently differ in their interpretation of a standard, the Commission used the various reports to present its opinion on the progress of standardization to the Internal Market Council in February 1998.[62]

The resulting discussion paper again cited concerns about efficiency and transparency.[63] Efforts to produce timely standards through a more systematic use of qualified majority, overcoming entrenched interests and shorter implementation or transposition periods, seemed to be at odds with providing increased access to representatives of European workers, consumers, and environmental associations. But in contrast to the Green Paper, the Commission discussion paper was clearly written with assistance from the European standards bodies, tackling such thorny issues as management of the standards process. Because standardization has become an instrumental element of the European legislative programme for the single market, 'standards bodies are not entirely free to decide what standards to develop.'[64] While the Commission supported existing institutional arrangements, it repeated its appeal for greater use of sectoral associations and industry federations in the early stages of negotiations, rather than the traditional reliance upon representatives from the national standards bodies. Although this seemed at odds with its professed interest in transparency and representativeness, the Commission was careful not to sanction cartels or private consortia of companies as alternative venues for agreement on new approach standards, acknowledging that they 'lack the democratic legitimacy and accountability offered by the standardization process'.

The issue of representation has also persuaded the Commission to sign a memorandum of understanding in 1995 with the European standards bodies not only to increase the awareness of European standardization among small and medium companies but also to improve their participation in the process. Because the internal costs of compliance are high for small and medium companies, the Commission has found through its own surveys that more needs to be done to aid small firms in taking advantage of the single market.[65]

The Commission also suggested that the European standards bodies 'carefully consider' the possibility of speeding up the standardization process by voting at earlier stages to prevent vested interests from blocking progress and 'showing no willingness to compromise'.[66] To put further pressure on the European standards bodies, the Commission advocated greater monitoring progress made by including standardization mandates in the Internal Market Scoreboard. The Commission was anxious to pre-empt further member state interference in such a crucial area. Knowing that member states were keen to participate in reforming the standards bodies, the Commission did not want public authorities to seek increased involvement in standardization for fear that this would further politicize the process. Somewhat disingenuously, the Commission sought to differentiate the role of public authorities by arguing that, although their participation in standard-setting must clearly be equal to that of workers, consumers, environmental groups, and industry, they should leave 'technical solutions' to interested parties and devote their energies to the broader task of protecting the public interest.

To convey the severity of the political pressures surrounding completion of the single market, the Commission also indicated that suggestions had been made for CEN and CENELEC to merge. The Commission voiced reluctance rather than outright opposition to this idea, arguing that it would require corresponding reorganization at the national level. Not wanting to further antagonize national standards bodies after their earlier reactions to the Green Paper, the Commission was also unwilling to countenance new standards bodies for fear that this would disrupt activities at both the regional and international level.[67]

During discussion of the Commission's proposal at the Internal Market Council in February 1998, member states were divided over possible reform strategies. The debate pitted Denmark, wishing to increase the priority of higher public safety standards, against Britain, arguing for a reduction in the number of standards, enhanced mutual recognition and simplified legislation. Germany sought to depoliticize the process by insisting that standardization should remain a responsibility of experts and industry, while Belgium took the opposing view that it was necessary to propose a political solution and merge the three existing institutions, CEN, CENELEC, and ETSI into a single European standards institute.[68] No agreement was reached, but the European standards bodies were put on notice that their work was under increased scrutiny in an environment of renewed political commitment to the single market.[69]

Monitoring the single market: effectiveness and efficiency

The Commission's approach to reform of European standardization highlighted concern about the credibility of its own policy objectives. Against the backdrop of calls for subsidiarity and proportionality, as well as increased criticism of its technocratic tendencies, the debate on European standardization has become caught up with the critical rethinking of European regulation in the post-Maastricht period. With a number of criticisms from member states and the business community, the issue of regulatory reform raised increased concerns about market governance.[70]

The following key problems emerged from these debates about the growth of European regulatory activity:

- Difficulties surrounding mutual recognition which lessen mutual trust and credibility. This undermines one of the important trading principles of the single market and highlights problems in realizing the gains from removing barriers to trade.
- Poor performance in implementing European legislation at the national level, joined by the continued expansion of national regulatory production in spite of their potential trade restricting effects.

Though standardization has received substantial attention, less attention has been given to the problems of product approval and conformity assessment, despite continued complaints from firms in this area.[71] Firms continue to experience difficulties in persuading other economic operators or suppliers to accept the results of conformity assessment from bodies they do not know, or to accept national standards and marking arrangements that they are not familiar with.[72] According to the Commission, 'the real life problems of conformity assessment have brought to light a whole series of problems which the standardizing and conformity assessment communities are not fully able to solve on their own', and the lack of public confidence in products tested and certified elsewhere continues to be a major problem.[73] Since this reflects consumer or customer preference for certain products, such non-regulatory barriers can only be addressed through changes in market behaviour. The Commission has clearly recognized this,[74] promoting market-led initiatives to encourage mutual recognition of testing and certification through EOTC, including the idea of common certification marks. However, this has met considerable resistance from some national standards bodies, in part due to the reluctance of profit-making bodies, including national standards bodies, who wish to protect their commercial interests. Only if they perceive advantages from either mutual recognition of existing national certification marks or the development of a common European mark will they be willing to cooperate.[75]

While problems related to standardization continually came up on the agenda, market access was also hampered by the regulatory and administrative obstacles imposed by member states that undermined mutual recognition.[76] It would be naïve to assume that the concept of mutual recognition would work without constant monitoring and oversight. Part of the problem is the lack of responsiveness on behalf of member states in notifying suitable bodies to undertake testing, certification, and accreditation based on established European standards.[77] Administrative delays, dissuasive measures, and the inability of national authorities to accept complex or innovative products and services involving health, safety, or consumer protection, often accompanied by a mutual lack of confidence in the regulations adopted by another member state have been notable in foodstuffs, electrical engineering, vehicles, precious metals, construction, and chemicals sector.[78]

Although the European Commission continues to police the single market, compliance is difficult to monitor because the Commission has little direct power in either area, depending instead on collaboration with member states to ensure the effectiveness of its regulatory policies. Though the lack of uniformity in implementation hampers the actual operation of the single market, the Commission has few management tools at its disposal to deal with this. More problematically, the lack of compliance with efforts to prevent new trade barriers from emerging points to the ineffectiveness of existing regulatory tools in this area. With the reports on the operation of the mutual information directive, the difficulties of enforcing the single market became readily apparent.[79] National standards bodies continued to inform the European standards bodies far too late in the process,[80] and requests to stop working on a national standard through imposing the standstill rule were clearly not monitored.

However, the Commission was also faced with member states continuing to adopt many technically complex national product regulations, specifying the conditions in which they could be used and the tests, certificates, and approvals that they must undergo before being placed on the national market.[81] As a Commission spokesman noted, 'the threat posed to the integrity of the internal market by both the volume and the character of these national regulations [which far exceed the measures adopted at the level of the EU] is a cause for serious concern.'[82] Between 1992 and 1994, the then twelve member states notified over 1,300 proposals for new national regulations. This number expanded dramatically with the admission of Austria, Sweden, and Finland, who notified over 400 measures pending their accession. The number of regulatory measures adopted by the member states in one year regularly exceeded the entire existing body of European regulations.

Clearly the nature and volume of national regulations poses a serious threat to the smooth operation of the single market.[83] The Commission was particularly worried about the management of the single market because many new regulations were emanating from Germany, France, and Britain, key members in promoting the single market programme. Even the Netherlands and Denmark continued to adopt new national regulations, presenting a political dilemma as these two members had also complained vociferously about the increased burden on industry resulting from excessive European regulations.[84] The Commission has continued to initiate infringement proceedings against member states that were unwilling to alter or amend discriminatory legislation.[85] While seeking informal understandings with members before seeking judicial redress, one trade association pointed out that it 'has been difficult to dismantle certain aspects of the old system'.[86]

Improving compliance with mutual recognition will be aided though by the insistence of the Court of Justice that member states have an obligation to include mutual recognition clauses in national legislation.[87] This formalizes the legal commitment towards mutual acceptance of regulation, ensuring it will receive better attention among public authorities in member states.

Market management and regulatory reform

Increased political commitment to regulatory reform and market management has been evident throughout the 1990s. Several of these initiatives have been crucial in tackling barriers to trade and market distortions, especially the Action Plan for the single market, the Simpler Legislation for the Internal Market (SLIM) project, and intervention mechanisms. While these are ex-post efforts to tackle problems, a host of ex-ante instruments not dealt with here are aimed at improving the outcomes of market-building efforts.[88] These include rules of procedure, impact analysis, coordination, and transparency.

To address these and other regulatory gaps, the Commission sought to bolster its 'Communication on the Impact and Effectiveness of the Single Market' by drafting an Action Plan in April 1997.[89] This focused on a broad number of objectives, such as making the single market rules more effective, dealing with market distortions, and removing sectoral obstacles to market integration. Its discussion of proper enforcement of the single market clearly highlighted problems of implementation and transposition of standards in member states that hampered business efforts to make use of common regulatory rules and practices. Emphasis was also placed on policing the single market to ensure that common rules for industrial and consumer products were respected, and that the application of mutual recognition, European standards, and conformity assessment were applied properly. The Action Plan also highlighted specific sectors such as public procurement and construction products, where problems in setting European standards had generated controversy and opposition.

Approved at the Amsterdam European Council Summit in June 1997, the Action Plan brought renewed focus to the single market, which had been overshadowed by the negotiations on economic and monetary union.[90] The Internal Market Council gave strong backing to the Commission's initiative and focused on progress that had been made by member states to fulfil their obligations. European Commissioner Mario Monti, then in charge of the single market, argued that 'there was no point in member states agreeing to single market rules if they don't implement the necessary directives at the national level within the deadlines they themselves have set'.[91] Having established a clear deadline of January 1999 for implementing outstanding directives, member states were under some pressure from the Commission to meet their obligations. Among the Commission initiatives boosting compliance was the introduction of a single market 'scoreboard' aimed at measuring the performance of member states in transposing single market initiatives into national law. Additional measures included an annual business survey, questionnaires and guides, and dialogues with business and citizens.[92]

Secondly, the Commission secured political agreement on reducing legislative burdens through its SLIM initiative that had been launched on an experimental basis in 1996. This ex-post monitoring and evaluation of legislative proposals is designed to amend, consolidate, or simplify existing legislation.[93] It does not represent deregulation but rather better law-making to deal with the complexities of many legislative proposals. Although efforts to include new approach directives on electromagnetic compatibility and construction products as part of SLIM were warmly received by businesses who had found existing legislation overly restrictive and costly to implement, the Belgian, Italian, and Portuguese delegations expressed concern that simplification not result in dismantling of European legislation.[94] Given that these two areas had been the subject of much political opposition and technical difficulties within the

European standardization process, discussed in detail in Chapter 8, the Internal Market Directorate General hoped that regulatory changes would enable agreement to be reached more quickly. Even within the Commission, however, there has been considerable internal opposition within the several directorates general about perceived interference in policies under their jurisdiction.[95]

To increase regulatory compliance, the Amsterdam Council also gave the Commission encouragement to tackle impediments to the free movement of goods. Following such highly publicized incidents as the 1993 refusal of French farmers to allow access for Spanish perishables, and the 1997 Spanish exclusion of all but one type of television decoder into their markets, the Commission was asked to submit proposals for sanctions against non-compliance with single market rules. Despite such an influential statement of support, however, these 'fast track' sanctions have proved controversial.[96] The Commission welcomed the intervention mechanism, as 'in the past we have faced situations such as the destruction of goods or bans on imports from other member states without being able to intervene'.[97] With its proposed regulation, the Commission hoped to safeguard the credibility of the single market and make it easier for private individuals or firms who had suffered damages to seek compensation before national courts.[98] The Commission wanted to be able to start legal action within a matter of days if a member state is unwilling or unable to take necessary political action to remove obstacles to free trade.

Although Italy, Spain, Portugal, and Ireland strongly advocated such a mechanism during the Amsterdam negotiations, the cool reception given to the proposal by the Internal Market Ministers in February 1998 was a clear indication that the issue was highly contested. France had expressed strong reservations including the question of legal basis and the compatibility of the measure with fundamental rights, including the right to strike. The plan to give the Commission powers similar to those it enjoys in the area of competition policy also generated concern among Denmark, the Netherlands, and the United Kingdom.[99]

What emerged was an expression of 'a strong political resolve' and the idea of the intervention mechanism was described as simply 'a yellow card system' rather than 'a red card' mechanism.[100] Council Regulation 2679/98 passed in late 1998 provided a framework under which the Commission could obtain information from states concerning obstacles to trade which constituted breaches of the Treaty leading to a serious disruption to free movement.[101] In effect, the Commission was proposing a sort of fast-track infringement proceeding in the area of goods. Decisions adopted by the Commission could provide a basis for bringing a case to the ECJ quickly, with the hope that this would aid private individuals in seeking damages in their national courts.

The Commission also sought to make the Mutual Information Directive more effective, and particularly that increasingly important sectors not be exempted from its scope. To this end, the Commission proposed and the Council and Parliament agreed in 1998 that the directive be expanded to cover services. The mechanism had previously covered only goods and did nothing to prevent new obstacles arising from the adoption of divergent national regulations in the service sector. Though this presents a formidable task to both national standards bodies and member governments, in light of their previous experience in this area, it is also indicative of a broader political effort to govern European markets.

Conclusion

Despite all the fanfare surrounding the new regulatory policy, the actual operation of the New Approach was problematic. Looking at both the process and outcome of European market-building, it is clear that the process of regulatory policy-making has shifted from legal conceptions to issues of single market governance.[102] This does not negate the importance of the rule of law for the functioning of the market, and the prevalence of legal and judicial mechanisms for resolving conflict. Instead it highlights the fact that markets are shaped in a variety of ways by public authorities—including ex-ante or ex-post measures in the case of standard-setting.[103]

The evidence in this chapter indicates that the mandating of European standards has not matched expectations, and the pace at which the standards have been adopted and implemented at the national level has created a backlog in bringing the single market into line with political objectives. The new regulatory environment was expected to ease the pressure on the Commission through the delegation of partial responsibility for setting the rules for market access to European standards bodies and the many actors interested in participating in these private and semi-private organizations. But the results have been mixed. Commission officials, recognizing that the structure and management of the standards bodies is somewhat outmoded, have pushed for radical reform and restructuring. Despite these efforts, deadlines for the standards necessary to implement the new approach directives continued to be missed, causing much uncertainty for firms both within and outside the EU. Though subsequent proposals and debates highlighted some of the weaknesses of the current regulatory system, it also revealed a gulf between the Commission and standards bodies over the locus of and solutions to the problem.

While attitudes thawed subsequently, the resurgence of political pressures to complete the single market made the need for new options and further regulatory reform more pressing. While certainly highlighting the 'regulatory gaps', the ongoing standardization debate has also had significant impact upon corporate behaviour and strategies, a crucial but often overlooked element of the single market programme. Whether the expectations mapped out in earlier chapters have been realized deserves further consideration. The effect of European standardization on corporate strategy and behaviour is discussed in the following chapter.

Strategic Firms in an Integrated Market

In studying European policy strategies designed to bring about industrial competitiveness, technological innovation, reduced transaction costs, and market access, previous chapters have illustrated that many of the difficulties surrounding market integration are coordination problems that condition the operation both of states and markets. Market competition cannot always reach Pareto optimal outcomes in standardization,[1] requiring institutional coordination because 'with many new technical standards being created, both domestic and international, firms may feel their cases for the adoption of particular technical standards may be improved by their promotion by a number of firms, rather than singly. . . . Collaboration provides an effective mechanism for the joint creation and promotion of standards.'[2]

However, the institutional environment cannot of course promote coordination in isolation from events in the market. Evolving technologies and market situations are highly mutable, so the process is one of bounded rationality and deliberation rather than the type of classic welfare analysis and static assumptions that underpinned much of the economic assessments of trade effects of integrated markets (see Chapter 3).[3] Because uncertainties can dominate, especially in new areas of standardization that cover broad generic processes rather than individual product standards, and because private gains need to be realized, the confidence in this regulatory strategy requires certain incentives and coercive effects to insure effective implementation as demonstrated in the previous chapter.

Although as principal agent analysis observes, hierarchical mechanisms can ensure some form of compliance and securing greater effort to prevent shirking and slippage, standards are agreements based on decision rules, shared values and beliefs, and deliberation regarding the appropriate means for attaining policy goals. In this sense, the strategies and policies of firms are crucial to understanding the construction of the market and the degree to which market integration has succeeded. However, we should not see them as simply shaping market developments (pro-active players), but also as responding to and inhibiting market developments, economic innovation, and technological change (reactive players) given that standardization, together with regulation, can reinforce current or past choices (so-called path dependency effects).[4] With this in mind, have the regulatory strategies pursued by the Commission actually produced significant adjustments by firms to meet the effects of increased competition?[5] What reactions have market-building efforts actually had on firm-level operations? These questions are crucial to understanding the impact of European efforts to create a single market and reconcile trade liberalization and regulatory objectives.

This chapter provides a firm-centred approach to market regulation, recognizing that firms are at the centre of adaptation and change in the European single market.[6] Governments have used firms to meet their regulatory goals, placing them at the centre of the market adjustment process in terms of production, marketing, distribution, and technological development.[7] While this process has been driven by the regulatory strategies chosen by the EU, the internal adjustment costs and benefits of firms, and the impact of standardization on corporate policies and strategies have rarely been addressed.

While the macro-political and economic implications of the integration project were widely touted, the organizational attributes and strategies of individual firms were largely 'black-boxed' under the neo-classical assumption that they were rational economic actors that would seek to maximize their competitive advantage according to established market structures and rules. This chapter seeks to provide a more accurate view of firm behaviour and reactions, not by providing a comprehensive overview of the 'outcome' of efforts to remove barriers to trade, but rather a 'snapshot' through observations provided by European firms in surveys, questionnaires, and interviews. It is those strategies and behaviours that ultimately dictate the impact of the single market.

Business scholars highlight the need for technological and regulatory adaptation to be complemented by appropriate changes in systems and procedures within companies, since competitive advantages in a more closely integrated market will shift from structural and locational advantages to firm-specific ones. These studies largely focus on what firms should do, however, rather than examining to what extent efforts at constructing a market have actually influenced company policies and strategy.[8] While much of the preceding analysis has focused on the process of attaining trade liberalization, this chapter shifts the focus towards economic restructuring as a result of market integration. It draws on a similar focus by business historians, in the American context, on transformations in company structure and strategy due to the consolidation of local markets.[9]

The American context is also important in assessing the impact of EU regulatory developments upon the policies and strategies of third country firms. An analysis of the causes and consequences of corporate responses to regulatory actions outside their territorial boundaries can lead to a better understanding of the efficacy of public policies. Because of the processes of interdependence and globalization, the internal market has exercised powerful pressures externally, where the fears of exclusion from regulatory decision-making have provoked images of European integration in partially negative terms ('fortress Europe'). A perspective that focuses on the dynamics of tackling barriers to trade must recognize that companies not located within Europe have also been faced with adapting to the changing system of market governance. Though some of the analysis below aggregates overall trends, we should be attentive to variations in corporate organization since this is tied to corporate strategies, and the ability to deal with necessary changes that can come in a variety of forms (quality control, production changes, sharing of proprietary information, independent verification, testing, and certification) as a result of European standardization.[10]

The chapter begins with macro-level EU official assessments, followed by individual company surveys, and compares these findings with trade association and member government reports. It concludes by assessing the external impact of standardization, which illuminates the interaction between international pressures and domestic politics since different levels simultaneously affect one another, and what happens at one level of negotiation resonates at other levels in shaping market access.[11]

Commission surveys and analysis

One important benchmark for measuring aggregate corporate reactions is the surveys of business perceptions concerning the impact and effectiveness of the single market carried out by the European Commission. Empirically, few would doubt that integration has had significant impact on most of the established industries in the manufacturing sector, as well as a growing range of service industries, including retail, transport and communications, finance and business. The growth of mergers and acquisitions, joint ventures, and strategic alliances are testimony to the awareness of strategic positioning among firms.

However, it should be apparent from developments within European standardization that business perceptions and responses to European integration are likely to be conditioned by the 'state of play' of the

TABLE 10.1 *Remaining obstacles to trade: goods and services frequently cited (%)*

Type of obstacles	SMEs	Large firms
VAT: heavy or complex rules	21.9	18.1
Testing, certification, or approval procedures	19.9	18.8
National specifications requiring modifications	19.2	25.0
Different labour or social legislation	16.7	15.7
Environmental regulations	14.8	19.4
Health and safety regulations	13.6	16.5
Other obstacles	11.1	14.1
Restricted access: special rights or licences	10.5	12.1
Regulations protecting public interest/consumers	9.9	14.6
Refusal of products/services from other member states	8.4	9.1
Tax obligations: off-putting/discriminatory	8.3	9.1
Poor protection of patents and intellectual property	6.3	6.4
Advertising/promotion/pricing restrictions	5.3	7.7

Source: Commission of the European Communities, Nov. 1997.

single market. In fact, the single market scoreboard published in October 1998 indicated that 80 per cent of businesses still believed that there were obstacles preventing the full benefits of the single market from being realized. Of those companies surveyed, 41 per cent mentioned differences in standards and technical regulations, and 34 per cent mentioned testing, certification, and authorization procedures.[12]

A 1997 opinion poll conducted by the Commission among more than 3,500 businesses, essentially confirmed that competition had increased and suggested most obstacles to trade were being addressed.[13] Table 10.1 documents the trade barriers that most troubled firms operating throughout Europe. While tax issues topped the agenda, it was clear that firms were still frustrated in two areas discussed in earlier chapters, namely product approval or testing and certification issues, and environmental, health, and safety regulations. With no sign of a decrease in national regulations, despite notification procedures aimed at stemming their growth, it is not surprising that firms still find that divergent regulations a considerable burden. Similarly, the perceived reluctance to accept testing and certification results is indicative of the lack of progress made in that area.

Despite best efforts to agree on European standards, without complementary product approval practices under the New Approach, and without the mutual acceptance of testing and certification as equivalent in areas where there was no need for regulatory harmonization, firms continued to encounter roadblocks.[14] Though the Commission has stepped up its policing of the single market, aided by compliance units in some member states, there are still problems of awareness about what the policies mean in practice. Here it is important to differentiate between regulatory hurdles and discriminatory market practices which result in trade barriers and business or commercial preferences that are non-discriminatory. Many firms continue to use local suppliers and distributors, even though foreign competitors are also in the market for new business. The impact of business habits, established networks and traditions, and preference for national quality marks are difficult to assess. Though these are not regulatory constraints, they can often be confused as technical barriers to trade.

In examining the effectiveness of measures to address those technical barriers, the Commission found that measures have been successfully implemented for products comprising 64 per cent of EU trade, but for two-thirds of this figure (46 per cent of EU trade), additional non-regulatory barriers are likely to remain. About 16 per cent of trade problems result from implementation difficulties, such as the development of harmonized standards for the machinery and construction products directives, and pressure equipment.[15]

Companies interviewed expressed concern about the lack of consistent enforcement and coordination between notified bodies responsible for testing and certification issues. Although firms could choose to have their products certified by third party independent assessors if no European standards were available, many complained that this was prohibitively expensive. In addition, supplier firms experienced great difficulty in convincing their customers that they met European regulatory requirements. This disrupted customer relations, and, because of the general lack of information regarding when these standards would be available and what the directives would entail, many companies worried about excessive or high costs.[16]

While firms recognized that products were subject to diverse regulations and standards, the Commission survey found a significant amount of misunderstanding about the role of certification marks for business practice. While the European certification mark (CE mark) is aimed at demonstrating conformity, many firms assumed this was similar to the national quality marks they often used to gain a marketing advantage. Though the Commission's surveys signalled that more needed to be done to improve the functioning of both capital and product markets,[17] especially as the Commission moves forward with ambitious plans for the single market, including exporting the single market as a tool of trade liberalization, and integrating environmental considerations into standardization and public procurement, those benefits will only accrue if a

TABLE 10.2 *Perceptions of the single market: opportunities and threats (% of enterprises)*

	Number of Workers				Total
	1–9	10–49	50–249	250+	
Opportunities					
Larger selling market	12	28	39	27	16
Simplified internat. collab.	17	17	18	23	17
Lower production costs	7	10	13	10	8
Other opportunities	16	17	18	29	16
No opportunities	51	37	34	37	48
Threats					
Greater competition	31	46	26	49	34
Increased regulation	10	10	12	12	10
Increased production cost	6	10	6	5	7
Other threats	13	16	12	20	13
No threats	45	36	52	29	43

Source: The European Observatory for SMEs: Fifth Annual Report, Directorate General XXIII (Enterprise Policy, Distributive Trades, Tourism, and Cooperatives) of the Commission of the European Communities (1997).

large proportion of firms actually pursue strategies congruent with these ambitious plans. This means that small and medium firms will have to become more aware of the changes necessitated by the single market. In fact, the European Observatory for SMEs (as part of the European Commission DG XXIII), focused on the impact of the single market on productivity and profitability levels in comparison to their larger counterparts.[18] In the Observatory's fifth report, small firms were asked whether they see the single market on balance as an opportunity or threat. Table 10.2 depicts the perceptions of firms, illustrating that in general, the smaller the enterprise the greater the concern. Very little variation was reported across sectors, so that distributive trades, manufacturing, and service industries all reported similar results.[19]

Moving beyond aggregate perceptions of the single market, gauging specific impacts on corporate strategy revealed some important trends. First, environmental issues have resulted in a striking amount of product or process adaptation and generated significant management attention. Although awareness of environmental norms and standards varied by company size, with larger firms more willing to invest in environmental protection and management systems, such as eco-audits and environmental management standards, surveys highlighted the influence of the single market. Although the figures are higher in large firms (over 250 workers), as would be expected given their greater access to resources and information, small and medium companies seemed to have been 'pushed' by public authorities, larger companies, trade associations, and competitors into compliance and adaptation.[20] Among small companies (less than 10 workers), over 40 per cent of manufacturing and construction companies, 27 per cent of trade, and 29 per cent of service industries modified their company practices between 1992 and 1997.[21] The situation varied across member states, reflecting the maturity of domestic environmental regulations and traditions, with Austrian, German, and Dutch firms being at the forefront of eco-industry standards in comparison to their southern European, Irish, and Belgian counterparts.[22]

Secondly, reactions to increased competition vary by sector and size.[23] The Commission study found that 17 per cent of respondents viewed the single market as promoting international collaboration, 8 per cent reported that production costs were lowered, and 16 per cent viewed the larger market more favourably. However, the survey also found that 34 per cent of small firms experienced or perceived increased competition, 7 per cent noted that production costs had increased, and 10 per cent saw a rise in regulation and red tape. Although the survey was designed to assess the overall impact of the single market, the results reflect the concern of small and medium firms in the changing regulatory environment, and substantiate the need for more micro-level analysis.

While the surveys provide good insight into remaining problems, however, they do not address in detail the extent to which firms have altered their internal and external policies and practices. A preliminary effort to do this follows, although more research needs to be done in this area.

Company assessments: industrial organization and market behaviour

Since few assessments have focused on changes in corporate strategy within individual sectors or firms,[24] the micro-foundations of change have been much less apparent.[25] Though standards bodies act as a 'conduit' for different interests to react to and influence the agenda, we do know that those involved render opinions, form alliances and coalitions, and portray national interests without undermining their own company interests in international and regional negotiations. This persuasion game is a bargaining problem and, as in any such situation, tactics can include commitments and concessions. Commitment to a particular technology, as occurred with third generation mobile phones, or conceding to low-cost licensing, hybrid standards, or combining technologies, as occurred with the competing high-definition television systems that merged their technologies and split licensing fees, can facilitate coordination.[26] While game theoretical models have focused on strategies and tactics in standardization, and have generated much theorizing about choosing a particular technology, less attention is given to the way that standards have impacted sectors of manufacturing and increasingly impact service sectors in terms of production, marketing, and distribution practices.[27]

An extended example illustrates this point. Dormont is a small manufacturer of flexible gas appliance connectors and related plumbing supplies. Its experience in exporting to Europe has become something of a *cause célèbre* in trade circles. The president Evan Siegel has aggressively pursued his case with a growing number of officials on both sides of the Atlantic, and his concerns illustrate the role of national standards as restrictive trade barriers.

Dormont developed an innovative gas appliance connector in the 1970s made from steel rather than brass. Shortly afterwards, the McDonald's Corporation adopted the connector, which allowed them to put their cooking equipment on casters or wheels to facilitate cleaning and service in a busy commercial kitchen. The product became the American standard for metal gas connectors for movable gas equipment. Since the early 1970s, Dormont has sold over 25 million stainless steel gas connectors for both the residential and commercial food service markets. Experienced in both manufacturing and standards development in the American context, Dormont hoped to influence the European standard-setting process by meeting with officials of the European Commission, many of the notified bodies, and several of the national standard-setting committees.

Dormont followed the American fast food companies as they expanded throughout Europe, and many continued to use Dormont's products until 1988. One by one, however, national standards bodies adopted gas connector standards with design criteria that excluded Dormont products. Dormont was consequently unable to convince national authorities regarding the suitability of their product in meeting necessary safety standards, and complained their competitors were essentially writing the rules to describe their own products. When McDonald's refused to accept Dormont products for their British chains, and then at Eurodisney in Paris, the company again sought certification and approval to meet national requirements. Now Dormont were told that they met French safety and performance criteria, but not design criteria, and were again refused the French NF approval (national certification mark). A similar decision was made by German authorities regarding the German certification mark.

Dormont needed another way of acquiring approvals for their connectors in Europe, as their bid to meet design and certification marks in each national market was proving unsuccessful and prohibitively expensive. Dormont had marketed their product via trade fairs, and used local staff to market and distribute their product. With large orders in place, the company chose to use the harmonized EU standards and gain approval to apply the CE mark for the New Approach gas appliance directive.

Dormont successfully sought approval with notified bodies in Belgium and Britain and began to market their products throughout the EU, with distribution and marketing facilities in each country. This would seem a perfect example of a New Approach success story, but then Dormont's problems began anew. In late 1993, the French authorities decided that the CE mark as issued by BSI was unacceptable. In January 1994, EU authorities informed Dormont that in the opinion of the Commission Services Working Group, known as GADAC and other experts in the comitology process, gas connectors fell outside the scope of the Gas Appliance Directive. The British Standards Institute (BSI) had been wrong to issue a CE mark for Dormont products, and member states were free to impose their own design standards. The Commission argued that each nation's gas distribution system was sufficiently different to warrant individual standards for gas connectors.

Dormont was confronted by a system of decision-making that was not notably transparent. Facing comitology committees composed of members from national standards bodies, gas industries, and notified bodies within members states, Dormont has been unable to market its product EU-wide. Evan Siegel argues that Dormont has 'tried everything' to gain standards and testing approval, with these problems significantly restricting its market share and export potential. The Dormont case has received widespread publicity in trade negotiations, national and industry press, and even US Congressional hearings, reinforcing concerns that European standards are being used as restrictive trade barriers.[28]

This example indicates the strategies some companies are willing to undertake to operate in the single market, and the importance of looking not just at the processes of standardization but their actual impact on corporate strategy. In fact, one of the few company studies on non-tariff barriers concluded that small firms lack adequate resources to respond to them. Arguing that small firms (like Dormont) cannot seize marketing opportunities because of the burdensome technical requirements of product approval and the often intense political pressures to use local firms when possible,[29] begs the question of whether, as the result of the single market programme and advances in European standardization, firms are actually able to take advantage of new opportunities.

To address this question, a survey questionnaire was distributed to the corporate, public, and regulatory affairs offices of over 150 large companies with a substantial presence in Europe. This was complemented by a questionnaire distributed to European trade associations, including those representing small and medium firms. Some problems in gathering data were encountered as many firms did not perceive any advantage in responding to the survey. Others recognized the existence of market distortions, but did not want to specify problems for fear of jeopardizing future toeholds in other markets by launching a complaint.[30] As a result, the information provided by individual firms was supplemented by interviews and additional data collected from government agencies, consultants, and various trade associations, and relevant secondary literature.[31]

Interviews and questionnaire responses indicate that firms use multiple sources for information on the changing regulatory environment in Europe. Many large, multinational firms find out about new or draft European standards through participation in the actual standard-setting process at the European and national level, and from information provided by national standards bodies, trade associations and industry federations, trade journals and newsletters, and other companies.[32] Some companies also rely on contacts with Commission officials, while others find that participation in European research enables them to keep abreast of new technological developments in the standards area.[33] This follows closely the survey results of Coen, who found that firms have adopted multiple lobbying strategies when seeking to influence the European policy process.[34]

Responses to questions about company involvement in European standardization produced a mixed picture. Some companies were involved in specific technical committees and working groups in sectors such as telecommunications, electronics, and computer systems. Others participated in business consortia in an effort to coordinate on pre-technology choices and prevent costly standards wars. When asked which issues have been most important for company policy and strategy, none of the firms chose only one option. All respondents highlighted several issues, with testing and certification and health and safety standards cited most frequently.[35] However, many companies that did not perceive problems also responded to the questionnaire, indicating that the issues of standards, testing, and certification were of considerable importance to them also.

Large companies followed a multi-pronged strategy in standardization. Some were actively involved in strategy groups within national standards bodies, while others followed the same approach at the regional level, working within various European forums including the Information Society Standardization System (ISS—formerly the European Workshop for Open Systems), European Computer Manufacturers' Association (ECMA), and notification bodies for coordinating testing and certification such as the European Organization for Technical Approval (EOTA), European Quality System (EQS), and umbrella groups within the European Organization of Testing and Certification (EOTC). Several companies altered their information strategies as the result of changes in their industries. This was particularly the case in the information technology sector, where companies have moved from being simply computer manufacturers to providers of computer services, making it imperative to work with *de facto* market leaders and involve themselves in business consortia. In this fast-changing sector, standardization needed to be considered carefully in terms of *de jure* versus *de facto* standards, since in many cases companies wanted technical compatibility. They did not view standards as altering their corporate strategy, but rather 'working the other way round' since they were able to influence standards at the international level. As one company official noted, the effect of European standardization has been relatively little since 'we have always tried to lead on those [issues] that concern us'. This suggests that a first-mover advantage strategy is particularly critical in areas of rapid technological development and change.[36]

Not surprisingly, the burden of activities for standardization fell on research and development (R&D), production, and engineering departments within firms. In most companies, standardization has still not moved 'from the backroom to the boardroom', despite industry analysts' perception that standards have become the new weapons of global competition.[37] Few companies indicated that standardization was of importance to management, with many of the questionnaires referred to staff in technical rather than management or public affairs departments. Several trade associations reported that they devoted a significant amount of time to helping their members cope with standardization, and that many of the problems encountered with the EU 'stem from a lack of understanding of how the European system works'.[38] Only one company mentioned its corporate standardization department, while providing the most detailed analysis of company participation in national, European, and international standards committees.

The survey found few complaints or concerns about the costs of economic restructuring among large companies. Asked whether these costs had been higher than expected, lower than expected, or about what they had anticipated, many firms chose the latter. Several firms noted that 'normally those changes are not unexpected', reflecting participation in working groups and technical committees at the national, regional, and often international level.[39] Many of the firms reported that they were affected by a number of standards issued by the EU. Perhaps more importantly, many respondents were not just concerned with standards under the New Approach, but construed standards more broadly to cover the entire range of regulatory requirements for their products. For example, respondents frequently referred to environmental emission standards and registration of chemical and environmental management systems as increasing in importance.

Firms often complained about problems related to private customer preferences, rather than to legislative barriers. This raises interesting questions about the degree to which the regulatory changes instituted by the single market have actually penetrated market practices and altered business relationships. Several sectoral studies have found that market preferences and specific company requirements are frequently cited as barriers to trade, and often confused with barriers stemming from divergent and uncoordinated national regulations.[40]

Perceived opportunities and constraints

Has the new regulatory strategy aimed at removing barriers to trade helped firms to realize the benefits of the single market? The specific issues that companies face make generalization difficult. However, in their survey responses many firms provided comments which go beyond the opportunities and problems that they face individually. In evaluating benefits, several firms stressed the impact of standardization on product rationalization, and the effect that such rationalization will have on cost reallocation within the company. While the ability to serve multiple markets meant that some firms would streamline and integrate different factors of production, such as research and development, others felt that the pressures of increased competition reduced lead times and increased the speed of technical development. Because of increased emphasis on internal quality management and certification, many larger companies had expanded this activity in-house or expressed increased interest in meeting these requirements company-wide. These and other findings were consistent with the Commission's goals in promoting greater competitiveness and efficiency in the single market.

However, not all respondents were satisfied with regulatory developments in Europe. Some companies saw the European level as an additional and unnecessary layer in the standardization process. This reflected concern that attention and resources could be diverted away from international standardization, which was viewed by some firms as more important than activity at the European level. The relationship between national, European, and international standard-setting was a frequent area of concern, with the multiple levels considered 'a complicating factor' placing additional burdens on company resources. This was in part due to the fact that some international committees did not mirror existing European ones, making it necessary to influence European standardization through participation at both the European and international levels.[41]

Some companies saw difficulties not in standard-setting *per se*, but in the absence of a coordinated testing and certification regime. While efforts have been made to promote mutual recognition among testing and certification bodies, the lack of competition in many domestic markets suggested that firms were frequently opting for multiple product approval. Companies still experienced problems that the single market was supposed to address in this area, and also expressed growing concern regarding intellectual property rights. This affected the European Telecommunications Standards Institute most directly, since ETSI standards were designed to be anticipatory, making use of emerging technologies from companies that were willing to cede intellectual property rights to get a common standard accepted. This was true in the case of mobile telephony standards, for example, where some firms were often unwilling to cede these rights and accept compromise solutions using technologies from various manufacturers.[42] Though subsequently resolved, it highlights the importance of proprietary technology in shaping and affecting corporate strategy. Since fewer complaints were recorded than expected, and some of the issues raised by companies in the author's questionnaire did, however, differ from that of official Commission surveys, the validity of the findings was further assessed against materials collected from trade associations, consultancies, and government agencies.

Making the single market work for business

Many existing surveys are striking in their emphasis on the negative aspects of market integration, and especially on persistent trade restrictions. The reports generally focused on problems encountered in the single market, with relatively few reports on impact on corporate strategy, which makes it hard to provide generalizations. Two detailed government reports by the British Department of Trade and Industry and the Danish Ministry for Business and Industry symbolized the national efforts to tackle single market breaches, resolving over fifty complaints per year on behalf of British and Danish companies, respectively. They provide good illustrations of market compliance problems.

The British Department of Trade and Industry Single Market Compliance Unit[43] found numerous problems related to the specific coverage of products under the New Approach.[44] British firms complained repeatedly about non-harmonized products that resulted in difficulties in gaining product approval, and also the absence of standards for many products. In assessing which member states caused British firms the most problems, most companies mentioned more than one, indicating that problems of market access were quite widespread. Germany was mentioned in over half the total number of the legislative problems, suggesting that penetrating the German market was still difficult.

Problems cited by British firms also extended beyond legislative barriers. Even though the survey concerned legislative barriers, for which the government could seek action through government channels such as the Internal Market Advisory Committee, many companies also complained about private customer preference for national standards or national certification marks. Thus standards can cause barriers to trade in the same way as regulatory barriers, forcing firms to seek additional approval or insurance cover to access certain markets. Industrial sectors varied. In chemicals, the overall impression was that the single market was functioning well, as it is a highly regulated sector at both the European and national level.[45] Biotechnology fared differently with companies seeking further action on product approval to ease market entry problems.[46] In the pharmaceutical sector, concerns about delays in product approval were coupled with complaints about differences in labelling and packaging requirements, and difficulties in bidding for government contracts due to the drug-pricing controls imposed by governments, and their bargaining over such issues as employment levels to funding for state-run research institutes.[47]

While many of these barriers should be resolved by mutual recognition, the awareness of national approval markets by many distributors, retailers, and customers is high. This leads many companies to promote either European standards or European-level agreements on testing. Part of the problem with this solution, as previous chapters have shown, is that the European standards bodies and the European Organization for Testing and Certification (EOTC) have already experienced difficulties in meeting the demands placed on them. In the case of testing and certification, national certification bodies have been reluctant to enter into negotiations that may increase competition and undermine their market share.[48] Companies have complained that some national governments, including Britain, France, Germany, and the Netherlands, have been reluctant to accede to European authority, and have placed roadblocks before efforts to transfer authority and oversight for testing and certification to a European agency. As a result, EOTC remains a little known organization that probably could not survive on its own without Community funding.[49] Because of threats from national bodies, notably in Britain, to stop participating in EOTC, the politics surrounding conformity assessment has made agreement difficult, and undermined some of the other benefits of the single market.[50] Acknowledging that real-life implementation of conformity assessment standards has encountered problems in terms of clarity, efficacy, and credibility, efforts have been made to clearly define accreditation and certification, standardize criteria through mandates to the European standards bodies, and improve coordination with other international organizations such as the OECD and ISO.[51]

The Danish Ministry for Business and Industry found similar problems. While recognizing that technical barriers were being addressed, companies and trade associations in electrical and electronic goods,[52] telecommunications equipment, and retail industries provided numerous examples of continuing problems at both the national and European level. Some of these issues rested with the member states, different levels of implementation of community legislation, and different interpretations of directives.[53] However, the lack of harmonization and standardization, and especially the lack of mutual recognition of non-harmonized standards, testing, and certification requirements was also a frequent barrier and cause for complaint.[54] This resulted in additional legal and regulatory requirements that went beyond harmonized community measures, with some Danish companies also frustrated by the lack of information provided by the Commission regarding the status of their complaint and the means of recourse available to them.[55]

The absence of standards was not the only problem affecting long-term Danish corporate strategies.[56] Several companies pointed to the constant amendments of legislative texts, which made it impossible to know which rules were actually applicable at a given time.[57] Some criticized the testing and certification agencies, where 'due to aggressive marketing on the part of certain test houses trying to exploit the insecurity of manufacturers, manufacturers are led to carry out unnecessary and costly third party tests' to show regulatory compliance.[58]

Other surveys conducted by the US Chamber of Commerce in Brussels and Eurochambres, the umbrella organization of the national Chambers of Commerce in Europe, found that their members were generally supportive of common standards, simplifying testing and certification processes, and extending product approval to non-EU authorities.[59] However, many firms provided examples of continuing problems with standards and regulatory practices, and complained that the member states frequently imposed additional requirements. The French Loi Toubon insistence on the use of French language on all products, the German preference for refill quotas for beverages, and the ban on sales of recyclable packaging in Denmark were all cited as violating free trade due to additional national restrictions.[60] Echoing many other surveys, both associations found that many firms believed that 'certain member states are deliberately attempting to protect their national standards,' resulting in considerable confusions about the relationship between national and European standardization. Because of the persistent complaints raised by individual companies, one trade association official estimated that, 'I spend half my time dealing with standards issues,' more than six years after the deadline for the single market programme.[61]

Though complaints were well documented, the legal, business, and regulatory environment has clearly changed. Companies with a good safety record and established product range frequently complain that the new directives are extremely bureaucratic, and costly to conform to.[62] Standards and product testing has become a billion-dollar industry and a hidden economic and political force in global trade. This may deter SMEs in particular, as high costs of certification in host country markets can undermine the commercial viability of promoting exports.

Exporting Europe: impacts on third country firms

Although removing barriers to trade was designed to aid intra-European trade, the effects of such policies have reverberated beyond the Community. The EU was anxious to avoid a recurrence of 'fortress Europe' imagery that characterized perceptions of the single market programme. However, the issue of market access for third country products and services was often treated as an afterthought, leading third countries to demand that the European policy process should be open and transparent.[63] European authorities sought to reassure their trading partners that 'any product, which is introduced on the Community territory, as long as it satisfies the legislation of the importing member country, and is admitted on its markets, will be entitled, as a matter of principle, to the benefits of free circulation in the Community.'[64]

In spite of efforts to stress non-discrimination, and the benefits of regulatory harmonization and mutual recognition within the EU for third country firms, the issue of standards, regulation, and conformity assessment has become an increasingly visible source of trade tensions.[65] EFTA countries were immediately offered extended mutual recognition,[66] direct participation in European standard-setting, and encouraged to frame their regulatory arrangements in terms of the single market. The applicant countries in Central and Eastern Europe have been pushed into pursuing regulatory alignment with the single market. Even with financial and technical assistance for their standards, testing, certification, and accreditation bodies, the transitional adoption of single market policies in this area focuses on alignment of product rather than process standards, alleviating the more costly burden of adjustment for companies to meet EU rules.[67] Technical assistance and aid has also been given to the Central and Eastern European countries through PraqIII (Phare), to the Gulf States through GCC (the Gulf Cooperation Council), and Soviet Republics through Tacis, as well as numerous individual standards, testing, and accreditation bodies in Europe, Asia, and Middle East to aid their efforts in meeting European requirements.

However, it has been the reaction and response of American firms that has placed the issue of standards and conformity assessment on the front-burner of trade issues for two reasons.[68] First, concerns about the transparency and openness of European standard-setting led American companies to lobby for greater influence in the negotiation. Though American efforts to gain a 'seat at the table' in European standardization were resolutely refused, concessions were made to allow American companies to comment on European standards under discussion.[69] Through an exchange of information with their American counterpart, the American National Standards Institute, ANSI, American companies were allowed to gain a preview of European discussions, although many companies still complained that this did not provide them with sufficient access to strongly influence the negotiations.

Second, and more importantly for many firms, the EU practice of independent third party (non-governmental) testing and certification meant only bodies notified by member state governments to the Commission had the authority to grant a CE mark. Because these notified bodies had to be located in Europe, it placed an additional burden on firms exporting to the EU to meet the necessary requirements for market access.[70] However, the Global Approach to Testing and Certification did address the issue of market access for third country parties. It provided that the EU should promote its relations with third countries, in particular by concluding mutual recognition agreements (known as MRAs) on the basis of Article 113 (now Article 133) of the Treaty.[71] Although the Europeans had found a method to accelerate trade liberalization and were willing to export it to the rest of the world,[72] the EU strategy was guided by concerns about reciprocity and mutual access.[73] Given the need to balance trade and regulatory concerns, the negotiations will be affected by calculations about the relative benefits of trade and market gains derived from regulatory recognition of different systems.[74] The demand for a balanced agreement with regard to the overall trade advantages meant that the European Union would link different sectors in negotiating mutual recognition agreements, and in doing so would seek to ensure that the regulations conditions of third countries be considered on a par with their EU counterparts. As Nicolaïdis notes, 'the 'recognition' involved here is of the 'equivalence', 'compatibility' or at least 'acceptability' of the counterpart's regulatory system; the 'mutual' part indicates that the real-location of authority is reciprocal and simultaneous so that governments agree to the general principle that if a product or service can be sold lawfully in one jurisdiction, it can be sold freely in any other participating jurisdiction, without having to comply with the regulations of these other jurisdictions'.

The coordination of European level testing and certification practices also meant that companies from third countries could not shop around and seek the easiest 'port of entry' into the EU. For European exporters, the idea was to extend the 'certified once, accepted everywhere' concept prevalent in Europe and gain the benefits of a regional market on a much larger scale. European companies, especially those with global production sites, were strongly supportive of these negotiations, and clearly recognized that it would provide them with leverage for opening up markets. One of the major European concerns regarding American market access was the large number of local and state standards over which the federal government had seemingly little control.[75]

For American companies, changes in Europe standardization and testing and certification has resulted in intense lobbying of Commission officials, domestic government agencies, and overseas trade representatives about their struggles to meet requirements that are often disadvantage to their industries (see *Dormont* case).[76] To alleviate such concerns, the European Commission put forward a Communication to the Council of Ministers which discussed in greater detail the conditions for entering negotiations, including the fact that negotiations could only be opened with countries that held technical and industrial competence comparable with that of the EU. Recognition of foreign regulatory authority was to be based on the same principles of trust and cooperation as had been the case internally in the single market program. In September 1992, the Council gave the Commission a formal mandate to start negotiations with the USA, Canada, Australia, and New Zealand.[77] Talks began initially with the United States in October 1992, with these negotiations considered the benchmark for further agreements, and reflecting the high profile that European trade liberalization activities in the areas of standards and mutual recognition of testing and certification had generated in the USA.

Along with pressures from the multilateral trade system to address non-tariff barriers to trade through the Agreement on Technical Barriers to Trade and the Agreement on the Application of Sanitary and Phytosanitary Standards, the transatlantic bilateral efforts to address the impact of standards and technical regulations on trade is at the forefront of policy discussions.[78] With the extension to other bilateral settings, as well as regionally within APEC, ASEAN, NAFTA, MERCOSUR, and the FTAA, its successful implementation will reverberate beyond the transatlantic marketplace. Although the WTO TBT Agreements encourage members to engage in bilateral mutual recognition agreements, the transatlantic case provides a good example not only of the bargaining dynamics and involvement of both the public and private sector in shaping outcomes, but also the importance and effect of enforcement and implementation on states and firms.

While the EU has concluded MRAs with the USA, Canada, New Zealand, Australia, Switzerland, and Israel, and is in the final stage of negotiations with Japan, the talks with the United States reached an impasse over accreditation. Sectors were originally selected on the basis of potential trade effects of liberalization for both sides and the feasibility of reaching an agreement. Many were areas covered under the new approach. And yet the negotiations highlighted not only the complexity of reaching agreement but also the regulatory differences between the two sides.

First, the demands by the EU that the authority of bodies in the USA certify to EU standards has resulted in substantial domestic adaptation within the American standards system, and altered the traditional arms-length relationship between business and government in this area. Under the mutual recognition agreements, if American testing and certification bodies are to be granted the same status as EU 'notified bodies', the US government will need to become more involved in guaranteeing the competence of conformity assessment bodies in the USA to enforce 'essential requirements' and certify to EU standards. Without such mechanisms, there would be no basis for mutual trust and credibility in the operation and equivalence of another trading partner. The US government has set up an accreditation programme, the National Voluntary Conformity Assessment Program (NVCASE) as a mechanism for addressing European demands. Recognition by NVCASE would prove sufficient to grant the US based testing and certification agencies the status of EU 'notified bodies'. Moreover, the American National Standards Institute (ANSI) has also responded to the changed situation by promoting a private sector-based national accreditation for testing and certification agencies engaged in quality and environmental management standards such as the National Cooperation for Laboratory Accreditation in 1998.[79] Though there was some private sector accreditation through ANSI, this is a shift in American regulatory practices since there has traditionally been less reliance on third party assessment and greater reliance on manufacturer's declaration of conformity (self-regulation), voluntary standards, and liability insurance. The new system is likely to foster greater uniformity in the American system, and streamline the fragmented accreditation system. This is important for those advocating the need for reciprocity. European complaints about the overlapping areas of jurisdiction at the national, state, and local level, as well as the host of private bodies involved, have in part been addressed by the new accountability system set up on the American side.

Secondly, the issue of compatible market access has generated substantial obstacles on the American side. With much of the regulatory oversight functions controlled by regulatory agencies such as EPA, FDA, and FCC, there was some initial reluctance to accept products and services accredited overseas. Although these agencies were recognized by a host of government agencies in European member states, there was reluctance about the technical competence of some of these bodies and their assessment standards. American negotiators felt that there was little oversight or control over notified bodies in Europe, and that there was little acknowledgment of the problems encountered in Europe that really required internal confidence-building measures to truly accept equivalence of each other member state's system. Though these issues proved to be a sticking point in the negotiations, the two sides differed sharply in how to resolve this impasse. The USA proposed to negotiate on an issue-by-issue basis in order to make some headway in certain sectors, but the EU refused arguing that the bilateral negotiations were part of a package deal that could not exempt certain sectors.

Yet negotiators managed to overcome such constraints right before their annual summit, to reach agreement in June 1997 on six key sectors including telecommunications, pharmaceuticals, medical devices, recreational marine craft, and electromagnetic compatibility. Yet despite the euphoria, MRA's represent a more restricted trade liberalization tool than exists in the single market. The MRA's cover only conformity assessment and do not address the heterogeneity of standards and regulations themselves.[80] Coverage of the first round of MRAs is estimated to cover about $47 billion in bilateral trade.[81]

The discussions about how to reduce the discrimination and foster greater cooperation received substantial support from multinational business. Concerned about the lack of concrete action in this area, multinationals under the auspices of the Transatlantic Business Dialogue (TABD) lobbied strongly for products approved by a European assessment body to be accepted into the USA without further testing and vice versa.[82] Given that many of the chief executives believed that 'competitiveness is hampered on both sides by excessive regulation and by differences between the EU and US regulatory systems,' their effort to raise the profile of bilateral mutual recognition agreements through a Transatlantic Committee on Standards, Certification and Regulatory Policy within the TABD placed clear pressure on the governments of both sides to reach agreement.[83] Small and Medium companies through their own parallel organization, TASBI, the Transatlantic Small Business Initiative, have lobbied strongly for such agreements since it is expected they would be the main beneficiaries.

The relative feasibility of implementing mutual recognition agreements will have an important effect, in the long run, on patterns of regulatory cooperation elsewhere. In the transatlantic context, the problem is how to secure mutual trust and credibility across regulatory systems, since the agreements did not provide for formal monitoring and sanctioning mechanisms to ensure compliance. The resulting joint committees set up to deal with problems and discuss market access issues involving stakeholders from the public and private sector, as well as the introduction of an early warning system is designed to minimize conflict when there are legitimate and entrenched differences in regulatory standards and practices. While the implementation process will provide a useful guide to the effectiveness of such policies in reducing the regulatory burdens for business, the successful bilateral negotiations have led to the extension of mutual recognition agreements in products (such as marine safety equipment) and services (such as insurance, architecture, and engineering services).[84] Yet even the selection of issues is contested, since there was initially a reluctance on the part of the federal government to negotiate for states and regulatory professions, and some sectors have been taken off the table in the early stages of the negotiation.

With the more ambitious proposals such as a transatlantic free trade area or new transatlantic marketplace being shelved, the largely technical subject matters such as regulatory cooperation and mutual recognition agreements have become increasingly important.[85] Building on the prior success of mutual recognition agreements, the most recent effort to deepen ties known as the Transatlantic Economic Partnership, has to do with overcoming regulatory obstacles through instruments such as scientific and regulatory dialogue, transparency and consultation. Such efforts are well suited to a bilateral framework, and although they backtrack from a more ambitious strategic commitment to trade liberalization, they do focus on what many policy-makers have described as 'deliverables'.

However, at the international level there is considerable difference between the United States and EU. American companies have been forced to confront the international implications of European activity in international standardization. Not only has European standardization engaged in widespread technical assistance to third countries, the EU members have fostered close ties with the international standards bodies through the Dresden and Vienna Agreements. These provide for accelerated procedures for the adoption of European standards as international ones, and enable the various different national standards bodies in Europe to continue to make themselves felt in international settings. Promoting a coordinated approach to international standardization where possible, American companies have expressed concern that such a concerted European strategy has undermined their influence on world markets.[86] While there are a number of efforts in Europe to build consortia of anticipatory standards through CEN, CENELEC, ETSI, and associate bodies, many American companies have been unwilling to participate in international standardization, with the exception of certain sectors such as medical devices and heavy equipment. There are growing concerns among trade associations and government agencies that American companies are falling behind in the standards race.[87] Industry representatives have testified in numerous congressional hearings and other fora that American companies are lagging behind on the standards front worldwide. Firms in the US have drawn the conclusion that they are disadvantaged by the current institutional structure of international standardization, and have difficulty in advancing their interests at the international and regional level.[88]

Proposals for a greater federal role in standardization, over the past four decades (1968, 1974, 1980, 1992), have failed to draw widespread support from industry. While some industry associations have complained about the lack of coordination exercised by ANSI, these concerns are heightened by the belief that the interlocking European system of industry, accreditation bodies, governments, and standards bodies represents a *de facto* industrial policy. Efforts to reform international standardization to reduce European influence and level the playing field within international standards bodies, where the USA has only one vote compared to the EU's fifteen, should not belie the fact that American firms have long been dominant in creating *de facto* industry standards that have shaped production patterns. Yet this tension reflects a sharp distinction between the more 'state-driven' European and 'market-driven' American approaches to standardization. With several high-profile failures to promote their standards in the international arena despite substantial investments (such as JAVA, OSI), American businesses are increasingly using alternative business consortia and other foras to establish common standards.[89] many of these consortia enable firms to keep proprietary control, while at the same time providing access to multiple users. American companies have come to think of standardization in more flexible institutional terms in response to the traditional institutional modes of standards coordination.

American corporate responses to changes in the European business and regulatory environment have primarily focused on three strategies: access, influence, and adaptation. In spite of difficulties with the governance of the single market, which has caused a good deal of uncertainty about the standards and conformity assessment policies for many American and European companies, the European regulatory regime is clearly shaping firm policies, perceptions, and strategies at the national, regional, and international levels. While the impact of the single market upon European firms is clearly being felt, it is also affecting American companies striving to keep ahead of developments in Europe to ensure that the 'gates of trade are not swinging shut as compliance with (European) standards developed overseas becomes the price of admission'.[90]

Conclusion

Corporate strategy is a crucial factor in shaping both the process and outcome of market integration. As this chapter documents, Europe's standardization strategy and its effects are not limited to companies within the single market, but also to those companies striving to exploit the commercial opportunities of an enlarged market. A number of reports, interviews, and surveys illustrate remaining problems in compliance and implementation with the EU's standardization regime, drawing attention to the importance of market governance. The material surveyed points to various adjustment strategies undertaken by firms and demonstrates the need for more research in this area. Since firms are at the forefront of adaptation, the study of European regulatory policy needs to take account of firm-level adjustments to understand the impact of efforts to construct a European market.

Just as scholars who focused on the changing nature of mass production highlighted the importance of customization and flexible specialization, and those who focused on product life cycles, just-in-time, and quality management, drew the attention of political economists to the internal dynamics of firms, so must research on European integration move beyond the undifferentiated view of the firm. Studies of regulation must also look not at the traditional lobbying activities of firms, but instead, how firms respond to and play a role in shaping their new regulatory environment. While studying the process and outcome of European market integration has resulted in attention being paid to implementation difficulties, and to the steps taken to improve the functioning of the single market, this has tended to focus on the public rather than private side of governance.[91]

Market governance is also related to the issues of legitimacy, accountability, and representation that are addressed in the conclusion. To date, the focus has been on public governance, with some of the solutions advocated by Majone, Dehousse, and others borrowed from the American context.[92] However, suggestions for federal administrative procedures that allow for widespread input from interested parties through notice and comment in the public sphere do not address the asymmetrical influence and access of private firms, as compared to other actors, in the standardization process.[93]

11

Conclusion:
Governance and Market-Building

The governance of the market has inspired considerable debate. Part of that discussion has focused on the relationship between states and markets, and their effectiveness as alternative mechanisms for coordinating economic activity, setting parameters, and simplifying and stabilizing conditions of choice. While the pendulum appears to have shifted towards markets, many neoliberal reforms, often touted as a means of 'rolling back the state', contain elements that actually strengthen the state in some ways. In fact, the divorce of markets from states is untenable, and markets are absolutely dependent on public authority.[1] The market-oriented reforms enacted by the European Union are particular striking in this regard since the effort to create 'freer markets' has resulted in 'more rules' and strengthened the authority of the European Union in exercising market governance.[2]

The analysis of market integration in this book has sought to explain this puzzle by demonstrating that the regulatory agenda of the EU has come to dominate the regulatory agendas of the member states, as the supply of and demand for European regulations has produced thousands of regulations in a host of policy areas. As the EU increasingly recognized the need to tackle the growing number of national regulations and standards, since these could threaten market integration, the central task facing the EU seemed to be finding the most efficient way to achieve its public policy goals and objectives. In trying to find an effective mechanism to bridge the gap between different regulatory traditions, European governments grapple with a double challenge. They have to reduce obstacles to trade to promote competition and find more efficient ways to regulate, while also protecting important welfare policy goals. In the end, however, there is more at stake in the discussion of regulation than the question of an efficient choice of instruments.[3]

Judgements of efficiency and effectiveness regarding market integration in previous chapters have focused on aggregate outputs. This concluding chapter addresses broader concerns about governance emerging from the choice of regulatory format and design by briefly summarizing the transformation of governance within the EU. It then examines the implications of these regulatory arrangements in terms of legitimacy, accountability, and power. The chapter concludes by comparing the European and American approaches to market-building. This provides a good comparative and historical perspective on experiences in dealing with both the distribution of regulatory competencies across different levels of government, and the distribution of regulatory competencies between the public and private sector.

The different arguments and perspectives on regulation laid out in Chapter 1 can then be evaluated in terms of their contribution to understanding the European system of governance. Stated differently, the issue of control by the public or private sector is at issue here. At the risk of oversimplification, the European view takes private involvement in regulatory policy as a given, while the American perspective struggles with the legitimacy of the regulatory regime, both in terms of the degree of administrative discretion and the degree of interest group influence over implementation of the law.[4] Yet the issues articulated by Lowi in the American context seem to be finding greater resonance at the European level, as the central problem of governing at the European level is how to combine a concern for accountability with a sensitivity to the full range of interests affected. We can see this clearly in the literature on the democratic deficit, as well as in the admonitions of the European Commission to the standards bodies to increase transparency, representation, and decision-making. Implicit in this view is that regulation is not just an instrument of production (as suggested by interest group theories) but is constitutive of other norms and values promoted by public interest theories that are described in Chapter 1 as market-correcting or market-modifying.[5]

The transformation of governance

Even though the single market was conceptualized as an economic project, the institutional design of the project has become increasingly important in understanding both the process and outcome of market-making. In evaluating the link between economic performance and political institutions, the importance of appropriate governance structures is crucial.[6] The European economic landscape has been transformed over the past four decades as regional efforts to establish a common framework of rules for interstate commerce and trade have been pursued within a setting of well-defined legal and judicial mechanisms, regulatory structures, and mechanisms of enforcement and compliance.[7]

In tackling impediments to cross-border trade, the European Union has embarked on a sustained effort to build, shape, and maintain a single market by coordinating divergent national standards and regulations. After reviewing these developments at length, several issues raised at the beginning of the book can now be more fully addressed. These include the effectiveness of policy mechanisms for coordinating regulatory traditions, the distribution of regulatory competencies, the interplay between the public and private sector, and the consequences of private sector governance.

Nowhere is the importance of effective governance structures more clearly demonstrated than in the harmonization approach. Past policy experience with harmonization has propelled the European Union into searching for alternative mechanisms. The notion that there was a 'regulatory mismatch' between policy objectives and outcomes, and that institutional arrangements do not always work out perfectly reminds us that we need to study the evolution of policies over time to understand the process of policy change.[8] Because policy-making takes place within a particular context of ideas, the lack of credibility of the harmonization approach in meeting expectations was reinforced by ideological trends in public policy and administration away from command and control legislation towards more flexible market-based instruments. The neoliberal discourse only served to emphasize the impotence of the interventionist approach, and the search for alternative solutions to tackle interstate barriers to trade has relied heavily on the law to shape the framework of relations between states. Trade liberalization has been painstakingly mapped out by legal rulings that have played a key role in resolving territorial conflicts over regulatory jurisdiction and competence.

Law and markets are inextricably intertwined. Law controls the capacity of states to exercise regulatory discretion, and in doing so shapes intergovernmental relations. Market-building as a result of intergovernmental politics is not surprising to scholars of European integration who have stressed the institutional self-interests of governments and the dilemmas of joint decision-making.[9] This relationship is not fixed or static, since member states seek to circumvent control through legal and treaty exemptions or exceptions while the European Commission seeks to ensure that such efforts do not undermine the collective thrust of the single market. The balance between territorial units is constantly being challenged by one or another unit, using the Court as the arbiter of conflicts over regulatory jurisdictions heightened by the principle of subsidiarity.[10] Intergovernmental politics shape regulatory policy and determine the parameters of political choices exercised by states, and economic theories of federalism that search for the optimal distribution of competencies underestimate the pressures of politics and law. The system of regulatory governance is not simply about the most efficient approach, but is also a political choice that is profoundly dependent on the legal order.[11]

Governance and private interests

That market, however, is also being constructed by private interests. Governance in the EU is no longer simply between a set of sovereign states, and the framework for institutional coordination is part of a larger global trend that has garnered increased notice in foreign economic policy.[12] Governance is not synonymous with government activity. The current trend towards business self-regulation through voluntary standard-setting and corporate codes of conduct is perhaps indicative of a shift from state to market.[13] At the very least, it suggests that business is interacting with governments and society in new ways, resulting in new forms of regulation.[14] While previous chapters have shown that private sector negotiations are expanding over a range of regulatory issues, such cooperation can take a variety of institutional forms. In the European case, governments have *chosen to use private actors* for public purposes, thereby incorporating market incentives, norms, and practices into the provision of public goods. Regulatory outcomes are not the result of private domination of the regulatory process but the products of *policy choices* exercised by governments. Though some argue that this substitution for direct governmental action may undermine governing capacity, others argue that this complements governmental efforts by facilitating the larger purposes of regulatory initiatives.[15]

A more convincing explanation may be borrowed from traditional analyses of the delegation issue. To ensure policy credibility and promote collective action, it may be rational for states to delegate regulatory authority to the regional level to enforce agreements that stabilize competition and constrain the ability of states to impose costs on one another through protectionist trade practices.[16] Particularly in the area of social regulation (health, safety, environment, and consumer protection), the delegation of certain responsibilities to the private sector may be due to the need for expertise to operationalize public policies. With the shift from command and control policies towards more flexible regulatory options such as process and management standards, the polluter pays principle, and ergonomics, standards bodies are well suited to performing rule-making functions since they can provide the necessary industrial and technical expertise to ensure enforcement and implementation.[17]

Such private sector coordination is rarely autonomous, since market relations are embedded in a complex set of contractual relations, and the rules and norms for regulating performance provided by the private sector are often legitimated by the public sector. Though this functional division of regulatory competencies is important in understanding European efforts to reconcile trade liberalization with domestic public policy objectives and goals such as health, safety, and environmental standards, much of the attention in regulatory studies has focused on the territorial distribution of regulatory competencies and the relationship between different levels of government in European policy-making.[18] Yet the transformation of governance has resulted in a distinctive model of regulation that is a hybrid of state and non-state actors.[19] Though private sector organizations taking on governmental functions is not a new phenomenon in Europe, given private interest government, corporatism, and *associative regulation*, the delegation of rule-making to European standard-setting bodies has raised concerns that more and more responsibility for governance is removed from public scrutiny.[20]

However, the transformation of governance does not simply mean the undue influence of private interests in European affairs. While the multi-level political system allows various interests to gain access and influence, as evidenced by the expansion of lobbying, private interests are playing a much more multifaceted role.[21] The 'outsourcing' of public sector activity and the effort to structure market outcomes to achieve both economic gains and political purposes suggest that the strategy employed by the European polity in pursuing market governance enables public actors to escape capture.[22] Instead of industry trying to exercise leverage and influence public policy-makers, the EU has instead chosen to engage in market-building by drawing on the resources of private actors, as regulations are likely to be more effective when those that must comply with them aid in their design.

That being the case, the empirical literature on the single market needs to support this claim that the transformation of governance is more effective in fostering free trade. One of the key findings in this study is that the politics of market-building within the European Union has proved extremely contentious and difficult. Though the transformation in European governance has increased the range of participants in decision-making, the resulting integration effort has not led to a frictionless, perfectly operating market as predicted by many neoclassical assessments. Regulatory gaps still remain, in part because private actors' perceptions of the standard-setting process influence their strategies in negotiations, and mutual trust and credibility are key factors in fostering agreement.[23]

Bargaining and negotiations in standardization

As previous chapters illustrate, addressing barriers to trade depends not only on formal institutional design and governance structures, but also on informal institutional dynamics, such as routines, norms, and operating practices.[24] Economic interactions among those involved in setting standards for market access include the formulation of shared rules and norms, which can be established legal practices or collective understandings, based on custom or explicit or tacit agreement. The *juridification and codification* of such rules and norms enable those participating in such private governance regimes in the European Union to organize themselves, to compete and cooperate, and to shape policy outcomes.[25]

Moreover, given that different kinds of market competition will produce different kinds of politics, large firms with greater resources are more likely than small firms, consumers, and labour interests to set the agenda. Political negotiations in standard-setting will usually reproduce the position of the advantaged group, with the integration of markets based on the ability to build a political coalition around an acceptable common standard. This depends on the political leadership exercised by those firms willing to bargain, persuade, and compromise. On many regulatory issues, agreement on rules governing market access may depend as much on the negotiating dynamics of firms as on the policies of governments. From a political economy perspective, as it is firms which must make the adjustments in production, marketing, and distribution practices to meet varying standards and rules to access different national markets, research on standard-setting suggests that more attention should be given to the role of corporate strategies and behaviour in shaping rules and outcomes.[26]

By focusing on the role of firms in the standards arena, we learn more about how trade differences are being tackled, and how these agreements can influence corporate strategies and regulatory policy-making. The survey results in the previous chapter provide a mixed picture regarding the impact of greater market integration. While it was expected that firms would rationalize and restructure to take advantage of a single market, a large degree of uncertainty remains. This is in part due to the continuing obstacles that many individual firms have found as a result of continued discriminatory standards, testing and certification practices, and also entrenched business practices that make it difficult for new entrants to establish local networks and ties. Markets still remain segmented in some areas as the principle of mutual recognition of standards, testing, and certification practices has not operated successfully in practice, and governments continue to impose additional regulatory requirements and demonstrate an unwillingness to accept the mutual equivalence of standards, regulations, and conformity assessment. Coupled with the absence of European standards in key sectors, the European regulatory regime has not yet achieved its end goal of securing trade liberalization and market access, eight years after the single market deadline.

Regulating delegation: accountability, oversight, and legitimacy

As noted earlier, the institutional intertwining between the public and private sector has serious effects on the nature of governance itself.[27] Though there has been much discussion about democratic governance and legitimacy in the context of European political institutions, and particularly to issues of accountability, representation, implementation, and problems of joint decision-making in interlocked systems, the same issues have received little attention in relation to non-governmental or private institutions.[28] Similarly, the legitimacy of devolving authority to the supranational level has led to concerns about the decreasing democratic accountability of such action given the effective reduction of national control.

Yet the operation and performance of private actors in the regulatory process deserves equal consideration. In theory, private institutions and actions, one step removed from the democratic process, are less accessible to public scrutiny.[29] The extensive reliance on private actors to assist in rule-making and compliance with regulatory objectives makes the issue of monitoring and oversight increasingly important to safeguard public interest objectives. While Majone argues that delegation to the European level is designed to increase the credibility of the regulatory process, and is often justified by the need for expertise in highly complex and technical matters, the result has been the growth of authority across a number of non-majoritarian institutions such as courts, central banks, and regulatory authorities.[30]

Though Majone's argument is reminiscent of the public interest perspective on regulation, it also separates administration from politics. Enabling such non-majoritarian institutions to exercise discretion to realize regulatory objectives may in principle improve efficiency, but it also reflects a deep ambivalence in the American context about the exercise of authority by the state.[31] In the European context, the delegation to non-majoritarian institutions may reduce transaction costs, but it also raises concerns about legitimacy and accountability.[32]

In searching for the optimal solution to achieve its regulatory objectives, the costs of legislative and executive oversight are not minimal. While Majone argues that accountability by results can provide sufficient legitimacy for efficiency-oriented policies and institutions, using a combination of control instruments, it is clear from the previous chapters that this takes sustained and active effort on the part of the EU.[33] Since negotiations in standardization may result in no agreement, protecting the status quo, much effort has been put into ensuring the credibility and effectiveness of the transfer of regulatory functions to standards bodies. While this does not represent 'regulatory capture', since regulatory activity has been explicitly delegated by the European Union, there are risks that private interests will pursue their own goals and objectives as principal-agent theorists have recognized, even when the outcomes are intended by public authorities to promote their broad policy objectives and interests. Under these circumstances, the institutional choices made by the European Union could be seen as highly discretionary, suffering from weak oversight and lacking incentives to force collective political outcomes.

The risks of failure and erosion of accountability are two of the most important factors that the European Union has been forced to address in delegating regulatory authority to non-governmental, standard-setting institutions. Case studies on toys, machines, medical devices, and construction products (see Chapter 8) highlight the possibilities of regulatory failure, not least the problems in reaching agreement on common European standards, and the mechanisms used by the European Commission to improve the pace and organization of European standard-setting. Though this has resulted in contentious disputes between the European standards bodies and the Commission regarding the cause of problems and the nature of solutions, the delegation to private actors has also enabled the Commission to shift the blame and offload problems of integrating diverse and sometimes intractable market differences.

With this shift in regulatory strategy, the European Commission has to focus more attention on monitoring and compliance. Delegation does not mean abdication: often an optimal amount of delegation will involve continuing oversight by public agencies, while giving private agents a certain amount of agenda-setting power.[34] In using private resources, the Commission has always maintained the credible threat of government intervention if this strategy fails to respond to the public interest. Oversight mechanisms are in place, and the combination of instruments including judicial review, budgetary sanctions, and procedural requirements is intended to foster compliance. Although the regulatory framework is designed to enforce an integrated market, facilitate intergovernmental competition, promote free trade, and provide certain regional-level public goods,[35] the shortcomings of the policy can be attributed only in part to the standards bodies. The credibility of the policy is also dependent on compliance by public authorities at the national level. This has proved problematic as some member states have been reluctant to accept regulatory equivalence through mutual recognition. As a result, the legal framework to create and sustain member state compliance is crucial.

European law has actively shaped markets, acting as the 'free trade umpire' in balancing the goals of market liberalization and market regulation, and fostered market compliance. The legal regime has shaped the market, creating a new legal order that is both market-preserving and market-correcting. Legal decisions are thus tied to conceptions about the nature of the market, the member–Community relationship, and the role of regulation in the economy. The end result is that the apparent lessening of trade authority at the domestic level does not mean stronger markets, weaker governments, since the capacity to shape, organize, and maintain markets has actually been reconfigured at the European level. What has changed is the method by which public authorities create and regulate markets.

Through a comparative lens: law and imperfect markets

In both the United States and Europe, the effort to construct an internal market has been a painstakingly difficult process. The United States federal system has proved a malleable but lasting institutional structure. Although the form of this system has changed considerably since its founding, and political, economic, and social forces have generated great changes in the overall scope of government activity, the legal and political efforts to foster interdependence among markets bears some resemblance to the European experience. A subsequent study, using a comparative-institutional approach to transatlantic market integration, will build on this work to explore the historical experiences of nineteenth-century American market-building with that of twentieth-century European Union market-building. It will assess similarities and differences in policy-making and institution-building in constructing 'internal' markets in goods, capital, services, and people.[36]

Comparisons of the growth of an integrated American economy and the European internal market have been made briefly at several junctures

TABLE 11.1 *Comparison of developments in US and EU single markets*

Key Issues	US	EU
Early references to interstate economic protectionism	US Constitution; *Federalist* No. 42; *Brown* v. *Maryland*	Spaak Report; Treaty of Rome; Marshall Plan
Obstacles to market consolidation	State police, proprietary, licence and tax powers; designed to protect health, safety, welfare, and morals	Health, safety, and environmental standards; licensing; testing and certification (non-tariff barriers)
Key legislation	Interstate Commerce Clause; Privileges and Immunities Clause; and Equal Protection Clause	White Paper on Single Market; New Approach and Global Approach
Key legal decisions	*Gibbons* v. *Ogden*	*Dassonville, Cassis,* and *Keck*
Role of business	Active (potential appearance of capture); arms-length relationship with government	Active (delegation); policy accommodation with government
Means of removing barriers	Pre-emption, reciprocity, and judicial decisions	Harmonization, mutual recognition, and judicial decisions
Market fragmentation in single market	Some sectors (e.g. insurance, trucking, agricultural, food)	Some sectors (e.g. tax, company law, intellectual property rights)

in this book. It is clear that public authorities in both Europe and the United States have been important 'market-builders'. Efforts to devise a uniform system of commerce and trade have been at the heart of American economic development. Using a variety of mechanisms including judicial decisions, reciprocal state statutes, and pre-emption statutes, the basic free trade premiss of the United States has a counterpart in the European Union.

Both the United States and European Union have legal clauses governing the free movement of goods. In their efforts to create internal markets, they have allowed states wide concurrent powers, provided they do not discriminate. Though the American single market has been established with much less interference upon the sovereign powers of individual states than in the European Union, legal and regulatory intervention has been crucial to removing persistent obstacles to free trade. Both European and American firms have used the law to achieve greater manœuvrability, with legal rulings carefully balancing states rights against protectionist politics. This has also involved consideration of providing an actual and demonstrable burden on interstate commerce.[37]

Judicial interpretations of the locus of regulatory authority have largely determined the shape of intergovernmental relations, and the boundaries of economic control over markets. Both the EU and USA allowed states to exercise regulatory control, or police powers, and were then forced to acknowledge the impact of such activities on their internal markets. The range of policy options of states has been restricted as the imperatives of economic growth, competition, and development have necessitated not only negative integration in areas of product regulation, safety, and environmental standards and competition policy, but also positive integration.

The pattern of market integration is similar in other, less conventionally recognized ways. The demand for rules to govern commerce in the United States has led to a variety of sources of supply, including the private sector itself. Though contemporary discussions on regulation have focused on the growth of 'big government' and the need to reduce 'red tape', this has ignored the wealth of regulations derived from private sector efforts at coordination. Business organizations, standards bodies, professional societies, and trade associations have often provided standards used by both the public and private spheres. In the nineteenth century, a range of private organizations carried out many of the responsibilities that we tend to associate with governments.

In the American system, use of the private sector to provide rules, standards, and codes resulted in the proliferation of private organizations to an extent not encountered in Europe.[38] Reflecting a system that is 'market-oriented' rather than 'state-oriented', the American standards system produced hundreds of organizations, with often overlapping jurisdictions and participants. This pluralistic but highly fragmented system has not been replicated in Europe, where the standardization strategy at the national and regional levels has been much more interventionist, often supported or funded by the state. Though the US government has made extensive use of private sector standards to achieve market integration and meet regulatory requirements,[39] the arms-length relationship between business and government in this area differs from the more concerted *strategic regulation* approach in Europe to promote standards as trade instruments. While European efforts have been criticized as a disguised form of industrial policy, the principles of trade liberalization, namely mutual recognition and standardization, are crucial components of the *expansionary regulation* effort to export the single market programme and enhance the strategic advantages for European industry globally.[40]

By contrast, the multiplicity of private organizations involved in setting standards means that, in some sectors, the American market is still fragmented and business is confronted with a range of choices about standards. Differences in interstate regulations and standards in the building sector, agricultural sector, trucking and transportation, and banking sector provide ample evidence that the American market is still 'imperfect'. The lack of coordination among standards bodies domestically can also hinder collective action and stymie efforts to exercise leadership in international standardization. Rather than take this more pluralist route and allow 'standards competition' among a number of different public and private organizations and agencies, the European Union has fostered a *strategic regulation* approach around a single set of European standards.

Though the USA and EU reflect different perspectives about the relationship between business and government, in other ways patterns of regulatory integration are similar. Both the EU and the USA have used law to shape markets, used private bodies to promote governance, and fostered interstate commerce by restricting state protectionism.

As a result, the politics of market-building in the USA and EU is both functional and territorial, involving both public and private actors. The conventional view of politics involving intergovernmental bargaining is only one side of the regulatory equation. The other side of regulatory politics is widely viewed as excruciatingly technical and involving arcane and tedious matters. These issues, such as the labelling of food additives, the safety level of electrical emissions, and the designation of appropriate hallmarking of precious metals, are now increasingly visible on the European internal and external trade agenda. Questions raised earlier concerning the importance of how, why, and at what level of regulation this occurs hopefully can now be addressed. The primary lesson in all of this is that viewing the discussion of regulation as 'industry capture' does not really convey the various alternatives available.[41] Business 'pressures' but it is also 'pressured'. Certainly industry influence is greater than that of consumers, trade unions, and other interests in the standardization process. But the European 'regulatory state' does not neatly fit into the theories of regulation outlined in Chapter 1. The European polity has a mixture of public interest objectives, administrative oversight and control, and interest group dynamics in establishing the rules governing the European market.

Viewing market integration this way does not necessarily mean that the capacity of the public authorities in shaping markets is declining, or that the most obvious illustration of liberalization is the retreat from regulation of the economy. Instead, it suggests that governance is being exercised in multifaceted ways. The various institutional mechanisms by which economic activity is coordinated and the circumstances under which those mechanisms were chosen to deepen integration have altered the relationship between states and markets in Europe.[42] Markets require highly sophisticated institutional arrangements to maintain their efficiency and effectiveness, and the organizational innovation of the EU has been to use the private sector in an *ancillary role* to the state. As the efforts of the EU increasingly shift from *market-making* to *market maintenance*, this will require mutual credibility and trust among both public and private actors, to ensure that the liberalizing effects of common standards and mutual equivalence of national regulations are adhered to in practice. The previous chapters make clear that markets are built and shaped in a variety of ways by governments, and that any assessment of the European experience reinforces Polanyi's argument that

there was nothing natural about laissez-faire; free markets could never have come into being merely by allowing things to take their course. . . . the road to the free market was opened and kept open by an enormous increase in continuous centrally organized and controlled interventionism. . . . Administration had to be continually on the watch to ensure the free working of the system.[43]

NOTES

Chapter 1

1. Karl Polanyi, *The Great Transformation: The Political and Economic Origins of our Time* (Boston: Beacon Press, 1944).
2. See the discussion in D. North, 'Markets and Other Allocation Systems in History: The Challenge of Karl Polanyi', *Journal of European Economic History*, 6 (1977), 703–16; K. Polanyi, 'The Economy as Instituted Process,' in Polanyi (ed.), *Trade and Markets in the Early Empires: Economies in History and Theory* (Chicago: Henry Regnery Company, 1957).
3. See the excellent article by W. Goldstein, 'The EU: Capitalist or Dirigiste Regime?', in A. Cafruny and G. Rosenthal (eds.), *The State of the European Community: The Maastricht Debates and Beyond*, vol. ii (Boulder, Colo.: Lynne Reinner, 1993).
4. P. Reuter, *La Communauté européenne du charbon et de l'acier* (Paris: Librarie Générale de Droit et de Jurisprudence, 1953), 142.
5. L. Tsoukalis, *The New European Economy*, 2nd edn. (Oxford: Oxford University Press, 1993), ch. 2.
6. See A. Prakash and J. A. Hart, *Globalization and Governance* (London: Routledge, forthcoming); J. H. Mittelman *Globalization: Critical Reflections* (Boulder, Colo.: Lynne Reinner, 1996).
7. For historical research on the role of the state in maintaining markets, see Polanyi, *The Great Transformation*.
8. P. Kapteyn, *The Stateless Market: The European Dilemma of Integration and Civilization* (New York: Routledge, 1993); see also S. Strange, *The Retreat of the State: The Diffusion of Power in the World Economy* (Cambridge: Cambridge University Press, 1996).
9. Regulation can be used for both market-making and market-correcting policy interventions, with the former aiming to harmonize national policies to eliminate barriers to trade and the latter mitigating negative externalities and providing public goods. See F. Scharpf, *Governing in Europe* (Oxford: Oxford University Press, 1999), 44–5.
10. Research on global governance provides further evidence that the Westphalian state is no longer the most efficient unit of aggregation for supplying various collective goods. See e.g. Prakash and Hart, *Globalization and Governance*.
11. S. K. Vogel, *Freer Markets, More Rules: Regulatory Reform in Advanced Industrial Countries* (Ithaca, NY: Cornell University Press, 1996).
12. See G. Majone, 'The Rise of the Regulatory State in Europe', *West European Politics*, 17, no. 3 (1994), 77–101; G. Majone, *Regulating Europe* (London: Routledge, 1996); 'From the Positive to the Regulatory State: Causes

and Consequences of Changes in the Mode of Governance', *Journal of Public Policy*, 17, no. 2 (1997), 139–67; 'A European Regulatory State?', in J. Richardson (ed.), *European Union: Power and Policy-Making* (London: Routledge, 1996). Majone's work is central to any discussion of EU regulatory policy, and is particularly useful for the discussion below as he draws upon many ideas developed in the American literature on regulation. A selective list of his other relevant publications includes: 'The New European Agencies: Regulation by Information', *Journal of European Public Policy*, 4, no. 2 (1997); 'Temporal Inconsistency and Policy Credibility: Why Democracies Need Non-majoritarian Institutions', EUI Working Paper No. 96/57, Robert Schuman Centre, European University Institute, Florence (1997); 'Mutual Recognition in Federal Type Systems', EUI Working Paper, SPS, European University Institute, Florence (1993); 'The Problem of Regulatory Legitimacy in the United States and the European Union', paper presented at the Conference on 'Rethinking Federalism in the US and EU', Harvard University, 19–20 Apr. 1999; See also J. Pelkmans, 'Regulation: An Economic Perspective', in H. Siebert (ed.), *The Completion of the Internal Market* (Tübingen: J. B. Mohr, 1990); S. Woolcock, M. Hodges, and K. Schreiber, *Britain, Germany and 1992: The Limits of Deregulation* (London: Pinter, 1991); G. Majone, 'The European Community as a Regulatory State', Lectures given at the Academy of European Law, European University Institute, Florence (July 1994); Special Issue on 'Regulation in the European Union', *Journal of European Public Policy*, 3, no. 4 (1996); R. Dehousse, 'Regulation by Networks in the European Community: The role of Regulatory Agencies', *Journal of European Public Policy*, 4, no. 2 (1997), 246–61.

13. See e.g. M. Huelschoff, 'Domestic Politics and Dynamic Issue Linkage: A Reformulation of Integration Theory', *International Studies Quarterly*, 38 (1994), 256.

14. 'Crossed Lines', *Financial Times* editorial, 20 Jan. 1999, 13.

15. K. Nicolaïdis and M. Egan, 'Regional Policy Externality and Market Governance: European, International and Transatlantic Regulatory Cooperation', in W. Mattli (ed.), Special Issue, *Journal of European Public Policy*, March 2001.

16. For an examination of such efforts in the service sector, see K. Nicolaïdis, 'Mutual Recognition among Nations: The European Community and Trade in Services', Harvard University, Ph.D. Dissertation, 1993; more generally E. Epstein, 'Resolving the Regulator's Dilemma: International Coordination of Banking Regulations', *International Organization*, 43, no. 2 (1989), 323–47; P. Genschel and T. Plümper, 'Regulatory Competition and International Co-operation', *Journal of European Public Policy*, 4, no. 4 (1997), 626–42; W. D. Coleman and G. R. D. Underhill (eds.), *Regionalism and Global Economic Integration: Europe, Asia, and the Americas* (London: Routledge, 1998).

17. The terms 'EC' and 'EU' are used in their appropriate historic and legal contexts. The terms EU and Community are used interchangeably since the

single market is positioned within Pillar I of the Treaty. Originally, European Economic Communities designated the three founding treaties, the Treaty of Paris establishing the Coal and Steel Community 18 Apr. 1951, the Treaty of Rome establishing the European Economic Community, 25 Mar. 1957, and the European Atomic Energy Commission, 25 Mar. 1957. The Single European Act of 1986 changed the designation to European Community, and the European Union was established by the Treaty of European Union, 7 Feb. 1992 (herein Treaty of European Union or Treaty of Maastricht). The Treaty of Maastricht established three separate pillars of activity, whereby the first pillar covers all traditional EU matters, the second pillar covers Common Foreign and Security Policy, and the third pillar covers Justice and Home Affairs. The EU covers all three pillars which were maintained by the Treaty of Amsterdam. The treaties were amended by the Treaty of Amsterdam Amending the Treaty of European Union, Treaties Establishing the European Communities, and Certain Related Acts, 7 Oct. 1997, OJ C 240 (1) 1997. For the consolidated version of the TEU see OJ C 340 145, 1997. Pillar I functions on the basis of the Community method allowing the exclusive right of initiative for the Commission, Council voting by qualified majority or unanimity, Co-decision by the European Parliament and legal jurisdiction and oversight by the European Court of Justice. Pillar I includes such topics as free movement of goods, capital, services, and people; competition policy; common commercial policy; social policy; industry, economic and social cohesion, public health, consumer protection, environment, education, employment, economic and monetary union, among other topics.

18. V. Haufler, 'Private Sector International Regimes', unpublished paper (Carnegie Endowment for International Peace, 1998).
19. For a similar perspective, see S. Wilks, 'Regulatory Compliance and Capitalist Diversity in Europe', *Journal of European Public Policy*, 3, no. 4 (1996), 538–9; A. M. Sbragia, 'Governance, the State and the Market: What is Going on?', *Governance*, 13, no. 2 (Apr. 2000), 243–50.
20. P. Cerny, 'The Politics of Transnational Regulation: Deregulation or Re-regulation', Special Issue of *European Journal of Political Research*, 19 (Mar./Apr. 1991).
21. D. Swann, *The Retreat of the State: Deregulation and Privatisation in the UK and US* (Hemel Hempstead: Harvester Wheatsheaf, 1988).
22. See Organization for Economic Cooperation and Development, *Regulatory Reform, Privatisation and Competition* (Paris: OECD Publications, 1992).
23. G. Underhill, 'Markets beyond Politics? The State and the Internationalisation of Financial Markets', *European Journal of Political Research* (1991), 197–225.
24. See S. Breyer, *Regulation and its Reform* (Cambridge, Mass.: Harvard University Press, 1982) for a detailed explanation of the economic justifications for regulation.
25. See Majone, *Regulating Europe*, esp. pp. 68–72; Majone, 'Independence vs Accountability? Non-majoritarian Institutions and Democratic Government

in Europe', EUI Working Paper, SPS 93/4, European University Institute, Florence, 1994.

26. See also Pelkmans, 'Regulation', in Siebert, *Internal Market*.

27. The question of whether these competitive economic pressures lead strict states to reduce the stringency of their regulations is the subject of extensive debate. See C. Barnard, 'Social Dumping Revisited: Some Lessons from Delaware', paper presented at the ECSA Biennial Conference, Pittsburgh, 2–5 June 1999; F. Scharpf, 'Economic Integration, Democracy and the Welfare State', paper presented at the GAAC Young Scholars Meeting, Bremen (Aug. 1996); D. Vogel, *Trading up: Consumer and Environmental Regulation in a Global Economy* (Cambridge, Mass.: Harvard University Press, 1995); A. Héritier et al., *Die Veränderun von Staatlichkeit in Europa: Ein regulativer Wettbewerb—Deutschland, Grossbritannien und Frankreich in der Europäischen Union* (Opladen: Leske & Budrich, 1994).

28. M. Cappalletti, M. Seccombe, and J. H. H. Weiler, *Integration through Law*, vol. i, book 1 (Berlin: De Gruyter, 1985); M. Conant, *The Constitution and the Economy: Objective Theory and Critical Commentary* (Norman, Okla.: University of Oklahoma Press, 1991); D. Kommers and M. Waelbroeck, 'Legal Integration and the Free Movement of Goods: The American and European Experience', in Cappalletti, Seccombe, and Weiler, *Integration through Law*, vol. i, book 1; T. Sandalow and E. Stein (eds.), *Courts and Free Markets* (Oxford: Clarendon Press, 1982).

29. P. Stewart, 'Foreword', in Sandalow and Stein (eds.), *Courts and Free Markets*, vii–viii.

30. See A. Berle and G. Means, *The Modern Corporation and Private Property* (New York: Macmillan, 1932).

31. See B. Kohler-Koch, 'Organized Interests in European Integration', in H. Wallace and A. Young (ed.), *Participation and Policy-Making in the European Union* (Oxford: Clarendon Press, 1997); B. Kohler-Koch, 'Catching up with Change: The Transformation of Governance in the European Union', *Journal of European Public Policy*, 3 (1996), 359–89.

32. See the excellent discussion by Grabosky about the variety of governance mechanisms to achieve regulatory compliance in P. Grabosky, 'Using Nongovernmental Resources to Foster Regulatory Compliance', *Governance*, 8, no. 4 (1995), 527–50.

33. A. M. Sbragia, *Debt Wish* (Pittsburgh: University of Pittsburgh Press, 1996), 14–16;

34. Majone, *Regulating Europe*; see also Haufler, 'Private Sector International Regimes'.

35. M. Egan, 'Comparing Markets across Time and Space: European and American Economic Integration', manuscript in progress; A. Chandler, *The Visible Hand: The Managerial Revolution in American Business* (Cambridge, Mass.: Harvard University Press, 1997); A. Chandler, 'The Beginnings of Big Business in American Industry', *Business History Review*, 33 (Spring 1959), 1–31.

36. The emphasis here is on the role of firms as institutions, reacting to and altering their policies in response to the politically driven process of market integration, which affects domestic production structures and regulatory regimes.

37. There has been a growth of literature on models of capitalism and corporate governance in Europe. These have focused primarily on the macro-level of analysis and there have been few systematic assessments of micro-level changes as a result of integration, an area which needs further empirical investigation.

38. See Ch. 4.

39. M. Egan, 'Modes of Business Governance: European Management Styles and Corporate Cultures', *West European Politics*, 20 (1997), 1–21.

40. C. Tiebout, 'A Pure Theory of Local Expenditure', *Journal of Political Economy*, 64 (1956), 416–24.

41. F. Scharpf, 'The Joint-Decision Trap: Lessons from German Federalism and European Integration', *Public Administration*, 66 (1988), 239–78; 'The Appropriate Level of Regulation in Europe: Local, National or Community-Wide? A Roundtable Discussion', *Economic Policy*, 9 (Oct. 1989), 465–82.

42. A. M. Sbragia, 'Asymmetrical Integration in the European Community: The Single European Act and Institutional Development', in D. Smith and J. L. Ray (eds.), *The 1992 Project and the Future of European Integration* (New York: M. E. Sharpe, 1993); See also C. Sunstein, 'Protectionism, the American Supreme Court, and Integrated Markets', in R. Bieber et al., *1992: One European Market. A Critical Analysis of the Commission's Internal Market Strategy* (Florence: European University Institute, 1988).

43. E. Kitch, 'Regulation, Federalism, and Interstate Commerce', in A. D. Tarlock (ed.), *Regulation, Federalism, and Interstate Commerce* (Cambridge, Mass.: Oelgeschlager, Gunn and Hain, 1981).

44. H. N. Scheiber, 'Federalism and the American Economic Order, 1789–1910', *Law and Society Review*, 10 (Fall 1975), 57–118.

45. See J. Pelkmans, in cooperation with M. Vanheukelen, *The Internal Markets of North America: Fragmentation and Integration in the US and Canada* (Luxembourg: Office for Official Publications of the European Communities, 1988).

46. For important exceptions, see D. North, *Institutions, Institutional Change, and Economic Performance* (Cambridge: Cambridge University Press, 1990); Polanyi, *Trade and Markets in the Early Empires*.

47. M. Egan, 'Regulatory Strategies, Delegation, and European Market Integration', *Journal of European Public Policy*, 5, no. 3 (1998); M. Egan and D. Wolf, 'Regulation and Comitology', in special issue on 'Regulatory and Administrative Reform in the EU', *Columbia Journal of European Law*, 4, no. 3 (1998).

48. H. Voelzkow, *Private Regierungen in der Techniksteuerung: Eine sozialwissenschaftliche Analyse der technischen Normung* (Frankfurt am Main: Campus Verlag, 1996).

Chapter 2

1. Giandomenico Majone, 'Market Integration and Regulation: Europe after 1992', paper presented the conference on at 'Production Organization, Dynamic Efficiency and Social Norms', Rome, 4–6 Apr. 1991; Jacques Pelkmans, 'Governing European Union', paper presented at the Conference on 'Federalism and the Nation-State', Center for International Studies, University of Toronto, 4–6 June 1992.

2. Welfare economics provides the theoretical foundation for such intervention. Welfare economics is characterized by a perfectly competitive market that leads to Pareto efficient outcomes in which prices equal marginal costs or there is no rearrangement of resources. See J. E. Alt and K. A. Crystal, *Political Economics* (Berkeley and Los Angeles: University of California Press, 1983).

3. In discussing 'commodification' (the commodity fiction) Polanyi was concerned about the need to subordinate the economy to society as a whole otherwise anything with intrinsic value would become generally acceptable for payment or exchange.

4. P. Grabosky, 'Using Non-governmental Resources to Foster Regulatory Compliance', *Governance*, 8, no. 4 (1995), 527.

5. V. Haufler, 'Private Sector International Regimes', unpublished paper (Carnegie Endowment for International Peace, 1998), 1; see also M. W. Zacher with B. A. Sutton, *Governing Global Networks: International Regimes for Transportation and Communications* (Cambridge: Cambridge University Press, 1996) and V. Haufler, 'Comparing Private Sector Initiatives: Labor Standards, Information Privacy and Environmental Management', discussion paper for the 'Project on the Role of the Private Sector', Carnegie Endowment for International Peace, Washington, 1998; V. Haufler, *International Business Self-Regulation* (Washington: Carnegie Endowment for International Peace, forthcoming); K. Ronit and V. Schneider, 'Global Governance through Private Organizations', *Governance*, 12, no. 3 (1999); V. Haufler, 'Crossing the Boundary between Public and Private: International Regimes and Non-state Actors', in V. Rittberger (ed.), *Regime Theory and International Relations* (Oxford: Clarendon Press, 1993).

6. For example, many core public functions have been undertaken in part or whole by the private sector in the past, including law enforcement, tax collection, defence and conscription, and colonial rule, as well as quasi-public associations that regulate markets in a variety of ways from guild systems to standard-setting bodies.

7. C. P. Kindleberger, 'Standards as Public, Collective and Private Goods', *Kyklos*, 36 (1983); for an early discussion of the public and private functions of organizations, see R. Dahl and C. Lindblom, *Politics, Economics and Welfare* (New York: Harper Bros, 1953), 9–16.

8. C. Allen, 'The Politics of Adapting Organized Capitalism: United Germany, the New Europe, and Globalization', photocopy, 1998; G.

Lehmbruch, 'The Organization of Society, Administrative Strategies, and Policy Networks', in Roland M. Czada and Adrienne Windhoff-Héritier (eds.), *Political Choice: Institutions, Rules, and the Limits of Rationality* (Boulder, Colo.: Westview Press, 1991), 121–58.

9. I. Ayres and J. Braithwaite, *Responsive Regulation* (Oxford: Oxford University Press, 1992); Ian Maitland, 'The Limits of Business Self-Regulation', *California Management Review* 27/3 (Spring 1985); B. G. Peters, 'Development of Theories about Governance: Art Imitating Life?', paper presented at the conference on 'Ten Years of Change', held at the University of Manchester, Sept. 1994; P. Self, *Governing by the Market: The Politics of Public Choice* (London: Macmillan, 1993).

10. See e.g. A. Héritier, 'Market-Making Policy in Europe: Its Impact on Member State Policies: The Case of Road Haulage in Britain, the Netherlands, Germany and Italy', *Journal of European Public Policy*, 4, no. 4 (1997), 539–55; S. Schmidt, 'Commission Activism: Subsuming Telecommunications and Electricity under European Competition Law', *Journal of European Public Policy* (1998), 169–84.

11. The usual focus in international relations is to examine the intergovernmental cooperation in public goods provision, and to compare this with private cooperation for private goods provision that provides selective benefits and incentives for members, see M. Olson, *The Logic of Collective Action: Public Goods and the Theory of Groups* (Cambridge, Mass.: Harvard University Press, 1965).

12. See G. Majone, 'Cross-national Sources of Regulatory Policy-Making in Europe and the United States', *Journal of Public Policy*, 11, no. 1 (1991). Majone's work is central to any discussion of EU regulatory policy. See also A. M. Sbragia, 'The European Community in English: A Preliminary Sketch', paper presented at 'The European Community after Maastricht', a seminar sponsored by the Research Committee on European Unification of the International Political Science Association, Berlin, 1993.

13. The Treaty of Rome assigns virtually no redistribution function to the Community, although the actual process of integration and bargaining has generated modest redistributive policies via regional and social funds. Pollack focuses on the expansion of policy competencies using Low's classification of redistributive, regulative, and distributive policies which in some sense overemphasizes the 'allocational' role of European policy. See M. Pollack, 'Creeping Competence: The Expanding Agenda of the European Community', *Journal of Public Policy*, 14, no. 2 (1994), 95–145.

14. Majone, 'Cross-national Sources'; B. G. Peters, 'Bureaucratic Politics and the Institutions of the European Community', in A. M. Sbragia (ed.), *Europolitics: Institutions and Policymaking in the 'New' European Community* (Washington: Brookings Institution, 1992), 75–122.

15. See V. Schmidt, 'European Integration and Democracy: The Differences among Member States', *Journal of European Public Policy*, 5 (1997), 169–84; K. Orfeo-Fiortes, 'Masks of Maastricht: Varieties of Capitalism

and the Domestic Sources of Multilateral Preferences in the European Community', in P. Hall and D. Soskice (eds.), *Varieties of Capitalism* (forthcoming).

16. See J. Pelkmans, 'The Assignment of Public Functions in Economic Integration', *Journal of Common Market Studies*, 21 (1982), 97–125; A. Shonfield, *Modern Capitalism* (Oxford: Oxford University Press, 1965).

17. See C. Crouch and W. Streeck, *Political Economy of Modern Capitalism* (London: Sage, 1997); H. Kitschelt et al., *Continuity and Change in Contemporary Capitalism* (Cambridge: Cambridge University Press, 1999); L. Pauly and S. Reich, 'National Structures and Multinational Corporate Behavior: Enduring Differences in the Age of Globalization', *International Organization*, 51 (Winter 1997), 1–30.

18. For cross-national comparisons, see D. Vogel, *National Styles of Regulation* (Ithaca, NY: Cornell University Press, 1985); S. Kelman, *Regulating America, Regulating Sweden* (Cambridge, Mass.: MIT Press, 1981); M. Moran, *The Politics of the Financial Services Revolution: The UK, UK and Japan* (New York: St Martin's Press, 1991); J. Francis, *The Politics of Regulation: A Comparative Analysis* (Oxford: Basil Blackwell Publishers, 1993); A. Peacock et al., *The Regulation Game: How British and West German Companies Bargain with Government* (Oxford: Basil Blackwell, 1984); S. K. Vogel, *Freer Markets, More Rules: Regulatory Reform in Advanced Industrial Countries* (Ithaca, NY: Cornell University Press, 1996).

19. W. Streeck, 'German Capitalism: Does it Exist, Can it Survive?', *New Political Economy*, 2, no. 2 (1997).

20. R. Boyer, 'French Statism at the Crossroads', in Crouch and Streeck, *Political Economy of Modern Capitalism*.

21. Several scholars point to the shift in French policy post under Mitterrand and the efforts to adopt elements of the Rhineland model. However the dense networks and interdependence of economic institutions explains the institutional and structural difficulties that make it difficult to transfer to France.

22. Shonfield, *Modern Capitalism*, 88; S. Blank, 'Britain: The Politics of Foreign Economic Policy, the Domestic Economy, and the Problem of Pluralistic Stagnation', in P. Katzenstein (ed.), *Between Power and Plenty* (Wisconsin: University of Wisconsin, 1978), 101.

23. The emergence of strategic trade theory has reinforced attention on the relationship between trade and regulation under imperfect competition. National regulations are considered part of comparative advantage, so that the special characteristics of national regulations that influence production in the home country are now open to intense scrutiny. The effort to expand the agenda of trade liberalization to include national regulations is controversial as the criteria for inclusion are broad notions of competitive effects. See P. Krugman, *Strategic Trade Policy and the New International Economics* (Cambridge, Mass.: MIT Press, 1986); H. Milner

and D. Yoffie, 'Between Free Trade and Protectionism: Strategic Trade Policy and a Theory of Corporate Trade Demands', *International Organization*, 43, no. 2 (1989); S. Woolcock, 'The European Acquis and Multilateral Trade: Are They Compatible?' *Journal of Common Market Studies*, 31, no. 4 (1993).

24. D. Vogel, *Barriers or Benefits: Regulation in Transatlantic Trade* (Washington: Brookings Institution, 1997); P. Nivola (ed.), *Comparative Disadvantages: Social Regulations and the Global Economy* (Washington: Brookings, 1997).

25. A growing number of cases exist where regulatory competition leads to a race to the top, the so-called 'California effect', with products made more attractive because they are highly regulated. See V. Eichener, 'Effective European Problem-Solving: Lessons from the Regulation of Occupational Safety and Environmental Protection', *Journal of European Public Policy*, 4, no. 4 (1997), 591–608. F. Scharpf, 'Negative and Positive Integration in the Political Economy of European Welfare States', in G. Marks et al., *Governance in the European Union* (London: Sage, 1996); cf. D. Vogel, *Trading Up: Consumer and Environmental Regulation in a Global Economy* (Cambridge, Mass.: Harvard University Press 1995); A. Héritier et al., *Die Veränderun von Staatlichkeit in Europa: Ein regulativer Wettbewerb: Deutschland, Grossbritannien und Frankreich in der Europäischen Union* (Opladen: Leske & Budrich, 1994).

26. E. Epstein, 'Resolving the Regulator's Dilemma: International Coordination of Banking Regulations', *International Organization*, 43, no. 2 (1989), 323–47.

27. P. Genschel and T. Plümper, 'Regulatory Competition and International Co-operation', *Journal of European Public Policy*, 4, no. 4 (1997).

28. Empirical studies have shown that cross-national institutional and ideological differences can affect cooperation. See Kelman, *Regulating America, Regulating Sweden*; Vogel, *National Styles of Regulation*; Vogel, *Freer Markets, More Rules*.

29. Genschel and Plümper, 'Regulatory Competition'; F. Scharpf, 'Introduction: The Problem-Solving Capacity of Multi-Level Governance', *Journal of European Public Policy*, 4, no. 4 (1997), 520–38; Robert O. Keohane, 'International Institutions: Two Approaches', *International Studies Quarterly*, 32 (1988), 379–96.

30. R. Keohane and L. Martin, 'Delegation to International Institutions', paper presented at the conference 'What is Institutionalism Now?', University of Maryland, 14–15 Oct. 1994; M. Pollack, 'Delegation, Agency, and Agenda-Setting in the European Community', *International Organization*, 5, no. 1 (1997), 99–134.

31. G. Majone, 'Market Integration and Regulation: Europe after 1992', *Metroeconomica* 43 (June 1992), 131–56.

32. K. Gatsios and P. Seabright, 'Regulation in the European Community', *Oxford Review of Economic Policy*, 5, no. 2 (1989).

33. Ibid.; Majone, 'Europe after 1992.'
34. The public choice approach emphasizes the economic debate about the division of economic functions among different levels of government. Its theoretical foundation is Tiebout's model of the provision of local public goods. C. Tiebout, 'A Pure Theory of Local Expenditure', *Journal of Political Economy*, 64 (1956), 416–24; see also S. Rose-Ackerman, 'Does Federalism Matter? Political Choice in a Federal Republic', *Journal of Political Economy*, 19 (1981), 152–65.
35. F. Scharpf points out that there are policy areas of crucial importance to the legitimacy of the European polity where European regulatory harmonization is blocked, and thus policies of positive integration are undermined. See F. Scharpf, *Governing in Europe* (Oxford: Oxford University Press, 1999), ch. 3.
36. Scharpf, 'Problem-Solving Capacity'; Scharpf, *Governing in Europe*.
37. J. H. H. Weiler, 'The Transformation of Europe', *Yale Law Journal*, 100 (1991).
38. See F. Scharpf, 'Economic Integration, Democracy and the Welfare State', paper presented at the GAAC Young Scholars Meeting, Bremen (Aug. 1996); see also C. Harlow, 'Francovich and the Problem of the Disobedient State', EUI RSC Working Paper No. 62 (1996), European University Institute, Florence; C. Harlow, 'Codification of EC Administrative Procedures? Fitting the Foot to the Shoe or the Shoe to the Foot', EUI RSC Working Paper No. 27 (1995), European University Institute, Florence.
39. See G. Majone, 'The Rise of the Regulatory State in Europe', *West European Politics*, 17, no. 3 (1994), 77–101; Majone, 'Cross-national Sources'; G. Majone, *Evidence, Argument and Persuasion in the Policy Process* (New Haven: Yale University Press, 1989); R. Dehousse et al., 'Europe after 1992: New Regulatory Strategies', EUI Working Paper No. 92, Florence: European University Institute (1992); A. M. Okun, *Equality and Efficiency: The Big Tradeoff* (Washington: Brookings Institution, 1975).
40. See S. Breyer, *Regulation and its Reform* (Cambridge, Mass.: Harvard University Press, 1982); B. Mitnick, *The Political Economy of Regulation: Creating, Designing and Removing Regulatory Forms* (New York: Columbia University Press, 1980).
41. M. Eisner, *Regulatory Politics in Transition* (Baltimore: Johns Hopkins University Press, 1993), xiii.
42. For an excellent assessment of the accommodation of diversity in the European regulatory context see A. Héritier, 'The Accommodation of Diversity in European Policy-Making and its Outcomes: Regulatory Policy as a Patchwork', *Journal of European Public Policy*, 3, no. 2 (1996).
43. M. Reagan, *Regulation: The Politics of Policy* (Boston: Little Brown & Company, 1987), 9; R. Noll, 'Governing Regulatory Behavior: A Multidisciplinary Survey and Synthesis', in R. Noll (ed.), *Regulatory Policy and the Social Sciences* (Berkeley and Los Angeles: University of California Press, 1985), 9.

44. S. Skronewek, *Building an American State* (Cambridge: Cambridge University Press, 1982), 13.

45. T. K. McCraw (ed.), *Regulation in Perspective: Historical Essays* (Cambridge, Mass.: Harvard University Press, 1981); K. T. Poole and H. Rosenthal, 'The Enduring Nineteenth-Century Battle for Economic Regulation: The Interstate Commerce Act Revisited', *Journal of Law & Economics*, 36 (Oct. 1993), 837–60.

46. See G. Wilson, 'Social Regulation and Explanations of Regulatory Failure', *Political Studies* (1984), 203–25.

47. See G. Majone, 'The European Community as a Regulatory State', Lectures given at the Academy of European Law, (July 1994); Majone, 'Controlling Regulatory Bureaucracies: Lessons from the American Experience', unpublished paper; Majone, *Regulating Europe*, esp. ch. 3.

48. G. Majone, 'The Agency Model', unpublished paper, European Institute for Public Administration, Maastricht, 1998.

49. The institutional structure of parliamentary systems (federal and non-federal) in Europe does not generate the same type of judicial policy-making—the commitment to private rights and judicial review has resulted in an American propensity to solve market disputes through adversarial litigation. By contrast, policy planning (dirigism) and corporatism has been the institutional basis for market disputes in Europe. See G. Majone for a discussion of different modes of governance (agency/centralized bureaucracy), 'From the Positive to the Regulatory State: Causes and Consequences of Changes in the Mode of Governance', *Journal of Public Policy*, 17, no. 2 (1997), 139–67.

50. For a detailed analysis of American regulatory agencies, see K. Meier, *Regulation: Politics, Bureaucracy and Economics* (New York: St Martins Press, 1985).

51. T. McCraw, 'Regulation in America', *Business History Review*, 39 (Summer 1975), 161.

52. See J. M. Landis, *The Administrative Process* (New Haven: Yale University Press, 1938).

53. While the ideological acceptance of the efficiency of the market economy has been, and still is, the basis of the deregulation movement in the United States, it is much less acceptable in explaining the emergence of social regulation—see Ch. 10. See also J. Q. Wilson (ed.), *The Politics of Regulation* (New York: Basic Books, 1980); Eisner, *Regulatory Politics in Transition*, esp. ch. 8; and G. Hoberg, *Pluralism by Design: Environmental Policy and the American Regulatory State* (New York: Praeger, 1992), esp. chs. 1, 9. David Vogel *National Styles of Regulation*.

54. This draws on L. Tsoukalis, *The New European Economy: The Politics and Economics of Integration*, 2nd edn. (Oxford: Oxford University Press, 1993), esp. chapter 2.

55. G. Majone, 'Deregulation or Reregulation? Policymaking in the European Community since the Single Act', paper prepared for the research project La Restructuration des États Européens, pp. 12 ff., no date.

56. For a discussion of transformations in governance, see G. Majone, 'The European Union: Positive or Regulatory State', paper, no date; Majone, 'From the Positive to the Regulatory State'.

57. See e.g. D. Swann, 'The Regulatory Scene: An Overview', in D. Swann and K. Button (eds.), *The Age of Regulatory Reform* (Oxford: Clarendon Press, 1989); C. Veljanovski, *Selling the State* (London: Weidenfield & Nicolson, 1987); G. Majone, *Regulating Europe* (London: Routledge, 1996)

58. Majone, 'Cross-national Sources'; G. Lehmbruch, 'The Institutional Framework of German Regulation', in K. Dyson (ed.), *The Politics of German Regulation* (Brookfield, Vt.: Dartmouth, 1992).

59. Majone, 'Cross-national Sources', 27.

60. T. Prosser, 'Regulation of Privatized Enterprises: Institutions and Procedures', in L. Hancher and M. Moran, *Capitalism, Culture and Economic Regulation* (Oxford: Clarendon Press, 1989).

61. See the excellent discussion in B. Eberlein, 'Regulating Public Utilities in Europe: Mapping the Problem', unpublished paper, European University Institute, Florence, Apr. 1998.

62. S. Wilks, 'Regulatory Compliance and Capitalist Diversity in Europe', *Journal of European Public Policy*, 3, no. 4 (1996), 536–59.

63. See e.g. Héritier, 'The Accommodation of Diversity'.

64. Vogel, *Free Markets, More Rules.*

65. Ibid. 16–18.

66. D. Levi-Faur, 'The Competition State as a Neo-mercantilist State: Restructuring Global Telecommunications', paper presented at annual conference of the American Political Science Association, Boston, Sept. 1998.

67. See Majone, *Regulating Europe*, 23–6.

68. See e.g. D. Swann, *The Economics of the Common Market* (London: Penguin, 1970).

69. B. Balassa, *The Theory of Economic Integration* (London: Allen & Unwin, 1961).

70. See J. Pelkmans, 'Economic Theories of Integration Revisited', *Journal of Common Market Studies*, 18 (1980), 333–54; J. Pelkmans, 'The Institutional Economics of European Integration', in M. Cappalletti, M. Seccombe, and J. H. H. Weiler, *Integration through Law*, vol. i, book 1 (Berlin: De Gruyter, 1985).

71. See Pelkmans, 'The Assignment of Public Functions'; also J. Pelkmans, *Market Integration in the European Community* (The Hague: Martin Nijhoff, 1984).

72. C. Lindblom, *Politics and Markets: The World's Political-Economic System* (New York: Basic Books, 1977), 5, 336; G. McConnell, *Private Power and American Democracy* (New York: Vintage, 1966), 51–2; G. Kolko, *The Triumph of Conservatism* (New York: Free Press, 1963).

73. M. Olson, *The Rise and Decline of Nations: Economic Growth, Stagflation, and Social Rigidities* (New Haven: Yale University Press, 1982).

74. A. M. Sbragia, *Debt Wish: Entrepreneurial Cities, U.S. Federalism, and Economic Development* (Pittsburgh: University of Pittsburgh Press, 1996).

75. See L. Cornett and J. A. Caporaso, 'And Still it Moves! State Interests and Social Forces in the European Community', in J. N. Rosenau and E.-O. Czempiel (eds.), *Governance without Government: Order and Change in World Politics* (Cambridge: Cambridge University Press, 1992), esp. 224–8.

76. This does not assume that all work on European integration focuses on the impact and preferences of firms on public policy. Intergovernmentalists such as Paul Taylor and Andrew Moravscik focus on domestic interests and state preferences that lead to interstate bargaining and negotiated policy outcomes. However, this view does not capture the mutual interdependence between states and markets anymore than the economic theory of politics captures the role of the state in managing the inputs to markets and setting the conditions on which exchanges are made. See P. Taylor, *The Limits of European Integration* (New York: Columbia University Press, 1983); A. Moravscik, 'Preferences and Power in the European Community: A Liberal Intergovernmentalist Approach', *Journal of Common Market Studies*, 31 (1993), 473–524.

77. M. Moran and M. Wright, 'The Interdependence of Markets and States', in Michael Moran and M. Wright (eds.), *The Market and the State: Studies in Interdependence* (New York: St Martins Press, 1991); A. Martin, 'Political Constraints on Economic Strategies in Advanced Industrial States', *Comparative Political Studies* (Oct. 1977), 323–51.

78. See also Sbragia, *Debt Wish*.

79. On the incentive system of regulators, see Mitnick, *The Political Economy of Regulation*, W. Niskanen, *Bureaucracy and Representative Government* (Chicago: Aldine Atherton, 1971), and A. Downs, *Inside Bureaucracy* (Boston: Little Brown, 1967); for an institutionalist perspective, see Hoberg, *Pluralism by Design*; for a neo-elitist state theory, see S. Krasner, *Defending the National Interest: Raw Materials Investments and US Foreign Policy* (Princeton: Princeton University Press, 1978).

80. See Majone, *Regulating Europe*; Dehousse et al., 'Europe after 1992'; Wilks, 'Regulatory Compliance'; G. Majone, 'Controlling Bureaucratic Accountability: Lessons from the American Experience', unpublished paper.

81. See P. Crowley, 'Incorporating the Administrative Process', *Columbia Law Review*, 98, no. 1 (1998), 1–168; M. Egan and D. Wolf, 'Regulation and Comitology', in a special issue on 'Regulatory and Administrative Reform in the EU', *Columbia Journal of European Law*, 4, no. 3 (1998), 499–523.

82. For a review, see P. Joskow and R. Noll, 'Regulation in Theory and Practice', in G. Fromm (ed.), *Studies in Public Regulation* (Cambridge: MIT Press, 1981), 1–65; Mitnick, *The Political Economy of Regulation*.

83. P. Quirk, *Industry Influence in Federal Regulatory Agencies* (Princeton: Princeton University Press, 1981).

84. See W. Niskanen, 'Bureaucrats and Politicians', *Journal of Law and Economics*, 18 (1975), 617–43; B. Weingast, 'Regulation, Reregulation and Deregulation: The Political Foundations of Agency Clientele Relationships',

Law and Contemporary Problems, 44 (1981); K. Shepsle and B. Weingast, 'The Institutional Foundations of Committee Power', *American Political Science Review*, 81 (1987), 935–45.

85. For a criticism of this approach, see Hancher and Moran, *Capitalism, Culture and Economic Regulation*; Leigh Hancher, *Regulating for Competition: Government, Law, and the Pharmaceutical Industry in the United Kingdom and France* (Oxford: Oxford University Press, 1990).

86. The following sections on regulatory theories draws upon M. Egan, 'Regulatory Strategies, Delegation, and European Market Integration', *Journal of European Public Policy*, 5, no. 3 (1998); Michelle Egan, 'Regulating European Markets: Mismatch, Reform and Agency', Ph.D. Dissertation, University of Pittsburgh, 1995; Egan and Wolf, 'Regulation and Comitology'; M. Egan and D. Wolf, 'Regulation and Comitology: The EC Committee System in Regulatory Perspective', in Christian Joerges and Ellen Vos (ed.), *European Committees: Social Regulation, Law and Politics* (Oxford: Hart Publishing, 1998). See also Vogel *Freer Markets*.

87. Breyer, *Regulation and its Reform*; S. Breyer, *Breaking the Vicious Circle: Towards Effective Risk Regulation* (Cambridge, Mass.: Harvard University Press, 1993); P. Herring, *Public Administration and the Public Interest* (New York: Russell & Russell, 1967).

88. McCraw, 'Regulation in America'; McCraw, *Regulation in Perspective*; Landis, *Administrative Process*.

89. Majone's discussion of the shift in policy deliberation towards efficiency rather than redistributive policies aimed at promoting aggregate welfare is reminiscent of much of the earlier discussions regarding public interest.

90. R. Rabin, 'Federal Regulation in Historical Perspective', in P. Shuck, *Foundations of Administrative Law* (Oxford: Oxford University Press, 1994), 45.

91. I thank Mark Pollack for this insight.

92. Pollack, 'Delegation'; see also E. B. Haas, *The Uniting of Europe; Political, Social, and Economic Forces, 1950–1957* (Stanford, Calif: Stanford University Press, 1958).

93. F. Scharpf, 'The Joint-Decision Trap: Lessons from German Federalism and European Integration', *Public Administration*, 66 (1988), 239–78.

94. G. Majone, 'Does Policy Deliberation Matter?', unpublished manuscript, European University Institute, Florence (no date), 3; L. Kohlmeier, *The Regulators: Watchdog Agencies and the Public Interest* (New York: Harper & Row, 1969).

95. Crowley, 'Incorporating the Administrative Process'.

96. M. H. Bernstein, *Regulating Business by Independent Commission* (Princeton: Princeton University Press, 1955); S. Huntington, 'The Masaramus of the ICC', *Yale Law Journal*, 61 (Apr. 1952), 467–509.

97. D. Truman, *The Governmental Process: Political Interests and Public Opinion*, 2nd edn. (New York: Knopf, 1971); A. Bentley, *The Process of*

Government: A Study of Social Pressures (Evanston, Ill.: Principia Press, 1949).

98. See also the discussion in Majone, *Regulating Europe*, 30–4.
99. G. Stigler, 'The Theory of Economic Regulation', *Bell Journal of Economic and Management Science*, 2 (1971), 3–21.
100. G. Stigler, *The Citizen and the State: Essays on Regulation* (Chicago: University of Chicago Press, 1975).
101. See D. North, *Institutions, Institutional Change, and Economic Performance* (Cambridge: Cambridge University Press, 1990); for a similar argument in the EU context, see R. Dehousse and G. Majone, 'The Dynamics of European Integration: The Role of Supranational Institutions', Paper presented at the Council for Europeanists, Washington DC, 27–9 May 1993; Majone, *Regulating Europe*, 69 ff.
102. S. Peltzman, 'Toward a More General Theory of Regulation', *Journal of Law and Economics*, 14 (1976), 109–48.
103. Ibid.; Niskanen, *Bureaucracy and Representative Government*; G. Becker, 'A Theory of Competition among Pressure Groups for Political Influence', *Quarterly Journal of Economics* (Aug. 1983), 371–400.
104. Olson, *The Logic of Collective Action*.
105. See also, G. Stigler, 'Free Riders and Collective Action: An Appendix to Theories of Economic Regulation', *Bell Journal of Economics and Management Science*, 5 (1974), 359–65.
106. Wilson, *The Politics of Regulation*; see also Graham Wilson, 'Social Regulation and Explanations of Regulatory Failure', *Political Studies*, 32 (1984), 203–25.
107. Quirk, *Industry Influence*.
108. M. Moran, 'Theories of Regulation and Changes in Regulation: The Case of Financial Markets', *Political Studies*, 34 (1986); Moran, *Financial Service Revolution*.
109. This approach to institutional choice and delegation of authority can be initially traced to the work of Berle and Means on the shareholder-management issue, and the separation of ownership by shareholders from control by management. See A. Berle and G. Means, *The Modern Corporation and Private Property* (New York: Macmillan, 1932).
110. Breyer, *Regulation and its Reform*; M. S. Ogul, *Congress Oversees the Bureaucracy: Studies in Legislative Supervision* (Pittsburgh: University of Pittsburgh Press, 1976).
111. M. Everson, 'Administering Europe', *Journal of Common Market Studies*, 36, no. 2 (June 1998), 2 .
112. A. Kreher, 'Agencies in the European Community: The Role of European Agencies', *Journal of European Public Policy*, 4, no. 2 (1997), 225–45; see also A. Kreher (ed.), 'The New European Agencies: Conference Report', EUI Working Paper no. 50 (1996), European University Institute, Florence.
113. T. J. Lowi, *The End of Liberalism* (New York: Norton, 1969; 2nd edn. 1976).

114. R. Stewart, 'The Transformation of American Administrative Law', *Harvard Law Review*, 88 (1975); M. Shapiro, *Who Guards the Guardians: Judicial Control of Administration* (Athens: University of Georgia Press, 1988); Cass Sunstein, 'Deregulation and the Courts', *Journal of Policy Analysis and Management*, 5 (Spring 1986), 517–34.

115. Stewart, 'The Transformation of American Administrative Law'; for an excellent assessment comparing rule-making procedures, see Norman Lewis and Ian Hardin, 'Privatization and Deregulation and Constitutionality: Some Anglo-American Comparisons', *Northern Ireland Legal Quarterly*, 34, no. 3 (1983), 207–29.

116. Stewart, 'The Transformation of American Administrative Law', 1670.

117. Dehousse et al., 'Europe after 1992'.

118. The literature on agency covers several disciplines. For major reviews, see Mitnick, *The Political Economy of Regulation*; K. Arrow, 'The Economics of Agency' in J. W. Pratt and R. J. Zeckhauser (eds.), *Principals and Agents: The Structure of Business* (Cambridge, Mass.: Harvard Business School Press, 1985); K. Eisenhardt, 'Agency Theory: An Assessment and Review', *Academy of Management Review*, 14 (1989), 57–74; S. A. Ross, 'The Economic Theory of Agency: The Principal's Problem', *American Economic Review* (1973); B. Mitnick, 'The Theory of Agency: The Policing "Paradox" and Regulatory Behavior', *Public Choice* 1975.

119. See Egan, 'Regulating European Markets'; Pollack, 'Delegation'; Keohane and Martin, 'Delegation to International Institutions'.

120. See esp. Mitnick, 'The Theory of Agency'; Berle and Means, *Modern Corporation and Private Property*. The proponents of the principal-agent view of the firm see the firm as a nexus of contracts. See R. Coase, 'The Problem of Social Cost', *Journal of Law and Economics*, 3 (1960), 1–33.

121. See e.g. M. McCubbins and T. Schwartz, 'Congressional Oversight Overlooked: Police Patrol vs Fire-Alarm', *American Journal of Political Science*, 28 (1984); B. Weingast and M. Moran, 'Bureaucratic Discretion or Congressional Control? Regulatory Policymaking by the Federal Trade Commission', *Journal of Political Economy*, 91 (1983), 765–800; M. McCubbins, Roger Noll, and B. Weingast, 'Administrative Procedures as Instruments of Control', *Journal of Law, Organization and Economics*, 3 (1987), 243–77; K. Bawn, 'Political Control versus Expertise: Congressional Choices about Administrative Procedures', *American Political Science Review*, 89 (Mar. 1995), 62–73.

122. See e.g. T. Moe, 'Control and Feedback in Economic Regulation: The Case of the NLRB', *American Political Science Review*, 79 (1985), 1094–117; D. Wood, 'Principals, Bureaucrats, and Responsiveness in Clean Air Enforcements', *American Political Science Review*, 82 (1988), 213–24.

123. See W. Gormley, 'The Bureaucracy and its Masters: The New Madisonian System in the US', *Governance*, 4, no. 1 (1991), 1–18.

124. McCubbins, Noll, and Weingast, 'Administrative Procedures'; Weingast and Moran, 'Bureaucratic Discretion'; M. McCubbins, 'The Legislative

Design of Regulatory Structure', *American Journal of Political Science*, 29 (1985).

125. See the interesting discussion in Gormley, 'The Bureaucracy and its Masters', where he describes the problems with this new Madisonian commitment to checks and balances.

126. M. Shapiro, 'The Problem of Independent Agencies in the United States and European Union', *Journal of European Public Policy*, 4, no. 2 (1997); M. Shapiro, presentation to the GAAC Workshop on 'Political Economy of European Integration', Berkeley, Calif., Aug. 1995.

127. M. Shapiro, 'Codification of Administrative Law: The US and the European Union', *European Law Journal*, 2, no. 1 (1996), 39.

128. See Majone, *Regulating Europe*.

129. Vogel, *National Styles of Regulation*.

130. Hancher and Moran, *Capitalism, Culture and Economic Regulation*.

131. See J. Greenwood et al., *Organized Interests and the European Community* (Newbury Park, Calif.: Sage, 1992); S. Mazey and J. Richardson (eds.), *Lobbying in the EU* (Oxford: Oxford University Press, 1993).

132. Lindblom, *Politics and Markets*; see also P. Cammerra Rowe, 'Lobbying in the New Europe: Firms and Politics in the Single European Market', Ph.D. Dissertation, Duke University, 1993.

133. See M. Green Cowles, 'Setting the Agenda for a New Europe: The ERT and EU1992', *Journal of Common Market Studies*, 13 (1995), 501–26.

134. W. D. Coleman and W. Grant, 'Business and Public Policy: A Comparison of Organisational Development in Britain and Canada', *Journal of Public Policy*, 4 (1984), 209–35; W. D. Coleman, *Business and Politics: A Study of Collective Action* (Kingston: McGill-Queens University Press, 1988); W. D. Coleman and G. R. D. Underhill (eds.), *Regionalism and Global Economic Integration: Europe, Asia, and the Americas* (London: Routledge, 1998).

135. W. Streeck and P. Schmitter, 'From National Corporatism to Transnational Pluralism: Organized Interests in the Single European Market', in W. Streeck (ed.), *Social Institutions and Economic Performance* (London: Sage, 1991), 197–231.

136. R. A. W. Rhodes, *Beyond Westminster and Whitehall: The Sub-Central Government of Britain* (London: Unwin Hyman, 1988).

137. See S. Hays, 'Political Choice in Regulation Administration' in McCraw (ed.), *Regulation in Perspective*.

138. See the discussion in Egan, 'Regulatory Strategies, Delegation, and European Market Integration'; H. Voelzkow, *Private Regierungen in der Techniksteuerung* (Frankfurtam Main: Campus Verlag, 1996).

139. M. Egan, 'Market Integration across Time and Space: Europe, America and Integration', unpublished paper, American University, 1999.

140. T. McGraw, *Prophets of Regulation* (Cambridge, Mass.: Belknap Press, 1984).

141. Meier, *Regulation*, 3.

142. Vogel, *National Styles of Regulation.*

143. Paul Quirk and Martha Derthick, *The Politics of Deregulation* (Washington: Brookings Institution, 1985); M. Eisner, J. Worsham and E. Ringquist, *Contemporary Regulatory Policy* (Boulder, Colo.: Lynne Rienner, 2000).

144. See special issue, *Journal of European Public Policy*, 1996; Majone, *Regulating Europe*; Dehousse et al., 'Europe after 1992'; G. Majone, 'The European Community: An Independent Fourth Branch of Government', unpublished paper, no date; G. Majone, 'Controlling Regulatory Bureaucracies: Lessons from the American Experience', Florence; EUI Working Paper SPS No. 93/3, 1993.

145. T. Freyer, *Producers versus Capitalist: Constitutional Conflict in Antebellum America* (Charlottesville: University of Virginia Press, 1994).

146. Shapiro, 'Codification'; Egan and Wolf, 'Regulation and Comitology'; Majone, *Regulating Europe*; G. Majone, 'The European Community: An Independent Fourth Branch of Government?', in G. Brüggemeier (ed.), *Verfassungen für ein Ziviles Europa*, 23 (1994); M. Everson, 'Independent Agencies, Hierarchy Beaters?', *European Law Journal*, 1, no. 2 (1995).

147. See J. Sheridan, 'The Déjà Vue of EMU: Considerations for Europe from Nineteenth Century America', *Journal of Economic Issues*, 30, no. 4 (1996).

148. For historical research on the role of the state in maintaining markets, see K. Polanyi, *The Great Transformation: The Political and Economic Origins of our Time* (Boston: Beacon Press, 1944).

149. H. Gillman, 'Reconnecting Modern Constitutional Law to the Historical Evolution of Capitalism', paper presented at the annual conference of the American Political Science Association, Boston, Sept. 1998.

150. *Gibbons* v. *Ogden*, 9 Wheat 1, 203 US 1824.

151. C. M. McCurdy, 'American Law and the Marketing Structure of the Large Corporation, 1875–1890', *Journal of Economic History*, 38, no. 3 (1978), 269.

152. See Albert S. Abel, 'Commerce Regulation before Gibbons v. Ogden: Trade and Traffic Part II', *Brooklyn Law Review*, (1940), 215–43.

153. Although I use the term 'courts' here to mean both state and local courts as well as the US Supreme Court, this does not mean that business organizations were consistently successful in their endeavours.

154. A. Chandler, 'The Beginnings of Big Business in American Industry', *Business History Review*, 33 (Spring 1959), 1–31.

155. See T. Freyer, 'The Paradox of Federal Judicial Power in Antebellum Alabama', *Alabama Law Review*, 44 (Winter 1993), 477–554.

156. See B. Cushman, *Rethinking the New Deal Court* (Oxford: Oxford University Press, 1998); Gillman, 'Reconnecting Modern Constitutional Law'.

157. McCurdy, 'American Law', 270.

158. Ibid. 283; Freyer, *Producers versus Capitalists*; H. Scheiber, 'Private Rights and Public Power: American Law, Capitalism, and the Republican Polity in Nineteenth-Century America', *Yale Law Journal*, 107 (1997), 823–61.

159. P. L. Hersch and J. M. Netter, 'The Impact of Early Safety Legislation: The Case of the Safety Appliance Act of 1893', *International Review of Law & Economics*, 10 (May 1990), 61–75; see also D. Hemenway, *Industrywide Voluntary Product Standards* (Cambridge: Ballinger Pub. Co., 1975).

160. S. Hayes, *Conservation and the Gospel of Efficiency: The Progressive Conservation Movement, 1890–1920* (Pittsburgh: University of Pittsburgh Press, 1999).

161. R. C. Cochrane, *Measures for Progress: A History of the National Bureau of Standards* (Washington: National Bureau of Standards, US Dept. of Commerce, 1966); A. I. Marcus, 'Setting the Standard: Fertilizers, State Chemists, and Early National Commercial Regulation, 1880–1887', *Agricultural History*, 61, no. 1 (Winter 1987), 203–29; Hemenway, *Industrywide Voluntary Product Standards*.

162. Lowi, *End of Liberalism*.

163. R. Chiet, *Setting Safety Standards* (Berkeley and Los Angeles: University of California Press, 1991); Samuel Krislov, *How Nations Choose Product Standards and Standards Change Nations* (Pittsburgh: University of Pittsburgh Press, 1997).

164. J. A. Caporaso, 'The European Union and Forms of State: Westphalian, Regulatory or Post-Modern?', *Journal of Common Market Studies*, 29 (1996).

165. See Scharpf, *Governing Europe*.

Chapter 3

1. *Comité Intergouvernemental créé par la Conférence de Messine*, Rapport des Chefs de Délégation aux Ministres des Affairs Étrangères, Brussels, 21 Apr. 1956, 9. This document is commonly known as the 'Spaak Report' after Paul-Henri Spaak who presided over the conference.

2. Economic Cooperation Act, 3 Apr. 1949 (Marshall Plan), Section 102.

3. E. Kitch, 'Regulation and the American Common Market', in A. D. Tarlock, *Regulation, Federalism, and Interstate Commerce* (Cambridge, Mass.: Oelgeschlager, Gunn and Hain, 1981).

4. Ibid. 15–17.

5. N. Owen, *Economies of Scale, Competitiveness, and Trade Patterns within the European Community* (Oxford: Oxford University Press, 1983).

6. The American model that the EU framers had in mind is one that has evolved over time since states have used their police, proprietary, licensing, and tax powers to create on occasion interstate trade barriers. See *Brown* v. *Maryland* 12 Wheaton 419 (1827) for an early assessment of interstate commercial problems.

7. For a detailed empirical analysis of the trade effects of removing tariff barriers to trade, see A. F. Kroner, 'An Analysis of the Static Welfare Effects of a Customs Union: The European Economic Community, 1958–1966', Ph.D. Thesis, Cornell University, 1971.

8. R. Baldwin, *Non-tariff Distortions of International Trade* (Washington: Brookings Institution, 1970).

9. M. Kahler, 'The Survival of the State in European International Relations', in Charles Maier (ed.), *Changing Boundaries of the Political* (Cambridge: Cambridge University Press, 1987); M. Richonnier, 'Europe's Decline is not Irreversible', *Journal of Common Market Studies*, 24 (Mar. 1988), 229–43.

10. W. Hager, 'Protectionism and Autonomy: How to Preserve Free Trade in Europe', *International Affairs* (Summer 1982), 413–28.

11. C. Crook, 'The Economist Survey of World Trade', *The Economist* (22 Sept. 1990); G. and V. Curzon, *Hidden Barriers to International Trade*, Thames Valley Essay No. 1 (London: Trade Policy Research Centre, 1970); E. Ray, 'Changing Patterns of Protectionism: The Fall in Tariffs and the Rise in Non-Tariff Barriers', in the symposium on 'The Political Economy of International Trade, Law and Policy', (Fall 1987), 285–327.

12. See A. Deardoff and R. Stern, *Methods of Measurement of Non-Tariff Barriers* (Geneva: United Nations Conference on Trade and Development, 1985); United States General Accounting Office, *The Difficulty of Quantifying Non-Tariff Measures Affecting Trade*, Report to the Chairman of the Subcommittee on International Economic Policy, Oceans and Environment, Senate Committee on Foreign Relations, NSIAD 85 133 (Sept. 1985).

13. See E. van Puyvelde, *Industry and the Battle for the EEC's Internal Market* (Brussels: Agence Européene d'Information, 1983); *The EEC as an Expanded Home Market for the United Kingdom and the Federal Republic of Germany* (London: The Anglo-German Society for the Study of Industrial Society, 1979).

14. Richonnier, 'Europe's Decline is not Irreversible'; J. Grieco, *Cooperation among Nations* (Ithaca, NY: Cornell University Press, 1990), 203.

15. New theories of strategic trade policy focus on trade under imperfect competition, see H. Milner and D. Yoffie, 'Between Free Trade and Protectionism: Strategic Trade Policy and a Theory of Corporate Trade Demands', *International Organization*, 43, no. 2 (1989).

16. P. Krugman (ed.), *Strategic Trade Policy and the New International Economics* (Cambridge: MIT Press, 1986); T. McKeown, 'Firms and Tariff Regime Change: Explaining the Demand for Protectionism', *World Politics*, 36 (1984), 215–33. Razeen, Sally *States and Firms* (Routledge, 1995).

17. See L. Pauly and S. Reich, 'National Structures and Multinational Corporate Behavior: Enduring Differences in the Age of Globalization', *International Organization*, 51 (Winter 1997), 1–30.

18. M. Rhodes and B. Van Apeldoorn, 'Capital Unbound? The Transformation of European Corporate Governance', *Journal of European Public*

Policy, 5 (1998); M. Egan, 'Modes of Business Governance: European Management Styles and Corporate Cultures', *West European Politics*, 20 (1997), 1–21. Razeen, Sally *States and Firms* (Routledge, 1995).

19. M. Peck, 'Industrial organization and gains from EU 92', *Brookings Papers on Economic Activity* 2 (Washington: Brookings Institution, 1989).

20. See the seminal work by A. Downs, *The Economic Theory of Democracy* (New York: Harper, 1957); M. Olson, *The Logic of Collective Action: Public Goods and the Theory of Groups* (Cambridge, Mass.: Harvard University Press, 1965).

21. In game theoretic terms, even though there may be gains from cooperation, it is often difficult to discriminate between different potential outcomes in terms of their efficiency. See S. Krasner, 'Global Communications and National Power: Life on the Pareto Frontier', *World Politics*, 43 (1991), 336–66. If multiple Pareto-efficient equilibria outcomes are possible, then reaching an agreement or durable bargain may take longer.

22. See Curzon and Curzon, *Hidden Barriers to International Trade*; V. Curzon-Price, 'Residual Obstacles to Trade in the Single Market', Institute Européen, University of Geneva, 1996. For more recent econometric studies that relate trade flows to standards, see Johannes Moenius, 'Information versus Product Adaptation: The Role of Standards in Trade', 26 Nov. 1999, mimeo; Peter Swann, Paul Temple, and Mark Shurmer, 'Standards and Trade Performance: the UK Experience', *Economic Journal*, 106 (1996), 1297–1313.

23. There are two studies that seek to use survey data to assess the role of standards in export dynamics. The US International Trade Commission under Section 232 of US Trade Laws is examining the economic impact of standards-related trade barriers for American firms in relation to the EU, and the Organization for Economic Cooperation and Development is undertaking a pilot project to examine the costs of divergent standards and conformity assessment systems through survey research.

24. K. Gatsios and P. Seabright, 'Regulation in the European Community', *Oxford Review of Economic Policy*, 5, no. 2 (1989).

25. R. N. Cooper, 'Europe without Borders', *Brookings Papers on Economic Activity*, 2 (Washington: Brookings Institution, 1989), 325–340; Rudiger Dornbusch, 'Europe 1992: Macro-economic Implications', *Brookings Papers on Economic Activity*, 2 (Washington: Brookings Institution, 1989), 341–62; H. Flam, 'Product Markets and 1992: Full Integration, Large Gains?', *Journal of Economic Perspectives*, 6, no. 4 (1992), 7–30; A. Sapir, 'Regional Integration in Europe', *Economic Journal*, 102 (1992), 1491–506; A. F. Bakhoven, 'An Alternative Assessment of the Macro-economic Effects of Europe 1992', in H. Siebert (ed.), *The Completion of the Internal Market* (Kiel: Institut für Weltwirtschaft an der Universität Kiel, 1990); Centre for Business Strategy Report Series, *1992: Myths and Realities* (London: London Business School, 1989); R. Baldwin, 'The Growth Effects of 1992', *Economic Policy*, 9 (1989), 248–81.

26. The overall results were documented in two books: P. Cecchini, *The European Challenge, 1992: The Benefits of a Single Market* (Aldershot: Gower, 1988); M. Emerson et al., *The Economics of 1992: The EC's Assessment of the Economic Effects of Completing the Internal Market* (Oxford: Oxford University Press, 1988).

27. This assumption ignores the distributional effects of market liberalization in the EC. Neven argues that the main beneficiaries are likely to be the southern member states, both in term of exploiting comparative advantage and economies of scale. See D. Neven, 'EEC Integration towards 1992: Some Distributional Aspects', *Economic Policy*, 10 (1990).

28. According to the Heckscher–Ohlin theory, factors of production are critical from comparative advantage. However, the focus of comparative advantage in the production of capital-intensive goods is static. It does not consider the dynamic possibility of change in economic structures and the possible build-up of comparative strength in new and emerging industries.

29. A. O. Hirschmann, *The Strategy of Economic Development* (New Haven: Yale University Press, 1958), especially ch. 10. This polarization was not addressed in the Cecchini Reports.

30. For an empirical assessment of inter-industry trade flows and their effect on comparative advantage, see Neven, 'EEC Integration towards 1992', and B. Belassa and L. Bauwens, 'The Determinants of Intra-European Trade in Manufactured Goods', *European Economic Review*, 32 (Sept. 1988), 1421–37.

31. In the political economy literature on comparative economic performance, there is great emphasis on the issue of historical timing. Neven's analysis reflects the Gerschenkron–Moore approach that different countries adopt different institutional responses depending on whether they were late or early industrializers.

32. Traditional analyses of the effects of European integration are based on Jacob Viner's theory of customs union formation, which expects trade creation and trade diversion. See J. Viner, *The Customs Union Issue* (New York: Garland Pub., 1983). Subsequent research has focused on alternative assessments of the effects of economic integration. Triffin argues that the preoccupation with trade diversion arguments has led to undue criticism of regional arrangements. This does not acknowledge the dynamic effects of integration that will push changes in the methods, scale, and organization of production in response to enlarged market opportunities. See R. Triffin, 'Economic Integration: Institutions, Theories and Policies', *World Politics*, 6, no. 4 (July 1954). Similarly, Scitovsky stresses the main benefits would result from increased productivity and greater competition. See T. Scitovsky, *Economic Theory and Western European Integration* (Stanford, Calif: Stanford University Press, 1958).

33. See Emerson et al., *Economics of 1992*, 6–7; Peck, *Brookings Papers on Economic Activity*, 289; D. Mayes, 'The Machine Tool Industry', in D. Mayes (ed.), *The European Challenge: Industry's Response to the 1992 Programme* (Hemel Hempstead: Harvester Wheatsheaf, 1991), 49. By contrast,

Dornbusch adopts the view that trade diversion will be highly significant. See Dornbusch, 'Europe 1992: Macro-economic Implications'.

34. Corporate slack or X-inefficiencies arise because competitive pressures are weak and firms operate below production efficiency. Though increased competition as a result of completing the internal market is expected to produce dynamic changes in firms' internal decision-making strategies, it is difficult to quantify and measure these sources of dynamic gains.

35. See P. Geroski, 'The Choice between Diversity and Scale', in John Kay (ed.), *1992: Myths and Realities* (London: London Business School, 1989).

36. Kitschelt provides a good analysis of the conditions under which industrial sectors conduct efficient innovation strategies. H. Kitschelt, 'Industrial Governance Structures, Innovation Strategies, and the Case of Japan: Sectoral or Cross-national Comparative Analysis', *International Organization*, 45, no. 4 (1991).

37. In the current economic debate about barriers to entry and the intensity of competition in markets, the theory of contestable markets has assumed increasing prominence. If the intensity of potential competition is sufficiently high, as entry barriers fall, then the result will discipline existing firms. See W. Baumol, 'The Theory of Contestable Markets', *American Economic Review*, 72 (1982), 1–15.

38. A. Jacquemin and D. Wright, 'Corporate Strategies and European Challenges post 1992', *Journal of Common Market Studies*, 31 (1993).

39. This is based on studies undertaken by the European Commission on the impact and effectiveness of the single market as well as my own interviews and data collected from individual companies.

40. Keith E. Maskus and John Wilson, 'Quantifying the Impact of Technical Barriers to Trade: A Review of Past Attempts and the New Policy Context', paper presented at the World Bank Workshop on 'Quantifying the Trade Effects of Standards and Technical Barriers: Is it Possible?', Washington DC, 27 Apr. 2000; see also, OECD, An Assessment of the Costs for International Trade in Meeting Regulatory Requirements, WP/99/8 Final, Paris, 1999).

41. Under Article 169 (the infringement procedure) the Commission has the task of investigating and prosecuting member states who fail to fulfil their obligations under the Treaty; Complaints about technical barriers account for 50% of all complaints lodged relating to the breach of Article 30 prohibition of measures having 'equivalent effect to quantitative restrictions'.

42. Business opinions on the expected effects on sales volumes differed among member states. A higher percentage expected a beneficial impact in Belgium, Netherlands, and Luxembourg, whereas in France, Spain, and Greece, respondents had more modest expectations of increased sales and expected a significant decline in domestic market shares.

43. Commission of the European Communities, 'The Economics of 1992', *European Economy*, no. 35 (Luxembourg: Office of Official Publications, 1988); G. Nerb, 'The Completion of the Internal Market: A Survey of European Industry's Perception of the Likely Effects', *The Costs of Non-*

Europe, vol. iii (Luxembourg: Commission of the European Communities, 1988); Interview by author with Swedish Standardization Official, London, 20 Dec. 1992.

44. C. K. Pralahad and G. Hamel, 'The Core Competence of the Corporation', *Harvard Business Review*, 68 (May–June 1990), 79–91.

45. See US Department of Commerce Subcommittee on Europe, *White Paper*, Nov. 1995; 'Hitting a Wall: US Firm's Troubles in EU Highlight a Lack of Integration', *Wall Street Journal*, 9 Apr. 1996; 'Stacking the Deck in Europe: One Company's Story', *ASTM Standardization News*, Aug. 1996; Department of Trade and Industry (United Kingdom), *Barriers to Trade in Chemicals in the Single Market* (London: HMSO, July 1995).

46. Nomenclature in the standards area is complex. Standards produced by non-governmental actors are often termed 'voluntary' standards; standards produced by state or federal government activity are classified as 'mandatory'. However, many voluntary standards are adopted or incorporated by 'reference' even in government legislation, thereby becoming mandatory even though they have been developed by private, non-governmental standards bodies. The phrase 'private standards' is sometimes used as a synonym for non-governmental standards. The term 'private standards bodies' is used hereafter to refer to a specific role that the private sector plays in developing standards for products, systems processes, and practices.

47. 'The European Community without Technical Barriers', CEPS Working Party Report No. 5 (Brussels: Centre for European Policy Studies, May 1992).

48. See D. Vogel, 'Regulatory Cooperation between the European Union and the United States', paper presented at the American Institute for Contemporary German Studies-European Community Studies Association Conference on US–EU Relations in Washington, Jan. 1997.

49. European Commission, *Impact and Effectiveness of Single Market*, COM (96) 520.

50. F. Abraham 'Building Blocks of the Single Market: The Case of Mutual Recognition, Home Country Control and Essential Requirements', *International Economics Research Papers*, no. 75, CES, 1991.

51. CEPS, 'European Community without Technical Barriers', 5; J. Waelbroeck, '1992: Are the Figures Right? Reflections of a Thirty Per Cent Policymaker', in Siebert, *The Completion of the Internal Market*.

52. H. Spruyt, 'Actors and Institutions in the Historical Evolution of Standard Setting', paper presented at the Political Economy of Standards Setting Conference, 4–5 June 1998, EUI Florence.

53. S. Krislov, *How Nations Choose Product Standards and Standards Change Nations* (Pittsburgh: University of Pittsburgh Press, 1996); D. Hemenway, *Industrywide Voluntary Product Standards* (Cambridge: Ballinger Pub. Co., 1975).

54. D. Vogel, *Barriers or Benefits: Regulation in Transatlantic Trade* (Washington: Brookings Institution, 1997); M. Egan, 'Bandwagons or Barriers: The Role of Standards in the European and American Marketplace', Center for West European Studies, University of Pittsburgh European Policy Paper

Series No. 1, Nov. 1997; P. Edelman, 'Japanese Product Standards as Non-Tariff Barriers: When Regulatory Policy Becomes a Trade Issue', *Stanford Journal of International Law*, 24 (1988), 389–446; M. Austin and H. Milner, 'Strategies of International and European Standardization', paper presented at the Political Economy of Standards Setting Conference, 4–5 June 1998.

55. See J. Pelkmans and D. Costello, *Industrial Product Standards*, UNIDO Report, 1991; For a more extensive analysis of these issues see, J. Farrell and G. Saloner, 'Competition, Compatibility and Standards: The Economics of Horses, Penguins and Lemmings', in H. Landis Gabel (ed.), *Product Standardization and Competitive Strategy* (Amsterdam: Elsevier, 1987).

56. Design standards specify exact conditions of use whereas performance standards set down targets, goals, and objectives.

57. Maskus and Wilson, 'Quantifying the Impact of Technical Barriers to Trade'.

58. Landis Gabel (ed.), *Product Standardization and Competitive Strategy*.

59. J. Farrell and G. Saloner, 'Coordination through Committees and Markets', *Rand Journal of Economics*, 19 (1988), 236–318.

60. See W. B. Arthur, 'Competing Technologies: An Overview', in G. Dosi, C. Freeman, R. Nelson, G. Silverberg, and L. Soete (eds.), *Technical Change and Economic Theory* (London: Frances Pinter, 1988).

61. There is a growing literature on the anti-trust implications of proprietary and dominant standards in the market place, see e.g. J. J. Anton and D. A. Yao, 'Standard-Setting Consortia, Antitrust, and High-Technology Industries', *Antitrust Law Journal*, 64 (1995), 247–65; S. J. Liebowitz and Stephen E. Margolis, 'Should Technology Choice be a Concern of Antitrust Policy?', *Harvard Journal of Law and Technology*, 9 (1996), 283–318.

62. This is a classic battle of the sexes problem.

63. R. Crane, *The Politics of International Standards: France and the Color TV War* (Norwood, NJ: Ablex, 1979); S. Schmidt and R. Werle, 'Technical Controversy in International Standardization', Working Paper 93/5, Max Planck Institüt, Cologne, Mar. 1993; J Pelkmans and R. Beuter, 'Standardization and Competitiveness: Public and Private Strategies in the EU Colour TV Industry', in Landis Gabel (ed.), *Product Standardization and Competitive Strategy*.

64. For an important exception see S. Schmidt and R. Werle, *Coordinating Technologies* (Boston: MIT Press, 1998).

65. The problem is illustrated by the case in which a procurement specification (government purchasing contract) for steel pipes required compliance with the Irish Standards Mark Licensing Scheme, in effect excluding competitive bids from non-Irish firms. See *EC Commission* v. *Ireland*, ECR 1369 (Luxembourg: Office of Official Publications, 1987).

66. See R. Mansell, 'Standards, Industrial Policy and Innovation', in R. Hawkins, Robin Mansell, and Jim Skea (eds.), *Standards, Innovation and Com-*

petitiveness: The Politics and Economics of Standards in Natural and Technical Environments (Aldershot: Edward Elgar, 1995); for a specific economic analysis in the British case, see P. Swann, P. Temple, and M. Shurmer, 'Standards and Trade Performance: The UK Experience', *Economic Policy* (Sept. 1996).

67. Pelkmans and Costello, *Industrial Product Standards*.
68. National Research Council, *Standards, Conformity Assessment and Trade: Into the 21ˢᵗ Century* (Washington DC: National Academy Press, 1995); Carmen Matutes and Pierre Regibeau, 'A Selective Review of the Economics of Standardization: Entry Deterrence, Technological Progress and International Competition', *European Journal of Political Economy*, 12 (1996), 183–209.
69. Raymond Werle's distinction between regulative and coordinative standards is a useful distinction since it focuses on the aim, economic effects, and governance mechanism. Coordinative standards concern interoperability and compatibility, and reduce transaction costs through either committees or markets. Regulative standards prevent externalities, results from hierarchical modes of governance, and are prohibitive mechanisms. See R. Werle, 'Institutional Aspects of Standardization: Jurisdictional Conflicts and the Choice of Standardization Organizations', paper presented at the Conference on the Political Economy of Standards Setting, Florence, June 1998.
70. D. Vogel, 'The New Social Regulation in Historical and Comparative Perspective', in T. K. McCraw (ed.), *Regulation in Perspective* (Cambridge, Mass.: Harvard University Press, 1981), 162.
71. See e.g. J. Hillman, *Technical Barriers to Agricultural Trade* (Boulder, Colo.: Westview Press, 1991).
72. See 'EU Firm on Beef Safety Rules', *Financial Times*, 11 Aug. 1997; 'US Presses for Change on Tallow Exports', *Financial Times*, 8 Aug. 1997.
73. 'US Challenges Europe's Food Safety Stance', *Financial Times*, 31 Mar. 2000.
74. See Vogel, *Barriers or Benefits*.
75. *The Economist*, 19 Apr. 1975; for good examples, see M. Elkes, 'Europe 1991: Its Impact on Non-Tariff Barriers and Trade Relations with the United States', *Food, Drug and Cosmetic Law Journal* (Sept. 1989).
76. A. O. Sykes, *Product Standards for Internationally Integrated Goods Markets* (Washington: Brookings Institution, 1995), 23.
77. The US–Japanese trade relationship is replete with examples in which the conformity assessment process in Japan has been a major obstacle to efforts by US manufacturers to gain market access. See Edelman, 'Japanese Product Standards as Non-Tariff Trade Barriers'. Much less has been written about EC–Japanese relations in this area.
78. See European Commission, *Europe 1992: Europe World Partner*, Spokesman's Service Press Release P-117, 19 Oct. 1988.
79. One of the problems with the Emerson report is its assumption of the autonomous increase of the export shares of the EC in world trade.
80. Jacquemin and Sapir provide convincing empirical evidence that competition from third country exports is an even more effective stimulus for

competitive behaviour on the part of European producers than intra-EC competition. See A. Jacquemin and A. Sapir, 'Europe post-1992: Internal and External Liberalization', *American Economic Review*, 81 (May 1991), 166–70.

81. See M. Egan, 'Tackling Barriers to Trade in Global and Regional Markets: Policy Patterns and Institutional Interactions', paper presented at the Conference on Europeanization in International Perspective, Pittsburgh, Sept. 1997; Egan, 'Bandwagons'.

82. See John Wilson, *Standards and APEC: An Action Agenda* (IIE: Washington DC, 1995); OECD, *Regionalism and its Place in the Multilateral Trading System* (Paris, 1996), esp. ch. by K. Nicolaïdis, 'Mutual Recognition of Regulatory Regimes: Some Lessons and Prospects'.

83. Wilson, *Standards and APEC*; Sherry M. Stephenson, *Standards and Conformity Assessment as Non-Tariff Barriers to Trade*, Policy Research Working Paper, no. 1826, World Bank, 1997.

Chapter 4

1. Some degree of legislative success has materialized in areas such as labelling of dangerous chemicals, cosmetics, and motor vehicles. See J. McCarthy, 'Protectionism and Product Harmonisation in the EEC', *Economic and Social Review*, 10 (Apr. 1979), 187–208.

2. S. Krislov, *How Nations Choose Product Standards and Standards Change Nations* (Pittsburgh: University of Pittsburgh Press, 1997); R. C. Cochrane, *Measures for Progress: A History of the National Bureau of Standards* (Washington, National Bureau of Standards, US Dept. of Commerce, 1966).

3. For a good description of national standards regimes, see J. J. Tate, 'Varieties of Standardization', in P. Hall and D. Soskice (eds.), *Varieties of Capitalism* (forthcoming).

4. Early examples of direct government action to harmonize state laws include bankruptcy provisions and uniform safety regulation of railroads. Later examples of harmonization include national labelling systems, automotive disclosure, nutrition labelling as examples of government pre-emption to harmonize diverse state laws.

5. See *Interstate Trade Barriers*, compiled by J. E. Johnsen (New York: H. W. Wilson Company, 1940); *Trade Barriers among the States*, the proceedings of the National Conference on Interstate Trade Barriers, 5, 6, 7 Apr. 1939, Chicago, Council of State Governments, 1939; G.Taylor et al., *Barriers to Internal Trade in Farm Products* (Washington: US Government Printing Office, 1939); R. H. Jackson, 'The Supreme Court and Interstate Barriers', *The Annals*, Jan. 1940.

6. For an excellent overview of harmonization from the mid-1960s to the early 1980s, see A. Dashwood, 'Hastening Slowly: The Community's Path Toward Harmonisation', in H. Wallace, W. Wallace and C. Webb (eds.), *Policymaking in the European Community* (London: John Wiley & Sons, 1983), 177–208.

7. C. Cosgrove Twitchett, 'Introduction', in Carol Cosgrove Twitchett (ed.), *Harmonisation in the EEC* (New York: St Martins Press, 1981), 1.

8. A. Dashwood, 'The Harmonisation Process', in Cosgrove Twitchett, *Harmonisation in the EEC*, 7.

9. It is often forgotten that EFTA was also pursuing a strategy of trade liberalization and harmonization, and in fact embarked on one of the earliest efforts at addressing non-tariff barriers through mutual recognition, see R. Middleton, *Negotiating on Non-tariff Distortions of Trade: The EFTA Precedents* (New York: St Martin's Press for the Trade Policy Research Centre, 1975).

10. Unless otherwise indicated, the term 'Treaty' refers to the Treaty of Rome establishing the European Economic Community, and subsequently amended.

11. H. von der Groeben, *the EC, the Formative Years: The Struggle to Establish a Common Market and the Political Union* (Luxembourg: Commission of the European Communities, 1985), 52.

12. See the statement of H. von der Groeben to the European Parliament, *Official Journal of the European Communities*, Annex 119, Nov. 1969, Debates of the European Parliament, 151–2. Reprinted in Select Committee of the European Communities, 'Approximation of Laws under Article 100 of the EEC Treaty', 22nd Report, HL 131, Apr. 1978.

13. To avoid conceptual confusion, reference is made to the treaty articles before the Treaty of Amsterdam. After Amsterdam, Article 30 EEC Treaty became Article 28 Treaty; Article 34 EEC Treaty became Article 29; Article 36 became Article 30, and other treaty articles were abolished.

14. Under the renumbering of the Treaty on European Union, Article 12 is now Article 25 and Articles 13–17 have been repealed. Given that the discussion is historically based, reference is made in the text to earlier numbering of the Treaty with explanatory footnotes referencing the new versions in the Treaty.

15. Articles 18–27 have been repealed. Article 28 is now Article 26, and Article 29 is now Article 27.

16. Article 30 has now become Article 28 and Article 36 has now become Article 30 in the new consolidated Treaty.

17. E. Stein and T. Sandalow, 'On the Two Systems: An Overview', in T. Sandalow and E. Stein (eds.), *Courts and Free Markets* (Oxford: Clarendon Press, 1982), 25.

18. F. Abb, 'Is Harmonisation of EC Economic Policy Necessary?', *Zeitschrift für die gesamte Staatwissenschaft* (Apr. 1967), 218–30. Author's translation of title.

19. A. Héritier, 'The Accommodation of Diversity in European Policy-Making and its Outcomes', *Journal of European Public Policy*, 3, no. 2 (1996), 149.

20. Ibid. 150.

21. T. W. Vogelaar, 'The Approximation of the Laws of the Member States under the Treaty of Rome', *Common Market Law Review*, 12 (1975), 211–30.

22. Article 3h and Article 100 refer to approximation, Articles 54 (3) g and 57 (2) to coordination and Article 99 refers to harmonization. Although there is a small distinction between the different meanings, the term harmonization is used consistently throughout the text.

23. For detailed accounts, see Dashwood, 'Hastening Slowly', and Cosgrove Twitchett, *Harmonisation in the EEC.*

24. Article 169 and 170 enable both the Commission and a member state to bring action against another member state for failing to fulfil obligations under the Treaty. Article 171 amended by the Treaty on European Union in 1993 provides the Court of Justice with the authority to impose a fine or penalty payment for non-compliance with European law. It should be noted that the ECSC Treaty under Article 88 allows the Council to impose sanctions on recalcitrant member states, though it has never actually been used.

25. The more restrictive interpretation of European policy competencies is outlined in the 22nd and 35th Reports of the House of Lords Select Committee on the European Communities on the Approximation of Laws. In this view, the adoption of directives in consumer protection or environmental policy areas transgresses the limits of Community competence. A detailed reply to these points is found in George Close, 'Harmonisation of Laws: Use or Abuse of the Powers under the Treaty', *European Law Review*, 3 (1978), 461–86.

26. Article 235 is reminiscent of the necessary and proper clause of the American constitution. Article 235 has been renumbered as Article 308 under the renumbered version of the Treaty on European Union.

27. See C. Sasse and H. Charles Yourow, 'The Growth of Legislative Power of the European Communities', in Sandalow and Stein, *Courts and Free Markets*, 95–7.

28. Ibid. 99.

29. For example, the United Nations Economic Commission for Europe has been actively pursuing automotive vehicle harmonization since 1958, and the European Convention concerning driving hours (AETR) negotiated by the UNECE in 1962 sparked efforts at harmonization within the EU.

30. N. Bel, 'L'Harmonisation de dispositions techniques dans le cadre de la CEE', *Revue du Marché Commun* (1966), 26–33; E. Lasnet, 'La eliminación de trabastéchnicas a los intercambios', *Derecho de la integración* 19, no. 4 (Mar. 1977).

31. P. Oliver, *The Free Movement of Goods in the EEC*, 2nd edn. (London: European Law Center Limited, 1982).

32. The initial success concerned additives, with the adoption of the first directive on food colourings in 1962. *Official Journal of the European Community*, 115/82/EEC, 23 Oct. 1962.

33. See Dashwood, 'Hastening Slowly', 184.

34. This included numerous product standards in agricultural products, but the first directive on industrial products was not adopted until 1970.

35. G. Jensen, 'Common Industrial Standards', *EFTA Bulletin*, 8, no. 3 (1967).
36. *Official Journal of the European Community*, no. 2611/65, Recommendation de la Commission 'aux états membres, relative à la communication préalable à la commission a l'état de projets, de certaines dispositions legislatives règlementaires et administratives'. See the assessment by F. Bonn, 'Les Entraves techniques aux échanges intracommunautaires', *Revue du Marché Commun*, 12 (1969), 369–87.
37. As Bonn points out, there is no reference to 'technical barriers to trade' in the Treaty. Bonn, ibid.
38. For a detailed review, see P. J. Slot, *Technical and Administrative Obstacles to Trade in the EEC* (Leiden: A. W. Sijhoff, 1975), 103–7.
39. General programme of 28 May 1969 for the elimination of technical barriers to trade which result from disparities between provisions laid down by law, regulation, or administrative action in the member states, *Official Journal of the European Communities*, Special Edition and Series, 9 (1969), 25–33. Translated from the French edition.
40. The EU's secondary legislation is often underestimated, and in 1999 alone it enacted 842 regulations, 55 directives, and 516 decisions in application of the treaties or secondary legislation. See Y. Devuyst, 'The European Union's Constitutional Order? Between Community Method and Ad Hoc Compromise', *Berkeley Journal of International Law*, 18, no. 1 (2000).
41. On the comitology process see M. Egan and D. Wolf, 'Regulation and Comitology: The EU System in Regulatory Perspective' *Columbia Journal of European Law*, 4, no. 3 (1998); F. Bignami, 'The Democratic Deficit in European Community Rule-Making: A Call for Notice and Comment in Comitology', *Harvard International Law Journal*, 40, no. 2 (1999); E. Vos, 'The Rise of Committees', *European Law Journal*, 3, no. 3 (1998), 210–29; R. H. Pedlar and G. F. Schaefer (eds.), *Shaping European Law and Policy* (Maastricht: EIPA, 1996).
42. G. Dennis, 'The Harmonisation of Non-Tariff Barriers', in Cosgrove-Twitchett, *Harmonisation in the EEC*, 19.
43. J. Pelkmans and A. Vollebergh, 'The Traditional Approach to Harmonisation', in J. Pelkmans and M. Vanheukelen (eds.), *Coming to Grips with the Internal Market* (The Hague: EIPA, 1986).
44. 'Technical Barriers to Trade, One Hundred Directives in Eleven Years', *Bulletin of the European Communities*, 6 (1978).
45. European Commission, *Thirty Years of Community Law* (Luxembourg: Office for Official Publications of the European Communities, 1983), 253.
46. See S. A. B. Page, 'The Revival of Protectionism and its Consequences for Europe', *Journal of Common Market Studies*, 20 (1981), 17–40; House of Lords Select Committee on the European Communities, *Internal Market Barriers to Manufacturers*, Seventeenth Report, 1981–2 Session.
47. W. Hager, 'Protectionism and Autonomy: How to Preserve Free Trade in Europe', *International Affairs* (Summer 1982), 416.
48. The dramatic six-month confrontation between the Commission and De Gaulle over the balance of sovereignty ended with the formalization

of a single veto method of policy-making. The effect was to deflate the Commission's status as a supranational body. See S. Hoffman, 'Obstinate or Obsolete: The Fate of the Nation-State and the Case of Western Europe', *Daedalus* 95 (1966).

49. *Industrial Policy in the European Community: Memorandum from the Commission to the Council*, COM (70) 100, 18 Mar. 1970 (Luxembourg: Office of Official Publications). This was named the 'Colonna report' after the Commissioner responsible for industrial policy in the newly created Directorate General for Industrial Affairs (DG III).

50. See e.g. Dashwood, who argues that harmonization has proceeded a long way in sectors such as motor vehicles, farm tractors, and measuring instruments. Dashwood, 'Hastening Slowly', 186.

51. *Agence Europe*, 5 Sept. 1973.

52. For a general review see A. M. Sbragia, 'Environmental Policy', in H. Wallace and W. Wallace (eds.), *Policy-Making in the European Union*, 4th edn. (Oxford: Oxford University Press, 2000); D. Vogel, 'Environmental Policy in the European Community', in S. Kamieniecki, *Environmental Politics and Policy: Some Recent Controversies and Developments* (Albany, NY: SUNY Press, 1993).

53. Stein and Sandalow, 'On the Two Systems', 23.

54. For a detailed description of the directives to be adopted in the revised programme, see *Agence Europe*, 10 May 1973.

55. J. Pelkmans, 'A Community without Technical Barriers? Accomplishments and Prospects', paper presented at the conference 'Europe 1992: Challenge or Opportunity', Center for International Business and Trade, Georgetown University, Washington, 8–9 Dec. 1988.

56. Krislov, *How Nations Choose Product Standards*, 144.

57. D. Vogel, 'Protective Regulation and Protectionism in the European Community: The Creation of a Common Market for Food and Beverages', paper presented at the biennial conference of the European Community Studies Association, George Mason University, Fairfax, Va. May 1991.

58. Ibid.

59. *Wall Street Journal*, 2 Sept. 1989; *New Republic*, 4 Nov. 1991.

60. Quoted in D. Welch, 'From "Euro-beer" to "Newcastle Brown": A Review of European Community Action to Dismantle Divergent Food Laws', *Journal of Common Market Studies*, 22 (Sept. 1983), 55.

61. 'Towards a Single European Sausage', *Wall Street Journal*, 26 Oct. 1993, B1. 'Wine by the Glass', *Financial Times*, 24 Dec. 1994; 'Climber's Safety Wedges', *The Independent*, 2 July 1995; 'Double Deckers', *The European*, 10 Mar. 1995.

62. 'Very Small Beer', *The Economist*, 2 Nov. 1974.

63. M. Lee, 'Commission v Germany and Article 36 Protection of Human Life and Health', *Northwestern Journal of International Law and Business*, 9 (1988), 444.

64. *Commission of the European Communities v. Federal Republic of Germany*, CMR 780 (Luxembourg: Office of Official Publications, 1988).

65. 'Very Small Beer'.
66. 'Industrial Policy: Status Report of the Community's Work', *Supplement to the EC Bulletin*, no. 6 (1972).
67. *Agence Europe*, 5 Sept. 1973.
68. 'Industrial Policy'.
69. For a detailed defence of the Community's method, see C. D. Ehlermann, then Director-General, Legal Services of the Commission of the European Communities, lecture given at Edinburgh, 18 Nov. 1977.
70. See reply to Written Question No. 142/74 in which the Commission stated 'the enlargement of the Community, however, necessitated a serious reappraisal of the situation as far as the elimination of technical obstacles to trade due to divergences of legislation is concerned.' See also the speech of R. Jenkins, then European Commission President, to the European Parliament, 'Commission Programme for 1977', *Bulletin of the EU* (Luxembourg: Office of Official Publications, 1977), 10.
71. Krislov, *How Nations Choose Product Standards*, 145.
72. F. Scharpf, 'The Joint-Decision Trap: Lessons from German Federalism and European Integration', *Public Administration*, 66 (1988).
73. In responding to a Parliamentary question, the Commission acknowledged the ad hoc basis stating that 'the Commission keeps in touch with all members of the Social Partners Group who have expressed an interest. To keep the consultation process within bounds however, the Commission endeavors to hold combined meetings for this purpose on aspects of Community interest to a number of these organizations.' Written Question No. 496/75, *Official Journal of the European Communities*, C 19/23 28 Jan. 1976.
74. For a good case study of the difficulties of compliance and implementation, see J. J. Beuve-Méry and A. Schaub, 'Die Beseitigung der technischen Handelschindernisse zwischen den EWG-Mitglied-staaten durch Richtlinien gemäss', Art. 100 EWGV. Ein praktischer Fall: die Lebensmittel Farbstoffe', *Europarecht* (1970), 135–60.
75. A. Morgan 'Pressure Groups and Harmonisation', in Cosgrove Twitchett, *Harmonisation in the EEC*, 103.
76. Dashwood, 'The Harmonisation Process'.
77. J. McMillan, 'La Certification, la reconnaissance mutuelle et le marché unique', *Revue du Marché Commun*, 2 (1991), 181–211. Author's translation.
78. For statistical evidence of non-compliance by member states by legal basis and policy area, see M. Mendrinou, 'Non-Compliance and the European Commission's Role in Integration', *Journal of European Public Policy*, 3, no. 1 (1996), 1–22.
79. Vogelaar, 'The Approximation of the Laws of the Member States under the Treaty of Rome'.
80. See J.-J. Servan-Schreiber, *Le Défi américain* (New York: Atheneum, 1968), esp. ch. 9.

81. S. Cohen and J. Zysman, *Manufacturing Matters: The Myth of the Post-Industrial Society* (New York: Basic Books, 1987).
82. See M. Piore and C. Sabel, *The Second Industrial Divide* (New York: Basic Books, 1983).
83. Dashwood, 'Hastening Slowly'.
84. D. Vogel, 'Trading up and Governing across: Transnational Governance and Environmental Protection', *European Journal of Public Policy*, 4, no. 4 (1997), 556–71.
85. S. Breyer, *Regulation and its Reform* (Cambridge, Mass.: Harvard University Press, 1982), 191–6; S. Breyer, 'Analysing Regulatory Failure: Mismatches, Less Restrictive Alternatives, and Reform', *Harvard Law Review*, 92 (1979), 549–609.
86. Sandalow and Stein (eds.), *Courts and Free Markets*; D. Kommers and M. Waelbroeck, 'Legal Integration and the Free Movement of Goods: The American and European Experience', in M. Cappalletti, M. Seccombe, and J. H. H. Weiler, *Integration through Law*, vol. i, book 1 (Berlin: De Gruyter, 1985); W. Hurst, *Law and Markets in United States History: Different Modes of Bargaining among Interests* (Madison: University of Wisconsin Press, 1982).
87. J. Zimmerman, *Interstate Relations* (Westport, Conn: Praeger, 1996), 126.
88. W. Hellerstein, 'Federal Limitations on State Taxation of Interstate Commerce', in Sandalow and Stein (eds.), *Courts and Free Markets*.

Chapter 5

1. The terms European Court of Justice, Court of Justice, and Court are used interchangeably in this chapter.
2. For a good comparison of the American and European experience see D. Kommers and M. Waelbroeck, 'Legal Integration and the Free Movement of Goods: The American and European Experience', in M. Cappalletti, M. Seccombe, and J. H. H. Weiler, *Integration through Law*, vol. i, book 1 (Berlin: De Gruyter, 1985); for the intersection of law and markets in the American case, see H. Scheiber, 'Federalism and the American Economic Order, 1789–1910', *Law and Society Review*, 10 (Fall 1975); and W. Hurst, *Law and Markets in United States History* (Madison: University of Wiscons in Press, 1982). For an extensive review of intellectual shifts in legal doctrine regarding the market see, M. Sklar, *The Corporate Reconstruction of American Capitalism 1890–1916* (Cambridge: Cambridge University Press, 1988), esp. 49–85.
3. M. Shapiro, *The Supreme Court and Administrative Agencies* (New York: Free Press/Macmillan, 1968), 25.
4. This does not mean that the Court has consistently pressed ahead at the expense of more specialized local needs and diversity. See cases *Commission* v. *Denmark* (recycling bottles), *Commission* v. *Germany* (woodworking machines), 1988.

5. See Kommers and Waelbroeck, 'Legal Integration'; M. P. Maduro, 'Reforming the Market or the State? Article 30 and the European Constitution: Economic Freedom and Political Rights', *European Law Journal* (Mar. 1997), 72–4.

6. T. Sandalow and E. Stein (eds.), *Courts and Free Markets* (Oxford: Clarendon Press, 1982), 25.

7. Article 3 of the Treaty and its broad phraseology indicate that the basic objectives of the common market include the elimination of discriminatory or otherwise unduly restrictive practices, whether imposed by governmental mandate or initiated by private action.

8. See e.g. S. Bruchey, *The Roots of American Economic Growth, 1607–1861: An Essay in Social Causation* (New York: Harper & Row, 1968); C. M. McCurdy, 'American Law and the Marketing Structure of the Large Corporation, 1875–1890', *Journal of Economic History*, 38, no. 3 (1978).

9. For an important exception, see G. Berk, *Alternative Tracks* (Baltimore: Johns Hopkins University Press, 1994).

10. See F. Frankfurter, *The Commerce Clause under Marshall, Taney and Waite* (Chapel Hill: University of North Carolina, 1937).

11. McCurdy, 'American Law'.

12. Research on the establishment of the American 'common market' usually focuses on either the development of an integrated transport network or the development of a single currency as critical for economic growth and a unified market. See e.g. J. Sheridan, 'The Déjà Vue of EMU: Considerations for Europe from Nineteenth Century America', *Journal of Economic Issues*, 30, no. 4 (1996); S. Skronewek, *Building an American State* (Cambridge: Cambridge University Press, 1982); C. Goodrich, *Government Promotion of American Canals and Railroads, 1800–1890* (New York: Columbia University Press, 1965).

13. It should be noted that alleged barriers have also been challenged on the grounds that they violate not only the interstate commerce clause but also the Privileges and Immunities Clause, and Equal Protection of the Law.

14. See Goodrich, *Government Promotion*.

15. See *Interstate Trade Barriers*, a report prepared by the Marketing Laws Survey and sponsored by the US Department of Commerce (US GPO: Washington, 1942); P. J. Slot, *Technical and Administrative Obstacles to Trade in the EEC* (Leiden: A. W. Sijhoff, 1975); A. S. Abel, 'Commerce Regulation before *Gibbons* v. *Ogden*: Trade and Traffic Part II', *Brooklyn Law Review* (1940), 38–77.

16. T. B. Spears, *One Hundred Years on the Road: The Traveling Salesman in American Culture* (New Haven: Yale University Press, 1995).

17. See B. Cushman, *Rethinking the New Deal Court* (Oxford: Oxford University Press, 1998); H. Gillman, 'Reconnecting Modern Constitutional Law to the Historical Evolution of Capitalism', paper presented to the American Political Science Association, Boston, Sept. 1998); A

similar distinction is that between business affected with a public interest and those which are not. See *Munn* v. *Illinois* (1877).

18. Spaak Report (see ch. 3 n. 1 above).

19. McCurdy makes this point in relation to the United States, but it is equally applicable to the European Court of Justice. For an extensive review of how American commerce law evolved, see Frankfurter, *The Commerce Clause*.

20. P. Stewart, 'Foreword', in Sandalow and Stein (eds.), *Courts and Free Market*.

21. See also M. Shapiro, 'The European Court of Justice', in A. M. Sbragia (ed.), *Europolitics: Institutions and Policymaking in the 'New' European Community* (Washington: Brookings Institution, 1992).

22. See R. Dehousse, 'Integration v. Regulation? On the Dynamics of Regulation in the European Community', *Journal of Common Market Studies*, 30, no. 4 (1992), 383–402.

23. Sandalow and Stein, *Courts and Free Markets*; E. Stein, 'Lawyers, Judges and the Making of a Transnational Constitution', *American Journal of International Law* (1981); J. H. H. Weiler, 'The Transformation of Europe', *Yale Law Journal*, 100 (1991); K. Alter, 'Who are the "Masters of the Treaty"? European Governments and the European Court of Justice', *International Organization*, 52 (Winter 1998), 121–47; D. Wincott, 'The Rule of Law or the Rule of the Court of Justice? An Institutional Account of Judicial Politics in the European Community', *Journal of European Public Policy*, 2, no. 4 (1995).

24. Weiler, 'The Transformation of Europe'; Stein, 'Lawyers, Judges'; S. Scheingold, *Law in Political Integration* (Center for International Affairs, Harvard University Occasional Paper Series, no. 27, 1971).

25. See Alter, 'Masters of the Treaty'; K. Alter and S. Meunier,' Judicial Politics in the EU: European Integration and the Path-Breaking Cassis de Dijon Decision', *Comparative Political Studies*, 26 (1994), 535–61; A.-M. Burley and W. Mattli, 'Europe before the Court: A Political Theory of Legal Integration', *International Organization*, 47 (1993); G. Bermann, 'Regulatory Federalism', unpublished manuscript, Columbia Law School; G. Bermann, 'Subsidiarity and the European Community', *Hastings International and Comparative Law Review*, 17 (Fall 1993), 97–112; H. Rasmussen, *On Law and Policy in the European Court of Justice: A Comparative Study of Judicial Policymaking* (Martinus Nijhof: The Hague, 1986); G. Garrett and B. Weingast, 'Ideas, Interests and Institutions: Constructing the EC's Internal Market', in J. Goldstein and R. Keohane (eds.), *Ideas and Foreign Policy: Beliefs, Institutions and Political Change* (Ithaca, NY: Cornell University Press, 1993).

26. See A. Stone Sweet and T. Brunell, 'Constructing a Supranational Constitution: Dispute Resolution and Governance in the European Community', *American Political Science Review*, 92 (Mar. 1998), 63–81.

27. J. H. H. Weiler, 'The Reformation of European Constitutionalism', *Journal of Common Market Studies*, 35, no. 1 (1997), 97.

28. J. H. H. Weiler, 'Community, Member States and European Integration: Is the Law Relevant?', *Journal of Common Market Studies*, 21 (1982), 55.

29. Shapiro, 'The European Court of Justice', 127–8.

30. Stone, Sweet, and Brunell, 'Constructing'.

31. Alter, 'Masters of the Treaty'; Frederico Mancini, 'The Making of a Constitution for Europe', *Common Market Law Review*, 25 (1989), 595–614.

32. J. Rasmussen, 'The European Court of Justice', in *Thirty Years of Community Law* (Luxembourg: Office of Official Publications of the European Communities, 1983), 172.

33. Burley and Mattli, 'Europe before the Court'; Jonathon Golub, 'Judicial Cooperation between National Courts and the European Court of Justice: The Politics and Patterns of Preliminary Reference', paper presented at the annual conference of the International Studies Association, Apr. 1996; Weiler, 'The Transformation of Europe'; Alter, 'Masters of the Treaty.'

34. Waelbroeck notes that pre-emption problems have arisen in the agricultural field, foreign commercial relations, and competition policy. He argues that pre-emption problems have not emerged in the free movement of goods because the Treaty does not give Community institutions a general power to 'regulate' trade between member states. See Michael Waelbroeck, 'The Emergent Doctrine of Community Pre-emption Consent and Re-delegation', in Sandalow and Stein, *Courts and Free Markets*; see also S. Weatherill, *Law and Integration in the EU* (Oxford: Clarendon Press, 1995).

35. George Bermann et al., *Cases and Material on European Community Law* (New York: West Publishing, 1993), 40; see also the discussion in W. Cohen, 'Congressional Power to Define State Power to Regulate Commerce: Consent and Pre-Emption', in Sandalow and Stein, *Courts and Free Markets*.

36. This is noticeable in the American case as different doctrinal formulations such as 'balancing standard', 'proportionality', and 'police powers' have evolved over time. For an excellent review, see 'The Legal Foundations of Regulatory Federalism: Constitutional and Judicial Perspectives', in The United States Advisory Commission on Intergovernmental Relations, *Regulatory Federalism: Policy, Process, Impact and Reform: A Commission Report* (Washington: ACIR, 1985). For a critical perspective on the Court's role in this area, see Donald H. Regan, 'The Supreme Court and State Protectionism: Making Sense of the Dormant Commerce Clause', *Michigan Law Review*, 84 (1986), 1092–174.

37. See Ch. 3. For other studies documenting the growth of non-tariff barriers in Europe, see Robert Baldwin, *Non-tariff Distortions of International Trade* (Washington: Brookings Institution, 1970); Gerard and Victoria Curzon, *Hidden Barriers to International Trade*, Thames Valley Essay no. 1

(London: Trade Policy Research Centre, 1970); Joseph Grieco, *Coopera-tion among Nations* (Ithaca, NY: Cornell University Press, 1990); Joan Pearce and John Sutton with Roy Batchelor, *Protection and Industrial Policy in Europe* (London: Routledge, 1986).

38. *Thirty Years of Community Law.*
39. This limited case law is due to the obligations under the transition period which provided the Commission with jurisdiction to issue directives for the elimination of quantitative restrictions and 'measures having equival-ent effect to a quantitative restriction' under Article 33(7). It is only after its jurisdiction in this matter expired in 1969 that the Court started to address the principles surrounding the free movement of goods.
40. Treaty Articles have been renumbered under the consolidated texts. Article 30 is now Article 28, Articles 31–3 have been repealed, Article 34 is now Article 29, and Article 36 is now Article 30. To avoid confusion since so many of the cases cite pre-consolidated treaty Articles, the former version of the Treaty on European Union is used.
41. Bernadette Kilroy, 'Member State Control of Judicial Independence: The Integrative Role of the European Court of Justice', paper presented at APSA, Chicago, 31 Aug.–3 Sept. 1995; Stone, Sweet, and Brunell, 'Constructing a Supranational Constitution'.
42. Slot, *Technical and Administrative Obstacles,* 66.
43. For a critical view of the Court's preference for a teleological, pro-integration approach, see Rasmussen, *On Law and Policy in the Euro-pean Court of Justice;* also Mauro Capelletti, 'Is the European Court of Justice Running Wild?', *European Law Review,* 12 (1987), 3–16.
44. See Bermann, 'Subsidiarity and the European Community'; Peter Oliver, *The Free Movement of Goods in the European Community,* 3rd edn. (London: Sweet & Maxwell, 1996).
45. See Directives 64/486/EEC, 66/682/EEC, and 66/683/EEC, *Official Journal of the European Community.*
46. Morton Horwitz, *The Transformation of American Law, 1870–1960* (Oxford: Oxford University Press, 1982), 19.
47. For a critical review suggesting that there is no need for protectionist effect balancing, see Regan, 'The Supreme Court and State Protectionism'.
48. Kommers and Waelbroeck, 'Legal Integration', 196.
49. Mr Deringer MEP, Written Question 118/1966, *Official Journal of the European Community;* and 64/1966, *Official Journal of the European Community.*
50. Slot, *Technical and Administrative Obstacles,* 73; Peter Oliver, *The Free Movement of Goods in the EEC,* 2nd edn. (London: European Law Center Limited, 1982), especially ch. 7.
51. Written Question 118/66, 1966; Written Question 64/67, 1967; Written Question 185/67. See Oliver, *Free Movement of Goods,* 3rd edn., 88–91.
52. Rene Barents, 'New Developments in Measures Having an Equivalent Effect', *Common Market Law Review,* 18 (1980), 272; Laurence Gormley, 'Actually or Potentially, Directly or Indirectly? Obstacles to the Free Movement

of Goods', *Yearbook of European Law*, 9 (1989); A. W. H. Meij and J. A. Winters, 'Measures Having an Equivalent Effect to a Quantitative Restriction', *Common Market Law Review*, 17 (1979), 79–104.

53. Barents, 'New Developments', 272–3.
54. Slot, *Technical and Administrative Obstacles*.
55. Directive 70/50, 1979.
56. Article 3 of Directive 70/50 covers measures governing the marketing of products, including shape, size, weight, composition, presentation, identification, or other characteristics which are indistinctly applicable to both domestic and imported goods, where the restrictive effect of such measures towards the free movement of goods exceeds the effect intrinisic to trade rules. *Cassis de Dijon* clearly took its reasoning from this 1970 directive.
57. The period leading up to 1970 was considered the transition period to make the common market operational.
58. Oliver, *Free Movement of Goods*, 3rd edn., 68.
59. A particularly striking example of the Court's initial focus on overt discrimination was the *Sekt-Weinbrand* case decided in 1975. Case 12/74 *Commission* v. *Germany*, ECR 141.
60. Case *Commission* v. *Germany*, ECR 181, 1975.
61. K. Armstrong, 'Regulating the Free Movement of Goods: Institutions and Institutional Change', in J. Shaw and G. More (eds.), *New Legal Dynamics of European Union* (Oxford: Clarendon Press, 1995), 174; see also Slot, *Technical and Administrative Obstacles*; Gormley, 'Actually or Potentially, Directly or Indirectly?'; Manfred A. Dauses, 'The System of the Free Movement of Goods in the European Community', *American Journal of Comparative Law*, 33, no. 2 (1985), 209–31.
62. *Procureur du Roi* v. *Dassonville*, Case 8/74, 1974 ECR 837.
63. *Charmasson*, Case 48/74, 1974 ECR 1383.
64. Directive 50/20/EEC 22 Dec. 1970. The Commission's interpretation is in fact much less cautious than that of the Court under *Dassonville*.
65. See Cases 56 and 58/64, 1966 ECR 299.
66. R. Barents, 'New Developments', 273.
67. See ibid. 274 for a more detailed description. Article 85 is concerned with collusive practices.
68. Case 68/76 *Commission* v. *France*, Mar. 1983.
69. Joined Cases 88-90/75, Sadam, 1976 ECR 323 and Case 65/75 Tasca, 1976 ECR 291.
70. For an early review of cases, see Peter Oliver, *Free Movement of Goods*, 2nd edn.; Laurence Gormley, *Prohibiting Restrictions on Trade within the EEC* (Amsterdam: Noth, 1985).
71. See *EC Commission* v. *Belgium*, CMLR 1979 216; *Fietje*, ECR 3839, 1980; *Openbaar Ministrie* v. *Danis*, CMLR 1979 492; *Rewe* Case 4/75 ECR 843, 1975; *Simmenthal* Case 35/76 ECR 1871, 1976.
72. See e.g. Case 82/77 1978 ECR 40.

73. See R. Joliet, 'Recent Trends in the Case Law of the European Court of Justice of the European Communities', Speech given 3 May 1993 to the US Supreme Court Justices.

74. *Iannelli* v. *Meroni*, Case 74/75 CMLR 1977 688.

75. Oliver, *Free Movement of Goods*, 74.

76. Armstrong, 'Regulating the Free Movement of Goods', 174.

77. Ibid. 175–6.

78. See J. Bourgeoine in R. Bieber et al., *1992: One European Market. A Critical Analysis of the Commission's Internal Market Strategy* (Florence: European University Institute, 1988).

79. A. Mattera, 'L'Arrêt Cassis de Dijon: une nouvelle approche pour la réalisation et le bon fonctionnement du marché intérieur', *Revue du Marché Commun*, no. 241 (Nov. 1980), 505.

80. See especially Alter and Meunier, 'Judicial Politics in the EU'; Mattera, 'L'Arrêt Cassis de Dijon'.

81. Barents, 'New Developments'.

82. The Commission's interpretation of the legal decision was largely responsible for raising the significance of mutual recognition as a trade liberalization principle, see Kalypso Nicolaïdis, 'Mutual Recognition among Nations: The European Community and Trade in Services', Harvard University, Ph.D. Dissertation, 1993; Kalypso Nicolaïdis, 'The Emergence of Managed Mutual Recognition: Legal Precedent and Political Innovation in the European Community', paper presented at European Community Studies Association, Charleston, May 1993.

83. Shapiro, 'The European Court of Justice', 129; Garrett and Weingast, 'Ideas'; David Vogel, *Trading up: Consumer and Environmental Regulation in a Global Economy* (Cambridge, Mass.: Harvard University Press, 1995).

84. See e.g. Directive 50/70.

85. Budesanzeiger No. 48, 11 Mar. 1958.

86. The Commission had begun in 1974 to study national rules on foodstuffs and alcoholic beverages to determine their restrictive impact on trade.

87. The Finanzgericht asked the Court of Justice whether the concept of measures having equivalent effect to a quantitative restriction on imports contained in Article 30 of the EEC Treaty be understood as meaning that the fixing of a minimum wine-spirit content for potable spirits laid down in the German Branntweinmonopolgesetz. The result of this would be that traditional products of other member states whose wine-spirit is below the fixed limit could not be put into circulation in the Federal Republic of Germany.

88. Case 13/77 GB *Inno* v. *ATAB*, ECR 2115, 1977.

89. For a detailed review, see Michelle Egan, 'Regulating European Markets', Ph.D. Dissertation, University of Pittsburgh, 1995.

90. ECR 649.

91. Case 120/78 23.

92. Kalypso Nicolaïdis, 'Comments', in Alan O. Sykes, *Product Standards for Internationally Integrated Goods Markets* (Washington: Brookings Institution, 1995).

93. Reversing the burden of proof was a significant shift in reasoning to that developed under Article 30 and Directive 70/50 discussed earlier.

94. ECR 649. Although the notion of mandatory requirements was used in translating from the French 'exigences imperatives', this has been better translated in later judgments as 'imperative state requirements'.

95. The Court's use of the phrase 'in particular' made it clear that the list was not exhaustive.

96. See later cases including *Commission* v. *Denmark*, ECR 4607, 1988; Case 145/88 *Torfaen* v. *B and Q plc*, ECR 3851, 1989.

97. Gormley, *Prohibiting Restrictions*, 51–7.

98. See Lawrence Tribe, *American Constitutional Law*, 2nd edn. (Mineola, NY: Foundation Press, 1988). For a critique of the balancing standard, see E. Martz, 'How Much Regulation is Too Much: An Examination of Commerce Clause Jurisprudence', *George Washington Law Review*, 50 (1981–2), 47–89.

99. Nicolaïdis, 'Comments'; see also V. Balsi, 'Constitutional Limits on the Power of the States to Regulate the Movement of Goods in Interstate Commerce', in Sandalow and Stein, *Courts*.

100. Mattera, 'L'Arrêt Cassis de Dijon', 509; see also Balsi, 'Constitutional Limits'.

101. Kommers and Waelbroeck, 'Legal Integration'.

102. See Joliet, 'Recent Trends'.

103. Friedbacher, 'Motive Unmasked: The European Court of Justice, the Free Movement of Goods, and the Search for Legitimacy', *European Law Journal*, 2, no. 3 (1997); Gormley, 'Actually or Potentially, Directly or Indirectly?'; Lawrence Gormley, 'Recent Case Law on the Free Movement of Goods: Some Hot Potatoes', *Common Market Law Review* (1990); E. L. White, 'In Search of the Limits to Article 30 of the EEC Treaty', *Common Market Law Review* (1989), 235.

104. Gormley, 'Actually or Potentially, Directly or Indirectly?', 205.

105. See David Vogel, 'Protective Regulation and Protectionism in the European Community: The Creation of a Common Market for Food and Beverages', paper presented at the European Community Studies Association Biennial Conference, George Mason University, Fairfax, Va., May 1991.

106. Case 788/79 *Gilli and Andres*, ECR 2021, 1980; Case 27/80 *Fietje*, ECR 3839, 1980; and Case 130/80 *Kelderman BV* ECR 527, 1981.

107. See Egan, 'Regulating European Markets' for a detailed survey of the cases.

108. Case 407/85 *Drei Glocken Gmbh et al.* v. *Unita Sanitaria Local Centro-Sud*, ECR 4233, 1988; Case 90/86 *Zoni* ECR 4285, 1988. The Court has generally considered these national policies excessive in view of their aim and available alternatives such as labelling and consumer information. See *Cassis*, paragraph 15.

109. A. Dashwood, 'Harmonisation Process', in C. Cosgrove Twitchett, *Harmonisation in the EEC* (New York: St Martins Press, 1981), 151.

110. The Court did in fact recognize that the establishment of a common market should take account of the traditions and interests of member states. The Court stated 'consumers' conceptions which vary from one member state to another are likely to evolve in the course of time . . .' However, the Court concluded that legislation of a member state 'must not crystallize given consumer habits so as to consolidate an advantage acquired by national industries'. See paragraph 31 of the judgment.

111. Case 53/80 *Eyssen BV* ECR 409, 1981; for a discussion see Tony Venables, 'The Impact of Consumer Protection on Trade', *OECD Symposium*, International Trade and the Consumer: Report on the 1984 OECD Symposium (Paris: OECD, 1986).

112. Case 174/82 *Sandoz*, ECR 2445, 1983.

113. Case 188/84, *Commission* v. *French Republic*, ECR 1986.

114. For a detailed review of this case, see Vogel, *Trading up*.

115. *Commission* v. *Denmark*, 1988.

116. The case has strong parallels with the balancing of interstate commerce and state environmental legislation in the USA. In *Minnesota* v. *Clover Leaf Creamery*, involving a state ban on the sale of milk in plastic, non-returnable bottles, the Supreme Court upheld the statute because it did not discriminate between in-state and out-of-state interests, and the reflected efforts to address environmental problems. See Kommers and Waelbroeck, 'Legal Integration', 188.

117. Gormley, 'Actually or Potentially, Directly or Indirectly?'

118. Alan Dashwood, 'Quantitative Restrictions and Measures Having Equivalent Effect', in *Discipline communautaire et politiques économiques nationales* (The Hague: Kluwer, 1984).

119. Case 155/80, *Oebel*, ECR 1983.

120. See *Blesgen* case; Armstrong, 'Regulating the Free Movement of Goods', 179.

121. Case 145/88 *Torfaen BC* v. *B and Q plc*, 1989; *W. H Smith Ltd & Payless DIY* v. *Peterborough City Council*, CMLR, 577, 1990.

122. Armstrong, 'Regulating the Free Movement of Goods', 180. This was especially the case in the Sunday trading cases.

123. L. Gormley, 'Reasoning Renounced? The Remarkable Judgement in Keck and Mithouard', *European Business Law Review*, 67 (1994), 199.

124. F. Schermers 'The Role of the European Court of Justice in the Free Movement of Goods', in Sandalow and Stein, *Courts and Free Markets*, 222.

125. Shapiro, 'The European Court of Justice'.

126. Gormley, 'Actually or Potentially, Directly or Indirectly?', 11.

127. R. Joliet, 'The Free Circulation of Goods: The Keck and Mithouard Decision and the New Directions in the Case Law', *Columbia Journal of European Law*, 1 (1995), 451.

128. See especially L. Gormley, 'Reasoning Renounced? The Remarkable Judgment in Keck and Mithouard', *European Business Law Review*, 67 (1994).
129. *Keck* and *Mithouard*, case C 267 and C 268/91, ECR, 6097, 1993.
130. Friedbacher, 'Motive Unmasked', 228.
131. See the judgments in *Keck* and *Mithouard*, cited below paragraphs 16 and 17, and in case C 292/92 *Hunermund and others* [1993] ECR I-6787, paragraph 21, and in case C 412/93 *Societé d' importation Edouard Leclerc-Siplec* [1995] ECR I-0179, paragraph 21.
132. Friedbacher, 'Motive Unmasked', 227; see also A. Mattera, 'De l'arrêt Dassonville à l'arrêt Keck: l'obscure clarté d'une jurisprudence riche en principes novateurs et en contradictions', Revue du Marché Unique Européen (1994); Joliet, 'The Free Circulation of Goods'; W. van Gerven, 'Articles 30, 48, 52, and 59 after Keck and Mithouard, and Protection of Rights Arising from Directives After Faccini Dori', *Columbia Journal of European Law*, 2 (Winter 1996), 217–40.
133. Resale at a loss was prohibited in France under Finance Law No. 63–28, July 1963 amended by Order No. 86–1423, 1 Dec. 1986. Traders selling below purchase price were liable to a FF 5,000 to 100,000 fine.
134. The French government referred to an old Court judgment, Case 82/77, *Openbar*, ECR 25, 1978 to justify that legislation prohibiting resale at a loss was compatible with Article 30.
135. Opinion in *Torfaen Borough Council* v. *B&Q*, case C 145/88, ECR 3865, 1989.
136. Joliet, 'The Free Circulation of Goods', 436.
137. *Keck* made the distinction on the basis of difference in treatment between product requirements (where a reduction in access is, as it were, presumed) and measures relating to sales methods or arrangements (where a reduction is not presumed but has to be proved).
138. Rules on selling arrangements would cease to be within the purview of Article 30 as long as they did not discriminate between domestic and imported goods.
139. The Court determined as effectiveness of fiscal supervision, protection of public health, fairness of commercial transactions, defence of consumer, and later protection of environment and cultural objectives (see above).
140. See Case 155/80 *Oebel*, 1981 ECR 2010; Case *Blesgen* v. *Belgium*, 1982, ECR 1211; and *Quietlynn*, Case 23/89, 1981, ECR 3081; see also the comments by Van Gerven, 'After Keck and Mithouard'.
141. Friedbacher, 'Motive Unmasked', 233.
142. Case C 258/93, *Punto Casa*, 1994 ECR, 2355.
143. See e.g. Case 412/93 *Edouard Leclerc-Siplec*, 1995 ECR 179; C 292/92 *Hunermund and others* [1993] ECR I-6787. As a sidenote, the Court has also dealt with the same question as to whether this reasoning could be analogously applied to services. It is likely that prohibitions and restrictions will only be dealt with which are interstate not internal to a member

state given that case law under Article 30 of the EC Treaty does not preclude different treatment of categories of domestic economic operators
(for example, importers and manufacturers established and carrying out
their activities in the member state), provided, at least, that the measures
in question do not affect the marketing of domestic and imported products noticeably differently.

144. Damian Chalmers, 'Repackaging the Internal Market: The Ramifications
of the Keck Judgment', *European Law Review*, 19 (1984), 385–403.
145. See *National League* v. *Usury*, 426, US 833, 1976 compared to *Garcia* v.
San Antonio Metro Transit Authority, 105 S Ct 1005, 1985.
146. W. Hellerstein, 'Federal Limitations on State Taxation of Interstate
Commerce', in Sandalow and Stein (eds.), *Courts and Free Markets*.
147. See the shifts in the US in *Garcia* v. *San Antonio*, 105 S Ct 1005, 1985.
148. S. Beer, 'The Modernization of American Federalism', *Publius: The
Journal of Federalism* (1973), 50–95.
149. A. M. Sbragia, *Debt Wish: Entrepreneurial Cities, US Federalism and
Economic Development* (Pittsburgh: University of Pittsburgh Press, 1996),
Conclusion.
150. Maduro, 'Reforming the Market or the State?', 55.
151. See also K. Polanyi, *The Great Transformation* (Boston: Beacon Press, 1944),
esp. chs. 16 and 17; W. Hurst, *Law and the Social Order in the United
States* (Ithaca, NY: Cornell University Press, 1977).

Chapter 6

1. See K. Alter and S. Meunier, 'Judicial Politics in the EU: European
Integration and the Path-Breaking Cassis de Dijon Decision', *Comparative Political Studies*, 26 (1994), 535–61; G. Garrett and B. Weingast
,'Ideas, Interests and Institutions: Constructing the EC's Internal Market', in J. Goldstein and R. Keohane (eds.), *Ideas and Foreign Policy:
Beliefs, Institutions and Political Change* (Ithaca, NY: Cornell University
Press, 1993).
2. Communication from the Commission concerning the Consequences of
the judgment given by the Court of 20 Feb. 1979 in Case 120/78 (*Cassis
de Dijon*), *Official Journal of the European Communities* C 256/2, 3 Oct.
1980; See also *Bulletin of the European Communities*, 7/8, 1980; *14ᵗʰ General Report of the European Communities, 1985–86* (Luxembourg: Office
of Official Publications of the European Communities, 1985); *Agence
Europe*, 18 July 1980.
3. For detailed legal assessment, see L. Gormley, 'Cassis de Dijon and the
Communication from the Commission', *European Law Review* (1981);
Faust Capelli, 'Les Malentendus provoqués par l'arrêt Cassis de Dijon',
Revue du Marché Commun, no. 421.
4. See J. Kingdon, *Agendas, Alternatives and Public Policies* (Boston:
Little Brown, 1984); M. Cini, *The European Commission: Leadership,*

Organisation, and Culture in the EU Administration (Manchester: Manchester University Press, 1996); M. A. Pollack, 'The Engines of Integration? Supranational Autonomy and Influence in the European Community', Working Paper No. 2, 41, Center for German and European Studies, Harvard University, Nov. 1996; see also B. G. Peters, 'Agenda Setting in the European Community', *Journal of European Public Policy*, 1, no. 1 (1994), 9–26; M. A. Pollack, 'The Commission as an Agent', in N. Nugent (ed.), *At the Heart of the European Union: Studies of the European Commission* (London: Macmillan, 1997).

5. *Bulletin of the European Communities*, 7/8 (1980).
6. See Capelli, 'Cassis'; Gormley, 'Cassis'; Alter and Meunier, 'Judicial Politics in the EC'; A. Mattera, 'De l'arrêt Dassonville a l'arrêt Keck', *Revue du Marché Unique Européen* (1994).
7. H. Siebert, 'The Harmonisation Agreement in Europe: Prior Agreement or Competitive Process?', in H. Siebert (ed.), *The Completion of the Internal Market* (Tübingen: J. B. Mohr; 1990); K. Gatsios and P. Seabright, 'Regulation in the European Community', *Oxford Review of Economic Policy*, 5, no. 2 (1989).
8. Opinion of the Consumer Consultative Council on the consequences of the judgment of the *Cassis de Dijon* case, CCC/29/31 Rev 4, Adopted on 16 Oct. 1981.
9. Ibid. 11.
10. *Agence Europe*, 8 Oct. 1981; Author interview, European Commission official, DG II.
11. See also M. Egan, 'Regulating European Markets: Mismatch, Reform and Agency', Ph.D. Dissertation, University of Pittsburgh, 1995.
12. Kingdon, *Agendas and Alternatives*.
13. For literature on the single market programme, see L. Tsoukalis, *The New European Economy*, 2nd edn. (Oxford: Oxford University Press, 1993); D. Cameron, 'The 1992 Initiative: Causes and Consequences', in A. M. Sbragia (ed.), *Europolitics* (Washington: Brookings Institution, 1992); W. Sandholtz and J. Zysman, '1992: Recasting the European Bargain', *World Politics*, 42 (1989); Jacques Pelkmans and Alan Winters, *Europe's Domestic Market* (London: Routledge & Kegan Paul; Royal Institute of International Affairs, Chatham House Paper No. 43, 1988); A. Moravscik, 'Negotiating the Single European Act: National Interests and Conventional Statecraft in the European Community', *International Organization* 45/1 (1991), 19–56; A. Moravscik, *The Choice for Europe: Social Purpose and State Power from Messina to Maastricht* (Ithaca, NY: Cornell University Press, 1998), esp. ch. 5; H. Wallace and A. Young, 'Single Market', in H. Wallace and W. Wallace (eds.), *Policy-Making in the European Union*, 4th edn. (Oxford: Oxford University Press, 2000).
14. Among the most important documents are the final communiqué of the Paris Summit of 1972 to complete economic and monetary union and establish a European Union by 1980; the 1975 Tindemans Report on the

needs of the European Union; and the Report of the Three Wise Men (Biescheuval, Marjolin, and Dell) on the subject of institutional and procedural reform in 1979.

15. Commission Communication to the Council on reactivating the European Internal Market, Internal Memorandum.

16. Ibid.

17. 'EEC Trade Evangelists Tackle Protectionism,' *Financial Times*, 1 Feb. 1983.

18. See 'Ten Look to Ease Trade Curbs', *Financial Times*, 2 Feb. 1983; 'Too Protectionist?', *The Economist*, 17 Sept. 1983.

19. UNICE issued a statement in support of the measures to be discussed by the Internal Market Council, 1 Mar. 1983; UNICE also issued a memorandum 'The Creation of a Genuine Internal Market as Regards Standards and Technical Regulations', 18 Oct. 1984, Brussels.

20. Author interview of American Chamber of Commerce in Brussels Official, 1993; 'France and Italy Operate Worst Trade Barriers', *Financial Times*, 22 Sept. 1983.

21. J. Richardson, 'Europe's Industrialists Help Shape the Single Market', *Europe: The Magazine of the European Community* (Dec. 1989), 18–20; 'The Self Help Seventeen', *Financial Times*, 15 Nov. 1983; M. Green Cowles, 'Setting the Agenda for a New Europe: The ERT and EU 1992', *Journal of Common Market Studies*, 13 (1995), 501–26; *Agence Europe*, 1 July 1983.

22. *The Economist* estimated that by October 1983, the Commission was grappling with 770 cases of suspected protectionism by member states against each other. *The Economist*, 22 Oct. 1983.

23. 'Paris Catalogues the EEC Tariff Trip Wires', *Financial Times*, 1 Mar. 1983.

24. See Solemn Declaration of the European Union, Stuttgart, 1983; Draft Treaty Establishing the European Union, OJ C 77, 19 Mar. 1984; O. Scmuck, 'The European Parliament's Discussion of the Draft Treaty Establishing the European Union', in R. Pryce (ed.), *The Dynamics of European Union* (Croom Helm: London, 1987); Commission of the EC, COM (80) 83 24 Feb. 1983; COM (81) 639 Oct. 1981.

25. See S. George, *Politics and Policy-Making in the European Community* (Oxford: Oxford University Press, 1991); Tsoukalis, *European Economy*; Wallace and Young, 'Single Market'.

26. See R. Corbett, 'The 1985 Intergovernmental Conference and the Single European Act', in Pryce, *Dynamics of European Union*.

27. Moravscik, 'Negotiating the Single European Act'; G. Bermann, 'The Single European Act: A New Constitution for the Community?', *Columbia Journal of Transnational and International Law*, 27 (1989), 529–87; Moravscik, *The Choice for Europe*.

28. European Commission, COM (185) 310 Final; see generally, R. Bieber et al., *1992: One European Market* (Florence: European University Institute, 1988); M. Emerson et al., *The Economics of 1992* (Oxford: Oxford University Press, 1988); B. van de Walle, G. van Gerven, and K. Platteua, 'The New Approach to the Elimination of Technical Barriers in the

European Community', *Brigham Young University Law Review* (Fall 1990), 1543–73.

29. Former ECJ Judge Pescatore criticized the target deadline as inconsequential, merely prolonging the transitional period for achieving the Community's original goals. See Pierre Pescatore, text published in *Agence Europe*, 27 Mar. 1986.

30. See J. Pelkmans and P. Robson, 'The Aspirations of the White Paper', *Journal of Common Market Studies*, 25, no. 3 (1987), 181–92.

31. Gormley, 'Actually or Potentially, Directly or Indirectly?', 9–20.

32. European Commission, *White Paper on Completing the Single Market*, COM (85) 310 Final, paragraph 13.

33. The Court of Justice in the insurance cases had only partly taken this approach of applying mutual recognition or home country control to services. See Cases 205/84 *Commission* v. *Germany*, 1986 ECR 3755; Case 206/84 *Commission* v. *Ireland*, CMLR 150; *Commission* v. *France*, 1986 CMLR.

34. Commission, *White Paper on Completing the Single Market*, paragraph 58.

35. European Commission, DG III, 'Completing the Single Market: The Removal of Barriers to Trade in Industry', Brussels, 1 Aug. 1990.

36. Briefing by T. Garvey, Director DG III, *Standards and Technical Harmonisation*, 27 July 1989, Background Report, Commission of the European Communities, ISEC/B22/89.

37. 83/189. OJ NO L 108, 26 Apr. 1983; amended OJ No L 81 26 Mar. 1998.

38. Sabine Lecrenier, 'Les Articles 30 et suivants CEE et les procédures de contrôle prévues par la directive 83/189 CEE', *Revue du Marché Commun et de l'Union Européenne* (Jan. 1985), 6–23.

39. The figures indicate the lack of compliance with this agreement. In 1975, a total of 8 new technical regulations were notified, 10 in 1976; 5 in 1977; 12 in 1978; 14 in 1979; 12 in 1980; 12 in 1981; 14 in 1983. Most of the notifications came from France and Germany, with no notifications during this period from either Britain or Luxembourg.

40. Directive 88/182 OJ L 81/75. In 1994, the directive was further amended, see OJ 1994 L 100/30.

41. Commission Communication Concerning Regulatory Transparency on the Internal Market for Information Society Services, COM (96) 392 Final.

42. If detailed opinions are offered, work is suspended on national drafts for six months; if the Commission decides to initiate its own regulatory action, work is suspended on national drafts for twelve months.

43. Answer to Written Question, No. 39/86, Mr G. de Vries, DR-NL.

44. S. Weatherill, 'Compulsory Notification of Draft Technical Regulations: The Contribution of Directive 83/189 to the Management of the Internal Market', *Yearbook of European Law*, 16 (1996); CEPS, *The European Community without Technical Barrier*, CEPS Working Party Report No. 5 (Brussels: Centre for European Policy Studies, 1992); J. Pelkmans and M. Egan, 'The Politics of the Green Paper on the Development of

European Standards', Center for European Policy Studies Working Paper, Brussels (1992).

45. OJ EC C 340, 23 Dec. 1997.
46. Report from the European Commission on the Operation of Directive 83/189 in 1992, 1993, and 1994, COM (96) 26 June 1996.
47. Ibid. 16.
48. Such geographical considerations include Edam and Feta cheese, Parma Ham, and Champagne.
49. J. McMillan, 'La Certification, la reconnaissance mutuelle et le marché unique', *Revue du Marché Commun*, 2 (1991), 181–211. In this case, the effort to guarantee equivalent conditions of competition between producers with Community protection for certain designated products has been extremely controversial.
50. COM (96) June 26 1996, Report from the Commission on the Operation of Directive 83/189 in 1992, 1993, and 1994, p. 24.
51. Article 169 infringement proceedings; author interview, European Commission, Head of Unit, DG III, 1993.
52. Securitel, Case 194/94, 1996 ECR L 2230; C. Joerges, H. Schepel, and E. Vos, 'Delegation and the European Polity: The Law's Problems with the Role of Standardisation Organisations in European Legislation', paper presented at the European University Institute conference 'The Political Economy of Standards Setting', Florence, 4–5 June 1998.
53. Decision 3052/95/EU OJ L 321/1, 1995 in effect 1 Jan. 1997.
54. OJ 1968 C 108/39 and OJ 1968 C 132/4.
55. OJ 1973 L 77/29. Directive 73/23/EC.
56. Joerges, Schepel, and Vos, 'Delegation and the European Polity'; OJ 1982 C 59/2.
57. See P. Stewart, 'Foreword', in T. Sandalow and E. Stein (ed.), *Courts and Free Markets* (Oxford: Clarendon Press, 1982); R. Chiet, *Setting Safety Standards* (Berkeley and Los Angeles: University of California Press, 1991); K. Opala, 'The Anatomy of Private Standards-Making Process: The Operating Procedures of the USA Standard Institute', *Oklahoma Law Review*, 45 (1969).
58. Case 133/76 *Commission* v. *The Italian Republic*, ECR 1449, 1977. See also T. Hartley, 'Consumer Safety and the Harmonisation of Technical Standards: The Low Voltage Directive', *European Law Review* (1982), 55–62.
59. J. Falke, 'The Role of Non-governmental Standardization Organizations in the Regulation of Risks to Health and the Environment', paper presented at the European University Institute, Florence (1996); J. Falke, 'Achievements and Unresolved Problems of European Standardization: The Ingenuity of Practice and the Queries of Lawyers', in C. Joerges et al., *Integrating Scientific Expertise into Regulatory Decision-Making* (Baden-Baden: Nomos, 1997), 187–224; C. Daelemans, 'The Legitimacy and Quality of European Standards: The Legitimation of Delegation of Powers and Standard-Setting Procedures', in Joerges et al., *Integrating Scientific*

Expertise into Regulatory Decision-Making; M. Egan, 'Regulatory Strategies, Delegation, and European Market Integration', *Journal of European Public Policy*, 5, no. 3 (1998), 485–506; K. Lenaerts, 'Regulating the Regulatory Process: "Delegation of Powers" in the European Community', *European Law Review* (1993).

60. Case 133/76 *Commission* v. *Italy*, 1977 ECR 1449 and *Cremoni and Frankovich*, ECR 3583, 1980.

61. S. W. Freemantle, 'Directive on Low-Voltage Equipment', *Trade and Industry*, Department of Trade and Industry (UK) Publication, Sept. 1973.

62. See Article 10 of the Low Voltage Directive.

63. See e.g. H. K. Tronnier, 'Standardization and Harmonization Effects in Europe: the role of CENELEC and the Experience with the Low Voltage Directive', in Jacques Pelkmans and Marc Vanheukelen (eds.), *Coming to Grips with the Internal Market* (The Hague: European Institute for Public Administration, 1986).

64. Ibid.

65. Communication from the Commission to the Council, *Technical Harmonisation and Standards: A New Approach* (COM) 85 19 Final.

66. Ibid.

67. COM (185), 31 Jan. 1995, 19.

68. Conclusions on Standardization, 16 July 1984, OJ C 136/2, 4 June 1985

69. OJ 1985 C/136/1, 7 May 1985.

70. *Guidelines for a New Approach to Technical Harmonisation and Standards*, Annex II, Conclusions on Standardization Approved by the Council, 16 July 1984; R. Lauwers, 'The Model Directive on Technical Harmonisation', in Bieber et al., *One European Market*; J. Pelkmans, *Opheffing van technische handelsbelemmeringen in de EG. Pilot-studie in opdracht van het UNO* (The Hague, 1985).

71. Outline of main elements of Model Directive published as Annex II to the Council Resolution on the New Approach.

72. See D. Kettl, *Government by Proxy* (Washington: Congressional Quarterly Press, 1988).

73. For reviews of the New Approach, see Egan, 'Regulating European Markets'; Egan, 'Regulatory Strategies, Delegation, and European Market Integration'; J. Pelkmans, 'The New Approach to Technical harmonization and Standards', *Journal of Common Market Studies*, 25 (1987), 249–69; K. Schreiber, 'The New Approach to Technical Harmonization and Standards', in L. Hurwitz and C. Lesquesne (eds.), *The State of the European Community: Policies, Institutions and Debates in the Transition Years* (Boulder, Colo.: Lynne Rienner, 1991); S. Farr, *Harmonisation of Technical Standards in the EC* (London, 1992); J. Falke, 'Technische Normung in Europa: Zieht sich der Staat wirklich zurück?', in G. Winter (ed.), *Die Europäischen Gemeinschaften und das Öffentliche* (Bremen: ZERP Discussion Paper 7/1991); Falke, 'Achievements and Unresolved Problems of European Standardization'; J. Falke and C. Joerges,

'Traditional Harmonization Policy', Working Paper no. 91/13 (Florence: Law Department, European University Institute, 1991); McMillan, 'La Certification'; N. Burrows, 'Harmonisation of Technical Standards: Reculer pour Mieux Sauter?', *New Perspectives in European Law*, 53, no. 5 (Sept. 1990).

74. See *Bulletin of the EC*, no. 1, 1985; *Agence Europe*, 4 Jan. 1985; *Agence Europe*, 2 Feb. 1985; J. Pelkmans, 'A Community without Technical Barriers? Accomplishments and Prospects', paper presented at the conference 'Europe 1992: Challenge or Opportunity', Georgetown University, Washington, 8–9 Dec. 1988; Pelkmans, 'The New Approach'.

75. Council Decision of 22 July 1993 (93/465/EEC).

76. G. Majone, 'The European Community as a Regulatory State', lectures given at the Academy of European Law, European University Institute, Florence (July 1994), mimeo.

77. See G. Majone, 'The Rise of the Regulatory State in Europe', *West European Politics*, 17, no. 3 (1994).

78. Jacques Repussard, 'Comments', in *The New Approach* (Brussels: CEN, 1994).

79. E. Previdi, 'The Organization of Public and Private Responsibilities in European Risk Regulation: An Institutional Gap between Them?', in Joerges et al., *Integrating Scientific Expertise into Regulatory Decision-Making*, 236.

80. See Egan, 'Regulatory Strategies, Delegation, and European Market Integration'.

81. See also Joerges et al., *Integrating Scientific Expertise into Regulatory Decision-Making*, 4.

82. Under the Meroni doctrine, the Commission can only delegate that power which it possesses and it is required to oversee that delegated competence.

83. This is known as the promulgation procedure.

84. Repussard, 'Comments'.

85. Organization for Economic Cooperation and Development, *Consumers, Product Safety Standards and International Trade* (Paris: OECD, 1991).

86. See (UK) Department of Trade and Industry, *White Paper on Standards, Quality and International Competitiveness* (London: HMSO, July 1992); French Decree 84–74, 26 Jan. 1984; The Gerätesicherheitsgesetz, Germany, 1968.

87. See H. Reilen, 'The Deutsches Institut für Normung (DIN): A National Standards Organization in Europe', *ASTM Standardization News* (Dec. 1986), 30–2; H. Voelzkow, *Private Regierungen in der Techniksteuerung: Eine sozialwissenschaftliche Analyse der technischen Normung* (Frankfurt am Main: Campus Verlag, 1996).

88. A. Thiard, 'Worldwide Standards: The Only Way: AFNOR and International Standardization', *ASTM Standardization News*, Dec. 1986, pp. 34–37; J. Pelkmans and D. Costello, *Industrial Product Standards*, UNIDO Report, 1991.

89. See Department of Trade and Industry, *White Paper*.

90. The notion that Commission Departments and Member States, with their designated experts, could review such activities under the New Approach was the subject of much discussion. The possibility that the Community would proceed along this path would mean that Committee procedures known as comitology would be used to check upon the implementing powers conferred upon the Commission.

91. British Standards Institute, 'Notes on UK and European Certification Developments', 22 Jan. 1991; UNICE, 'The Internal Market and Product Certification', memorandum, 30 Nov. 1988; COM (89) 209 Final, 15 June 1989.

92. Author interview, European Commission official.

93. UNICE, 'The Internal Market', 5.

94. Symposium on 'Organizing Certification and Testing for Europe', 21–3 June 1988, Brussels.

95. Opening remarks by T. Garvey, Director-General for the Internal Market, DG III, ibid.

96. See Egan, 'Regulating European Markets'; Previdi, 'Public and Private Responsibilities'.

97. McMillan, 'La Certification'.

98. G. Majone, 'The Agency Model', unpublished paper, European Institute for Public Administration, Maastricht, 1998; see also Previdi, 'Public and Private Responsibilities'.

99. European Commission Communication, 'A Global Approach to Certification and Testing', COM (89) 209, 24 July 1989.

100. See Commission Memorandum on Global Approach to Testing and Certification, Annex to Official Journal, COM (89) 209, C 267/20.

101. The modules are: Module A (internal product control); Module B EC-type examination; Module C (conformity to type); Module D (production quality assurance); Module E (product quality assurance); Module F (product verification); and Module G (unit verification and Module H (full quality assurance).

102. Council Resolution of 21 Dec. 1989 on the Global Approach to Conformity Assessment, OJ C 10/1, and Council Decision, 90/683/EC 13 Dec. 1990 on the module approach used in New Approach directives.

103. This could either be in the form of quality assurance systems or accreditation schemes based on European standards (EN 4500) that sought to ensure cross-national equivalence. The European Quality Assurance Standards: EN ISO 9000 and EN 45000) in the Community's New Approach legislation, Quality Series No. 4, European Commission, DG III.

104. See Framework for Coordination and Cooperation between Notified Bodies and Member States and the European Commission under the Community Harmonized Directives based on the New Approach and the Global Approach, DG III, CERTIF/94/6 Rev. 2, 10 Oct. 1994.

105. Previdi, 'Public and Private Responsibilities'.

106. For a detailed assessment, 'The European Quality Assurance Standards: EN ISO 9000 and EN 45000 in the Community's New Approach legis-

lation', Quality Series No. 4, European Commission, DG III Jan. 1997; for a general review, see S. Cooney, *EC-92 and U.S. Industry: NAM Report on the Major Issues for U.S. Manufacturers in the European Community's Internal Market Program* (Washington: National Association for Manufacturers, 1989).

107. While there is a synergy between international and European standards under the Vienna agreement, the same type of coordination does not exist between international and regional conformity assessment bodies.

108. For a detailed assessment, see Communication from the Commission, 'Community External Trade Policy in the Field of Standards and Conformity Assessment', COM (96) 6564 Final, 13 Nov. 1996.

109. The efforts by both CEN and CENELEC with the CENCER mark in the mid-1970s did not yield any tangible results and it was not widely used for commercial purposes.

110. See the *Guide to Implementation of Directives Based on the New Approach and Global Approach, European Commission*, DG II, 1999.

111. This includes medical device monitoring, rapid exchange of information, and injury data collection systems, as well as product liability and general consumer protection legislation.

112. OMB Circular A-119 is the common designation for the Federal Agencies to Use Voluntary Standards for regulatory purposes in lieu of developing in house standards (reference to standards technique).

Chapter 7

1. See J. Falke, 'The Role of Non-governmental Standardization Organizations in the Regulation of Risks to Health and the Environment', paper presented at the conference on 'Integrating Scientific Expertise into Regulatory Decision-making', European University Institute, Florence (1996), 1; see also CEPS Working Party Report, 'Technical Barriers to Trade' (Brussels: Centre for European Policy Studies, 1992); M. Egan, 'Regulatory Strategies, Delegation, and European Market Integration', *Journal of European Public Policy*, 5, no. 3 (1998), 485–506.

2. E. Previdi, 'The Organization of Public and Private Responsibilities in European Risk Regulation: An Institutional Gap between Them?', in Christian Joerges et al. *Integrating Scientific Expertise into Regulatory Decision-Making* (Baden-Baden: Nomos, 1997), 225.

3. *Financial Times*, 13 Oct. 1995; M. Egan and A. Zito, 'Policy Networks and International Standard-Setting', paper presented at the Annual Conference of the International Studies Association, Chicago, Mar. 1996.

4. See F. Nicolas and J. Repussard, *Common Standards for Enterprises* (Luxembourg: Office for Official Publications of the European Communities, 1988); V. Eichener, 'Social Dumping or Innovative Regulation?', EUI Working Paper, SPS 92/28, European University Institute, Florence (1992); H. Voelzkow, *Private Regierungen in der Techniksteuerung* (Frankfurt am Main: Campus Verlag, 1996); N. Brunsson 'Standardization as

Organization', in M. Egberg and P. Laegreid (eds.), *Organizing Political Institutions* (Oslo: Scandanavia University Press, 1999).

5. For an exception, see P. Genschel, 'How Fragmentation Can Improve Co-ordination: Setting Standards in International telecommunications', *Organization Studies*, 18, no. 4 (1997).

6. Ibid.

7. See K.-H. Laudeur, 'The Integration of Scientific and Technological Expertise into the Process of Standard-Setting According to German Law', in Joerges et al. *Integrating Scientific Expertise into Regulatory Decision-Making*, 77; F. Gambellini, 'Technical Standardization in France: Evolution of its Legal Aspects in the New European Framework', in Joerges et al., *Integrating Scientific Expertise into Regulatory Decision-Making*; R. Chiet, *Setting Safety Standards* (Berkeley and Los Angeles: University of California Press, 1991); R. Hamilton, 'The Role of Non-Governmental Standards in the Development of Mandatory Standards Affecting Health', *Texas Law Review*, 56 (1978); R. Hamilton, 'Prospects for the Non-Governmental Development of Regulatory Standards', *American University Law Review*, 32 (1983).

8. F. Gambelli, *Aspects juridiques de la normalisation et de la réglementation européenne* (Paris: Éditions Eyrolles, 1994).

9. See also Chiet, *Setting Safety Standards*, ch. 1.

10. M. Shapiro, 'The Problem of Independent Agencies in the United States and European Union', *Journal of European Public Policy*, 4, no. 2 (1997), 284–91.

11. Ibid.

12. J. Badarraco, *Loading the Dice* (Cambridge, Mass.: Harvard University Press, 1985).

13. CEN affiliates include Bulgaria, Cyprus, Latvia, Hungary, Croatia, Slovakia, Esotnia, Albania, Lithuania, Romania, Slovenia, and Turkey. The Czech Republic has become the latest full member.

14. The Greek standards body was for example created after joining the EU. The Luxembourg standards institute does not actually create its own national standards but implements European ones, and works closely with the Belgian national standards institute (BIN).

15. European Commission, Preparation of the Associated Countries of Central and Eastern Europe for Integration into the Internal Market of the Union COM (95) 163 final, 1995. For an empirical study of efforts to establish the single market in three central and East European states, see H. Grabbe, 'Accession and Transition: The Europeanisation of Public Policy in East-Central Europe', unpublished Ph.D. Dissertation, University of Birmingham, 2001.

16. The European standards bodies are classified as international associations governed by Belgian private law.

17. H. K. Tronnier, 'Standardization and Harmonization Efforts in Europe, the Role of CENELEC and the Experience with the Low Voltage Directive',

in J. Pelkmans and M. Vanheukelen (eds.), *Coming to Grips with the Internal Market* (The Hague: EIPA, 1986).

18. See S. Schmidt and R. Werle, *Coordinating Technology: Studies in the International Standardization of Telecommunications* (Cambridge, Mass.: MIT Press, 1998).

19. *Official Journal of the European Communities*, Written Question by Mr. Leonardi, No. 203/81, 17 Apr. 1981.

20. Interview, EU Official, 1993.

21. F. Raymond, 'Standards Related Activities', in *Friendship among Equals* (Geneva: International Standards Organization, 1997), 53.

22. This resulted in what are known as harmonized documents (HD). This means that identical national standards are unnecessary or not achievable, and results in the acceptance of national deviations.

23. See Memorandum No. 4 on the general guidelines for cooperation between the EC and standardization bodies, 13 Nov. 1984. This provides for the European standards bodies to invite the Commission to attend meetings of technical committees, although the Commission often designates consultants to act as their interlocutor as they do not have the administrative capacity or necessary technical expertise in many cases to actively contribute to the debate. Interview, EC Commission Consultant.

24. CEN/CENELEC, no date.

25. Information on the structure and operation of CEN and CENELEC is drawn from their Statutes and Internal Regulations.

26. CEN, Opening of CEN's Management Structures, 1992–7, Brussels; Interview, CEN official.

27. Interview, ETUC Official. See also C. Joerges et al., *Die Sicherheit von Konsumgütern und die Entwicklung der Europäischen Gemeinschaft* (Baden-Baden: Nomos 1988); republished Working Paper 91/10, European University Institute, Florence.

28. Schmidt and Werle, *Coordinating Technology*.

29. A special forum was held on European Testing and Certification in 1988; on the Future of European Standardization in 1992, and on Information Technology and Standardization in 1997.

30. CEN Statutes; see also Ellen Vos, 'Institutional Frameworks of Community Health and Safety Regulations: Committees, Agencies and Private Bodies', Doctoral Thesis, European University Institute, Florence, 1997.

31. Interview, CEN Official, 1993.

32. Vos, 'Institutional Frameworks', 277.

33. See CEN/CENELEC Internal Regulations.

34. L. C Verman, *Standardization: A New Discipline* (Hamden, Conn.: Ardon Books, 1973); Vince Grey, 'Setting Standards: A Phenomenal Success Story', in *Friendship among Equals*; author interview, US Delegate to UNECE Committee on Vehicle Standards, 1997.

35. G. Majone, 'Standard Setting and the Theory of Institutional Choice: The Case of Pollution Control', *Policy and Politics*, 4 (1975), 40.

36. See M. Egan and A. Zito, 'Regulation in Europe and the Globalization of the Economy: European Standardization at a Cross-roads', in Joerges et al., *Integrating Scientific Expertise into Regulatory Decision-Making.*
37. Majone, 'Standard Setting', 41.
38. Salter has argued that standardization in information technology is an excellent example of a policy community. See L. Salter, 'Do Reforms Make a Difference? A Methodological Analysis of IT&T Standardization', paper presented at the Workshop on Standards, Innovation, Competitiveness and Policy, Nov. 1993.
39. Ibid. 40.
40. Eichener, 'Social Dumping or Innovative Regulation?', 65.
41. Genschel, 'How Fragmentation Can Improve Co-ordination', 613–14; M. Egan, 'The Politics of European Regulation: Bringing the Firm back in', paper presented at the Conference of Europeanists, Chicago, Mar. 1994; A. O. Sykes, *Product Standards for Internationally Integrated Goods Markets* (Washington: Brookings Institution, 1995).
42. As one standards official commented, 'it can be a thankless task, trying to bring together mutually antagonistic forces.'
43. See P. A. David, 'Clio and the Economics of QWERTY', *American Economic Review*, 75, no. 2 (May 1985), 332–7.
44. See A. Héritier, 'The Accommodation of Diversity in European Policy-Making and its Outcomes: Regulatory Policy as a Patchwork', *Journal of European Public Policy*, 3, no. 2 (1996).
45. European standards officials point to the internal rules and regulations that indicate that committee chairs cannot vote and must act in an impartial and unbiased manner.
46. In the mid-1980s, Germany held 39% of these secretariats, Britain 20%, France 14%, and Italy 8%. See K. Schreiber, 'Technical Standards', in S. Woolcock et al., *Britain, Germany and 1992: The Limits of Deregulation* (London: Pinter, 1991).
47. V. Eichener, 'Effective European Problem Solving: Lessons from the Regulation of Occupational Safety and Environmental Protection', *Journal of European Public Policy*, 4, no. 4 (1997), 602.
48. Ibid. 601.
49. See Falke, 'Role of Non-Governmental Standardization Organizations'.
50. A. Link, 'Market Structure and Voluntary Product Standards', *Applied Economics*, 15 (1983), 400.
51. The *Bulletin* of the European Standards Bodies provides information on European standards and other documents, drafts submitted to public inquiry, decisions, official citations in Official Journal, and standardization mandates. It also provides information on the date of withdrawal of existing national standards and their replacement with European standard(s) on a monthly basis.
52. Genschel, 'How Fragmentation Can Improve Co-ordination'.
53. Ibid.
54. Author interview, CEN official, 1993.

55. *Electrotechnical Standards for Europe*, CENELEC, Brussels, no date.
56. Author interview, National Standards official, Dec. 1993; see also Commission Report on the Operation of Directive 83/189.
57. Wayne Sandholtz, 'Institutions and Collective Action', *World Politics*, 45, no. 2 (1993), 258.
58. For examples of European and Japanese barriers in this area, see Michael Oppenheimer and Donna Tuths, *Non-tariff Barriers: The Effects on Corporate Strategy in High-Technology Sectors* (Boulder, Colo.: Westview Press, 1987).
59. The Commission considered the telematics industries as critical for European competitiveness. This comprised semiconductors, computers, and telecommunications. See Framework Programme of Community Activities in the Field of Research and Development, 'Development of Telematic Systems of General Interest', COM/90/221/Euratom, EC OJ 117, 8 May 1990.
60. Commission of the EC, 'Standards Organizations and Technical Bodies in Brief', Nov. 1990, DG XIII.
61. 'Standardization: Reference Sheet', Commission of the European Communities, Nov. 1990; see also W. Sandholtz, *High-Tech Europe: The Politics of International Cooperation* (Berkeley and Los Angeles: University of California Press, 1992).
62. Sandholtz, 'Institutions and Collective Action'; S. Besen, 'The European Telecommunications Standards Institute—A Preliminary Analysis', *Telecommunications Policy* 14, no. 6 (1990); Bargiola, 'ETSI—Offene Kommunikation, einheitliche Normen', *XIII Magazin* (Apr. 1991), 22–3.
63. Commission of the EC, *Green Paper on the Development of the Common Market for Telecommunications Services and Equipment*, COM 87 (290) Final, 30 June 1987. The Commission stated, 'jointly staffed, the institute based on a small core of permanent staff and independently managed to best business practice, should draw flexibly on experts from both the Telecommunications Administration and Industry, in order to substantially accelerate the elaboration of standards and technical specifications.'
64. For a good overview, see W. Drake, 'The Transformation of International Telecommunications Standardization', in C. Steinfield et al., *Telecommunications in Transition: Policies, Services and Technologies in the European Community* (London: Sage, 1994), 71–97.
65. Sandholtz, 'Institutions and Collective Action'.
66. Ibid. 261.
67. ETSI, 'ETSI Meets the Challenge', Document D/149/91/ST/FA/skw, Valbonne, 4 Apr. 1991.
68. See Besen, 'The European Telecommunications Standards Institute'.
69. Ibid. 538.
70. S. Besen and J. Farrell, 'Choosing How to Compete: Strategies and Tactics in Standardization', *Journal of Economic Perspectives*, 8, no. 2 (Spring 1994), 129.
71. 91/263/EC, Apr. 1991.

72. See e.g. H. Kroger, 'Opportunities and Threats for Innovative Industries in the European Community', UNICE, 11 Sept. 1990; UNICE, 'The Internal Market and Product Certification', memorandum, 30 Nov. 1988; BSI, 'Notes on UK and European Certification Developments', 22 Jan. 1991.

73. A Draft Memorandum of Understanding between the Commission of the European Communities, EFTA and CEN/CENELEC for the Setting up of a European Organization for Testing and Certification, CERTIF 89/1 Rev. 4.

74. Author interview, EOTC official, 1993.

75. K. Petrick, 'The Objectives of the Newly Established EQS within the European Framework for Testing and Certification', Mar. 1990, Washington. Presentation to NIST/ANSI and Commerce Department.

76. Author interview, national standards official, Dec. 1993.

77. Interview, CEN Official, 1993.

78. Salter, 'Do Reforms Make a Difference?', 40.

79. Information provided by CEN Secretariat, Brussels.

80. See R. Putnam, 'Diplomacy and Domestic Politics: The Logic of Two-Level Games', *International Organization*, 42 (1988), 427–60.

81. This policy of allowing deviations characterized European standard-setting prior to the New Approach and represented one of the major reasons why European firms did not use European standards. There were too many deviations or exceptions granted for specific circumstance or interests.

82. See 'Deadlines Draw Closer', *Financial Times*, 13 Oct. 1995, 4; 'A Shock to the System', *Financial Times*, 7 Dec. 1995; 'Plugs Plan Prompts Cost Fears', *Financial Times*, 30 Oct. 1995.

83. See CEN, 'Règles pour la rédaction et la présentation des normes européennes', July 1990.

84. Author interview, national standards official, 1993.

85. Author interview, European Roundtable of Industrialists, 1993.

86. See T. Bundgaard-Pedersen, 'States and EU Technical Standardization: Denmark, the Netherlands and Norway Managing Polycentric Decision-Making 1985–95', *Journal of European Public Policy*, 4, no. 2 (1997). Bundgaard-Pedersen describes this system as polycentric, comprising state agencies, national standards bodies, and industries. While standard-setting is a quasi-regulatory system, states have lost some measure of policy-making influence and there is a larger majority of private actors participating and setting European standards.

87. R. Crane, *The Politics of International Standards: France and the Color TV War* (Norwood, NJ: Ablex, 1979); S. Schmidt and R. Werle, 'Technical Controversy in International Standardization', Working Paper 93/5, Max Planck Institüt, Cologne, Mar. 1993; J. Pelkmans and R. Beuter, 'Standardisation and Competitiveness: Public and Private Strategies in the EU Colour TV Industry', in H. Landis Gabel (ed.), *Product Standardization and Competitive Strategy* (Amsterdam: Elsevier, 1987).

88. See Besen and Farrell, 'Choosing How to Compete'; P. Grindlay, *Standards Strategy and Policy* (Oxford: Oxford University Press, 1995), ch. 2; Schmidt and Werle, *Coordinating Technology*; J. Farrell and G. Saloner, 'Coordination through Committees and Markets', *Rand Journal of Economics*, 19 (1988), 235–52; K. Abbott and D. Snidal, 'Standardization, Legalization and Governance', paper presented at the Workshop on the Political Economy of Standards Setting, June 1998, European University Institute, Florence.

89. See Grindlay, *Standards Strategy and Policy*; Farrell and Saloner, 'Coordination through Committees and Markets'.

90. See K. Abbott and D. Snidal, 'Standardization, Legalization and Governance', in Walter Mattli (ed.), *The Political Economy of Standardization* (Cambridge: Cambridge University Press, forthcoming); H. Milner, 'Internationalization and Domestic Politics: A Conclusion', in R. O. Keohane and H. V. Milner (eds.), *Internationalization and Domestic Change* (Cambridge: Cambridge University Press, 1996).

91. K. Arrow, 'Alternative Approaches to the Theory of Choice in Risk Taking', *Econometrica*, 17 (1951), 404–37; K. Arrow, *Social Choice and Individual Values* (New Haven: Yale University Press, 1970).

92. See C. Blankart and G. Knieps, 'State and Standards', *Public Choice*, 19 (1993), 39–52.

93. T. Risse-Kappen, 'Exploring the Nature of the Beast: International Relations Theory and Comparative Policy Analysis Meet the European Union', *Journal of Common Market Studies*, 34, no. 1 (Mar. 1996), 53–80.

94. C. Antonelli, 'Localized Technological Change and the Evolution of Standards as Economic Institutions', *Information Economics and Policy*, 6 (1994), 213.

95. F. Scharpf, 'Political Institutions, Decision Styles and Policy Choices', in R. M. Czada and A. Windhoff-Héritier (eds.), *Political Choice: Institutions, Rules, and the Limits of Rationality* (Boulder, Colo.: Westview, 1991); for a similar description of the standards process, see N. Brunnson and B. Jacobsson et al., *A World of Standards* (Oxford: Oxford University Press, 2000).

96. See J. March and J. Olson, *Rediscovering Institutions: The Organizational Basis of Politics* (New York: Free Press, 1989).

97. Eichener, 'Effective European Problem Solving'; Bundgaard-Pedersen, 'States and EU Technical Standardization'.

98. See J. L. Badaracco, *Loading the Dice* (Boston: Harvard Business School Press, c. 1985); G. Majone, 'The New European Agencies: Regulation by Information', *Journal of European Public Policy*, 4, no. 2 (1997), 262–75.

99. Majone, 'New European Agencies'; G. Majone, 'Temporal Inconsistency and Policy Credibility: Why Democracies Need Non-majoritarian Institutions', EUI Working Paper No. 96/57, Robert Schuman Centre, European University Institute, Florence (1997).

100. G. Majone, *Evidence, Argument and Persuasion* (New Haven: Yale University Press, 1989).

101. Héritier, 'The Accommodation of Diversity'.
102. Salter, 'Do Reforms Make a Difference?', 17.
103. See Brunnson and Jacobsson, *World of Standards*.
104. Eichener, 'Effective European Problem Solving', 603.
105. Majone, *Evidence, Argument and Persuasion*; John Kingdon, *Agendas, Alternatives and Public Policies* (Boston: Little Brown, 1984).
106. The development of these para-bureaucratic communities of policy specialists drawn together by their interest and knowledge in a particular area has broad similarities to epistemic communities. See Peter Haas, 'Introduction: Epistemic Communities and International Policy Coordination', *International Organisation*, 46, no. 1 (Winter 1992), 1–35.
107. The internal rules of the European standards bodies include appeals to the board to ensure procedural fairness in standard-setting. See for example K. Opala, 'The Anatomy of Private Standards-Making Process', *Oklahoma Law Review*, 45 (1969).
108. Author interview, European Roundtable of Industrialists, 1993.
109. Genschel, 'How Fragmentation Can Improve Co-ordination', 614.
110. Schmidt and Werle, 'Technical Controversy'; P. Genschel and R. Werle, 'From National Hierarchies to International Standardization: Modal Changes in the Governance of Telecommunications', *Journal of Public Policy*, 13 (1993), 203–25.
111. As Pelkmans points out, this also enabled the Commission to crack open the door of telecoms monopolies and extend competition into telecoms services by promoting the importance of interoperability, open standards, and market fragmentation. See Jacques Pelkmans, 'The GSM Standard', paper presented at the Workshop on Political Economy of Standards Setting, European University Institute, Florence (June 1998), 16.
112. *International Herald Tribune*, 'Europe, Asia, and US Argue over Solving Mobile Phone Jam', 25 Mar. 1999.
113. For a good discussion of the role of the ITU and reform efforts, see Paul A. David and Mark Shurmer, 'Formal Standards-Setting for Global Telecommunications and Information Services: Towards an Institutional Transformation?', *Telecommunications Policy*, 20 no. 10 (1996) 789–815.
114. Indeed in this situation, the problem has the pay-off structure of a battle of the sexes game.
115. Farrell and Saloner, 'Coordination through Committees and Markets'; Opala, 'Private Standards-Making Process'.

Chapter 8

1. The analogy is drawn from E. E. Schattschneider, *The Semisovereign People: A Realistic View of Democracy in America* (Hinsdale, Ill.: Dryden Press, 1975).

2. J. Falke, 'The Role of Non-governmental Standardization Organizations in the Regulation of Risks to Health and the Environment,' paper presented at the European University Institute, Florence (1996).

3. V. Eichener and H. Voelzkow (eds.), *Europäische Integration und verbandliche Interessenvermittlung* (Marburg: Metropolis Verlag, 1994).

4. G. Gaddes, Director-General of CENELEC, as quoted in *ISO Bulletin*, Sept. 1997, 16.

5. D. Foray, 'Users, Standards and the Economics of Coalitions and Committees', *Information Economics and Policy*, 6 (1994), 269.

6. See F. Scharpf, 'Die Politikverflechtungs-Falle: Europaïsche Integration und deutscher Foederalismus im Vergleich', *Politische Vierteljahrreschrift*, 26, no. 4 (1985).

7. C. F. Cargill, *Information Technology Standardization: Theory, Process and Organization* (Bedford: Digital Press, 1989).

8. P. A. David, 'Clio and the Economics of QWERTY', *American Economic Review*, 75, no. 2 (May 1985), 332–7.

9. Author interview, European Commission official, May 1998.

10. The sample from which cases could be drawn was limited by the number of New Approach directives adopted. The cases chosen varied in terms of economic importance and market structure, number of mandated standards, and industrial strategies and corporate structure.

11. *Reuters*, 3 May 1988.

12. Spokesman's Service of the European Commission, 1 Oct. 1991; *Reuters*, 23 Jan. 1993.

13. *South China Seas*, June 1992.

14. Braun-Moser, Debates of the European Parliament, No. 2-354/122 8/7/87.

15. Organization for Economic Cooperation and Development, *Safety of Toys Report of the Committee on Consumer Policy* (Paris: OECD, 1975).

16. Commission of the EC Background report, ISEC/B45/80.

17. British Toy and Hobby Association, correspondence with author, 22 June 1993.

18. *European Report*, Business Brief, 16 Mar. 1988, 2.

19. British Toy and Hobby Association, correspondence with author, 22 June 1993.

20. Letter to E. Davignon, on the Commission proposal for a Council directive on the approximation of laws of member states concerning toys, no date.

21. Letter to M. Carpentier, Director-General, 29 Oct. 1980.

22. European Parliament, PE 69.935 19 Dec. 1980; 7 Jan. 1981; and 27 July 1981.

23. Comments of Worch, Secretary-General of CEN to Working Group on Technical Barriers, 14 Apr. 1991.

24. *Agence Europe*, 25 Oct. 1986.

25. Ibid.

26. Metten, Debates of the European Parliament, No. 2-354/122, 8 July 1987.

27. Hammerich, Debates of the European Parliament, No. 2-363/26, 8 Mar. 1988.
28. Directive 88/378/EU, Official Journal of the European Communities, No. L 187, 16 July 1988.
29. See Opinion of the Consumers' Consultative Committee relating to a technical assessment of the new CEN standards for toys, CCC/51/82XI/358/82-en.
30. *Reuters*, 7 May 1992.
31. W. S. Adkins, *Technical Barriers to Trade*, vol. i, subseries iii: *Dismantling of Barriers* (Luxembourg: Office of Official Publications of the European Communities, 1998), 118.
32. *Reuters*, 20 Jan. 1993.
33. Official Journal C 264, 1992.
34. *Sunday Telegraph*, 17 Oct. 1993.
35. *International Herald Tribune*, 17 Oct. 1992.
36. Ibid.
37. Manufacturers have two options of compliance under the Global Approach: module A (self-certification and technical file available for national authorities); and module B (EC approval where a sample is submitted for testing to a Commission approved notified body).
38. K. Schreiber, 'Technical Standards', in S. Woolcock et al., *Britain, Germany and 1992* (London: Pinter, 1991).
39. This section draws heavily on the report by W. S. Adkins, *Technical Barriers to Trade*, for the European Commission. It was also supplemented by interviews and data collection.
40. Despite the European Broadcasting Directive, differences in regulations remain regarding television advertising. Greece has restricted the broadcasting time on advertising for children which has led to complaints that importers are at a considerable advantage in marketing their products compared to Greek manufacturers.
41. For example, the Grune Punkt in Germany, Point Vert in France, and Fost Plus in Belgian, are all mandatory recycling schemes.
42. Author interview with representative of Danish multinational firm, 1992.
43. Adkins, *Technical Barriers to Trade*, 97–8.
44. P. Makin, Consultant to CEN and Chairman of ISO Technical Committee for Safety of Machinery, in *European Standards: A Win-Win Situation*, published by CEN/CENELEC and ETSI in 1998.
45. D. Mayes, 'The Machine Tool Industry', in D. Mayes (ed.), *The European Challenge: Industry's Response to the 1992 Programme* (Hemel Hempstead: Harvester Wheatsheaf, 1991); A. Baxter, 'US Machine Tool Makers Stage a Revival', *Financial Times*, 24 June 1993.
46. For a comparative assessment, see A. Daly and D. T. Jones, 'The Machine Tool Industry in Britain, Germany and the United States', *National Institute Economic Review*, 53–63.
47. Commission of the EC, *Strategic Study on EC Machine Tool Sector*, prepared by W. S. Adkins Consultants, May 1990.

48. See CECIMO, 'First Follow-up Report on the Boston Consulting Group Report', Brussels, 1989.
49. The industry is divided between cutting and forming tools. Cutting tools include lathes, and tools for drilling, boring, and grinding. Forming tools include presses, and shearing, forging, and threadrolling tools.
50. See CECIMO, 'First Follow-up Report'; C. Batchelor, 'Caught in the Cross-Fire', *Financial Times*, 23 June 1993; European Roundtable of Industrialists, 'Towards a Single European Export Control System: Harmony or Chaos', June 1991.
51. See European Commission COM (74) 2195 Final on approximation of laws relating to construction plant and equipment, laws relating to sound level of construction plant and equipment and laws relating to sound level of pneumatic concrete-breakers and jackhammers.
52. COM (77) 656 Final, 21 Dec. 1977.
53. Written Question No. 2149/82, Wedekind, European Parliament, 27 Apr. 1983; USITC, 'The Effects of Greater Economic Integration within the European Community and the United States', Washington, July 1989, pp. 6–26.
54. V. Eichener, 'Social Dumping or Innovative Regulation?', EUI Working Paper, SPS 92/28, European University Institute, Florence (1992), 51.
55. Ibid. 54; Interview Commission Official, May 1998.
56. Eichener, 'Social Dumping or Innovative Regulation?'; Karlheinz Zachman, 'Sicherheit von Maschinen—Werdegang einer Richtlinie', *DIN-Mitteilungen*, 67, no. 9 (1988), 538–40.
57. Case No. 188/84 ECR, 1986.
58. W. Dawkins, 'Machinery Rules Spark EC Power Struggles', *Financial Times*, 13 June 1988.
59. Ibid.; Schreiber, 'Technical Standards'.
60. Eichener, 'Social Dumping or Innovative Regulation?'
61. Article 100 (4) of the EC Treaty.
62. Dawkins, 'Machinery Rules Spark EC Power Struggles'.
63. Comment of ESC, 27 Oct. 1988, OJ 88/C 337/11; First Reading, European Parliament, 16 Nov. 1988 OJ 88/C 326/40.
64. Eichener, 'Social Dumping or Innovative Regulation?'
65. European Parliament Debates, No. 2-371/86-92.
66. Lord Cockfield, Debates of the European Parliament, No. 2-371/92.
67. Official Journal 93/44/EU.
68. Directive 98/37/EC 22 June 1998.
69. Eichener, 'Social Dumping or Innovative Regulation?', 38.
70. Circular saws listed in Annex IV of the machine directive, and woodworking machinery listed in Annex I paragraph (2) 3 both have special requirements.
71. Official Journal, Article 1 89/392/EU. For a detailed elaboration see British Department of Trade and Industry, 'Machinery Safety'.
72. Machinery Update, Nov. 1993; European Commission's Guide to the Directive.
73. Eichener, 'Social Dumping or Innovative Regulation?', 11; see also C. Joerges, K. Ladeur, and E. Vos, *Integrating Scientific Expertise into*

Regulatory Decision-Making: National Traditions and European Innovations (Baden-Baden: Nomos, 1997).

74. 'Machine Safety in the Twenty-First Century', in *European Standards: A Win-Win Situation*.
75. V. Eichener, 'Effective European Problem Solving', 338.
76. Ibid.
77. Source CEN; see also CEN, 1998; Makin, *Win-Win*.
78. 'Technical Standards Machinery Grinds Exceedingly Slow', *Financial Times*, 14 May 1990.
79. Makin, *Win-Win*.
80. CEN *Annual Report*, statistics for mandates for the new approach and related directives, June 1999.
81. M. B. Lieberman and D. B. Montgomery, 'First-Mover Advantages', *Strategic Management Journal*, 9 (1988) 41–58.
82. Debates of the European Parliament, No. 3-404/12-16.
83. Bangemann, Debates of the European Parliament, No. 3-404/14.
84. J. Pelkmans and M. Egan, 'The Politics of the Green Paper on the Development of European Standards', Center for European Policy Studies Working Paper, Brussels (1992); 'Tackling Technical Barriers', paper presented at the CEPS/CSIS conference 'Reconciling Regulation and Free Trade', Brussels, (Dec. 1992).
85. Adkins, *Technical Barriers to Trade*, 118.
86. 84/539/EU.
87. Commission Proposal for directive on the approximation of the laws of the member states relating to active implantable electromedical devices, COM (88) 717 Final, 12 Dec. 1988.
88. Survey Results attached to COM (88) 71 Final, 12 Dec. 1988.
89. OJ No. C 18/13, 22 Jan. 1996.
90. For example, France is considered exceptional in the medical health community because of the degree of protection offered in conditions for the conduct of clinical trials and product safety using human subjects. See C. Altenstetter, 'European Integration and National Governance: A Comparative Analysis of the Implementation of EU Regulatory Policy on Medical Devices', paper presented at ECSA Biennial Conference, Pittsburgh, May 1999, p. 29.
91. 93/42/EU, OJ No. L 169, 12 July 1993.
92. 90/385/EU, OJ No. 189, 20 July 1990.
93. Commission Communication to the European Parliament, SEC (1998) 26 Mar. 1998; 98/79/EU Dec. 1998.
94. Adkins, *Technical Barriers to Trade*, 74–5; Health Industry Manufacturers' Association (HIMA), 'The European Market for Medical Technology Products', no date.
95. Health Industry Manufacturers' Association, 'The European Market'; see also Mike Phillips, *Financial Times Management Report: The European Medical Device Industry*, Oct. 1996.

96. Proposal for a European Parliament and Council Directive on In Vitro Diagnostic Medical Devices, presented by the Commission, COM (95) 130 Final, 19 Apr. 1995.

97. C. Altenstetter, 'Collective Action of the Medical Devices Industry at the Transnational Level', paper presented at the 17th World Congress of the International Political Science Association, Seoul, Korea, Aug. 1997.

98. Information provided by European Diagnostics Manufacturers' Association (EDMA).

99. See 'Medical Devices in Europe', European Commission (DG-III), Apr. 1994.

100. Medicinal products are regulated by 65/65/EC.

101. Altenstetter, 'Collective Action', 14–15.

102. Ibid. 18.

103. CENELEC standards HD 395-1.

104. 'A European Quality Mark to Guarantee the Safety of Medical Products and Equipment', Spokesman's Service of the European Commission, 1 Aug. 1991.

105. Medical devices refers to any product, other than medicines, which are used in the healthcare environment for the diagnosis, prevention, monitoring, treatment, or alleviation of illness or injury.

106. European Commission, MEDDEV 2.1/3 Rev 5, 1 Mar. 1998. Guidelines for conformity assessment bodies known as MEDDEV documents can be obtained from European Commission, national governments, or industry associations.

107. E. Previdi, 'The EEC Directives for Harmonization of Medical Devices Regulatory Environment', presentation to the Conference on European Regulation of Medical Devices and Surgical Products, New Orleans, 14–15 Nov. 1988.

108. N. Anselmann, Address to Conference on the European Quality Systems Standards, Brussels, 30 Aug. 1990.

109. Meeting of Scientific Committee on Medicinal Products and Medical Devices, 24 June 1998.

110. See also Altenstetter, 'European Integration and National Governance', 19.

111. Anselmann, Address to Conference on the European Quality Systems Standards, 1990.

112. B. Maassen and R. Whaite (eds.), *In Vitro Diagnostic Medical Devices: Law and Practice in Five EU Member States: France, Germany, Italy, Spain and the United Kingdom* (Dordrecht: Kluwer, 1994).

113. See Altenstetter, 'European Integration and National Governance', 12.

114. Commission Proposal, COM (95) 130 Final, 19 Apr. 1995.

115. OJ C18/13, 22 Jan. 1996.

116. This applies to all incidents which might led to or have led to a patient's death or injury. The manufacturer must activate the vigilance system and notify the surveillance authority.

117. SEC (89) 555 Final, 26 Mar. 1998; COM (96) 643 Final, 20 Dec. 1996, Amending Directive Proposal on In Vitro Diagnostic Medical Devices.

118. The French had adopted legislation on human tissue in 1994 and in the end the issue had to be decoupled from the IVD directive to move forward.
119. 8134/97, Presse 156-G 21, May 1997.
120. *European Report*, 24 May 1997.
121. *European Report*, 29 Nov. 1997.
122. D. Sherratt, 'The Medical Devices Directive: Are you Ready?', *Compliance Engineering*, July/Aug. 1994.
123. Altenstetter, 'Collective Action', 30.
124. The Medical Devices Agency in the UK was established in 1994. It was formerly the Medical Devices Directorate, which became an Executive Agency of the Department of Health assigned to enforce the medical device directives and act as a competent body.
125. The market surveillance and vigilance system (*socialstyrelsen*) in Sweden is one example. See the Medical Devices Agency Competent Authority (UK) Medical Devices Vigilance System, European Commission Guidelines.
126. See the excellent discussion in Altenstetter, 'European Integration and National Governance' and ecole Nationale d'Administration (ENA) Séminaire ENA sur la sécurité sanitaire, 1998, www.ena.fr.
127. Federal Institute for Drugs and Medical Devices.
128. See Previdi, 'The EEC Directives for Harmonization of Medical Devices Regulatory Environment'; G. Dash, 'EU Regulation of Medical Devices: Are You Ready to Comply?', *Compliance Engineering*, July/Aug. 1997.
129. Brussels, 5 Aug. 1993, DOC 41/93/EN. Mandate BC/CEN/CE ELEC/ 09/89; BC/CENELEC/02/89; and BC/CEN/03/91.
130. Ibid.
131. CEN, Annual Report 1998–9.
132. EUCOMED information provided to author.
133. Adkins, *Technical Barriers to Trade*, 73.
134. Case C 239/95, 1996 ECR 1-1459.
135. Adkins, *Technical Barriers to Trade*, 74.
136. N. Anselman, 'Mutual Recognition and Global Harmonization', *Medical Devices Technology*, Jan./Feb. 1997.
137. See K. Nicolaïdis, 'Negotiating Mutual Recognition Regimes: A Comparative Analysis', Working Paper Series, Cambridge, Mass., Center for International Affairs, Harvard University, WP 6, Spring 1998.
138. 'Compromises pave way for FDA Reform', *Financial Times*, 21 Dec. 1997.
139. Anselman, 'Mutual Recognition'.
140. For an overview, see D. Vogel, 'The Globalization of Pharmaceutical Regulation', *Governance*, 2, no. 1 (1998), 1–22. Vogel discusses the International Conference on Harmonization of Technical Requirements for Registration of Pharmaceuticals (ICH).
141. This includes representatives from CEN, COCIR, European Medical Device Industry, European Notified Body (BSI), EFTA (Norwegian Board of Health), HIMA (US), FDA (US), Ministry of Health and Welfare (Japan), Health Canada, and TGA (Australia).
142. Anselman, 'Mutual Recognition'.

143. COM (74) 2195 Final, 20 Dec. 1978. Proposal for a Council Directive of the law relating to constructional plant and equipment, relating to the measurement of the sound level of constructional plant and equipment, and the permissible sound level for pneumatic concrete-breakers and jackhammers.

144. *Euroforum*, no. 42/78, 28 Nov. 1978, Annex 1, 1.

145. For example, see the Directive on Permissible Sound Power Level of Tower Cranes, COM (86) 491 Final.

146. Ibid.

147. *Agence Europe*, 15 Mar. 1980, p. 2.

148. Communication from the Commission to the European Parliament, Council, Economic and Social Committee and the Committee of the Regions on Competitiveness of the Construction Industry, COM (97) 539 Final.

149. *European Report*, 21 May 1980.

150. COM (74) 2195 Final.

151. Ibid.

152. *European Report*, 15 Nov. 1978.

153. *Agence Europe*, 24 Nov. 1978.

154. European Parliament Opinion, 8 May 1979, OJ C 140 5 June 1979; ESC Opinion, 18 July 1979, OJ C 247 1 Oct. 1979; *Agence Europe*, 8/9 Oct. 1979.

155. In response to a specific question on nail plates in house construction from the European Parliament, the Commission focused on the broader problems of decision-making power in internal market questions. See Question No. 55 Basil De Ferranti, No. 1/296/153, 9 Mar. 1983.

156. Ibid.

157. Ibid.

158. The Commission sought implementing power under Article 155 to avoid delays experienced with implementing directives. This would be accomplished by the Commission drafting directives on individual construction products without having to go through the Council.

159. *European Report*, 21 May 1980.

160. *Agence Europe*, 29 Oct. 1980.

161. Amended Proposal on Limitation of Noise by hydraulic and rope-operated excavators and by bull dozers, loaders, and excavator loaders, COM (81) Final, 5 Oct. 1981.

162. European Commission Press Release Presse e/84 (Presse 142) che/MCK/jw.

163. *Agence Europe*, 25 Apr. 1984.

164. T. Bundgaard-Pedersen, 'States and EU Technical Standardization', *Journal of European Public Policy*, 4, no. 2 (1997), 212.

165. Ibid.

166. European Organization for Technical Approval, no. 7 (1995).

167. European Technical Approvals are a route to enable manufacturers to show that their products meet the criteria set out in the CPD's essential requirements, providing the products concerned have been successfully assessed by a European Technical Approvals-issuing body.

168. Annual Report, Subcommittee, TEC-1, FIEC (European Federation of Construction Products Industry), 'Directives, Standards and Quality Assurance', 1998.
169. Ibid.
170. See the discussion in Helmut Hertel, 'Erläuterungen zum Grundlagendokument "Brandschutz". Bindegleid zwischen Bauproduktenrichtlinie und harmonisierten Normen sowie europäischen Zulassungen', Mittelungen (Deutsches Institut für Bautechnik) 25 (1994).
171. FIEC, Position Paper on certification of quality management systems to ISO 9000 and 14000 series, 1996.
172. Directive 89/106/EEC.
173. *The New Approach*, CEN, Brussels, 1994, 60.
174. *Official Journal of the European Communities*, 94/C62/01, 28 Feb. 1994.
175. Commission Report on the Construction Products Directive, COM (96) 202 Final, 15 May 1996.
176. COM (96) 205 Final, 15 May 1996.
177. Hertel, 'Erläuterungen zum Grundlagendokument "Brandschutz" '.
178. P. Laycock, S. Graham, and P. Fewings, 'The Effective Implementation of the Construction Products Directive: An Update', *Building Research and Information*, 23, no. 2 (1994), 119–24.
179. As quoted in European Commission, 'Report of the Group of Independent Experts on Legislative and Administrative Simplification', COM (95) 288 Final. Also known as the Molitor Group Report.
180. *Financial Times*, 14 Oct. 1993.
181. FIEC, Position Paper, Technical Commission on proposed revision to construction products directive, 1996.
182. Commission Report on the Construction Products Directive, COM (96) 202 Final, 15 May 1996.
183. See Better Lawmaking Report, COM (97) 626, 27 Nov. 1997; Communication from the Commission, 'Legislate to Act Better: The Facts', COM (98) 345 Final, 27 May 1998.
184. US Mission (Brussels) Reports from H. Delaney to US Department of Commerce. On file at National Institute of Standards and Technology, Gaithersburg, Maryland.
185. European Parliament, 5 Nov. 1997, A4-0350/97, Rapporteur, Langen.
186. Ibid. See also *Agence Europe*, 2 Dec. 1997.
187. See Bundgaard-Pedersen, 'States and EU Technical Standardization'. Bundgaard-Pedersen describes this system as polycentric, comprised of state agencies, national standards bodies, and industries. While standard-setting is a quasi-regulatory system, states have lost some measure of policy-making influence and there is a larger majority of private actors participating and setting European standards.
188. C. Antonelli, 'Localized Technological Change and the Evolution of Standards as Economic Institutions', *Information Economics and Policy*, 6 (1994), 213.

189. C. P. Kindleberger, 'Standards as Public, Collective and Private Goods', *Kyklos*, 36 (1983); J. Farrell and G. Saloner, 'Coordination through Committees and Markets', *Rand Journal of Economics*, 19 (1988), 235–52.

190. See Farrell and Saloner, 'Coordination through Committees and Markets.'

Chapter 9

1. See C. Radaelli, 'Governing European Regulation: The Challenges Ahead', EUI Working Paper, 98/3 Florence; L. Metcalfe, 'After 1992: Can the Commission Manage Europe?', *Australian Journal of Public Administration*, 51, no. 2 (1992), 117–30.

2. See also the critical comments by H. Schmitt von Sydow, 'Die Angst der Deutschen vor der Euro-Norm', *EGMagazin*, 6 (1991).

3. *Green Paper on the Development of European Standardization: Action for Faster Technological Integration in Europe*, COM (90) 456 Final, *Official Journal of the European Communities*, C20, 28 Jan. 1991.

4. C. Radaelli and B. Dente, 'Evaluation Strategies and the Analysis of the Policy Process', *Evaluation*, 2, no. 1 (1996), 51–66.

5. See the discussion in Michelle Egan, 'Regulatory Strategies, Delegation, and European Market Integration', *Journal of European Public Policy*, 5, no. 3 (1998), 485–506.

6. See Report to the Secretary of Commerce, Federal Advisory Committee on the EC Common Approach to Standards, Testing, and Certification in 1992, May 1991; Office of Technology Assessment, *Global Standards*, Washington, 1992; for an early assessment of the American standardization system, see American Standards Association, 'Does Industry Need a National Standardization Agency?' New York: ASA, 1932.

7. European Commission, DG-3 Working Paper, 'The Need for a Single European Standards Organization', 1 Nov. 1989.

8. Ibid.

9. Official Journal C 291/45, 16 Oct. 1980.

10. *Green Paper on the Development of European Standardization*, 15.

11. Ibid. 16.

12. Ibid. 23.

13. Ibid. 36.

14. Ibid. 29.

15. Ibid. 30.

16. See OJ COM (96) 564 Final, 'Community External Trade Policy in the Area of Standards and Conformity Assessment'.

17. *Green Paper on the Development of European Standardization*, 32.

18. Associate status enabled states to attend all committee meetings but provided them with no voting rights.

19. Then Secretary of Commerce Mosbacher had requested this in 1989 from Commissioner Bangemann.

20. European Commission, 'Europe 1992: Europe World Partner', *Communiqué of the European Commission*, 19 Oct. 1988, p. 3.
21. The formalized agreements coordinating work between the European and International Standards bodies are known as the Lugano and Vienna Agreements.
22. *Green Paper on the Development of European Standardization*, 32.
23. See ISO/IEC Response to Green Paper, 1991.
24. *Green Paper on the Development of European Standardization*, 49.
25. See e.g. H. Kroeger, 'What Industry Expects from European Standards Bodies', Union of Industrial and Employer's Confederations of Europe (UNICE), Apr. 1991; 'Development of European Standardization: Comments on the Commission Green Paper', European Roundtable of Industrialists (ERT), Apr. 1991; BDI comments on Green Paper in letter to Commissioner Bangemann, 8 July 1991.
26. Institute of Directors, 'Technical Standardization in the European Community', London, June 1991, 14.
27. Author interview with representative of British multinational firm, 1993.
28. Kroeger, 'What Industry Expects'; see also American Chamber of Commerce (Brussels) EC Committee, 'Position Paper on the Commission Green Paper on the Development of European Standardization', 3 Apr. 1991.
29. 'EC Green Paper on European Standardization: Orgalime Position', Orgalime (the liaison group of the European Mechanical, Electrical, Electronic and Metalworking Industries Association), Apr. 1991, Brussels.
30. See also the letter from the BDI to Commissioner Bangemann, 8 July 1991.
31. Ibid.
32. See BDI's Comments on the Green Paper: 'Kleine und mittlere Unternehmen können nur in nationalen Ausshüssen mitarbeiten. Personnel, finanziell und sprachlich sind sie kaum in der Lage, in europaïschen gremien aktiv mitzuarbeiten.'
33. M. Olson, 'The Logic of Collective Action', in J. Richardson (ed.), *Pressure Groups* (Oxford: Oxford University Press, 1993).
34. See the comments of the British, French, and German standards bodies.
35. Author correspondence with British Standards Institute official. The figures of number of participants varies, though a recent Commission report (1998) puts the number of participants at 50,000.
36. Author interview with official at Deutsches Institut für Normung e.V (DIN), 1992.
37. European standards are transposed into national ones so that they are readily available in all languages. National standards bodies remove any conflicting standards and are responsible for the implementation, oversight, and sale of European standards in their domestic markets.
38. Cited in 'Survey of International Standards', *Financial Times*, 14 Oct. 1993, p. 23.
39. 'BSI response to EC Commission Green Paper on the Development of European Standardization', British Standards Institute, Mar. 1991.

40. European Telecommunications Standards Institute, 'ETSI Meets the Challenge', Document D/149/91/ST/FA/skw, Valbonne, 4 Apr. 1991.

41. Author interview with CEN official, 1993; CENELEC Commentary on the Commission's Communication on the Development of European Standardization, Annex I, CLC/AG(SG)623.

42. Author interview with British Standards Institute official; author interview with representative of European Roundtable of Industrialists, 1993.

43. 'ETSI Meets the Challenge'.

44. Correspondence of Joint Presidents Group Gnetti with Commissioner Bangemann, 26 May 1991, CLC/AG(Copenhagen/SG)06.

45. CEN/CENELEC/ETSI Joint President Group, Open Letter to EC Commission Vice-President, M. Bangemann, 26 Apr. 1991.

46. The results of the debate were summarized on the Communication from the Commission on Standardization in the European Economy, 16 Dec. 1991, OJ EC C 96, 15/4/91.

47. See e.g. Josef Falke, 'The Role of Non-governmental Standardization Organizations in the Regulation of Risks to Health and the Environment', paper presented at the European University Institute, Florence (1996).

48. Official Journal 92/C 172/EC.

49. See Communication from the Commission to the Council and Parliament on the Broader Use of Standardization in Community Policy, COM 11/95/EN.

50. Author interview with European Commission official, May 1998.

51. See European Commission, 'Reinforcing the Effectiveness of the Internal Market', Communication from the Commission to the Council and the European Parliament, COM (93) 256, 2 June 1993; European Commission, 'The Impact and Effectiveness of the Single Market', Communication from the Commission to the European Parliament and the European Council, COM 96, 30 Oct. 1996.

52. Resolution of the European Parliament on the report from the Commission to the Council and European Parliament, 'Efficiency and Accountability in European Standardization under the New Approach', COM 98 0291 Official Journal C 150 28 May 1999; Council Resolution on the Role of European Standardisation, 28 Oct. 1999.

53. This includes mandates already underway in the domain of public utilities (93/38/EC) for water supply, production, transport, and distribution of electricity, transmission and distribution of gas, and telecommunications.

54. Communication from the Commission to the Council and Parliament on the Broader Issue of the Use of Standardization Policy in Community Policy, 11/95 EN. Communication drawn up under the terms of the Strategic Programme for the Internal Market.

55. 'Internal Market Council: Ministers make Key Progress with Heavy Agenda', *European Report*, 29 Nov. 1997.

56. See AFNOR, *Normalisation des services: le milieu du gué enjeux* No. 155, June 1995. The French standards body, AFNOR, has been promoting the

distinction between services induced by a product and services associated or linked with a product or service.

57. Because services are difficult to define given that they are so broad and diversified, the standardization of services is more general and generic to a whole sector. See Special Issue on Services, *ISO Bulletin*, Oct. 1996; 'Servicing the Service Industry', *ISO Bulletin*, Sept. 1995; 'Survey of International Standards', *Financial Times*.

58. European Commission Staff Working Paper, 'Report on the Progress of European Standardization', SEC (95) 2104, 28 Nov. 1995, 4.

59. European Commission, 'Impact and Effectiveness of the Single Market', 12.

60. European Commission, 'Progress of European Standardization'.

61. 'The European Standardization Work: Analysis and Recommendations for Efficiency Considerations', Report Prepared for the Danish Agency for Trade and Industry, Oct. 1997.

62. See 'Once on its Feet, EOTC will play Key Role in Harmonizing EU Assessment', *Journal of Commerce*, 2 Sept. 1998; see 'Progress and Problems in Mutual Recognition', National Forum Discussion Paper by the Quality Unit, 94/008577 BSI UK.

63. 'Efficiency and Accountability in European Standardization under the New Approach', SEC (98) 291, 13 May 1998.

64. Ibid. 2–3.

65. See Commission Recommendation on Improving and Simplifying the Small Business Environment for Business Start-Ups, C (97) 116 Final, Apr. 1997; C. Dannreuther, 'Discrete Dialogues and the Legitimation of EU SME Policy', *Journal of European Public Policy*, 6, no. 3 (Sept. 1999), 436–56.

66. European Commission, 'Efficiency and Accountability', 10.

67. Ibid. 13.

68. 'Internal Market Council: Ministers Seek Concrete Solutions at Informal Gathering', *European Report*, 18 Feb. 1998.

69. Author interview, May 1998.

70. See e.g. UNICE, 'Releasing Europe's Potential through Targeted Regulatory Reform', Brussels, 1995.

71. See British Department of Trade and Industry, 'Generic Study on Standards, Testing and Certification Barriers in Non-Harmonised Areas of the Single Market', May 1995; 'Exporter Swerves Past Cones Obstacle', *Financial Times*, 14 Nov. 1995. The Commission acknowledged that the complaints registered in this area represent only a fraction of problems encountered under mutual recognition.

72. Author interview with European Commission official, 1993; author interview with National Institute of Standards and Technology official, Washington, 1998.

73. 'Strategy note on the EN 45000 series of standards', Certif. 94/529, June 1994, DG III Brussels.

74. Author interview with European Commission official, May 1998.

75. Business preference for conformity with national standards to ensure approval by national inspection bodies is a commercial rather than legal requirement. However, it often results in more advantageous conditions for those conforming to local standards, testing, and certification practices. See also British Department of Trade and Industry, 'Standards, Testing and Certification Barriers'; Action Single Market Success Stories, Mimeo, Apr. 1997, London, UK; 'Marks and Labels; Difficulties with Diversity', *ISO Bulletin*, Sept. 1996.

76. See Communication from the Commission to the Council and the European Parliament, 'Mutual Recognition in the Context of the Follow-up Action Plan for the Single Market', COM (1999) 299 Final.

77. See 'Progress and Problems in Mutual Recognition'.

78. Ibid. 5.

79. Report from the Commission on the Operation of Directive 83/189/I EC in 1992, 1993, and 1994. COM (96) 286 Final, 26 May 1996. This was not the first time that the EU had reported on the problems surrounding the operation of Directive 83/189. The single market trade transparency procedures adopted by a decision in 1995 (3052/95) does not replace 83/189 but is designed to address many of the problems mutual recognition has encountered in practice.

80. Ibid. 9. The report noted that in Britain and Germany, half of the notifications that the national standards body was working on an issue came at the public screening stage.

81. Recent efforts have been made under the SLIM simplification of the single market project to tackle this issue at the national level. Under the Internal Market Advisory Council representatives of the member states along with those on a SLIM project report on the situation regarding national legislation in the sector in question. See Spokeman's Service of the European Commission, 'Commission Moves to Simplify Single Market Legislation', 6 Mar. 2000.

82. Spokesman's Service of the European Commission, IP 96/91.

83. For a detailed statistical analysis, see Report from the Commission on the Operation of Directive 83/189/EC in 1992, 1993, and 1994.

84. Ibid.

85. For example, in July 1997 the Commission referred a number of cases to the European Court of Justice, requesting reasoned opinions (second stage of infringement procedure) in 26 cases where member states had failed to transpose single market directives into national legislation. Among the measures highlighted as restricting trade were an Italian Law of 1968 on precious metals which did not permit marketing without specific hallmarks, thus violating the principle of mutual recognition, and a Dutch refusal to permit marketing of foodstuffs enriched with iron and vitamins because national legislation requires a technical or nutritional demonstration of need. This despite the existence of previous case law, e.g. the *Nisin* case, in this area—see Ch. 5. Infringement cases reached 228 in the 1996–9 period and

63 cases were resolved. The largest number of cases were against France and Germany.

86. Marino Marcich, Director of Investment for the National Association of Manufacturers, quoted in Amy Zuckerman, 'Product Standards', *Journal of Commerce*, 15 Oct. 1997.

87. Case C 184-96 *Commission* v. *France*, ECR 1998.

88. See Radaelli, 'Governing European Regulation'.

89. Spokesman's Service of the European Commission, 'Single Market: Commission Agrees Outline of Action Plan', 30 Apr. 1997. Jacques Santer had indicated to the European Council in Dec. 1996 that the Commission would produce such a document.

90. CSE (971) 1 Final, June 1997, 'Action Plan for the Single Market', 4 June 1997.

91. Spokesman's Service of the European Commission, 'Single Market—Commissioner Monti Recalls first Action Plan Deadline', 30 Sept. 1997.

92. See Communication from the Commission to the European Parliament and Council, 'The Strategy for Europe's Internal Market', COM (99) 464, 28 Sept. 1999 for the broader rationale for the internal market strategy.

93. See COM (96) 204 Final; COM (96) 559 Final and Commission Staff Working Paper, 'Review of SLIM: Background Material to the Communication of the Commission', COM (2000) 104, 28 Feb. 2000.

94. *Agence Europe*, 17–18 Mar. 1997.

95. *European Voice*, 10–16 Apr. 1997; see also the excellent discussion on regulatory reform by Radaelli, 'Governing European Regulation'.

96. 'Brussels Acts on Trade Obstacles', *Financial Times*, 20 Nov. 1997.

97. Spokesman's Service of the European Commission, 'The Commission Proposes an Intervention Mechanism to Safeguard Free Trade in the Single Market', 19 Nov. 1997.

98. The ECJ had given judgment in *Commission* v. *France* concerning the alleged failure of France to take steps to prevent private individuals from disrupting trade in goods.

99. 'Internal Market Council: Ministers Seek Concrete Solutions at Informal Gathering', *European Report*, 18 Feb. 1998.

100. The attribution comes from Lord Simon, British Minister for Trade and Competitiveness in Europe, after the Internal Market Council Meeting in Cambridge in February. Quoted in *European Report*, ibid.

101. Council Regulation on the Functioning of the Internal Market in relation to the free movement of goods—Official Journal L337, 12 Dec. 1998.

102. See Radaelli, 'Governing European Regulation'.

103. See also A. M. Sbragia, 'Governance, the State and the Market: What is Going on?', *Governance*, 13, no. 2 (Apr. 2000), 243–50.

Chapter 10

1. See for example, J. Farrell and G. Saloner, 'Coordination through Committees and Markets', *Rand Journal of Economics*, 19 (1988), 235–52;

for empirical illustrations, see J. Pelkmans and R. Beuter, 'Standardization and Competitiveness: Public and Private Strategies in the EU Colour TV Industry', in H. Landis Gabel (ed.), *Product Standardization and Competitive Strategy* (Amsterdam: Elsevier, 1987).

2. M. Dodgson, *Technological Collaboration in Industry: Strategy, Policy, and Internationalization in Innovation* (London: Routledge, 1993).

3. For a similar critique, see A. David, 'Standardization Policies for Network Technologies: The Flux between Freedom and Order Revisited', in R. Hawkins et al., *Standards, Innovation and Competitiveness* (Aldershot: Edward Elgar, 1995).

4. See R. Mansell, 'Standards, Industrial Policy and Innovation', in Hawkins et al., *Standards, Innovation and Competitiveness*; W. B Arthur, 'Competing Technologies, Increasing Returns and Lock in by Historical Events', *Economic Journal*, 99 (Mar. 1989), 116–31.

5. Following the work on corporate strategy by Michael Porter, the chapter recognizes that a firm's competitive strategy is obviously affected by factors both internal and external to the company. See M. Porter, *Competitive Advantage* (New York: Free Press, 1985) and M. Porter, *The Competitive Advantage of Nations* (New York: Free Press, 1990).

6. See P. Hall and D. Soskice, 'Varieties of Capitalism: The Institutional Foundations of Comparative Advantage', draft article manuscript.

7. See also R. Sally, *States and Firms: Multinational Enterprises in Institutional Competition* (London: Routledge, 1995).

8. A. De Meyer, 'New Manufacturing Strategies' and Y. Doz, 'Aligning Strategic Demands and Corporate Capabilities', in S. G. Makridakis (ed.), *Single Market Europe: Opportunities and Challenges for Business* (San Francisco: Jossey-Bass Publishers, 1991).

9. A. Chandler, *Strategy and Structure: Chapters in the History of the Industrial Enterprise* (Garden City, NY: Doubleday, 1966).

10. Several companies alluded to the problems of responding to questionnaires due to the diversity of product ranges, conglomeration of companies, and multinational structures that made generalization difficult.

11. R. Putnam, 'Diplomacy and Domestic Politics: The Logic of Two-Level Games', *International Organization* 42 (1988), 427–60.

12. Single Market Scoreboard results cited in COM (1999) 299 Final, 16 June 1999.

13. 'Single Market: Business Survey Reveals Cautious Optimism', Spokesman's Service of the European Commission', 19 Nov. 1997.

14. There are no statistics where mutual recognition works without any problems nor are there any data on how many companies chose to comply with the additional requirements of the country of destination or simply decide not to market their goods or services in another member state.

15. W. S. Adkins, *Technical Barriers to Trade* (Luxembourg: Office of Official Publications of the European Communities, 1998).

16. Ibid.

17. See COM (1999) 10 Final, Report on the Functioning of Community Product and Capital Markets, 20 Jan. 1999.

18. See the European Observatory for SMEs, *Annual Reports*, Presented to Directorate General XXIII (Enterprise Policy, Distributive Trades, Tourism and Cooperatives) of the European Commission.

19. European Observatory for SMEs, DG XXIII of the European Commission, *Fifth Annual Report*, Oct. 1997.

20. See M. Egan and A. Zito, 'Environmental Management Standards, Corporate Strategies and Policy Networks', *Environmental Politics*, 7, no. 3 (1998), 94–117.

21. European Observatory for SMEs, *Fifth Annual Report*.

22. Ibid.; see also A. Héritier et al., *Die Veränderung von Staatlichkeit in Europa: Ein regulativer Wettbewerb—Deutschland, Grossbritannien und Frankreich un der Europäischen Union* (Opladen: Leske & Budrich, 1994).

23. K. Van Elk, 'SMEs in the Single Market', EIM Small Business Research and Consultancy, Report to European Commission, DG-XXIII.

24. See X. Dai, *Corporate Strategy, Public Policy, and New Technologies: Philips and the European Consumer Electronics Industry* (Oxford: Oxford University Press, 1996).

25. For exceptions see M. Egan, 'Regulatory Policy, Corporate Strategies and Market Integration', *European Union Review*, 3, no. 1 (Mar. 1998); J. Cantwell, 'The Effects of Integration on the Structure of Multinational Corporation Activity in the EC', in M. W. Kelin and J. J. Welfens, *Multinationals in the New Europe and Global Trade* (Springer-Verlag, 1992); J. A. Cantwell, 'The Reorganization of European Industries after Integration: Selected Evidence on the Role of the Multinational Enterprise Activities', *Journal of Common Market Studies*, 26, no. 2 (Dec. 1987); A. Jacquemin and A. Sapir, 'Europe post-1992: Internal and External Liberalization', *American Economic Review*, 81 (May 1991), 166–70; P. Buigues and A. Jacquemin, 'Strategies of Firms and Structural Environments in the Large Internal Market', *Journal of Common Market Studies*, 28 (1989), 53–67.

26. S. Besen and J. Farrell, 'Choosing How to Compete: Strategies and Tactics in Standardization', *Journal of Economic Perspectives*, 8, no. 2 (Spring 1994), 117–31.

27. Service is obviously an important component of the single market. However, like goods, it is difficult to obtain data on the application of mutual recognition to services. One problem area is financial services, where the concept of general interest to justify exemptions to mutual recognition has in some cases prevented the marketing of financial services, other areas such as business communications and electronic trade have also encountered legal and regulatory obstacles.

28. 'Hitting a Wall: US Firm's Troubles in EU Highlight a Lack of Integration', *Wall Street Journal*, 9 Apr. 1996; 'Stacking the Deck in Europe: One Company's Story', *ASTM Standardization News*, Aug. 1996; author interview, company president; US Congress, House Subcommittee Hearing, on International Standards: Technical Barriers to Free Trade, 28 Apr. 1998 US Government GPO, http://www.house.gov/science/hearing.

29. M. Oppenheimer and D. Tuths, *Non-tariff Barriers: The Effects on Corporate Strategy in High-Technology Sectors* (Boulder, Colo.: Westview Press, 1987), 20.

30. Survey questionnaires distributed by author; see also British Department of Trade and Industry (DTI), 'Generic Study on Standards, Testing and Certification Barriers in Non-Harmonized Areas of the Single Market', May 1995; Oppenheimer and Tuths, *Non-tariff Barriers*.

31. Twenty-five companies responded to the questionnaire, providing much of the data used in this assessment. Due to the small sample size, further information was gained from interviews, reports, and other published material.

32. Questionnaire, German company, 29 Oct. 1997; British company, 18 Nov. 1997; Dutch company, 27 Oct. 1997; American multinational, European Affairs Office, 24 Nov. 1997. Questionnaire response from British pharmaceutical firm, Sept. 1998.

33. American multinational, European Technology Division, no date.

34. Coen's data is derived from a 1994 survey of European Affairs Directors. See D. Coen 'The Evolution of the Firm as a Political Actor in the European Union', *Journal of European Public Policy*, 4, no. 1 (1997); D. Coen, 'The European Business Lobby', *Business Strategy Review*, 6, no. 4 (1997).

35. Companies were asked to select from the following categories: competition policy; health and safety standards; testing and certification; labour relations; tax and financial services provision; public procurement; utility/service liberalization; and other (please specify).

36. Questionnaire response, 10 Nov. 1997.

37. Sergio Mazza, ANSI President, Testimony before the House Subcommittee on Technology, Environment and Aviation, 101st Congress, Second Session, 22 Sept. 1994.

38. Marino Marcich, Director of Investment for the National Association of Manufacturers, quoted in Amy Zuckerman, 'Product Standards', *Journal of Commerce*, 15 Oct. 1997.

39. Questionnaire response from German engineering company, 29 Nov. 1997.

40. See Department of Trade and Industry, 'Barriers to Trade in Chemicals in the Single Market', July 1995.

41. Questionnaire response from Dutch multinational, 17 Dec. 1997.

42. Author interview with European Commission official, May 1998; author interview with EU trade official, Sept. 1998; *Business Week*, 31 Aug. 1998; J. Pelkmans, 'The GSM Standard: A Success Story without Lessons?', paper presented at the Workshop on Political Economy of Standards Setting, European University Institute, Florence (June 1998).

43. This was set up in 1994 to monitor trade complaints and assist companies in negotiating their resolution. It differs from the Technical Help for Exporters Programme provided by the British Standards Institute.

44. British Department of Trade and Industry (DTI), 'Generic Study on Standards, Testing and Certification Barriers'.

45. DTI, 'Chemicals and Biotechnology Division, Barriers to Trade in Chemicals in the Single Market', July 1995.

46. Questionnaire response from British pharmaceutical company, Sept. 1998.
47. See 'Hopes Dwindle that EU will Dismantle Draconian Price Controls on Medicines', *Wall Street Journal*, 7 Dec. 1998.
48. 'Once on its Feet, EOTC will Play a Key Role in Harmonizing EU Assessment', *Journal of Commerce*, 2 Sept. 1998.
49. A. Zuckerman, 'EU Officials Fight for Accountability among Agencies in Charge of Testing', *Journal of Commerce*, 10 Dec. 1997.
50. Author interview with EOTC official, Brussels, 1993.
51. For an acknowledgement of problems, see European Commission, 'Strategy Note on the EN 45000 Series of Standards', Certif. 94/5, 29 June 1994.
52. Comments by Chairman F. Arzano, Senior VP International Affairs, Ericsson, SPA in 'Conference Report on Technical Barriers to Trade in Europe', 13 Sept. 1994, Copenhagen.
53. J. Rosted, Permanent Secretary, Danish Ministry of Business and Industry, ibid. 34–5.
54. T. Stoll, Director for the Internal Market, European Commission, ibid. 30–1; Comments from the Toy Manufacturers of Europe, in ibid. 27; Comments from CEI Bois on the woodworking sector, ibid. 26.
55. Comments by Chairman J. Ardagh, Director EU and International Policy, Food and Drink Federation, ibid. 15–17.
56. See e.g. Eurochambres, 'Non-tariff Barriers in the European Union', Oct. 1994.
57. Opinion of the European Cleaning Industries Association Regarding the Directives in the Chemical Sector on Dangerous Substances. The Directive had been amended fifteen times under the traditional harmonization approach.
58. European Federation of Material Handling Machinery, Comments, ibid. 24.
59. Eurochambres, 'Non-Tariff Barriers in the European Union', 9.
60. EU Committee of AMCHAM, Position Paper on Single Market, 24 Apr. 1997, Brussels.
61. Marcich quoted in Zuckerman, 'Product Standards'.
62. Interview with M. Masri, SGS, *Financial Times*, 14 Oct. 1993.
63. S. Woolcock, M. Hodges, and K. Schreiber, *Britain, Germany and 1992: The Limits of Deregulation* (London: Pinter, 1991); M. Egan, 'Bandwagons or Barriers: The Role of Standards in the European and American Marketplace', Center for West European Studies, University of Pittsburgh European Policy Paper Series No. 1, Nov. 1997.
64. 'Europe 1992: Europe World Partner', Communiqué of the European Commission, Brussels, 19 Oct. 1988, 3.
65. See M. Egan, 'Mutual Recognition and Standard-Setting: Public and Private Strategies for Governing Markets', in M. Pollack and G. Schaffer (eds.), *Transatlantic Governance in a Global Economy* (Boston: Rowman & Littlefield, forthcoming).
66. At the Tempere Meeting of 1988.
67. See Preparation of the Associated Countries of Central and Eastern Europe for Integration into the Internal Market of the Union, COM (95) 163 Final, 3 May 1995; U. Sedelmeier and H. Wallace, 'Eastern Enlargement: Strategy

or Second Thought?', in H. Wallace and W. Wallace (eds.), *Policy-Making in the European Union*, 4th edn. (Oxford: Oxford University Press, 2000).

68. See P. Eeckhout, *The European Internal Market and International Trade: A Legal Analysis* (Clarendon Press: Oxford, 1994), ch. 6; National Research Council, *Standards, Conformity Assessment, and Trade* (National Academy Press: Washington, 1995).

69. Secretary of Commerce Mosbacher proposed this to Commissioner Bangemann in 1989.

70. The EU did allow some subcontracting of certain testing practices to overseas-based independent testing bodies, but these were limited to certain procedures.

71. Council Resolution of 21 Dec. 1989 (OJ 1990 C 10/1).

72. For a detailed analysis of the negotiations, see K. Nicolaïdis, 'Mutual Recognition of Regulatory Regimes: Some Lessons', Jean Monnet Working Paper No. 7 (1997), Harvard University; M. Egan and K. Nicolaïdis, 'Regulatory Co-operation and Market Governance: Alternative Patterns of Standardisation and Mutual Recognition', paper presented at the Political Economy of Standard-Setting Conference, May 1998, European University Institute, Florence. This section draws extensively on Nicolaïdis.

73. See K. Nicolaïdis, 'Negotiating Mutual Recognition Regimes: A Comparative Analysis', Working Paper Series, Cambridge Mass., Center for International Affairs, Harvard University, WP 6, Spring 1998.

74. See 'Regional Policy Externality and Market Governance: European and Transatlantic Regulatory Cooperation', K. Nicolaïdis and M. Egan Special Issue, Governance in International Standards Setting, *Journal of European Public Policy* (forthcoming 2001).

75. There are no official statistics on how many state and local standards exist. State and local standards cover a diversity of issues including building codes, some agricultural produce, truck weights, axles, and sizes.

76. Author interview with National Trade Association official, Washington, Sept. 1998; Author interview with EU trade official, Aug. 1998; Presentation of H. Delaney, US Mission in Brussels, 'Towards a National Standards Strategy to Meet Global Needs', 23 Aug. 1998.

77. Mutual recognition agreements have become an important trading tool outside Europe as well, as evidenced by discussions within APEC, ASEAN, NAFTA, MERCOSUR, and the FTAA.

78. See D. Victor, 'Risk Management and the World Trading System: Regulating International Trade Distortions Caused by National Sanitary and Phytosanitary Policies', paper presented at the National Research Council Conference Board on Agriculture and Natural Resources, 23–7 Jan. 1999, Irvine, Calif.

79. There are more than 110 private-sector certifiers in the USA.

80. Egan, 'Mutual Recognition and Standard-Setting'; M. Egan, 'Transatlantic Trade and Market Governance', American Institute for Contemporary German Studies (AICGS) Working Paper, Washington, 1999.

81. Dept. of Commerce, Press Release, 13 June 1997.

82. For a general discussion, see P. Stern, Testimony before the Subcommittee on Trade, House Committee on Ways and Means, Hearing on New Transatlantic Agenda 23 July 1997.

83. Conclusions of First Meeting of TABD, Seville, 1995; see also Jacques Pelkmans, *Atlantic Economic Cooperation: The Limits of Plurilateralism* (Brussels: CEPS, Working Document No. 122, 1998).

84. See Egan, 'Mutual Recognition and Standard Setting'.

85. For a discussion of trade policy initiatives, see J. Pelkmans, CEPS, 1998; A. Gardner, *A New Era of Transatlantic Relations? The Clinton Administration and the New Transatlantic Agenda* (Aldershot: Avebury, 1997); European Commission, *The New Transatlantic Marketplace*, Brussels COM 125 Final, 11 Mar. 1998; John Peterson, 'Get Away from Me Closer, You're Near Me Too Far: Europe and America after the Uruguay Round', Paper presented at the New Transatlantic Dialogue Conference, 31 May–2 June 1999, Wisconsin-Madison.

86. IFACS, 'Report on Standards, Testing and Certification to the Secretary of Commerce', Washington, May 1991; 'Toward a National Standards Strategy to Meet Global Needs', Conference organized by the National Institute for Science and Technology and the American National Standards Institute, Washington, 23 Sept. 1998. See also 'Playing Catch up in the Global Game of Standards', *Journal of Commerce*, 6 July 1998.

87. 'The Media and Standards: An Example of Ignorance over Enlightenment', *Journal of Commerce*, 26 Aug. 1998.

88. See Congressional Hearings, April and June 1998, esp. F. Vargo, presentation to the House Committee on International Relations, US Congress, 7 May 1998; Congressional Hearing, 'International Standards and US Exporters: The Key to Competitiveness or Barriers to Trade?', before the Subcommittee on Technology, Environment, and Aviation of the Committee on Science, Space, and Technology, 22 Sept. 1994; IFACS, 'Report on Standards, Testing and Certification'; White Paper, US Department of Commerce Subcommittee on Europe, Nov. 1995; 'Global Standards', Office of Technology Assessment, Washington, 1992.

89. See J. J. Tate, 'Varieties of Standardization', in Peter Hall and David Soskice (eds.), *Varieties of Capitalism* (forthcoming).

90. R. Krammer's testimony to the House Science Committee, Technology Subcommittee, www.house.gov/science/welcome.htm, 28 Apr. 1998; see generally National Research Council, *Standards, Conformity Assessment, and Trade*.

91. See E. Previdi, 'Making and Enforcing Regulatory Policy in the Single Market', in H. Wallace and A. Young (eds.), *Participation and Policy-Making in the European Union* (Oxford: Clarendon Press, 1997), 69–90.

92. R. Dehousse et al., 'Europe after 1992: New Regulatory Strategies', EUI Working Paper, Law 92/31, 1992.

93. There have been efforts by the USA to move the European Commission to a notice and comment process along the lines of the American Procedure Act (APA).

Chapter 11

1. See A. M. Sbragia, 'Governance, the State and the Market: What is Going on?', *Governance*, 13, no. 2 (Apr. 2000), 245.

2. S. K. Vogel, *Freer Markets, More Rules* (Ithaca, NY: Cornell University Press, 1996). See also N. Fligstein, *The Transformation of Corporate Control* (Cambridge, Mass.; Harvard University Press, 1990); N. Fligstein, 'Markets as Politics: A Political-Cultural Approach to Market Institutions', *American Sociological Review*, 61 (1996), 656–73.

3. S. Elkin, 'Regulation and Regime: A Comparative Analysis', *Journal of Public Policy*, 6, no. 1 (1986), 55.

4. T. J. Lowi, *The End of Liberalism* (New York: Norton, 2nd edn., 1976).

5. Here I am borrowing and adapting Scharpf's concern with both input and output legitimacy. See F. Scharpf, 'Economic Integration, Democracy and the Welfare State', Cologne, 10 Aug. 1996, unpublished paper; Fritz Scharpf, *Governing in Europe* (Oxford: Oxford University Press, 1999).

6. See J. Rodden and S. Rose-Ackerman, 'Does Federalism Preserve Markets?', *Virginia Law Review*, 83 (1997), 1521–69.

7. See Sbragia, 'What is Going on?', 243–50.

8. S. Breyer, *Regulation and its Reform* (Cambridge, Mass.: Harvard University Press, 1982).

9. S. Beer, 'The Modernization of American Federalism', *Publius*. (1973), 50–95.

10. A. M. Sbragia, *Debt Wish* (Pittsburgh: University of Pittsburgh Press, 1996), 219 and, more generally, 210.

11. Under economic theories of federalism, regulation is often thought of as an economizing problem that leads to clear-cut preferences for institutional solutions based on market-like instruments.

12. For a good discussion, see K. Ronit and V. Schneider, 'Global Governance through Private Organizations', *Governance*, 12, no. 3 (1999), 243–66.

13. V. Haufler, 'Crossing the Boundary between Public and Private: International Regimes and Non-state Actors' in V. Rittberger (ed.), *Regime Theory and International Relations* (Oxford: Clarendon Press, 1993); D. Spar, *The Cooperative Edge: The Internal Politics of International Cartels* (Ithaca, NY: Cornell University Press, 1994).

14. V. Haufler, 'Beyond Government: Business Self-Regulation in International Affairs', Discussion Paper No. 1, 29 Sept. 1998, Carnegie Endowment for International Peace, Washington.

15. Ibid. This section draws on Haufler.

16. Because the evolution of cooperation is a fragile mechanism, which can easily break down under conditions of ambiguity, states may be willing to delegate due to concerns about misinterpreting each others moves, and without the secure knowledge that others are cooperating, they may be concerned about defectors. See K. Gatsios and P. Seabright, 'Regulation in the European Community', *Oxford Review of Economic Policy*, 5, no. 2

(1989), 37–60; G. Majone, 'Independent Agencies and the Delegation Problem: Theoretical and Normative Considerations', in B. Steuenenberg and F. Van Wright (eds.), *Political Institutions and Public Policy*, (Amsterdam: Kluwer, 1997), 143.

17. Ibid.
18. C. Tiebout, 'A Pure Theory of Local Expenditure', *Journal of Political Economy*, 64 (1956).
19. See B. Kohler-Koch, 'Catching up with Change: The Transformation of Governance in the European Union', *Journal of European Public Policy*, 3 (1996), 359–80.
20. C. Joerges, H. Schepel, and E. Vos, 'Delegation and the European Polity: The Law's Problem with the Role of Standardization Organizations in European Legislation', paper presented at the conference 'Political Economy of Standards Setting', European University Institute, Florence, 4–5 June 1998; H. Voelzkow, *Private Regierungen in der Techniksteuerung: Eine sozialwissenschaftliche Analyse der technischen Normung* (Frankfurt am Main: Campus Verlag, 1996).
21. Kohler-Koch, 'Catching up with Change', 366–7.
22. Ibid.
23. See D. North, 'Institutions and Credible Commitment', *Journal of Institutional and Theoretical Economics*, 149 (1993); G. Majone, 'Temporal Inconsistency and Policy Credibility: Why Democracies Need Non-majoritarian Institutions', EUI Working Paper No. 96/57, Robert Schuman Centre, European University Institute (1997).
24. N. Fligstein, 'Markets as Politics', 658.
25. Ibid.
26. M. Egan, 'Regulatory Policy, Corporate Strategies and Market Integration', *European Union Review*, 3, no. 1 (Mar. 1998).
27. See M. Egan, 'Regulatory Strategies, Delegation, and European Market Integration', *Journal of European Public Policy*, 5, no. 3 (1998), 485–506.
28. See F. Scharpf, 'The Joint-Decision Trap: Lessons from German Federalism and European Integration', *Public Administration*, 66 (1988), 239–78; G. Majone, 'Independence vs Accountability? Non-Majoritarian Institutions and Democratic Governance in Europe', mimeo European University Institute, Florence.
29. P. Grabosky, 'Using Non-governmental Resources to Foster Regulatory Compliance', *Governance*, 8, no. 4 (1995), 538.
30. See among others, Majone, 'Independent Agencies'.
31. For a discussion of such trade-offs in the European context, see Majone, 'Independence vs Accountability'.
32. Ibid.
33. Ibid.
34. R. Keohane and L. Martin, 'Delegation to International Institutions', paper presented at the Conference 'What is Institutionalism Now?', University of Maryland, 14–15 Oct. 1994.

35. Ibid.
36. Michelle Egan, 'Comparing Markets across Time and Space: European and American Economic Integration', manuscript in progress, American University.
37. This does not mean that the courts have been inherently dogmatic and expansive in their approach to removing barriers to trade. See also G. Bermann, 'European Community Law from a US Perspective', *Tulane Journal of International and Comparative Law*, 4 (Winter 1995), 1–11.
38. S. Krislov, *How Nations Choose Product Standards and Standards Change Nations* (Pittsburgh: University of Pittsburgh Press, 1997).
39. See especially R. Chiet, *Setting Safety Standards* (Berkeley and Los Angeles: University of California Press, 1991).
40. M. Egan, 'Mutual Recognition and Standard-Setting: Public and Private Strategies for Governing Markets', in M. Pollack and G. Schaffer (eds.), *Transatlantic Governance in a Global Economy* (Boston: Rowman & Littlefield, forthcoming).
41. I. Ayres and J. Braithwaite, *Responsive Regulation: Transcending the Regulation Debate* (Oxford: Oxford University Press, 1992); D. Kettl, *Sharing Power: Public Governance and Private Markets* (Washington: Brooking Institution, 1993).
42. Most of this recent work has focused on different trajectories of nation-states and the variation in the role of market coordination mechanisms, see e.g. J. R. Hollingsworth and R. Boyer (eds.), *Contemporary Capitalism: The Embeddedness of Institutions* (Cambridge: Cambridge University Press, 1997); C. Crouch and W. Streeck (eds.), *Varieties of Capitalism* (London: Pinter Press, 1996).
43. K. Polanyi, *The Great Transformation* (Boston: Beacon Press, 1944), 139–40.

INDEX